Merry Christmas '21
All the best
[signature]

NUNO

Reiko Sudo

NUNO

Visionary Japanese Textiles

Edited by Naomi Pollock

Over 600 Illustrations

Contents

8   Foreword by Caroline Kennedy
10   Introduction by Naomi Pollock

18   **FUWA FUWA**
Fuwa Fuwa by Haruki Murakami
Portrait of a Textile: *Jellyfish*

66   **SHIWA SHIWA**
Shiwa Shiwa by Kenya Hara
Portrait of a Textile: *Origami Weave*

114 **SHIMA SHIMA**
Stripes of all Colours by Brooke Hodge
Portrait of a Textile: *Colour Plate*

162 **KIRA KIRA**
Shining Within by Akane Teshigahara
Portrait of a Textile: *Amate*

208 **SUKE SUKE**
Three Transparencies by Toyo Ito
Portrait of a Textile: *Turkish Wall*

258 **ZAWA ZAWA**
Four Poems by Arto Lindsay
Portrait of a Textile: *Paper Rolls*

306 **BORO BORO**
Boro Boro by Anna Jackson
Portrait of a Textile: *Threadstray*

352 **IRO IRO**
The Arrow of Time: The Magical
Transformation of Surface and Colour
by Adam Lowe and Charlotte Skene Catling

362 Chronology of Textiles
374 Glossary
376 Authors Biographies
378 Picture Credits
379 Acknowledgments

Foreword

Caroline Kennedy

When I arrived in Japan as Ambassador of the United States in late 2013, Naomi Pollock was one of the first people I met. Over the next three years, she shared with me her deep knowledge and love of Japanese architecture, design and craftsmanship. We went to a different exhibition almost every weekend, and she introduced me to box-makers, ceramicists, jewelry designers, architects, collectors and curators who are reinterpreting Japan's rich traditions for the twenty-first century.

The very first place she took me was NUNO, where I met the irrepressible creative force known as Reiko Sudo. I was Christmas shopping for my family, and I wanted to get them something that they had never seen before. I couldn't decide between iridescent bags made of fishing line, scarves of traditional and modern woven rainbows, cloud-like pillows that eventually brightened the dour family quarters of the Ambassador's Residence, coats that harked back to the shapes of Kesa Buddhist robes and bolts of fabric that wove the strength and lightness of the natural world – plantain leaves, bark fibre – into our lived environment, or tempered industrial materials into decorative gossamer. I was thrilled when Reiko surprised me with a tablecloth of traditional *kozo* mulberry fibre and recycled cotton to brighten the Embassy's formal reception hall – and perplex some of its more traditional visitors.

But it isn't just that the textiles themselves are thought-provoking and beautiful. It is that, through them, Reiko allows us to share her sense of infinite possibility and connect more closely with the world around us. She is one of those rare geniuses who has mastered the strict and demanding Japanese conventions of her field and transformed them through the force of her innovative spirit.

This book is the gift of two remarkable women whom I am honoured to call my friends. I will treasure it always, and look forward to returning to it often in the years to come.

'Koinobori Now!', installation view at The National Art Center, Tokyo, 2018.

Introduction

Naomi Pollock

Rubber Band Scatter, 1997.
By Reiko Sudo.
Loopy shapes printed in an acrylic-silicone mix on linen mimic how old rubber bands change colour and melt onto paper.

Double-barrelled, onomatopoeic words are among the most expressive in the Japanese lexicon. Bypassing conscious thought, these phrases communicate sounds, physical sensations or even emotions without requiring the brain to first assign descriptors. Just the mention of *shin shin* calls up the calm of snow wafting gently to the ground, *kira kira* the image of twinkling stars, or *fuwa fuwa* the feel of a fluffy wad of cotton. Even their lettering – using angular *katakana* syllabary for harsh expressions and rounded *hiragana* for softer ones – cuts through the complexity of the written Japanese language.

The ability of these expressions to evoke the visceral, tactile or audial makes them ideal for describing the unique textiles created by the NUNO Corporation, a team of ten textile, fashion and graphic designers spearheaded by Reiko Sudo. This Tokyo-based group has been producing some of the world's most wondrous bolts of cloth since its establishment by Junichi Arai in 1983. Their pockets of puckered polyester, see-through spirals of ribbon and tightly woven lengths of silk laced with thin strips of Japanese *washi* paper are unparalleled in elegance, beauty and, above all, originality.

It is NUNO's unfettered creativity that drives these results – industry rules and regulations simply do not apply. For NUNO, standard weaving structures are meant to be reconfigured; the behaviour of fibres, natural or artificial, is to be exploited; and just about anything, be it a rusty nail, dinner fork or rubber band, can be a design tool. The only restrictions are the capabilities of the machinery used for fabrication and the designers' own imaginations.

In many ways, NUNO's experimental approach is a direct descendant of Japan's homegrown textile traditions. A small cluster of islands stretching from snowy Hokkaido to sunny Okinawa, the country encompasses multiple climatic zones and, consequently, a wide variety of flora and fauna. All but closed to the world during the Edo period (1603–1868), Japan developed as an isolated, agrarian land, where farmers and craftspeople, including carpenters, potters and basket-makers, as well as weavers and dyers, had to rely on locally available resources and their own ingenuity. For the most part, what they could grow or forage became their food, clothing and shelter.

Thanks to these limitations, people developed sophisticated skills and a deep understanding of obtainable materials. Over time, this knowledge was passed from generation to generation, evolving ever so slightly with each iteration. In the process, different locales developed their own techniques and areas of expertise. This traditional system of teaching and learning became deeply entrenched, and continued even after Japan opened its doors to the West in 1868 and industrialization swept the country.

The Gunma Prefecture town of Kiryu, a centuries-old centre of sericulture, was a flourishing hub for the craft of *kimono* production until its handlooms were replaced by machinery and its workshops supplanted by factories with saw-tooth roofs. After the Second World War, few Japanese people could afford such ornate garments, and many Kiryu mills began swapping costly silks for the cheap synthetics used for Western-style clothing. The factory owned by Junichi Arai's family was no exception. Trading *kimono* for cocktail dresses, they began manufacturing metallic lamés that could be exported to the United States and Europe.

Though Arai had no intention of taking over the family business – he wasn't even a weaver – when duty called, he had no choice. The experience instilled a lifelong love of metallized fabrics and acquainted him with mass-production processes. But he was not cut out to run a factory, and left after a few years to become an independent consultant. Working out of his Kiryu home, Arai undertook a variety of textile-related projects, but it was his collaborations with Japan's then newly emerging fashion designers, such as Issey Miyake, Kansai Yamamoto and Yohji Yamamoto, that put him on the proverbial map in the 1970s and 1980s. Arai's expressive cloth was the perfect medium for their avant-garde garments.

Keen to have more direct contact with consumers, Arai dreamed of opening his own shop. That chance came in the early 1980s, when he was offered space in the Axis Building, a newly developed, design-oriented retail centre in the heart of Tokyo. Working with carpenters from Kiryu, Arai turned the shop's concrete shell into a textile treasure trove, lining the walls with wooden shelving for rolls of fabric and outfitting it with rustic furnishings. Using the simple Japanese word for 'cloth', he called his shop NUNO, and calligraphed the brand's distinctive logo, which is still in use today.

For NUNO, standard weaving structures are meant to be reconfigured; the behaviour of fibres, natural or artificial, is to be exploited; and just about anything, be it a rusty nail, dinner fork or rubber band, can be a design tool.

The interior of Junichi Arai's NUNO shop in Tokyo's Axis Building.

INTRODUCTION

The shop featured a broad selection of handmade and original textiles, many designed and created in Kiryu by Arai himself. Given his background, Arai had a deep understanding of the tools of his trade, but it was imagination that fuelled his inventive spirit. 'He was always dreaming', recalls Reiko Sudo. This stimulated the creation of something entirely new. Part-anthropologist, part-alchemist, part-artist, Arai was inspired by technology as well as tradition, using both in unprecedented ways. Jacquard looms, transfer-dye presses, heavy-duty dryers and even Xerox machines were among his many tools.

Arai saw opportunity in materials where others saw flaws, mistakes or accidents. Wool's tendency to shrink and polyester's propensity to crease were variables to be manipulated. Fibres with different properties could be blended. Cloth density or weaving tension could be inconsistent. He applied labour-intensive techniques to cheap synthetics and mass-production methods to costly natural materials. Unorthodox strategies like these were Arai's métier. Some of the resulting fabrics had a uniform texture or pattern, while others had a highly irregular, even organic appearance. Yet every Arai textile, even if machine-made, was created with a craftsman's care and sensibility.

Arai's hands-on knowledge of cloth structure and quest for innovation often yielded results that surprised even the designer himself. But that did not matter in the slightest. He gave little thought to the end use of his textiles; they have neither front or back, nor a right or wrong side. For Arai, and later for Reiko Sudo, the making of textiles was the passion. It was up to the consumer to give purpose and form to the cloth – a stance that may stem from *kimono* culture. Made from standard-sized strips of fabric sewn together in set patterns, Japan's traditional garments vary relatively little in shape or style. The artistry of *kimono* comes from the quality of the raw materials and the cloth created by the weaver.

Shortly after the planning for NUNO began, Arai enlisted Sudo to help set up the shop and assist with the creation of his new textiles. 'I was shocked when I saw his works, but it was really exciting', she recalls. Given her drawing skills and solid understanding of colour, Sudo was the perfect creative partner for NUNO. At the same time, the opportunity to work with Arai propelled Sudo's career in an entirely new direction. Previously, she had envisioned herself as a craftsperson who made everything by hand. But exposure to Arai's way of working convinced her to think otherwise: design may be a collaborative process, but it can also be a medium for one's own expression.

Like Arai, Sudo's knowledge of and affinity for cloth can be traced back to her upbringing. Raised in a large, traditional house in rural Ibaraki Prefecture, Sudo was surrounded by skilled needleworkers: her grandmother was an avid embroiderer and her mother sewed all of her daughter's clothing, both talents that Sudo picked up as a young girl. Biannual visits from a Kyoto *kimono*-maker left an equally indelible impression. Every visit, she watched as the merchant laid out his colourful bolts in her home's sprawling, *tatami*-matted sitting room and, while the women of the family looked on, her grandfather selected the silks that would be made into garments for each one.

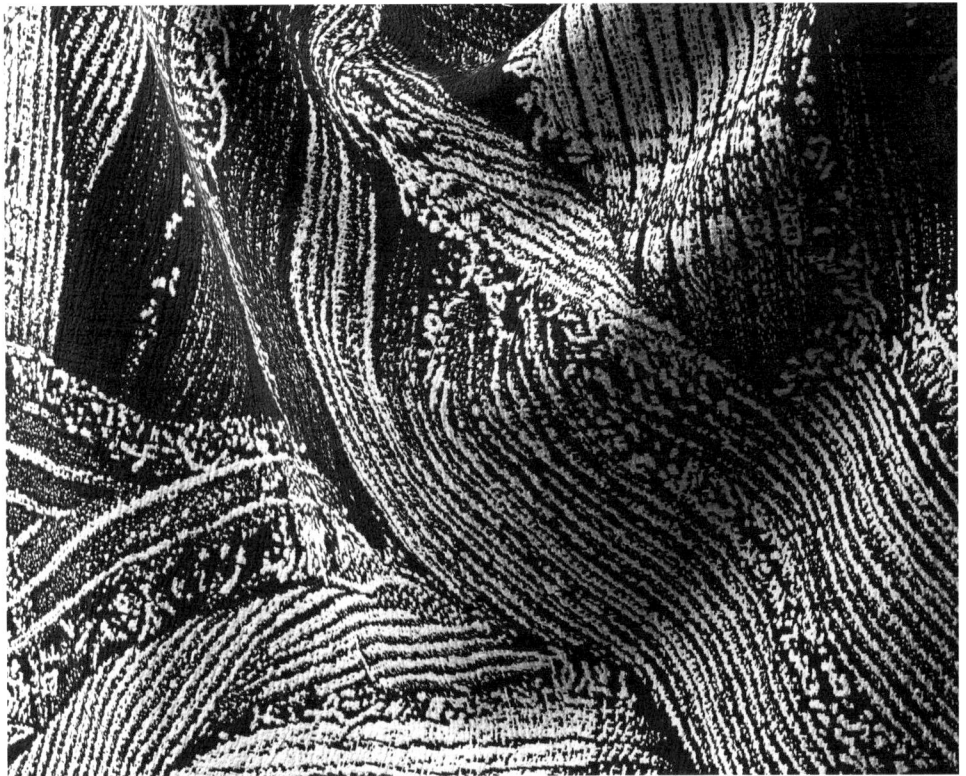

Though Sudo's mother hoped her daughter would become a pianist, Sudo decided to pursue *kimono*-making instead. In preparation, the Nihonga painter Kogaku Kobayashi was hired to teach the teenage Sudo how to paint birds, flowers, trees and other traditional motifs used to decorate *kimono*. This led to Sudo's enrollment in Tokyo's Musashino Art University, where she joined the craft department. The curriculum familiarized Sudo with various materials – wood, plastic, iron and clay – but did not include *kimono* design or cloth-making.

After graduation, Sudo fortified her understanding of textiles by winning a fellowship to study tapestry weaving with Kyoto craftsmen – one of several activities that fostered her creative and career development. She also worked as a freelance textile illustrator for large fabric manufacturers such as Kanebo and Nishikawa, and undertook hand-weaving projects, mainly tapestries for architectural installations. But Sudo's focus did not shift to design itself until she began working with Arai.

Participating in Arai's process from design through to production, Sudo sketched up his concepts and faxed him alternatives from which to choose. Weekly car journeys to Kiryu enabled discussions about colour and texture, meetings with representatives from the local mills producing NUNO's fabrics and transport of inventory back to Tokyo. Working with Arai not only built up Sudo's practical skills, it also broadened her vision of what textiles could be. By the time Arai left NUNO in 1987, Sudo was ready to assume the lead. But she also wanted to forge her own path.

Over the years, this path has taken multiple forms, such as discovering new sources of inspiration, expanding methods of design and production,

Woven Structure Pattern, 1984.
By Junichi Arai.
A pattern from a rumpled piece of West African *kente* cloth was photocopied over and over again until the image pixelated into a distinctive design that human hands could never have produced.

and taking on large-scale collaborations with manufacturers and commissions from world-famous architects. Arai's experimental approach and innovative spirit are still evident in every NUNO project. But their delicacy, tactility and imagery bear Sudo's distinct imprint. In contrast to Arai's penchant for the antique or traditional, from West African textiles to handmade furniture from Southeast Asia, Sudo tends towards the precise or exacting. Where Arai favoured exuberance and dynamism, Sudo opts for more control, more consistency. And in contrast to the weight and density of many Arai works, Sudo's creations can be so light and diaphanous that they are barely fabric at all.

Attuned to every aspect of cloth-making, Sudo and her staff experiment with spinning, dyeing, weaving, printing and finishing. Enlisting factories all over Japan, they work within convention, but often reach beyond the textile world. In terms of materials, fishing line, feathers and even foodstuffs are all fair game. And where technique is concerned, Sudo borrows freely from other industries. She has woven fabric from super-thin strands of steel produced by a tyre company, metallized metres of polyester with a spatter-plating technique normally used for car parts and stiffened cotton threads with a paste made from the root vegetable *konyaku*, a traditional waterproofing agent.

Sudo is equally committed to preserving and repurposing Japan's rich textile heritage, be it by weaving fabric from *bashofu*, a material made with Okinawa's indigenous banana plants, or making use of *kibiso* fibres from Tsuruoka, one of Japan's few remaining silk-producing towns. Strands spun by silkworms to protect their cocoons, *kibiso* are considered too coarse for cloth and ordinarily discarded. Convinced of their utility, NUNO devised ways to ready the material for mechanized loom-weaving, and also set up collaborations with local craftspeople, who turn the rough yarn into *zori* sandals, bags and hats.

Revitalized with indigo dye, ReMUJI garments are readied to be re-sold.

In the same vein, NUNO is committed to supporting and helping to secure the future of Japan's small manufacturers and specialized workshops, many of which are threatened by cheap labour available elsewhere or a decline in demand for their services. Unchanged for decades, their cramped spaces are filled with clanking looms and other devices from another era. Straddling the line between the handmade and the mass-produced, those vintage machines churn out metres of fabric at a time, but require the labourer's close attention, sound judgment and nimble fingers.

One such establishment is the one-man embroidery factory in Kiryu tasked with stitching spirals of polyester ribbon onto white backing for NUNO. While a row of heavy-duty needles works its magic, the factory owner's hands are always ready to offer guidance or replace empty spools. Once the sewing is finished, the base cloth is dissolved in water by NUNO staff, leaving the swirling, lacy fabric called *Paper Rolls* in its wake.

Like *Paper Rolls*, many NUNO textiles come off the sewing machine or loom incomplete. Their finish often requires trimming, cutting, melting or even burning by hand. With her boundless enthusiasm, Sudo has a knack for persuading fabricators to try something new – but, when needed, the designer and her team never hesitate to roll up their sleeves and get to work. In addition to the Roppongi shop, now double its original size, NUNO maintains studios in Tokyo and Kiryu partly for this purpose.

The studios are also where NUNO members fashion some of their fabric into the selection of clothes, cushions and other merchandise sold in their store and other retail outlets. 'We like to make things from the ground up', Sudo explains. But scraps are an inevitable by-product of cutting cloth down to size. Instead of throwing out these bits and bobs, Sudo's staff trims the pieces uniformly and then sews them artfully onto base fabric, generating entirely new textiles from their own discards.

Practical as well as philosophical, Japan's *mottainai* mentality – the notion of not letting anything go to waste – has a long history, dating back to times when resources were scarce. Even when no longer wearable, cloth can be incorporated into quilts, bags and other items for daily use. NUNO's prioritization of recycling and reuse bows to this heritage, but is also a commentary on Japan's more recent appetite for disposable goods.

In addition to their own remnants, the unwanted cloth, leftover thread and even garments produced by others find their way into many NUNO projects. Like the *kibiso* fibres, some of these materials are incorporated into fabrics. Others are reinvented completely. When lengths of damaged denim arrived from a maker in Okayama Prefecture, Sudo sent the yardage out to an apparel factory in Yamanashi Prefecture in the hope that their needle-punch machine would breathe new life into the sturdy cloth. By pulling up loops of the denim's white weft threads, the myriad needles gave the cloth a nubby texture, transforming its appearance dramatically and turning it into another NUNO success story.

As an advisory board member of the retail giant MUJI, Sudo has been able to promote recycling on an even bigger scale through the company's ReMUJI initiatives. Based on the tradition of re-dyeing *kimono* or *yukata* as a means of imbuing them with new life, one such project collects used clothing, colours it at indigo-dyeing workshops and resells the deep-blue tops and bottoms (opposite). Another investigated the possibility of repurposing used woollen garments by sending them to a processing plant in Aichi Prefecture that would reduce them to fibres, which could then be respun and turned into textiles for MUJI products.

Practical as well as philosophical, Japan's mottainai *mentality – the notion of not letting anything go to waste – has a long history, dating back to times when resources were scarce.*

Revitalization and repurposing are both important missions for NUNO. But Sudo engages in a variety of other kinds of collaborations as well. Expanding the applications of NUNO textiles, she has teamed up with manufacturers and retailers as well as interior designers and architects. Unlike the bolts of fabric sold at the NUNO shop, these works are purpose-driven, such as the textiles created for the German umbrella-maker Knirps and the Japanese casual clothes-maker Steteco, or site-specific, such as the curtains, upholstery and lighting elements developed for Toyo Ito, Shigeru Ban and Gwenael Nicolas.

One of NUNO's biggest interior commissions arose when the Mandarin Oriental Hotel Group erected a new building in downtown Tokyo and awarded the design of all of its textiles to Sudo. Over the course of five years, she created everything from wall coverings and carpets to hand towels and guest robes. Based on the theme of 'Wood and Water', each piece evoked Japan's rich cultural heritage while addressing the needs of the hotel's international clientele and image.

Outside the commercial realm, Sudo spreads NUNO's message through teaching, exhibitions and other forms of media. NUNO works are included in the permanent collections of venerated institutions such as New York's Museum of Modern Art, London's Victoria and Albert Museum and the Los Angeles County Museum of Art. In addition, NUNO works appear regularly in temporary, textile-themed shows and exhibits around the globe. Meanwhile, installations organized by NUNO have offered the designers the chance to present textiles on their own terms. One of the group's most dramatic and dynamic installations was 'Koinobori Now!', held in Tokyo in the spring of 2018. The latest iteration of an exhibition format initially developed with the French scenographer Adrien Gardère, it presented NUNO's interpretation of Japan's fish-shaped flags, known as *koinobori*, which are flown in honour of Children's Day, held in May each year. For the Tokyo exhibit, NUNO created 319 fish from different fabrics, which were arranged in a rainbow spectrum and suspended invisibly from the ceiling. As if swimming in formation, the fish entered the cavernous hall through one door and exited through another. Below sat clusters of beanbag chairs, where gallery-goers of all ages could relax while gazing up at the colourful creatures overhead.

Like 'Koinobori Now!', this book is a celebration of NUNO's achievements, based on another benchmark in NUNO history: the publication of the NunoNuno Books. To mark the company's ten-year anniversary, Sudo had planned to build a NUNO archive. When this proved impossible as a result of the loss of certain textiles and fabrication techniques, she set her sights on documenting select works instead. Published in sequence over a period of fifteen years, the onomatopoeic, expressive titles of the Nuno Nuno volumes connect NUNO's textiles inextricably to Japan, but also underscore the universal, visceral reactions elicited by many of their designs.

Unravelling, re-weaving and expanding on the material in those earlier books, this comprehensive volume is the first to share the beauty, creativity and wonder of NUNO textiles with a broad, international audience.

Suspended lanterns created by NUNO for the Oita Prefecture Art Museum, which opened in 2015 and was designed by architect Shigeru Ban.

FUWA
FUWA

fuwa fuwa (ふわふわ)

1. Soft, spongy, downy, cottony, flossy, fluffy, lightweight
2. Lightly, buoyantly, in a fluttering manner
3. Unsteady, unstable, vacillating, fickle, frivolous
4. Offhand, flimsy (as an excuse); negligible, dismissible (as a reason)

Strictly lightweight fluff

The Japanese onomatopoeic term *fuwa fuwa* leads a double life. It can conjure up an image of light and carefree fluffy clouds, or a good-for-nothing person with no commitment to anything.

What these *fuwa fuwa* textiles lack in dramatic presence or sharply defined design, they more than make up for in cuddly creature comfort, softness and body-warmth. While NUNO believes that originality is the fountainhead of strong design and always strives for distinctive approaches, these *fuwa fuwa* fabrics make light of the commonly held 'myth of originality': they're original without making a show of themselves, relaxed, full of humour, even — dare we say it? — a little silly. For all the effort that goes into their creation, *fuwa fuwa* textiles are quite modest about their design pedigrees, homebodies seemingly oblivious to the fashion footlights. We might even say that blanket blankness is their trademark. Those who dare to wear such fabrics may run the risk of appearing 'soft' themselves — but when it feels so wonderful, who cares?

p. 18:
Cotton Candy, 1985.
By Reiko Sudo.
Light, airy and sweet, but not too sugary, there is no need for a carnival to enjoy this.

right:
Baby Hairs, 2006.
By Reiko Sudo.
Fibres with phosphorescent pigments that store sunlight to glow in the dark, widely used for safety devices, create the soft waves of light given off by this fabric.

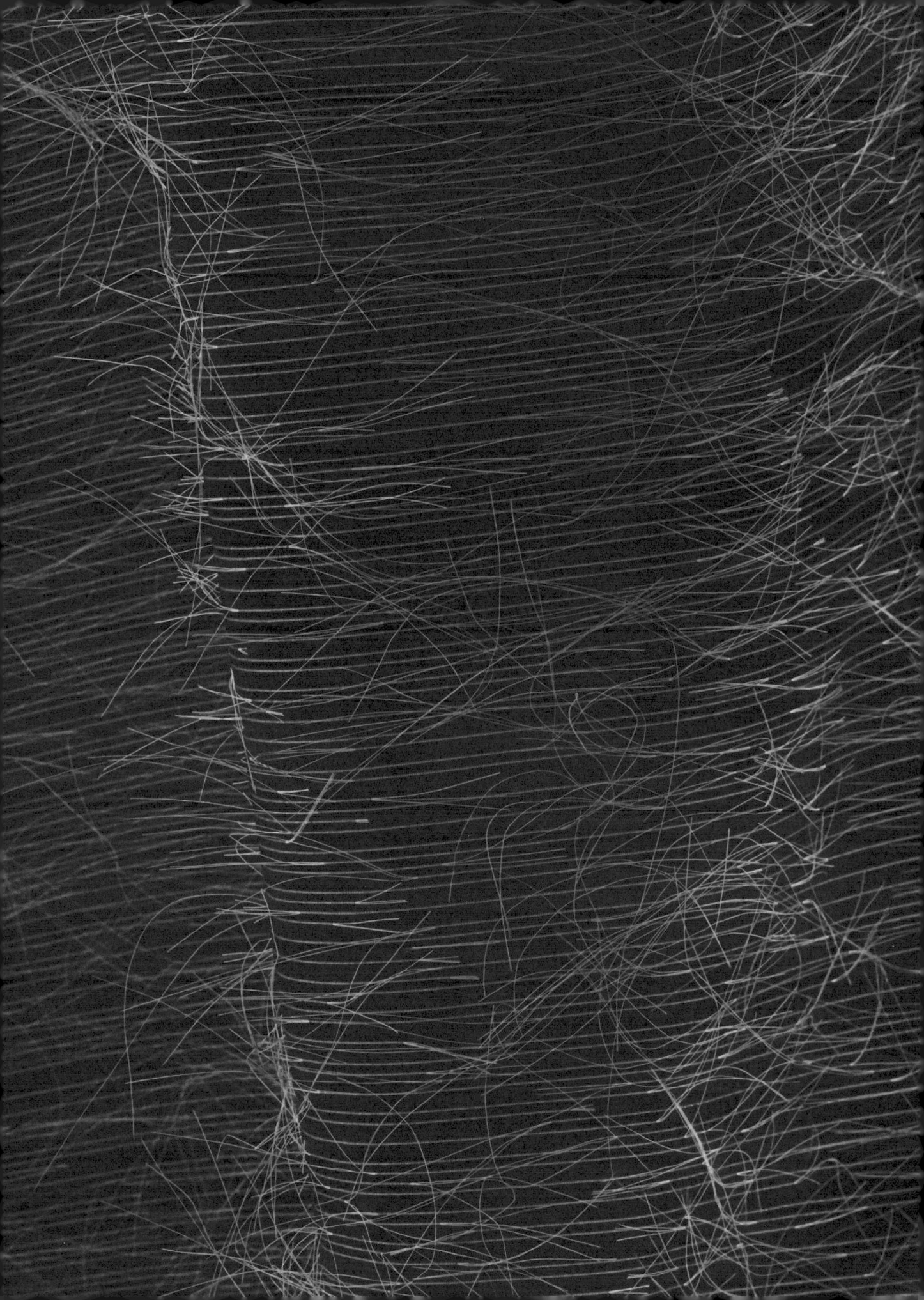

Fuwa Fuwa

Haruki Murakami

Of all the cats living in this world, one big old female is my favourite.

This cat, when she's napping in the sun on the *engawa* deck-floor on a really hushed afternoon, I like to snuggle up right next to her. The afternoon seems mysteriously vacant, like a big bath that nobody's used for a long time – everything sounds just a little off from normal. I just lie there beside the cat, feeling myself almost a part of the puss, smelling her fur.

The cat's fur just soaks up the sun's warmth like a carpet, revealing to me (very likely) one of the most beautiful things in this life. These countless particles of life coming together to create a part of the great big world, it's an important lesson in living. Everything here in this one little space has got to be, by the same rule, also inside another, greater space. This is something I'm eventually going to find out for myself, someplace else.

I reach out to touch the fluffy, soft fur, gently run my hand over the broad nape of the neck, the chill rounded sides of the ears, until finally the cat starts to purr. So nice to hear. At first she's so quiet I can hardly tell she's purring at all. Then the *purr-purr* gets louder, deeper, like a marching band coming closer and closer from far off. Finally, I press my ear to the cat's body and I can hear a rumbling like the roar of the sea at summer's end. The side of the cat's belly rises up, then eases down like bellows with each breath. Up again, then down again.

Though I'm just a little kid, there's not such a big difference between me and this old she-cat. Differences in size, even in how we think, really count for next to nothing. Whatever the gap, it's really not so much at all. We just lie there, still, two of a single lump. In a pool of afternoon sunlight. No one saying a thing. As if we two were the only ones in the world.

I reach out to touch the fluffy, soft fur, gently run my hand over the broad nape of the neck, the chill rounded sides of the ears, until finally the cat starts to purr. So nice to hear.

On a hushed afternoon like this, it's some other special time, a current apart from the time that paces our world, that steals through the cat's body. We're on 'cat time'.

My tiny kid's fingers can sense that time-flow in the cat's fur. Like schools of slender secretive silvery fish, or else like an unscheduled ghost train, destination unknown, all windows sealed tight, time slips through the warm cat-shaped darkness inside a cat, undetected by humankind.

I breathe in, then breathe out in rhythm with the cat's breathing. Softly, ever so softly – so nobody suspects. If I'm careful, not even cat time can tell I've tuned in. That's the best of all.

The cat puts out her two front paws, pat together as if pushing something out ahead, then rests her big triangular jaw on top and shuts her eyes, all mellowed out. Her long, straight, white whiskers sometimes twitch, as if picking up the after-vibrations of old memories. Her wonderfully long tail curves around her body very chastely. Just looking at that tail, I can tell she knows a thing or two about what's what.

Over in a corner of the yard, white and pink cosmos are in bloom, so the season must be autumn. There's music, barely audible, from somewhere far off. A distant piano – somebody's simple practice piece. And high in the sky, an elongated wisp of cloud. Someone is calling someone. The cosmos, the music, these echoes of many different worlds all exist in cat time. Me and the cat, unknown to anyone, we're united as one by the hidden workings of cat time.

I loved that cat. That big old hen of a cat.

I was maybe six or seven when I lived with that cat in an old house near the coast. The cat's name was Tantsu – after a type of very expensive Chinese carpet. A dense coat of fur, really soft and fluffy, patterned all over and beautiful, so Father gave her that strange name. She never made a sound, she was a smart cat. And I loved to touch her more than anything.

ふわふわ

She was quite old when, for one reason or another, we got her from someone. She was already close to fifteen, I think. Her first owner was a paediatrician, a short man with a moustache. After coming to us, twice she returned to her former home, a distance that would take an adult human more than an hour to travel on foot – no one had a clue how she could possibly remember the way. She was put in a cardboard box, tied onto the back of a bicycle, and pedalled over to us. But the cat just went straight back without a word (well, obviously), without getting lost, in the course of one night. Crossing over two train lines and a river – I tell you, she was one smart cat.

After twice being brought back to our house, always on a bicycle, the same way, she seemed to get the idea. *All right, all right. So this is to be my new home.* After that, she never ventured out anywhere. She sat down on her haunches and began a new life. Given the very un-cat-like name 'Tantsu', she became a member of the family and my special friend. Well-behaved and gentle, you could leave fish out on a serving tray and she would never ever set paw on it.

Maybe it was because I had no brothers or sisters, but often when I came home from school, it was the cat I'd play with. And I learned so much, so many things important to every living creature, from that cat. No joke, I really and truly learned many lessons from playing with that smart old cat. So that one day when, with no warning, with no farewell, she vanished forever from our sight – she never found her way back – I lost one true link to the world.

The cat had lovely old velvet fur. Drinking in the smell of the afternoon sun, shining beautiful gold. That's why even now, of all the cats living in this world, one big old female is still my favourite.

Puffed Blocks, 1979 (reissued 1987). By Junichi Arai. Four contrasting yarns – tightly overspun, less tightly spun, shrinking polyester and plain untwisted yarn – combine to make alternating blocks of shrinking and swelling puckers.

Papillon, 2018.
By Reiko Sudo.
Wispy spume seems to sprout from the surface of the fabric. A revival of one of NUNO's very first fabrics.

Paper Honeycomb, 2004.
By Reiko Sudo.
Threads of manila hemp paper are woven in a honeycomb pattern.

Azumino Wild Silk, 2013.
By Reiko Sudo.
Wispy wefts of Japanese wild silk curl up naturally when cut by hand, like skeins sprouting all over the gauzy plain-weave ground.

Shuro, 1984 (reissued 1997).
By Junichi Arai;
reissued by Reiko Sudo.
This rough fabric has all the itchiness of hemp fibre, but not the stiffness. Woven in a tubular weave, a long-standing favourite technique.

Fluff, 2002. By Reiko Sudo. Overspun silk and Spandex™ wefts play creative havoc with otherwise soft surface patterns.

opposite:
Bagheera Velvet Rounds, 2000.
By Reiko Sudo.
Using an old-fashioned technique, sharpened wires are woven in and then pulled out, cutting the weft loops and forming a velvet pile.

below:
Bell and Ivy, 1995.
By Sayuri Shimoda and Reiko Sudo.
Warps and wefts overspun in two different tensions and directions create a sculptural effect when woven.

Sweet Pea, 2016.
By Reiko Sudo.
A Raschel warp knit in a romantic two-petal sweet pea motif, with a raised nap and soft, fluffy texture.

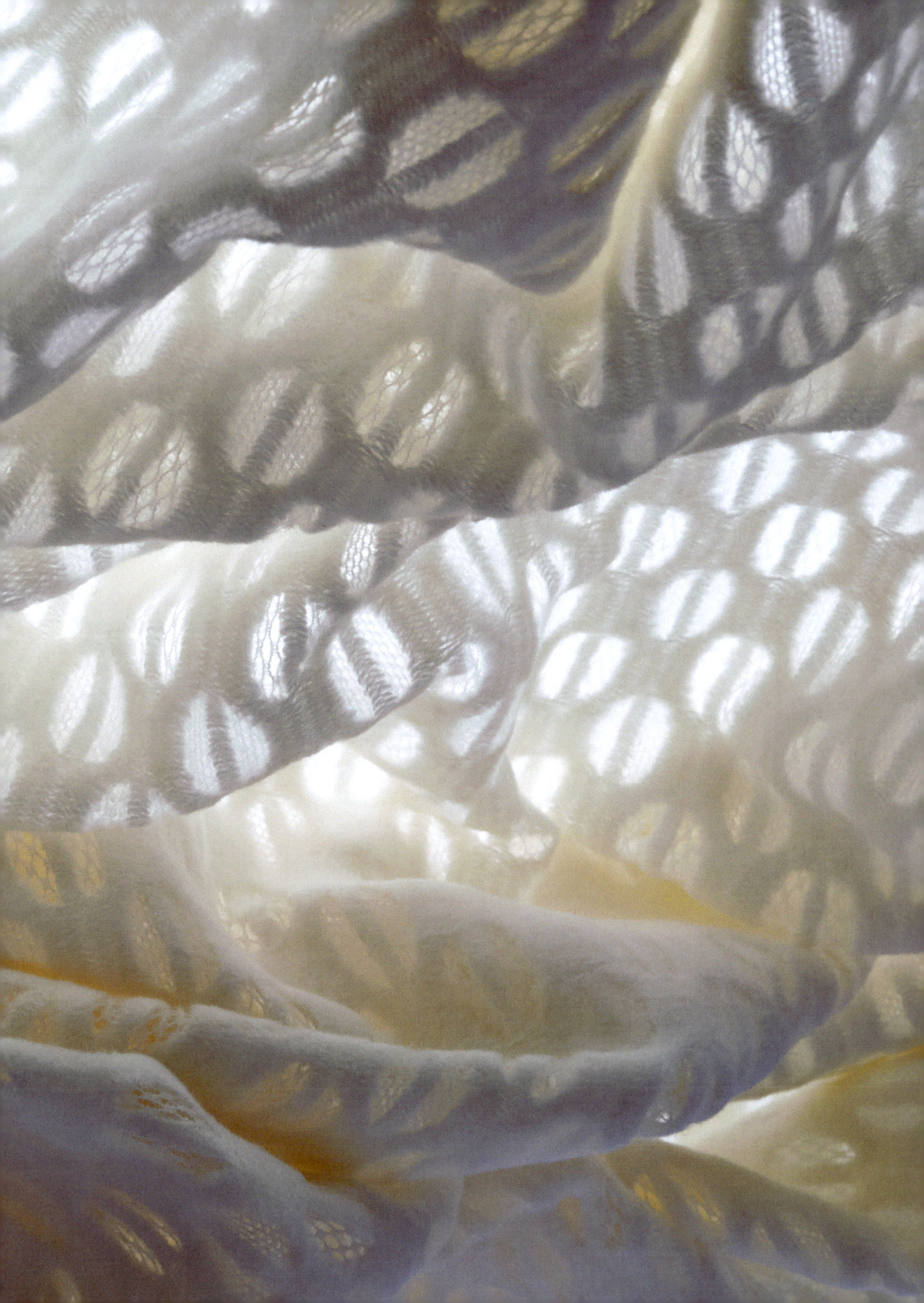

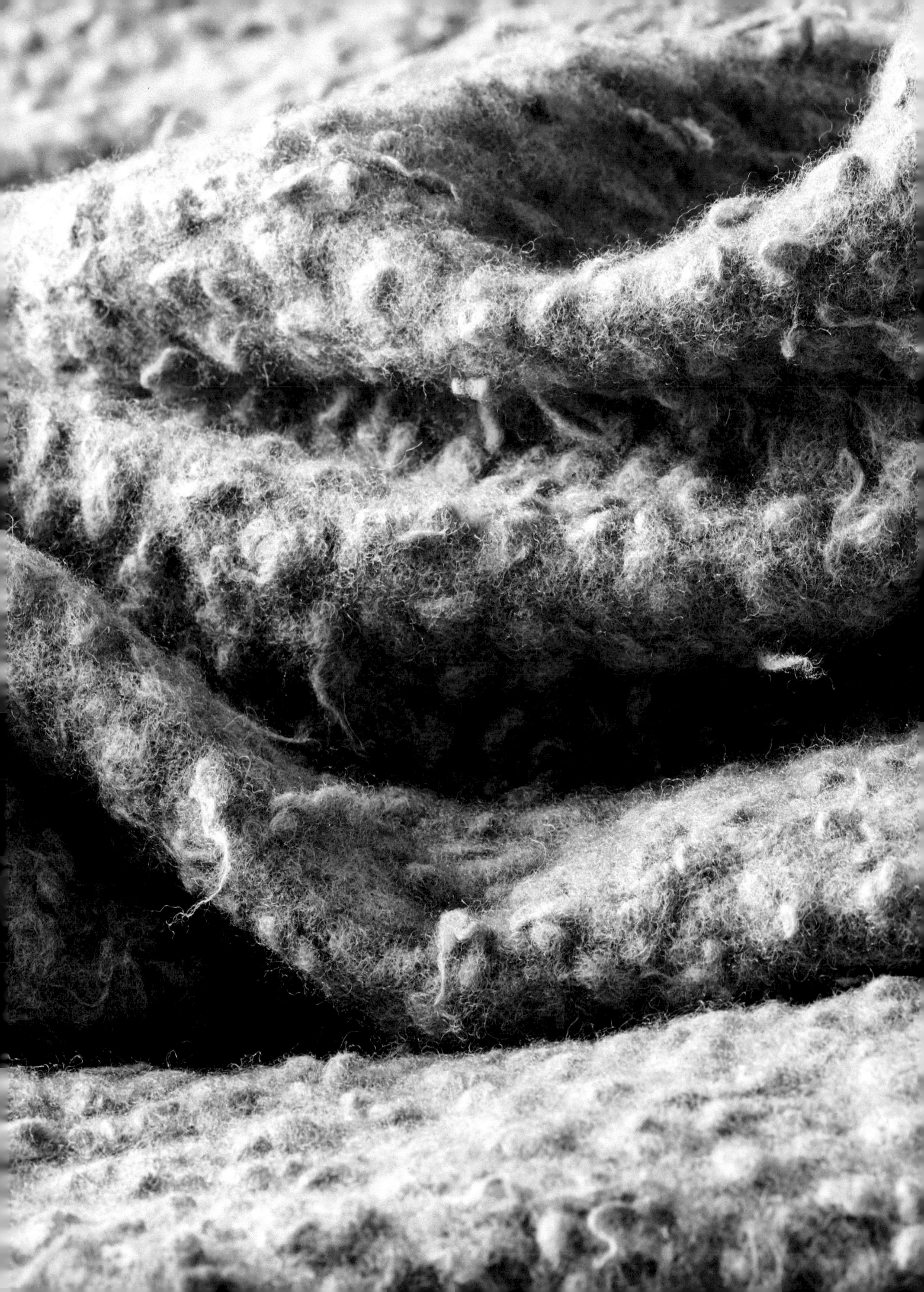

opposite:
Hairball, 2020.
By Reiko Sudo.
A loopy sportswear pile knit is steamed, trimmed, steamed again, brushed, shaved, steamed and brushed yet again, until the fur comes alive.

above:
Fluffy Hair, 1989.
By Reiko Sudo.
Soft, sleek swards of silk cover a polyester ground, heat-treated to keep the silk firmly attached.

following spread:
White Noise (Boom Bass), 1991.
By Reiko Sudo.
Masuori weaves have small square patterns with uneven surfaces. In Japan, squares are said to bring good luck.

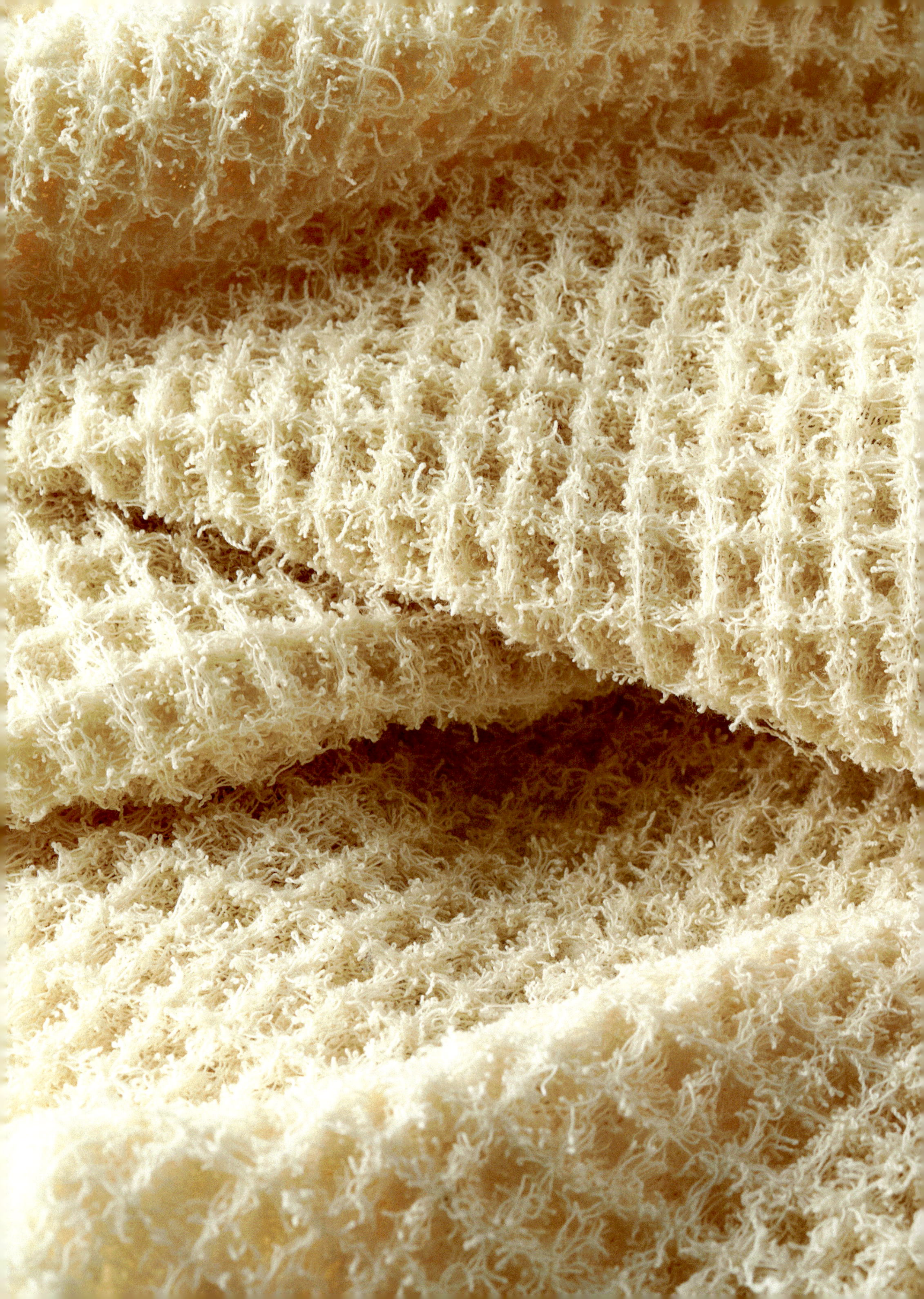

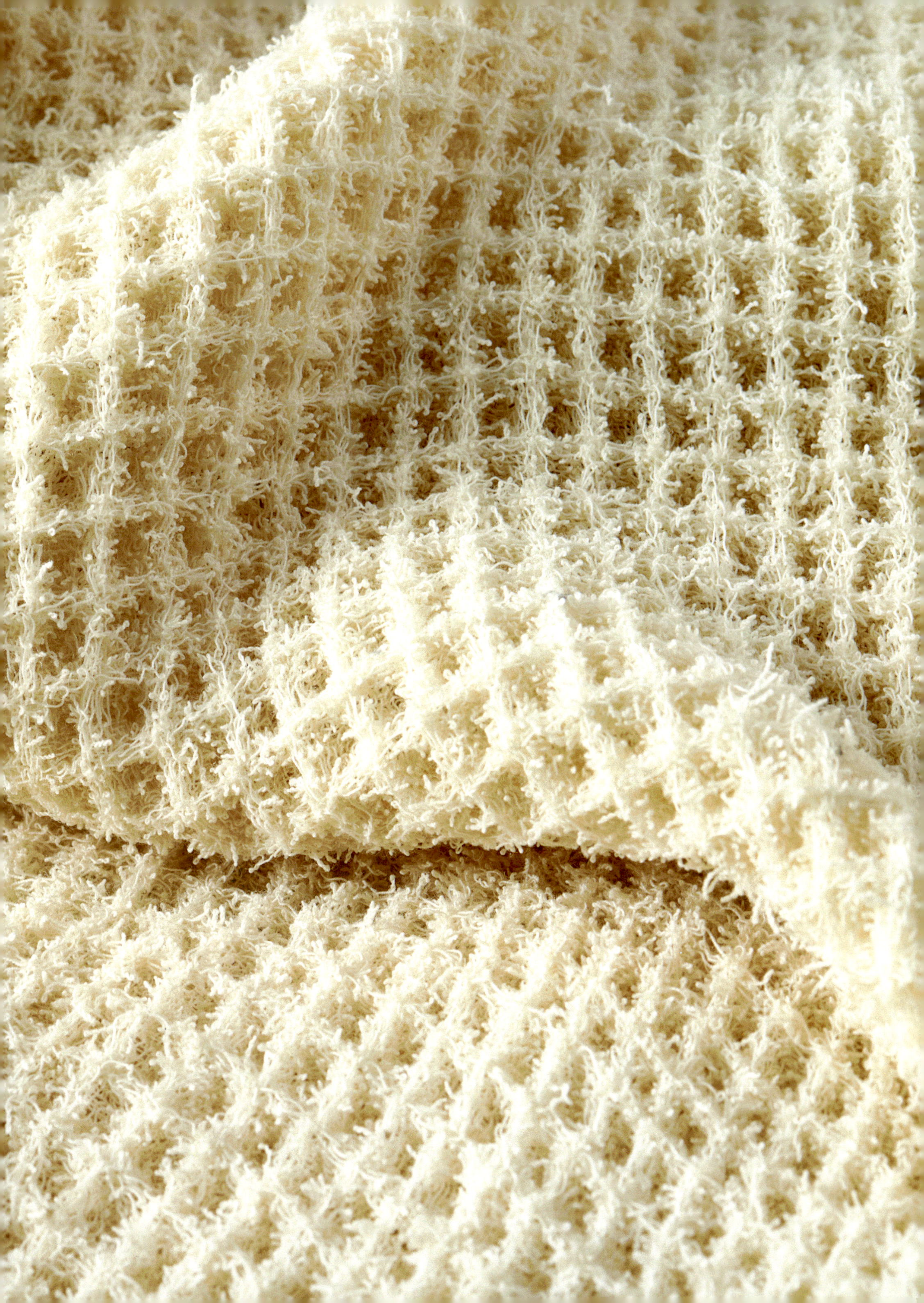

below:
Honeycomb Plaid, 1994.
By Reiko Sudo.
Two lightweight, traditional honeycomb weaves, using tightly twisted wool yarn warps and even more tightly twisted wefts. This unprecedented degree of twisting is underscored by subtle, complementary colours.

opposite:
Bias Puff, 1985 (reproduced 2010).
By Reiko Sudo and Junichi Arai.
A clever double-weave of comforting cotton layered on soft polyester, the design mimics *chigiri-e* torn-paper pictures.

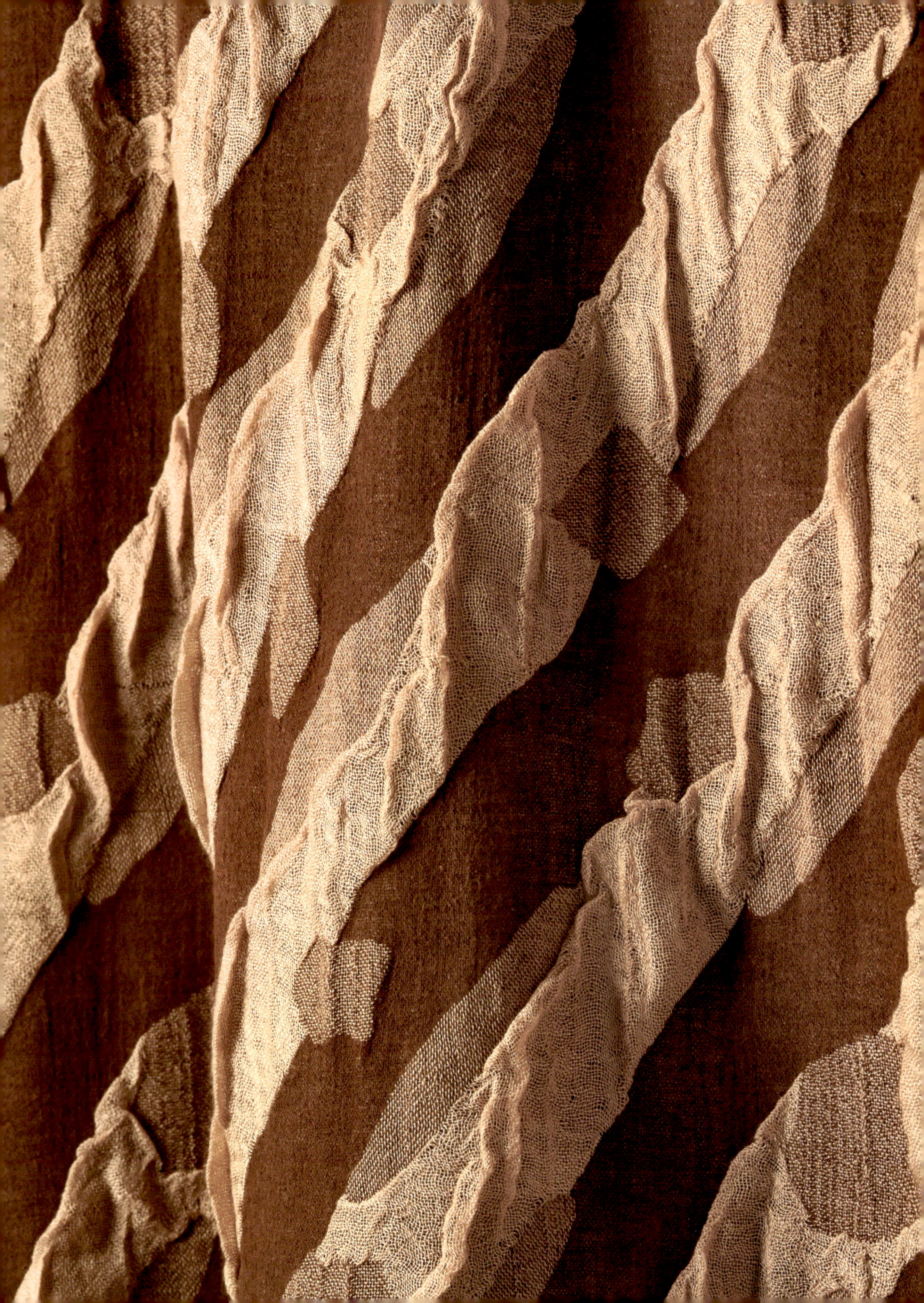

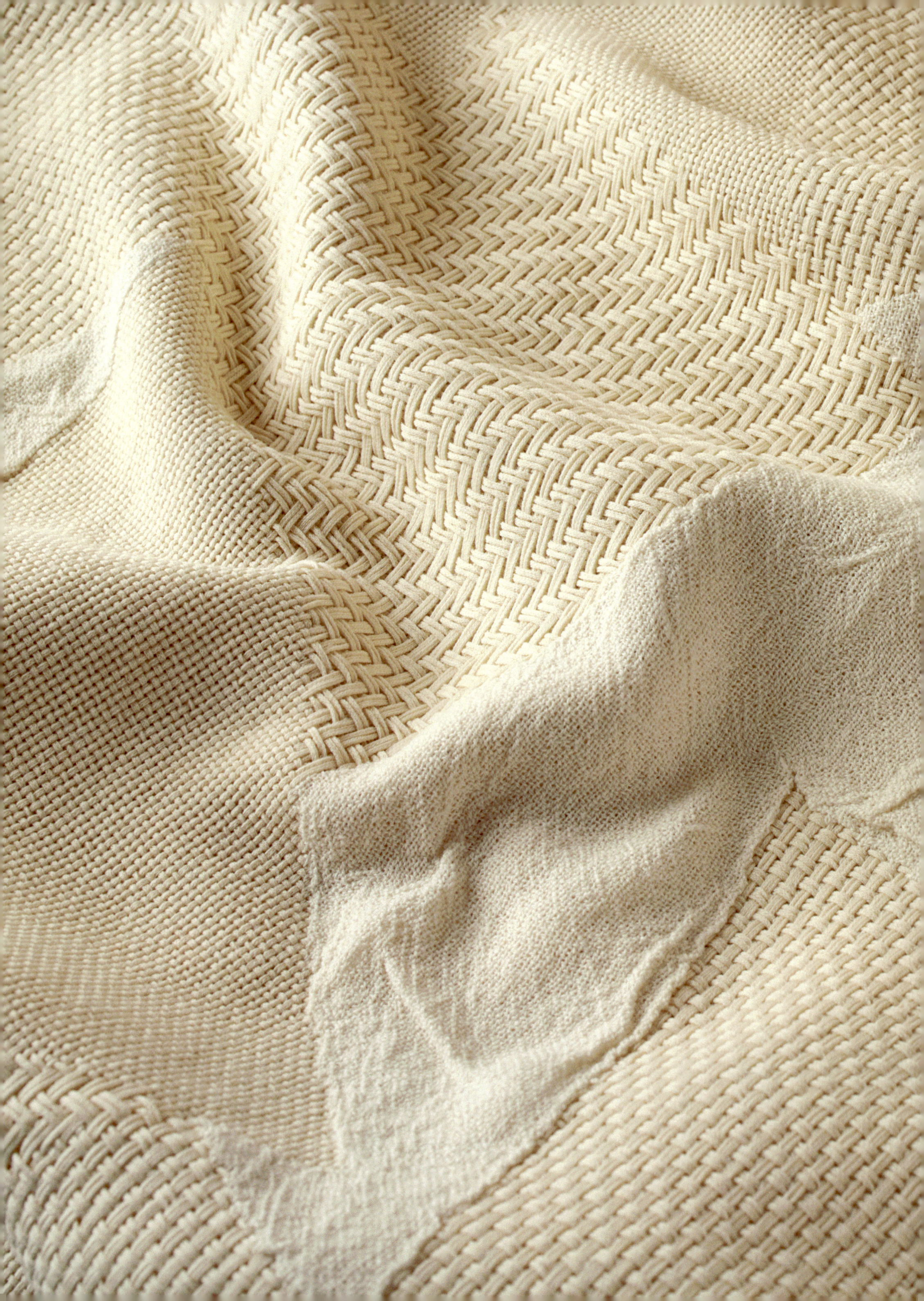

opposite:
Basket Weave Big Pocket, 1984.
By Junichi Arai.
Flat machine-knitting ribbons contrast with regular cotton thread ground in this technique patented by Junichi Arai.

above:
Ice House, 1993.
By Reiko Sudo.
Delicate *sha* gauze, traditional for elegant summer *kimono*, gains a fuller translucent volume reminiscent of an ice drift when interwoven with alternating wool yarn and cotton tape.

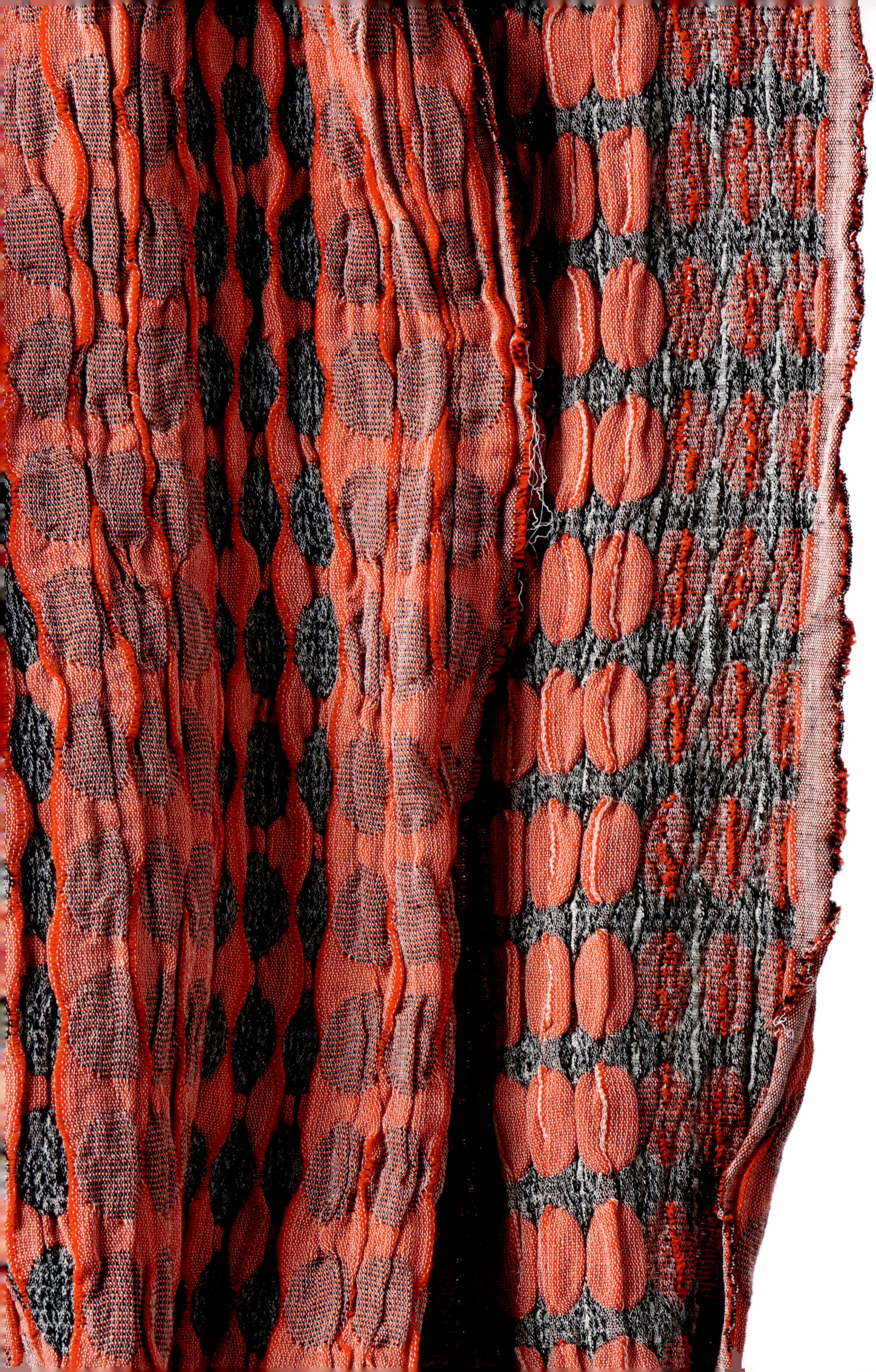

opposite:
Trap Circle, 2015.
By Reiko Sudo.
Stretch yarns woven into this repeating disc-pattern textile give it a full-bodied texture.

above:
Moss, 1994.
By Reiko Sudo.
A double-weave of silk warps and wool wefts. As the wefts contract tighter, the warps hang loose like tropical undergrowth.

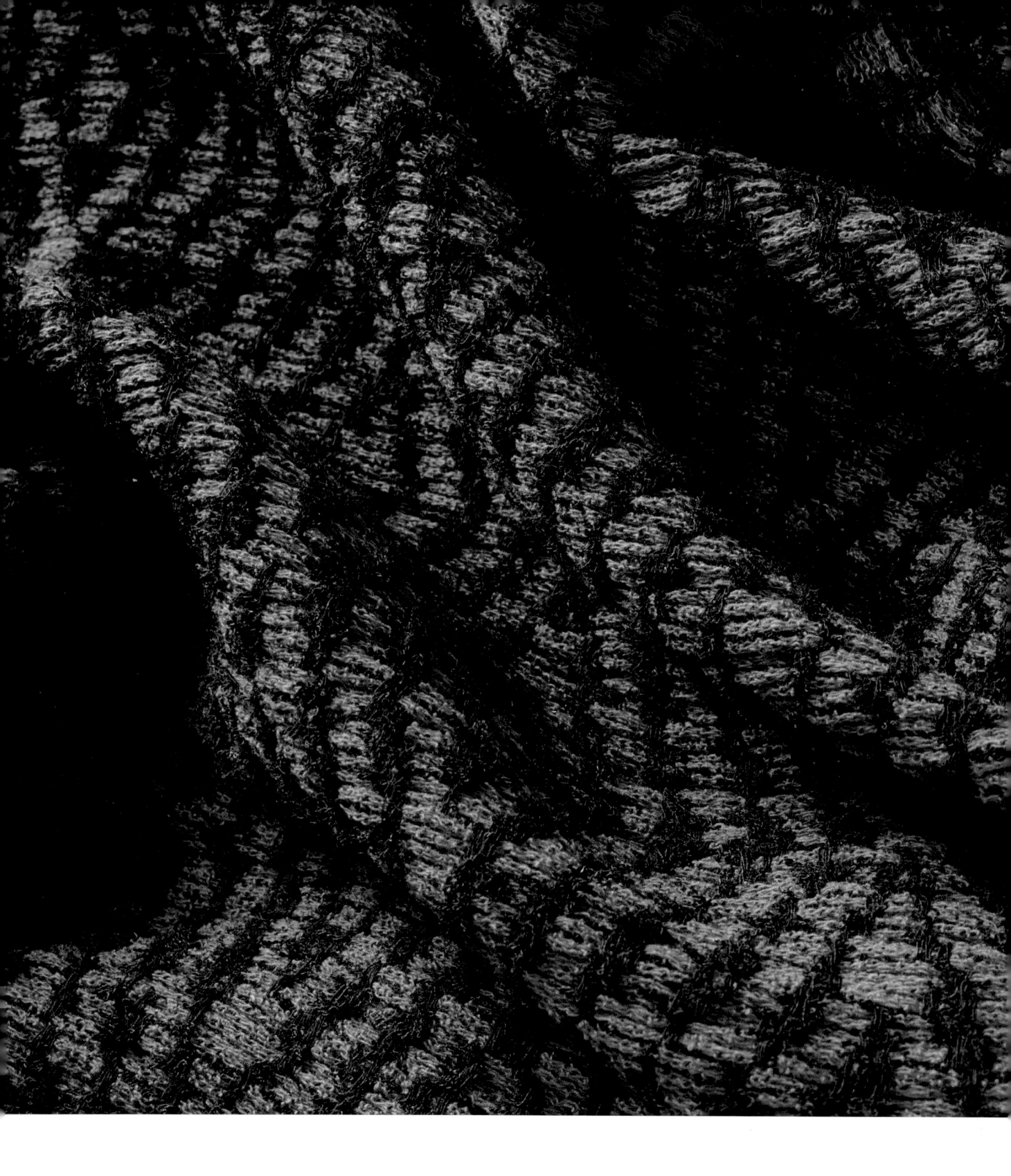

Shii Tree, 1997.
By Reiko Sudo.
Delicious *shiitake* mushrooms sprout from the base of the *shii* tree, the woodgrain of which looks like Tibetan tiger stripes.

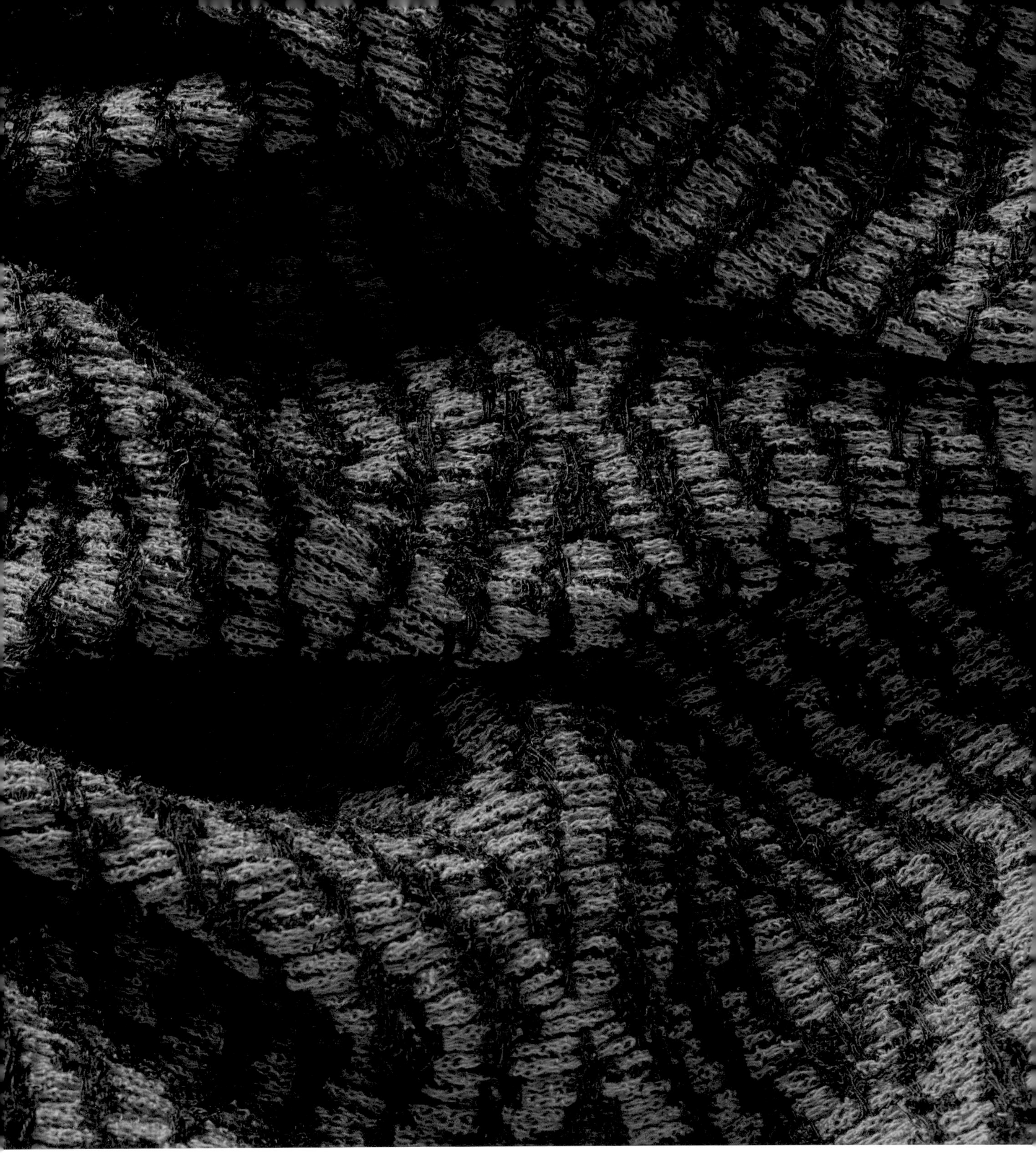

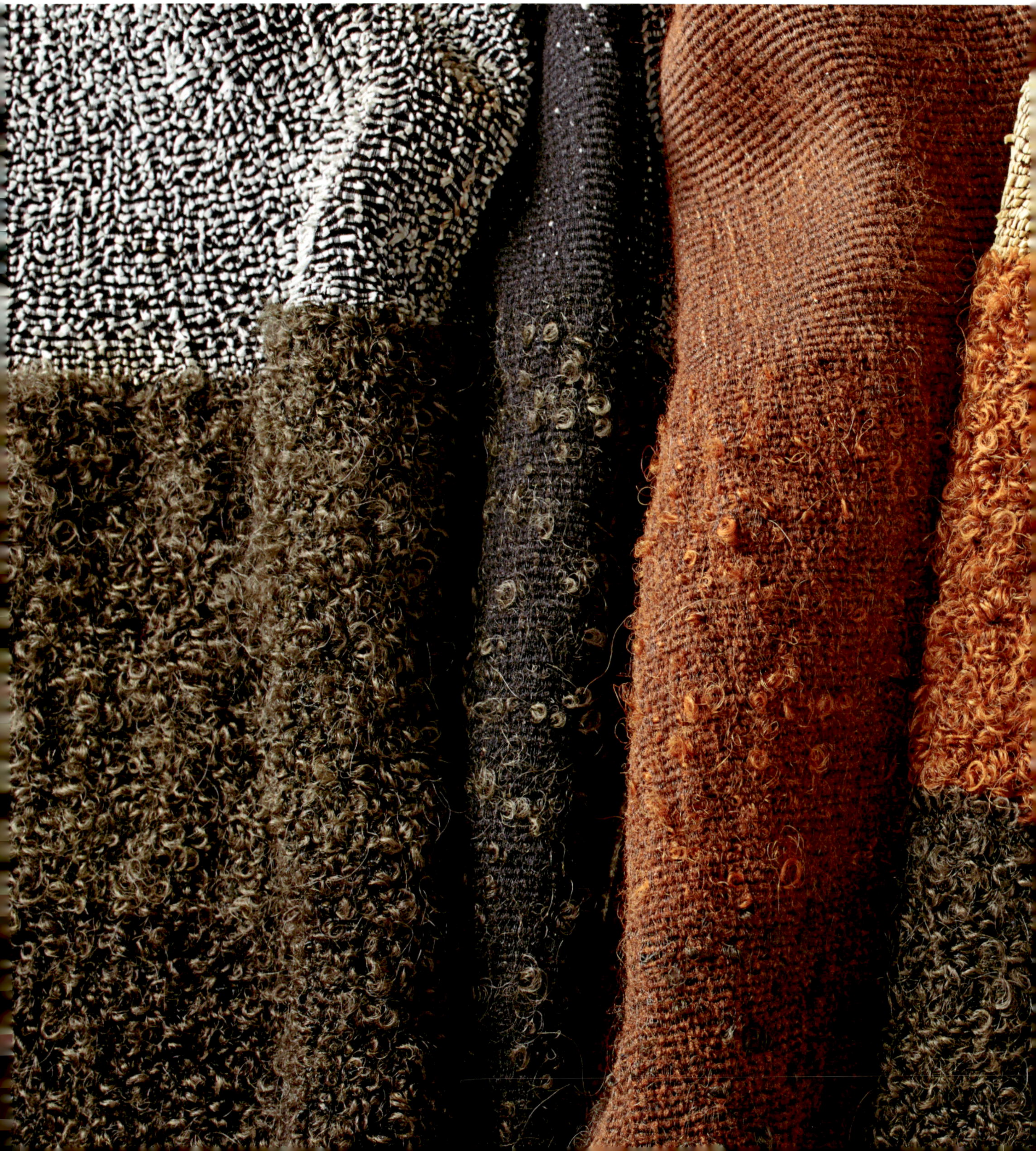

K9 Clip, 1996.
By Reiko Sudo.
Many dog owners favour the velvety feel (not to mention the disciplinary authority) of the doggy crew-cut. Diverse materials weave into this bristling, fun fabric.

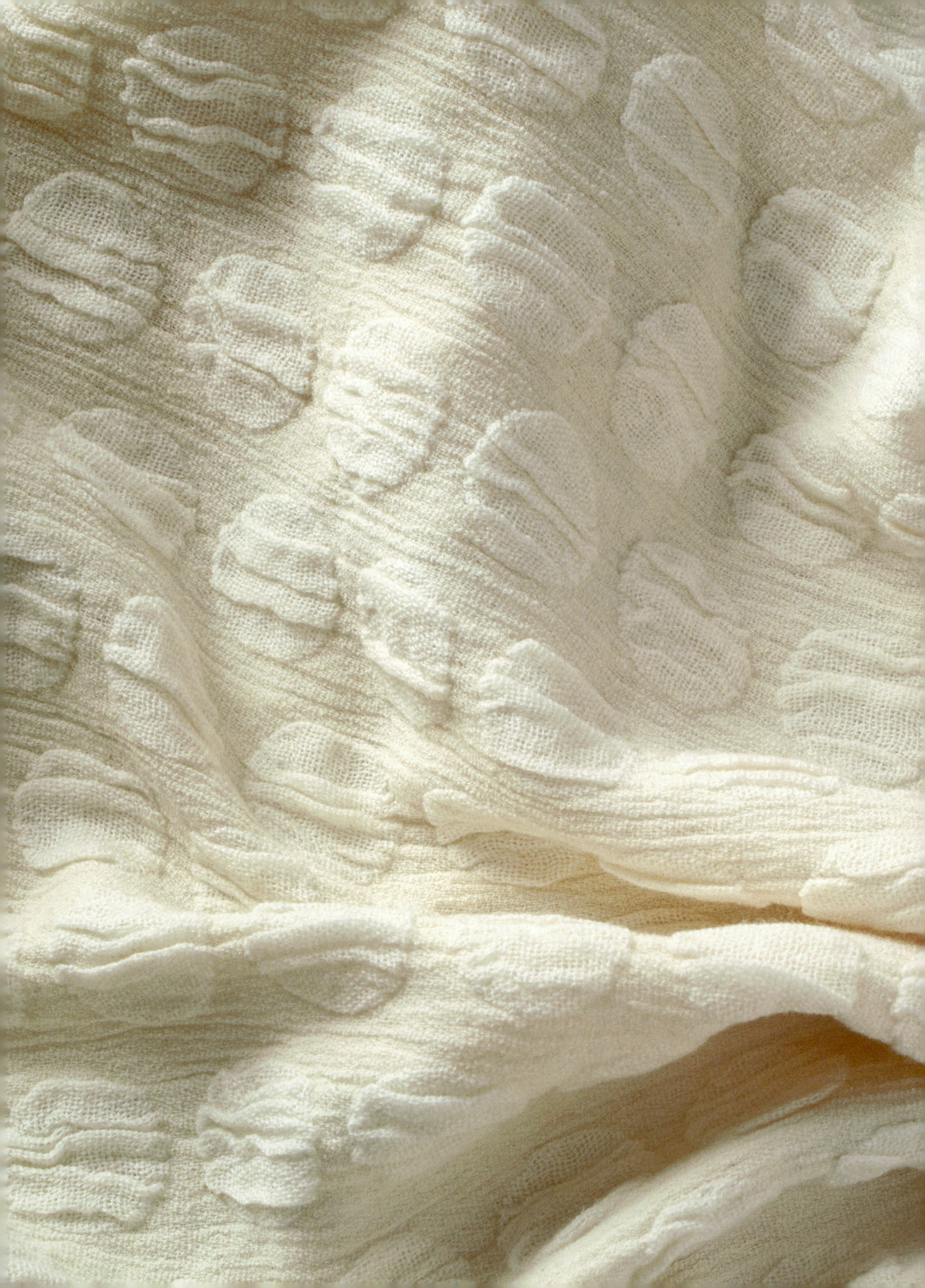

left:
Nesting Instinct, 1998.
By Kazuhiro Ueno and
Reiko Sudo.
A double-weave of regular
and overspun cotton yarns
with a fluff-and-circle pattern
reminiscent of eggs in nests.

following spread:
Loop de Loop, 2009.
By Reiko Sudo.
Bouclé yarns, made by
wrapping a core strand in a
loose tangle of filaments, are
pulled out front and back after
weaving to finish this cuddly,
warm, resilient fabric.

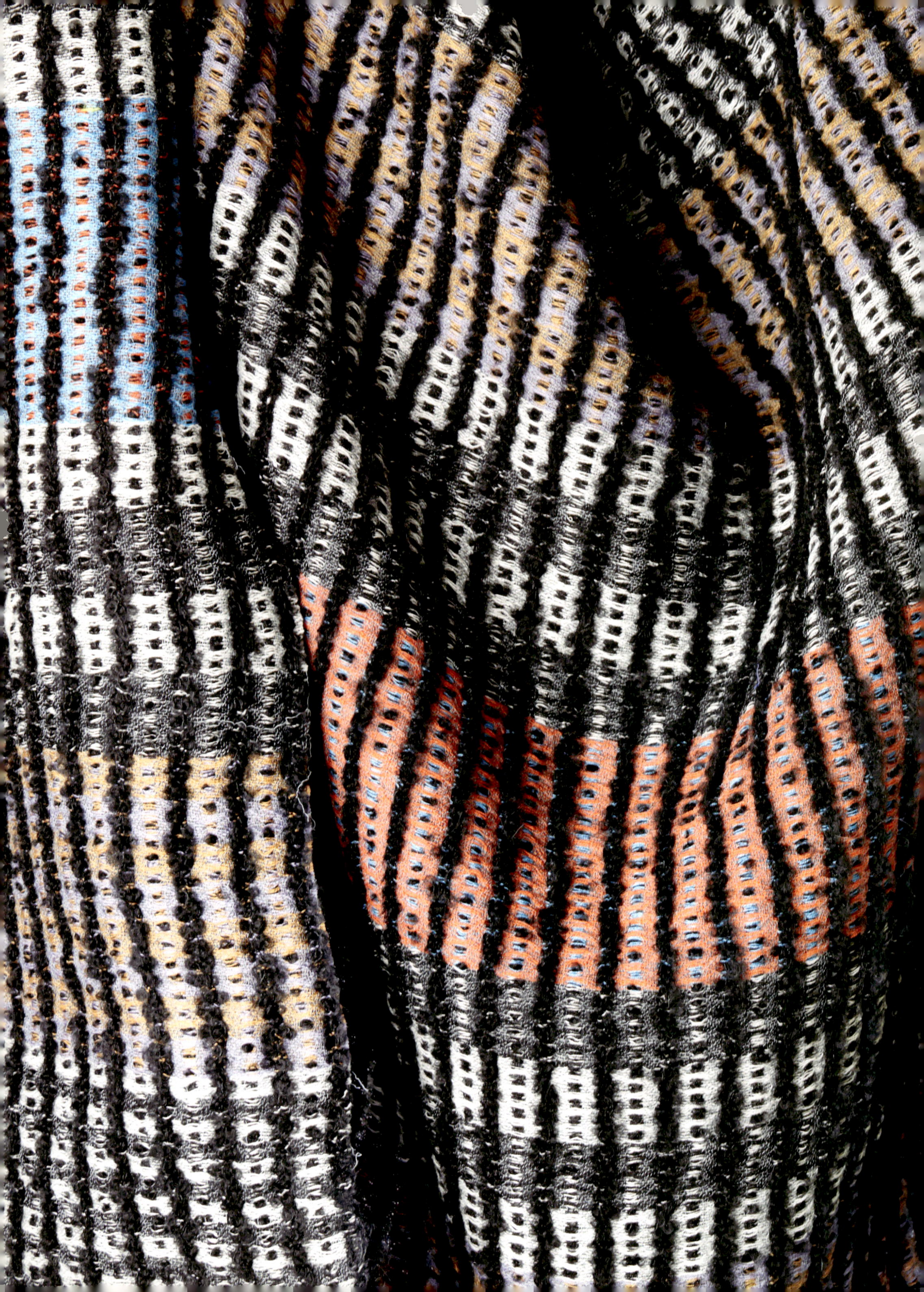

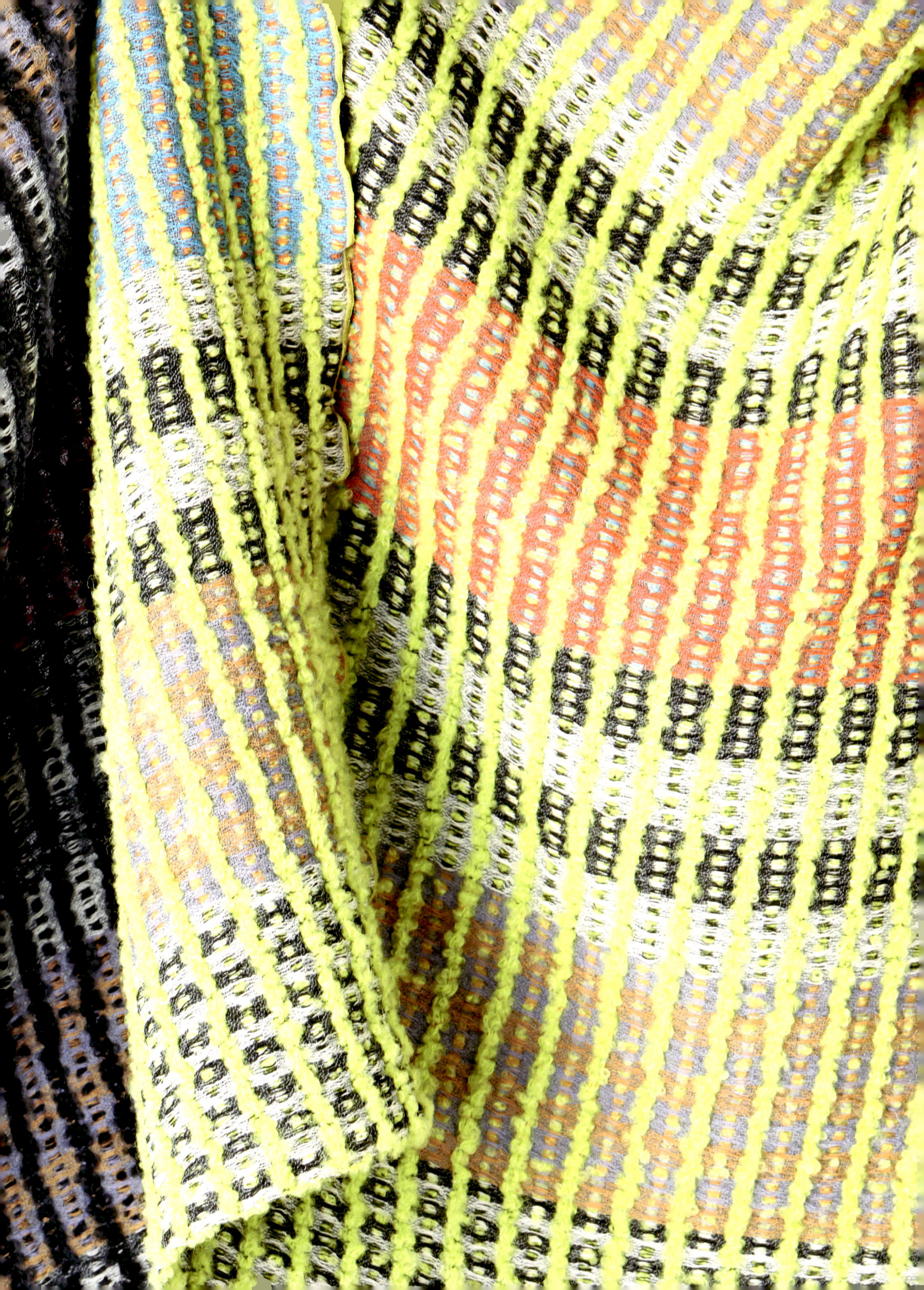

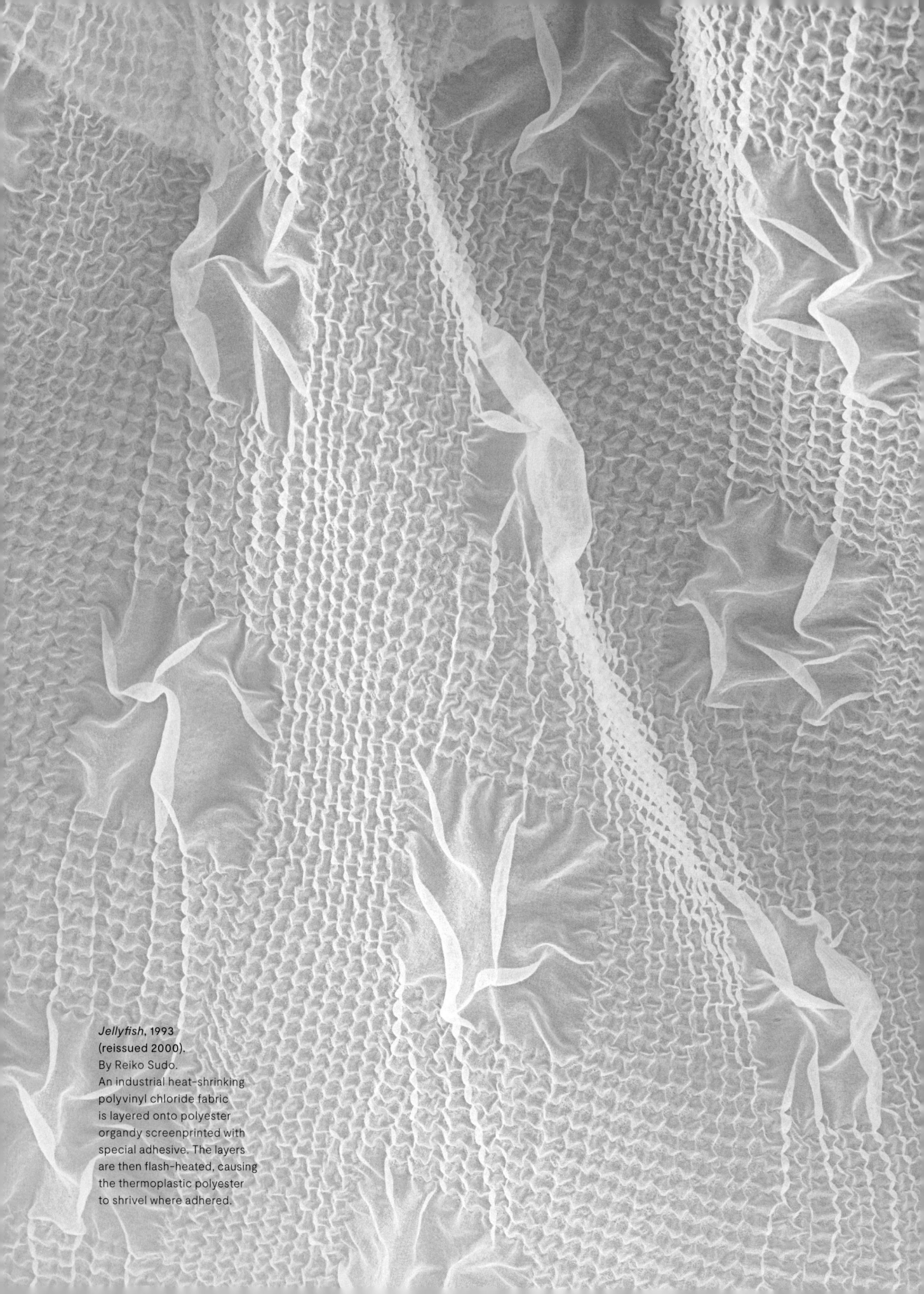

Jellyfish, 1993 (reissued 2000). By Reiko Sudo. An industrial heat-shrinking polyvinyl chloride fabric is layered onto polyester organdy screenprinted with special adhesive. The layers are then flash-heated, causing the thermoplastic polyester to shrivel where adhered.

Portrait of a Textile: *Jellyfish*

What would a heat-shrinking material do to a thermoplastic fabric?

Polyvinyl alcohol is a functional resin first developed by Japanese fibre manufacturer Kuraray. Composed of carbon, hydrogen and oxygen, it does not produce toxic materials like dioxin or ammonia when burned. Strong, durable, chemical-resistant textiles woven with this fibre are widely used in industry, agriculture and fishing.

    At NUNO, we love to adapt industrial materials from other fields for making textiles. We found out that polyvinyl alcohol shrinks at 60°C (140°F), and decided to utilize that characteristic in combination with highly thermoplastic polyester taffeta to create a sculpted textile. We stitched the two fabrics together and heated them in an oven to 85°C (185°F), whereupon the entire mass shriveled before our eyes. So, we experimented further in the kitchen, baking little textile 'cookies' at different temperatures until we discovered the ideal control conditions. We then took the project to Nakanishi Senko Dye Works, a leafing specialist in Shiga, who agreed to reproduce our stitched needlework with printing. The result of all this trial and error was a now-patented process, and luminous, jellyfish-like drifts of translucent organdy.

Original design collage, **with** cut and reduced *washi* paper in large and small patterns.

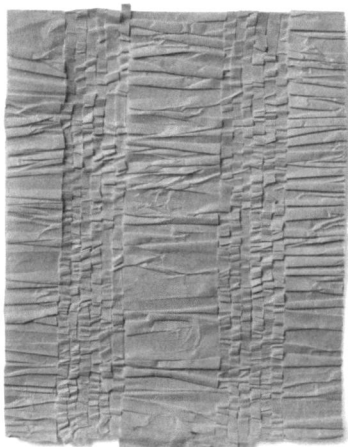

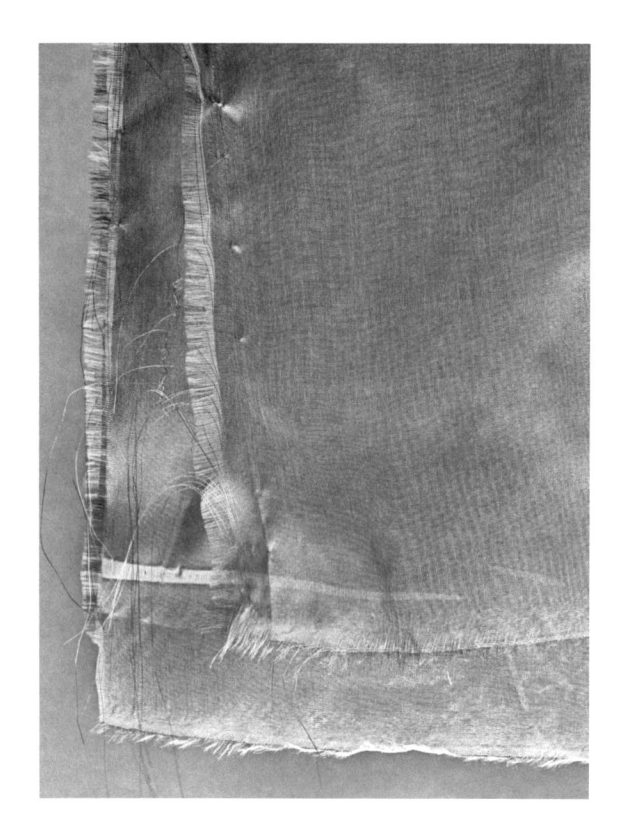

above left
Heat-shrinking Vinylon
(polyvinyl alcohol fabric)
developed by Kuraray Co. Ltd.

top right
Water-soluble thread.

above right
A hand-embroidered sample
border pattern.

below
Testing the shrinkage
of josette fabric.

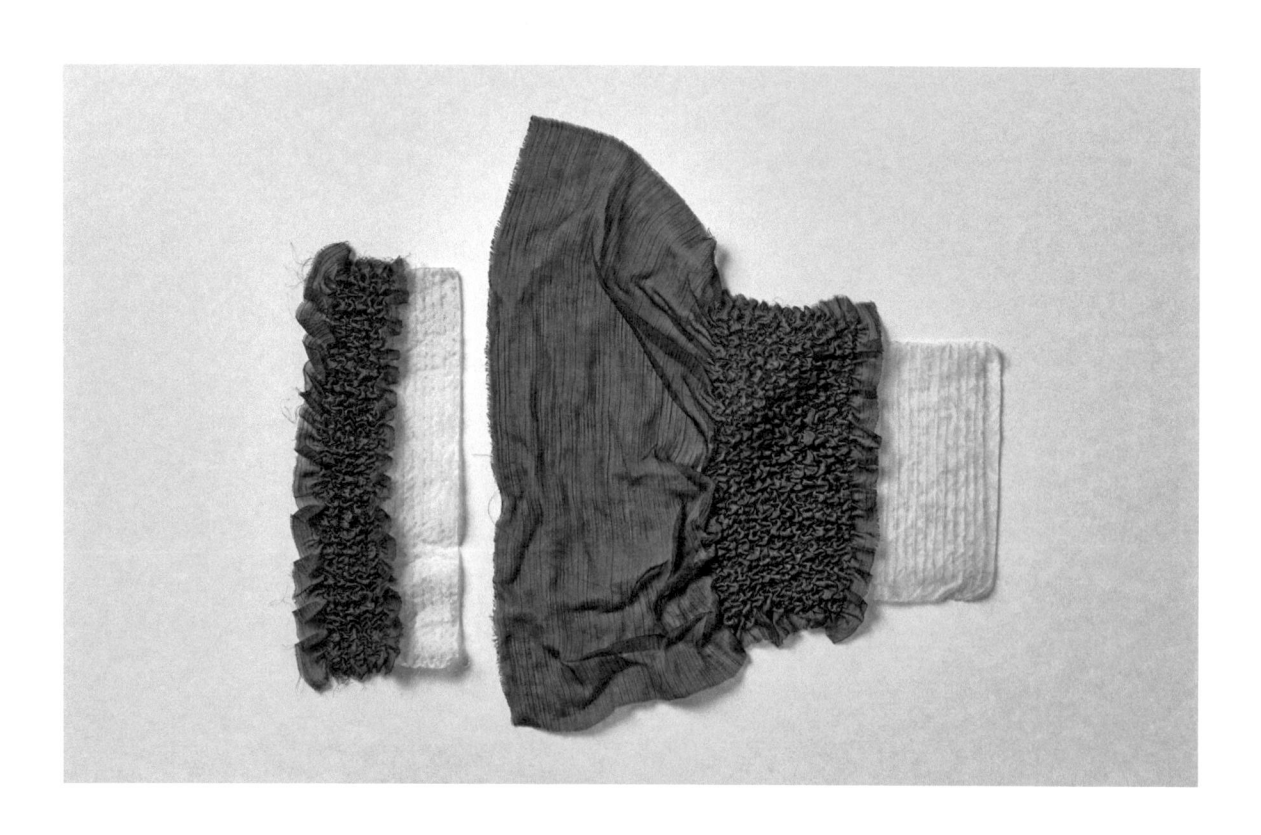

58

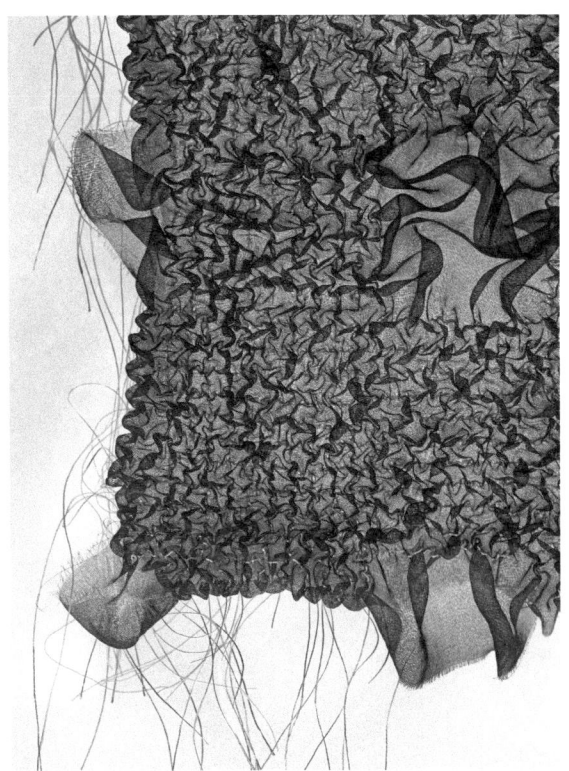

above left
A trial using heat-shrinking polyvinyl alcohol fabric stitched onto polyester organdy.

above right
Embroidered test fabric roasted in an oven to check the shrinkage.

below left
Checking the shrinkage by dissolving a corner of the test piece in water.

below right
Water-soluble threads are dissolved and heat-shrinking fabric removed to reveal finished test fabric.

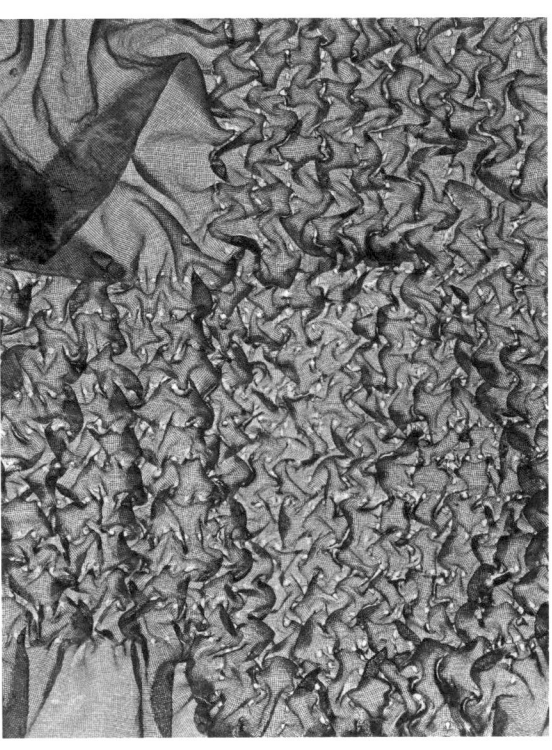

FUWA FUWA

59

left to right
Oven-roasted test; heat-shrinking fabric test-stitched onto organdy with water-soluble thread; heat-shrunken fabric and organdy after removal.

Polymer aesthetics
In 1993, I learned of an industrial heat-shrinking polyvinyl chloride (PVC) material, and experimented by baking it in an oven together with thermoplastic polyester until we obtained production-level results, which we patented as our 'Jellyfish' process. In 2000, we switched to a more eco-friendly biodegradable polyvinyl alcohol (poval), which was found to have similar heat-shrinking characteristics.

FUWA FUWA

ふわふわ

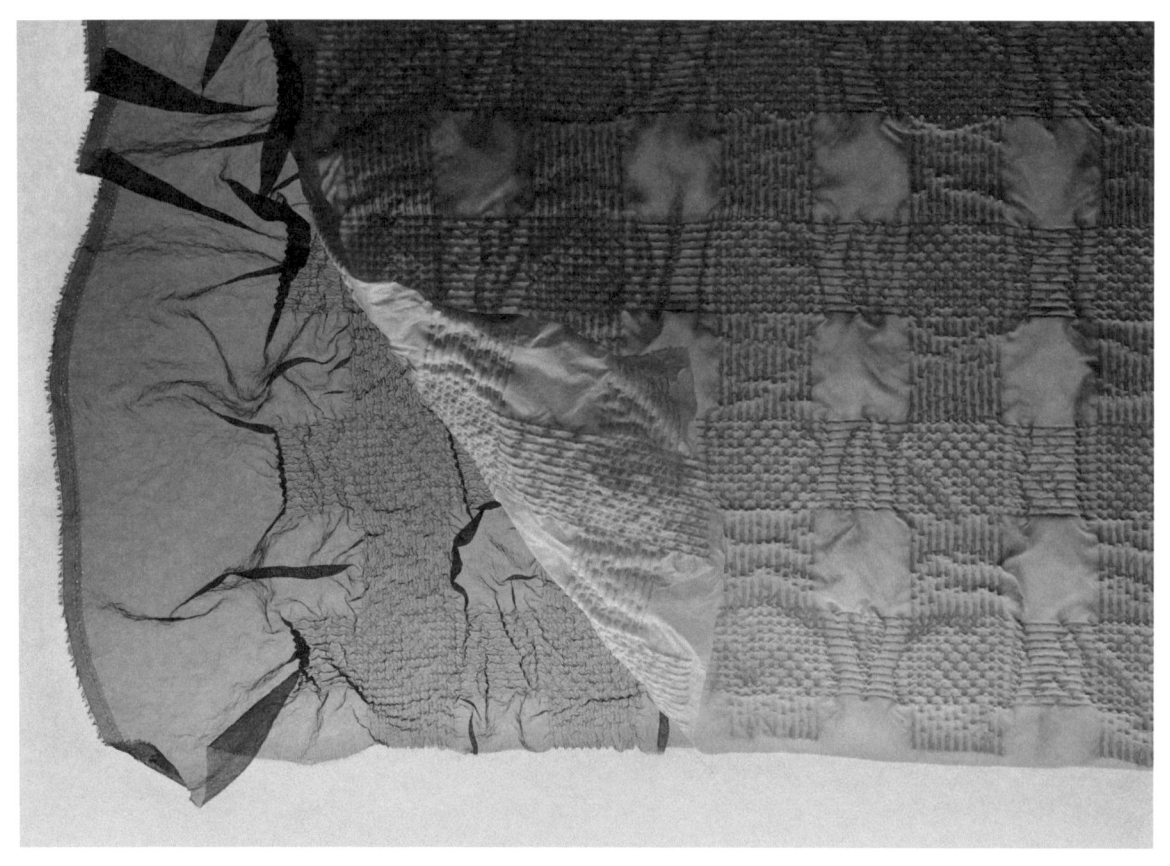

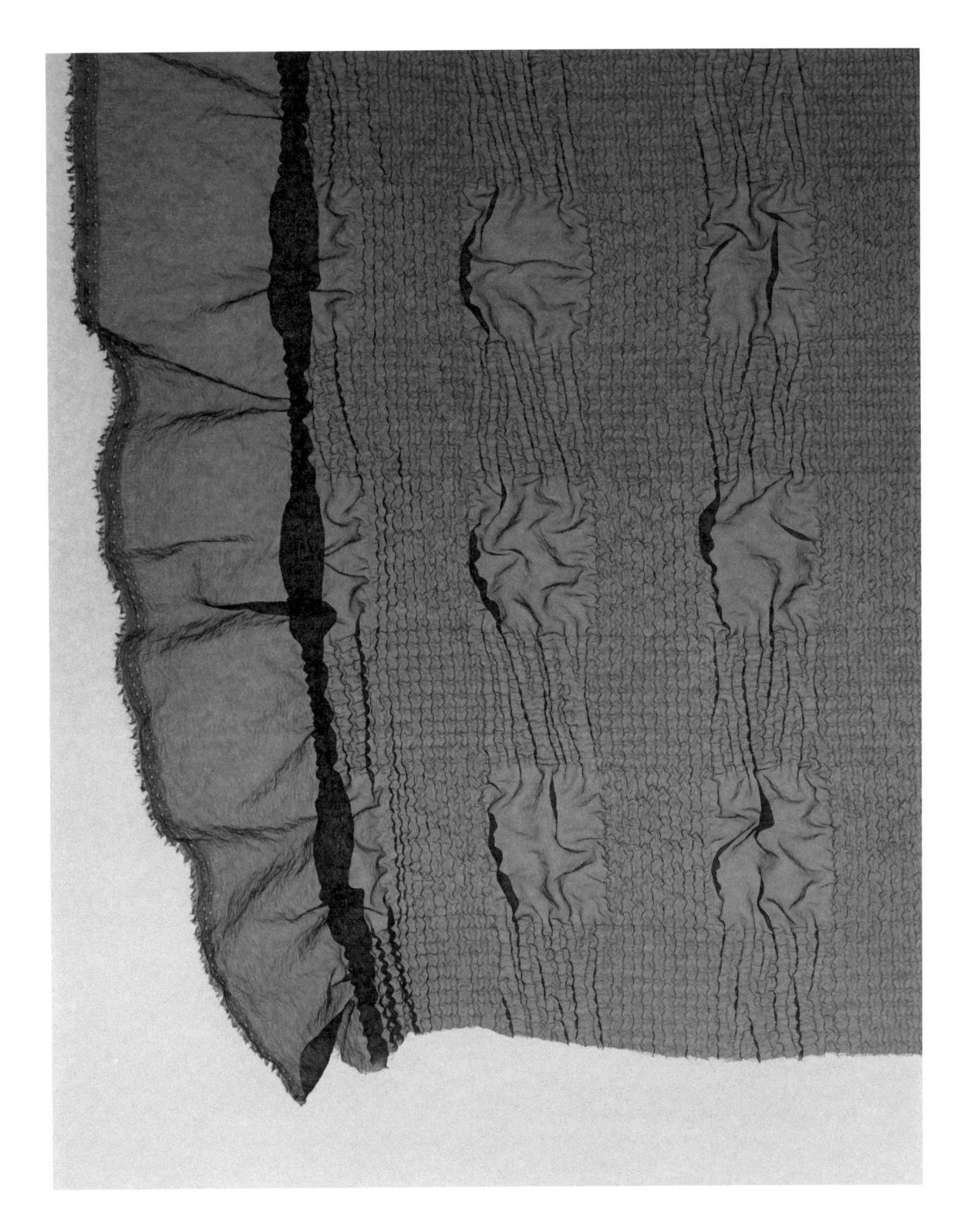

opposite top
A printed production sample.

opposite bottom and above
Removing heat-shrinking fabric from the sample to check shrinkage and finish.

following page, top
Heat-shrinking fabric is laid out with organdy layered on top, then overprinted in a grid pattern with water-soluble adhesive.

following page, bottom left
Fabric is covered with plastic and brushed to ensure even adhesion.

following page, bottom right and p. 65
Heat-set *Jellyfish* emerges from the oven.

ぜんまい

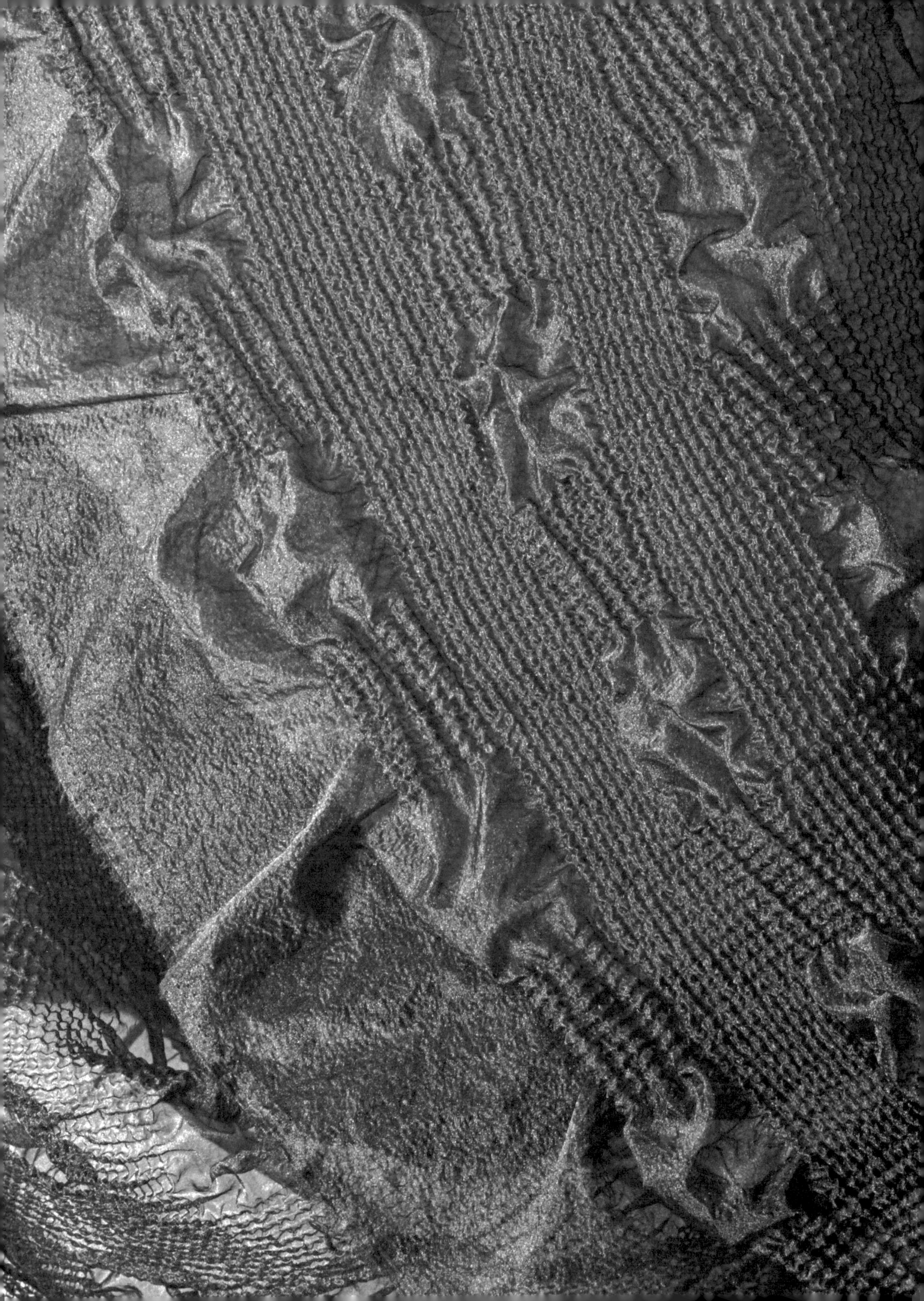

SHIWA
SHIWA

shiwa shiwa (シワシワ)

1. Wrinkled, rumpled, crumpled, creased, unironed (as in clothing)
2. Furrowed, corrugated, channelled, grooved, creviced
3. Puckered, crinkled, crimped; bunched, gathered; tucked, folded
4. Bedraggled, messy, untidy

Reverse, inverse, increase

Depending on who you ask, wrinkles are either the hard-earned hallmarks of age and repositories of ingrained wisdom, or anathema to all things pure and clean and new. A quick web search for 'wrinkle', or *shiwa*, instantly pulls up hundreds of thousands of beauty tips and remedies. Apparently hardly anyone likes to have wrinkles – not even smile lines.

And yet, wrinkles are the very essence of texture and surface aesthetics. Crinkly, wriggly, bunched-up and gathered, *shiwa shiwa* textiles offer entry into a labyrinth of sensory stimulation, a deeply rewarding immersive experience of countless moments folded into a physical analogue of memory. It is as though we could drop a phonograph needle onto the lines of each fabric and play the life stories of weavers and textile towns, themselves very often hidden away in the folds of mountain valleys. The scratchy soundtrack of those grooves might well resonate in every halcyon hollow around the world.

NUNO's *shiwa shiwa* textiles all bear witness to time-honoured tastes and techniques – plus a few new tricks – as precious mantles of heritage lost and regained. From humble and honest to crevassed and convoluted, there is depth in these layers. Wear your worldliness with pride.

p. 66:
Polygami, 2010.
By Reiko Sudo and Hiroko Kobayashi.
A lengthy trial and error experimentation process finally yielded this 'origami weave' technique that lets us weave folded pleat patterns.

right:
Delphi, 1996.
By Reiko Sudo.
Pleated horizontally over and over, different warp and weft colours create beautiful iridescent surface effects on this polyester organdy.

Shiwa Shiwa

Kenya Hara

People are drawn to 'smooth'. Box-fresh clothes, just-bloomed flowers, youthful complexions, newly completed buildings, crisp-laid stationery, steaming white rice, everything nice and neat. Feel-good images all, bright, clean, blank sheets of perfection virtually synonymous with pristine purity. Things taut to the touch – just the sight of them makes us want to stand to attention, with our backs straight.

Yet any honest observation of the world will tell us that 'smooth' is but a one-time state, never to be repeated. The hard knot structure of a flower bud before it blooms enfolds countless wrinkles that will open out into petals, gleaming with blessings. Even so, their flawlessly smooth beauty doesn't last long. Sooner or later the petals wrinkle up and wilt into shrivelled decay – a process people have come to associate with their own ageing and ultimate demise.

Then again, further observation reveals a vast *shiwa shiwa* world of folding phenomena. The plump little hands of a newborn baby are already creased with lines, fingertips uniquely whorled with identifiable swirls. Under the microscope, at high magnification, wrinkles spread and multiply, layer upon layer. From far above, the Earth's crust is seen to buckle and fold, the oceans roil with waves and currents, atmospheric motions spawn wrinkles we know as clouds. The cosmos crackles and stirs with electromagnetic waves; our Milky Way galaxy is a pinwheel of bending light.

Picture a pair of images: one, the beginnings of form emerging from chaos, converging towards an apex of tensile cohesion through the vector of creation; the other, forms losing cohesion and

Yet any honest observation of the world will tell us that 'smooth' is but a one-time state, never to be repeated. The hard knot structure of a flower bud before it blooms enfolds countless wrinkles that will open out into petals, gleaming with blessings.

There is a special Japanese aesthetic sensibility known as mono no aware, *'pathos toward things', a poetic appreciation of impermanence premised on a Buddhist awareness that all phenomena shift and change, reaching their peak for only a fleeting moment.*

SHIWA SHIWA

dispersing back into chaos through the vector of regression. While science has yet to fully explicate the ultimate origins of everything, these two movements, out of primordial chaos and back again, are thought to be the coiling and uncoiling mainspring of all life and the universe itself.

We humans are actually quite adept at perceiving these two movements in the dizzying array of changes folding and unfolding around us. Rarely do we apprehend the singular peak of the fullness of creation; but if we look carefully at the folds and wrinkles, the *shiwa shiwa* phenomena that propel the drive towards creation, we may see a vast store of latent possibilities.

I once had some art-school students do an experiment, asking people to send them thirty-square-centimetre parcels wrapped in white paper from around the globe. One after another, the parcels arrived by land and sea and air, wracked by wind and waves, tossed about by nameless hands, battered and scarred by their journeys. Seeing all the wear and tear of their travels served to inspire flights of imagination.

There is a special Japanese aesthetic sensibility known as *mono no aware*, 'pathos toward things', a poetic appreciation of impermanence premised on a Buddhist awareness that all phenomena shift and change, reaching their peak for only a fleeting moment. Knowing the beauty of flowers, scenery, love and glory all fade and pass away gives us pause to reflect on our shared, evanescent fate. Accordingly, we tend to avoid expressions of perfection and fulfilment, preferring instead to find visions of 'withered grace' in the waxing moon, warped asymmetric ceramics, craftwares lovingly worn just-so; the diverse minutiae of the *shiwa shiwa* workings of life in flux.

p. 71, left:
Demon Crepe, 1985.
By Reiko Sudo and
Junichi Arai.
This double-action weave
pits wool on one side against
cotton on the other, sending
shockwaves through both
and causing the wool to
shrink in defence.

p. 71, right:
Kumihira Stripes, 2007.
By Reiko Sudo.
Woven with old-fashioned
'coil yarns' that poke up
from the surface, this soft
wool josette is a study in
textural contrasts.

above:
Mountain (Pinch Puff), 1997.
By Reiko Sudo and
Hiroko Kobayashi.
The time-honoured *shibori*
'tie-dyeing' technique is
emulated in pleating,
without using knots.

Circle Z, 2019.
By Reiko Sudo.
This textile, with its repeating oval design, is woven with two types of tightly twisted yarns in the back side of the cloth to give it a varied and full-bodied texture.

75

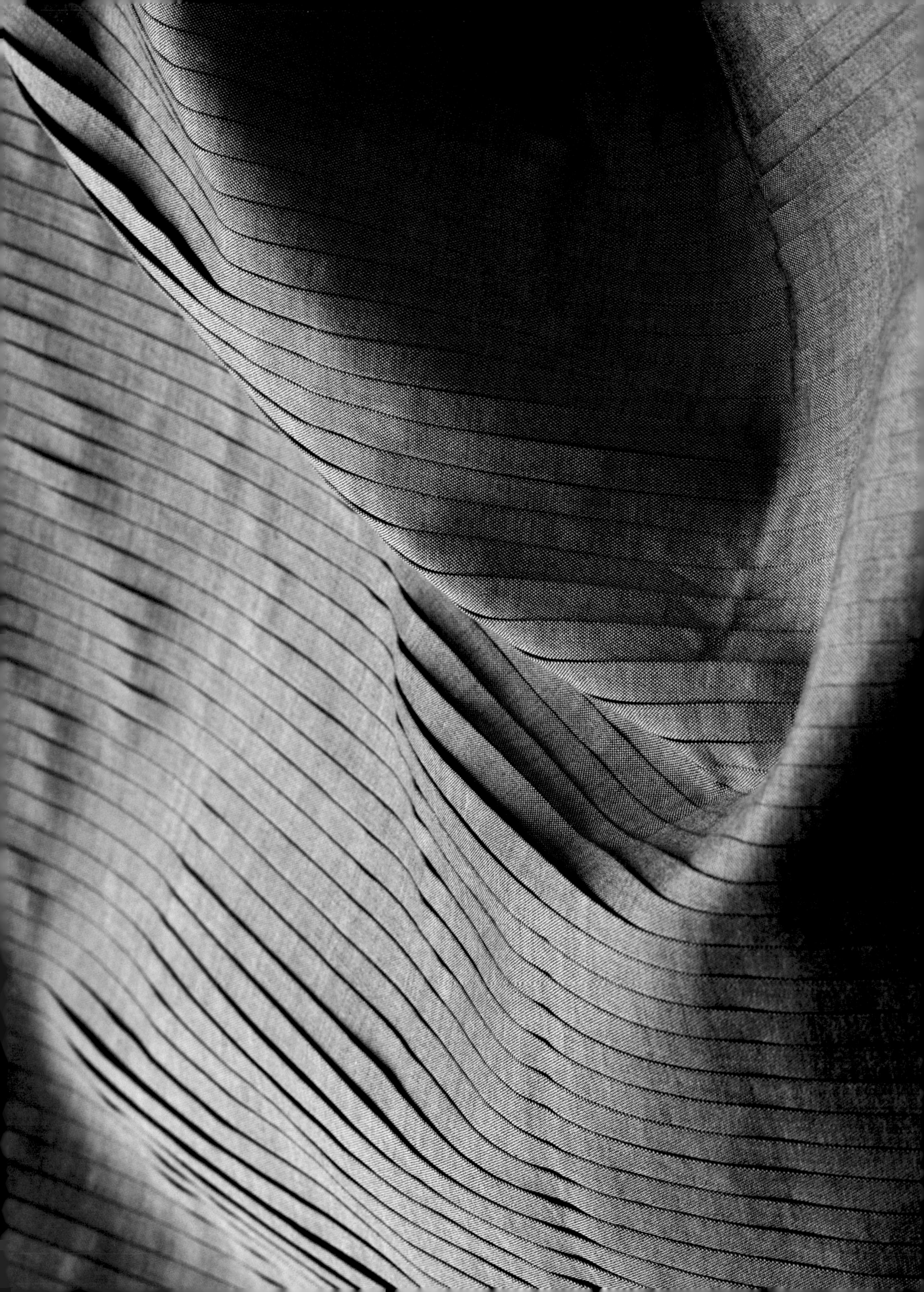

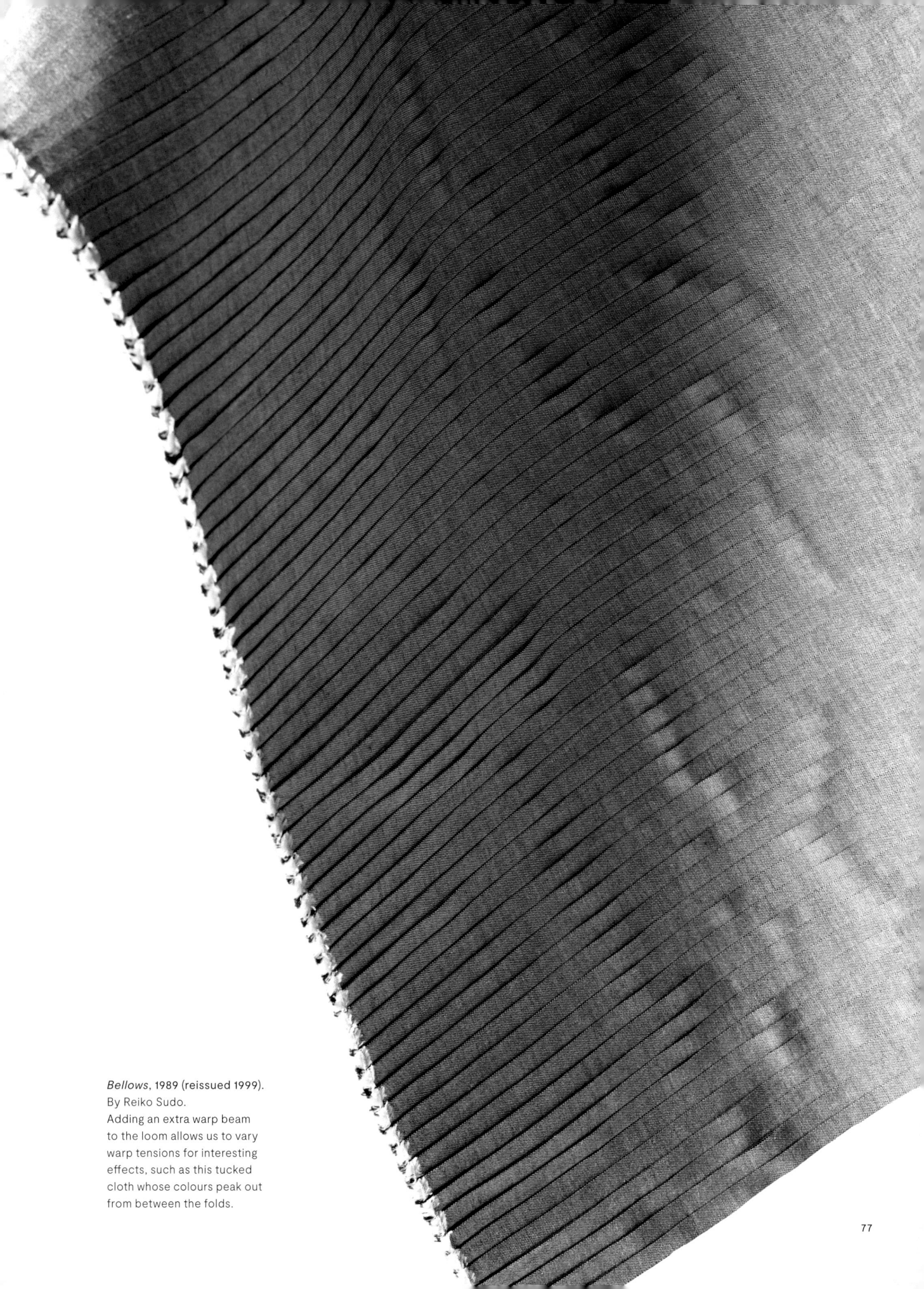

Bellows, 1989 (reissued 1999).
By Reiko Sudo.
Adding an extra warp beam to the loom allows us to vary warp tensions for interesting effects, such as this tucked cloth whose colours peak out from between the folds.

Crostata, 1996.
By Reiko Sudo.
This bi-directional stretch jacquard weave of cotton-covered Spandex™ warps and wefts takes its design motif from Italian baking tins.

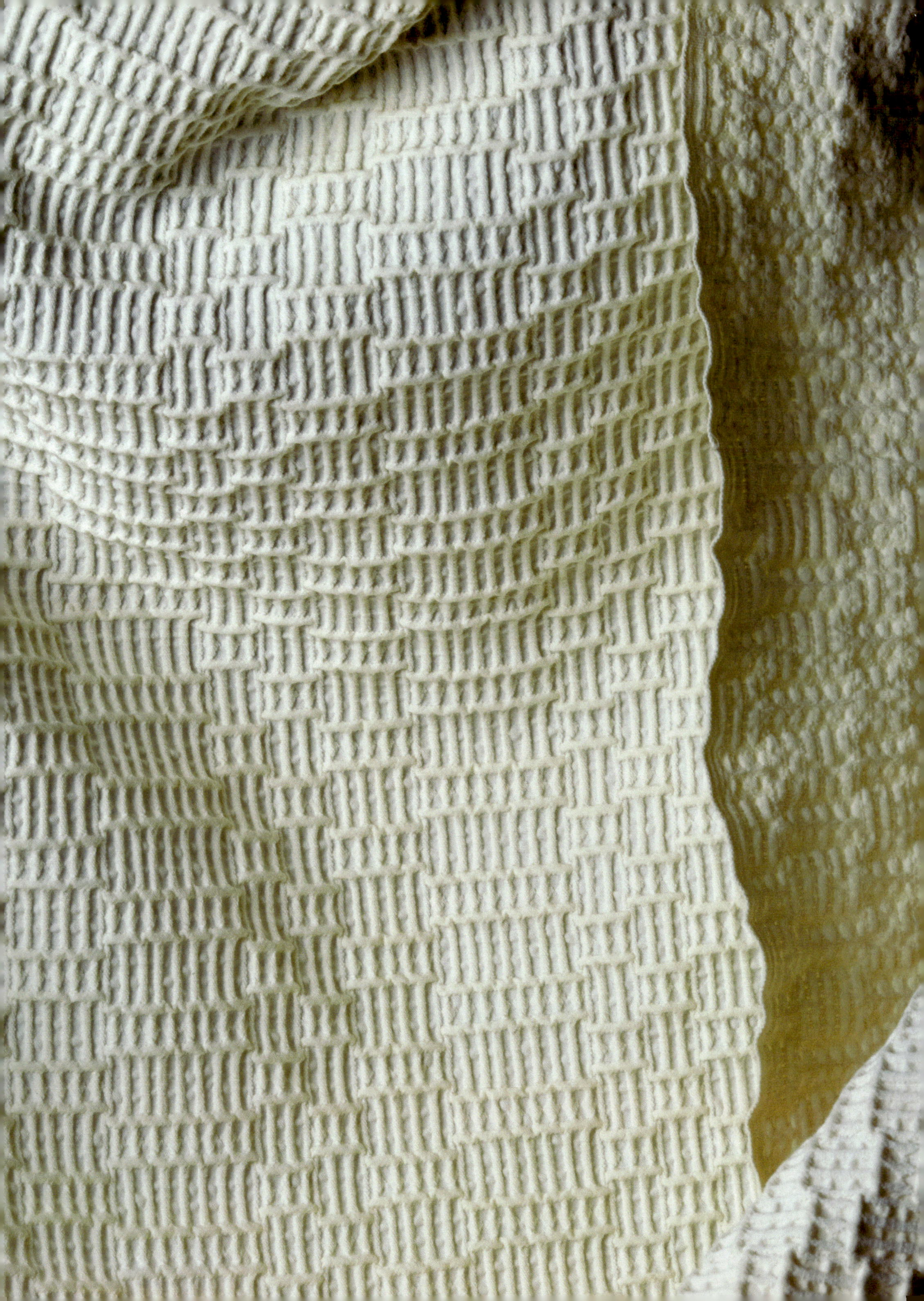

below:
Wave Head, 1997.
By Reiko Sudo.
Overspun silk ridges criss-cross diagonally to give this fabric a dynamic vibrancy.

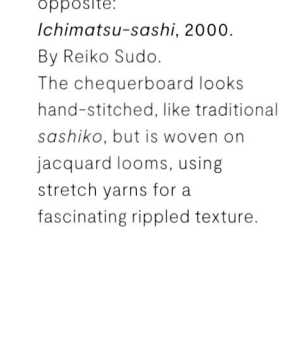

opposite:
Ichimatsu-sashi, 2000.
By Reiko Sudo.
The chequerboard looks hand-stitched, like traditional *sashiko*, but is woven on jacquard looms, using stretch yarns for a fascinating rippled texture.

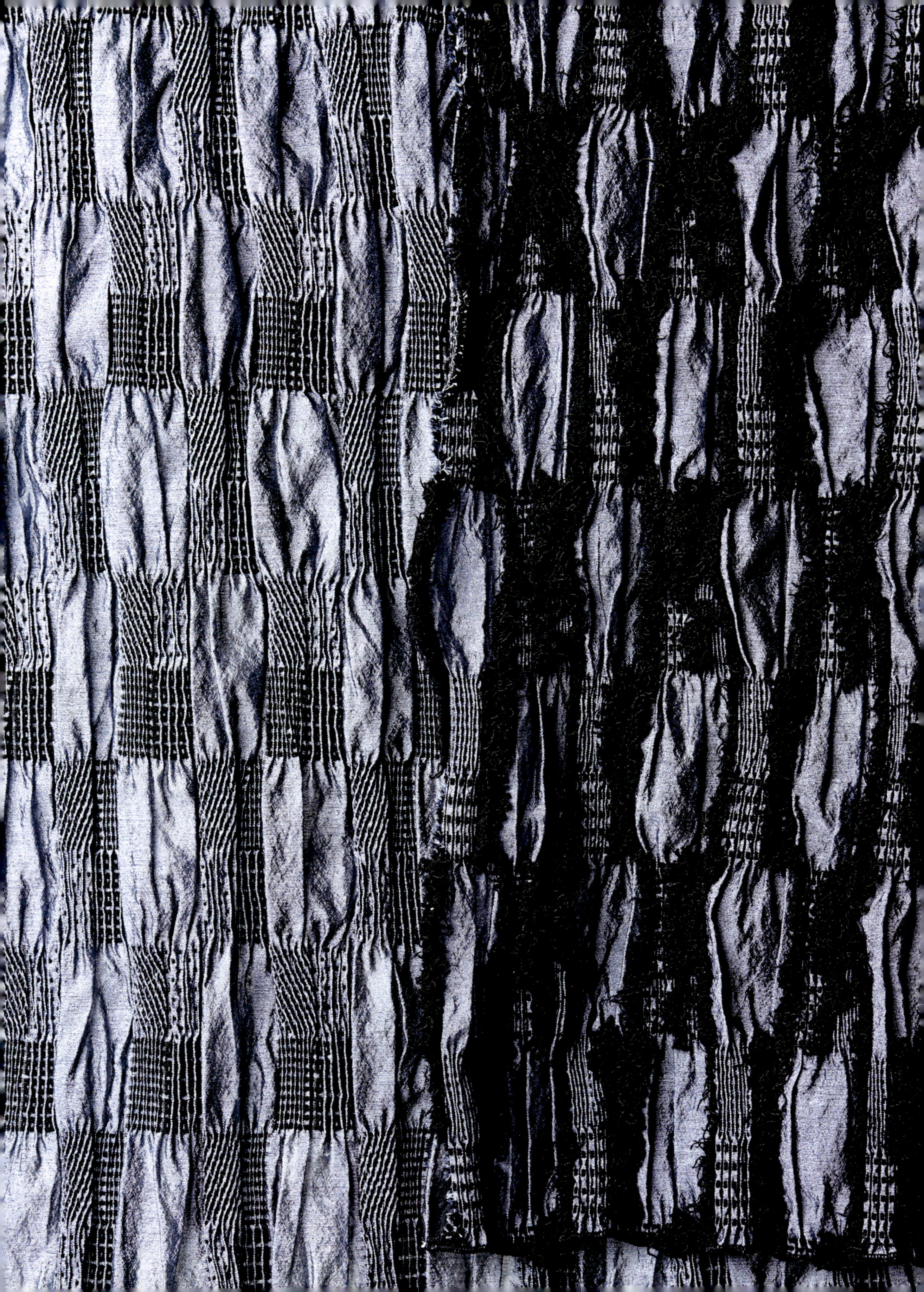

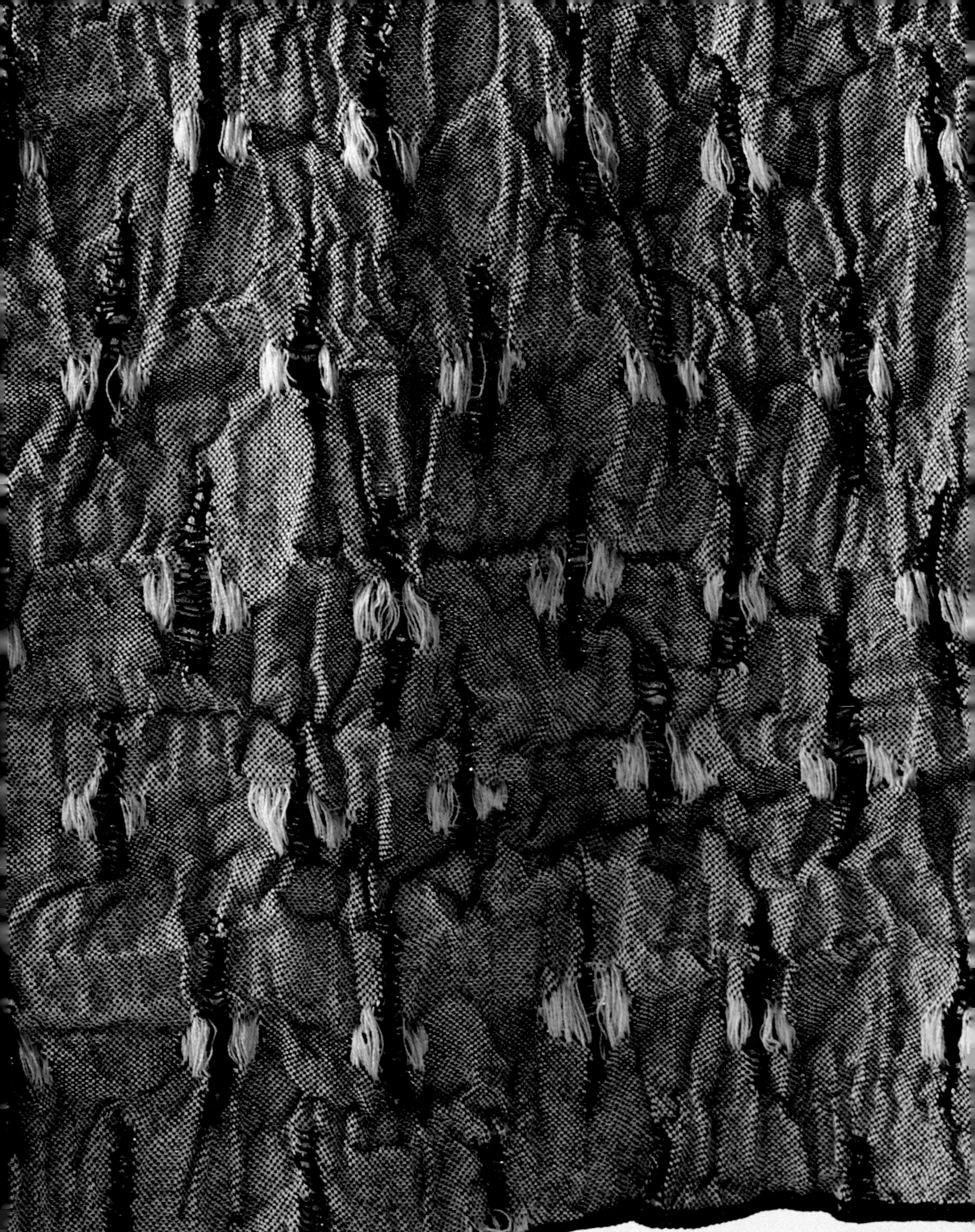

SHIWA SHIWA

Inutadé, 2008.
By Reiko Sudo.
Loosely weaving with highly twisted, overspun yarns creates a soft knit effect with plenty of stretch. The design here emulates wild *inutadé* field grass, with its tiny pink flowerlets.

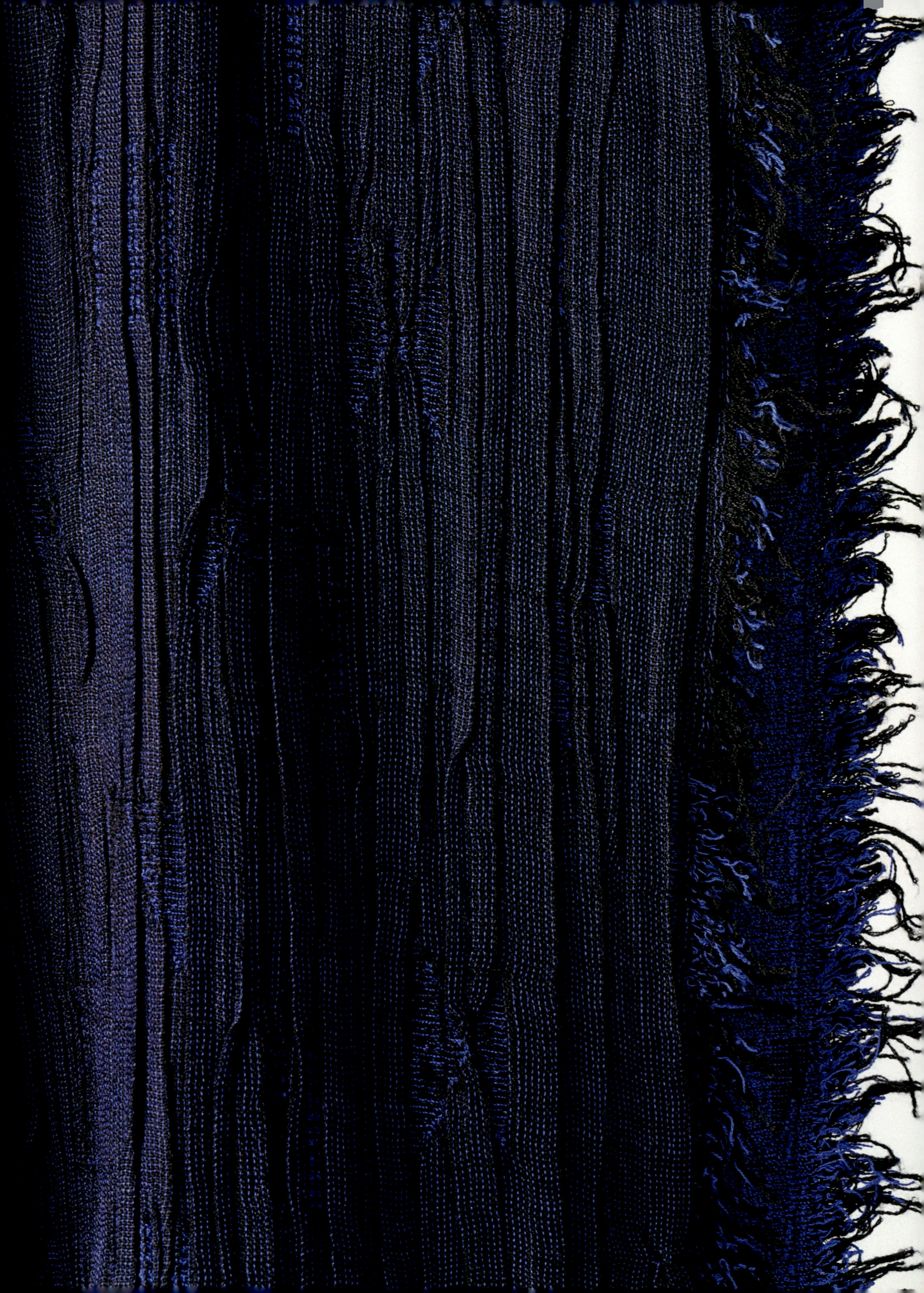

opposite:
Kakuré Cho (Hidden Butterflies), 1985.
By Reiko Sudo and Junichi Arai.
Minute wrinkles from overspun yarns in a fine merino gauze excite the butterflies woven on the reverse side.

below:
Chilly Wind, 1998.
By Reiko Sudo.
Silk *saki-zomé* threads weave an intricate iridescence. The reverse side is woven with overspun cotton yarns, which bulge out in irregular crinkles that resemble windblown leaves.

following spread:
Eulalia Crepe / Cicada, 1996.
By Reiko Sudo.
Inspired by eulalia plants swaying in the breeze, the pleat in this fabric is created by repeating several different highly twisted yarns in narrow stripes, side by side.

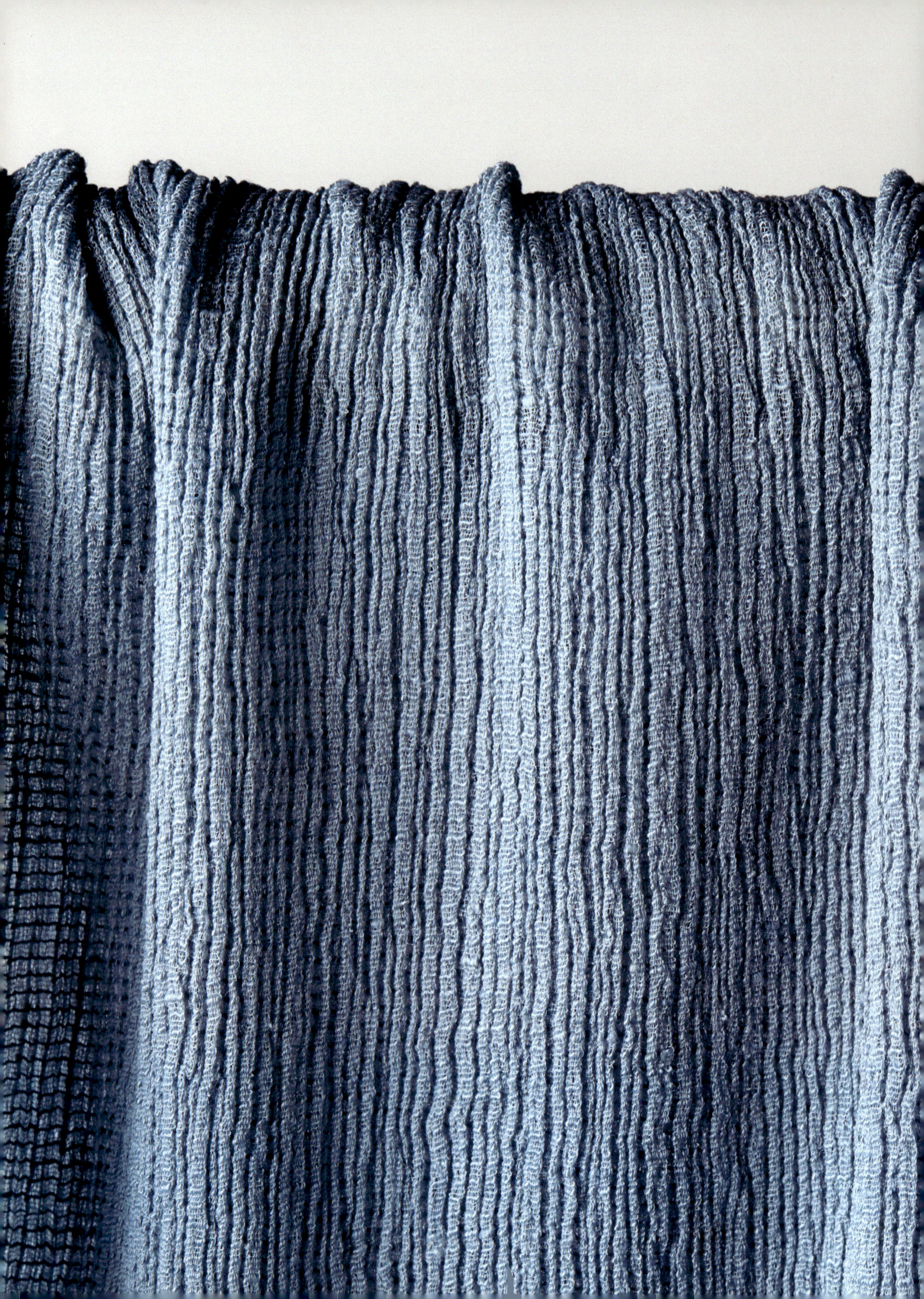

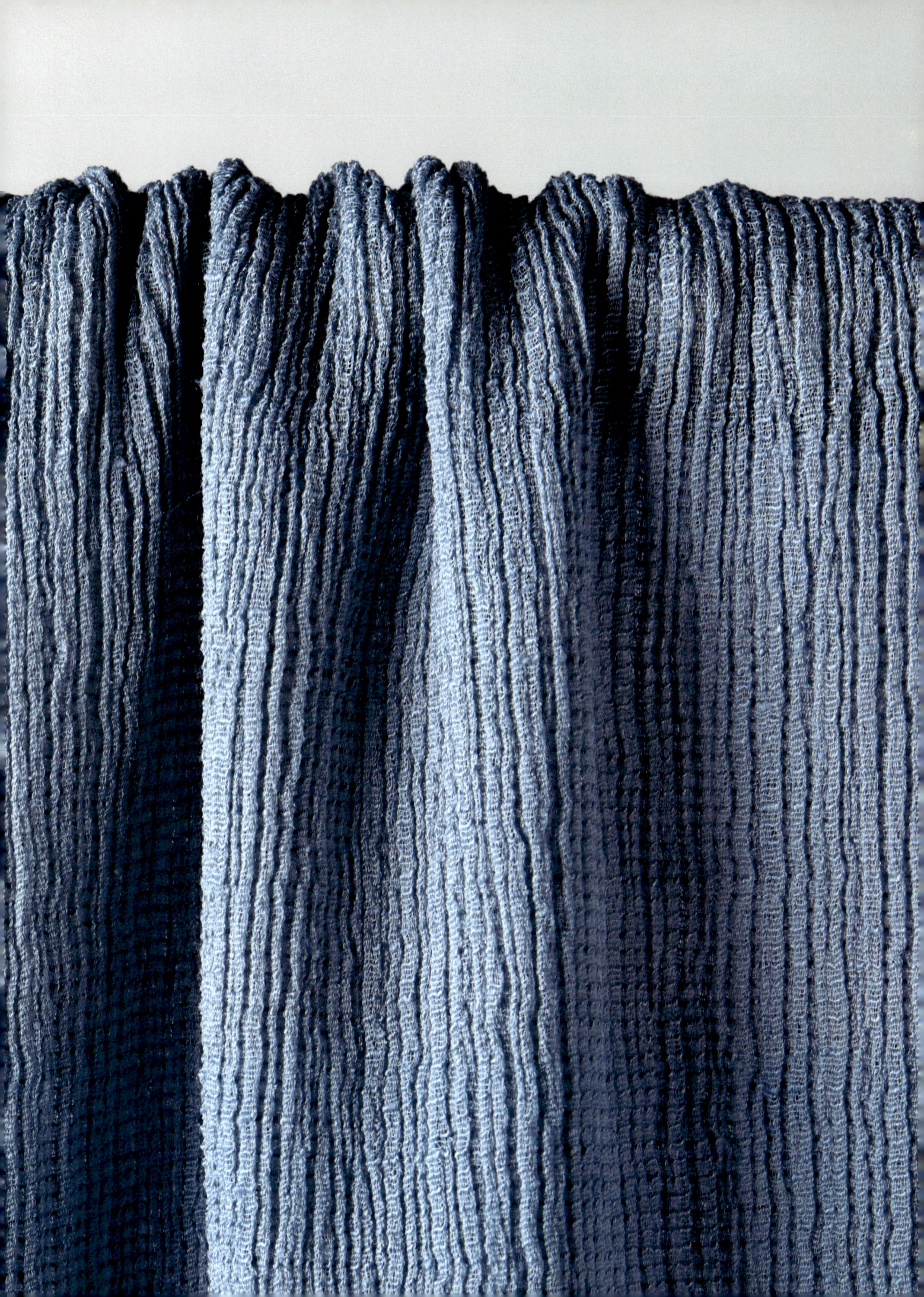

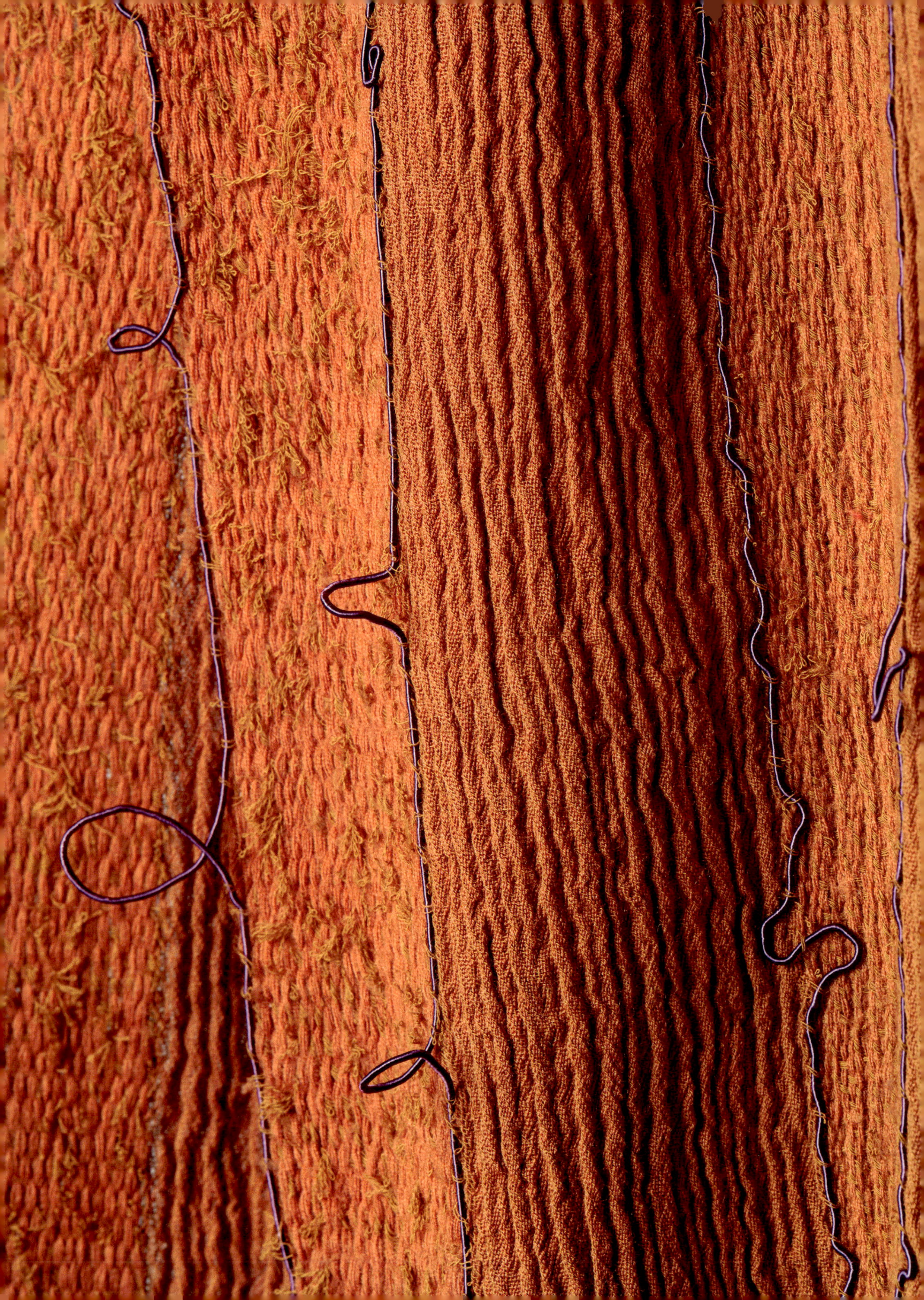

opposite:
Whalebone, 1997.
By Reiko Sudo.
Overly thick, hard string yarns used as warps incidentally distort the woven structure, creating wonderfully twisted and skewed 'imperfections'.

this page:
Shifu (Paper Cloth), 1994.
By Reiko Sudo.
Wefts of handmade *washi* paper were traditionally used to make lightweight, tough *shifu* 'paper cloth'. Here, warps of silk combine with Mino paper wefts, with Spandex™ woven in for elasticity.

following spread:
Peak (Pinch Puff), 1997.
By Reiko Sudo and Hiroko Kobayashi.
Using our patented no-sew, no-tie *tsumami shibori* process, we pinch up little peaks before transfer-dyeing the exposed tips.

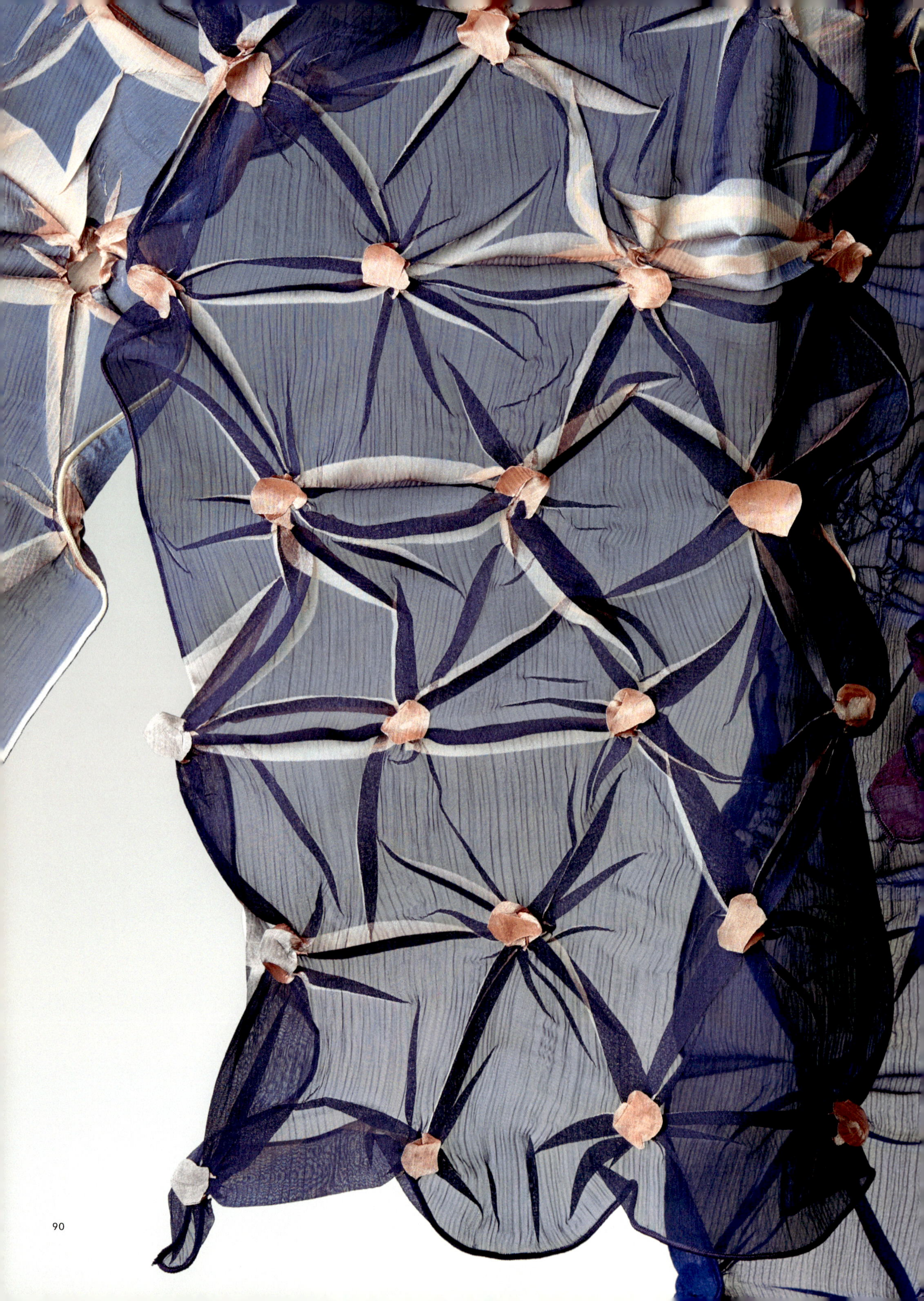

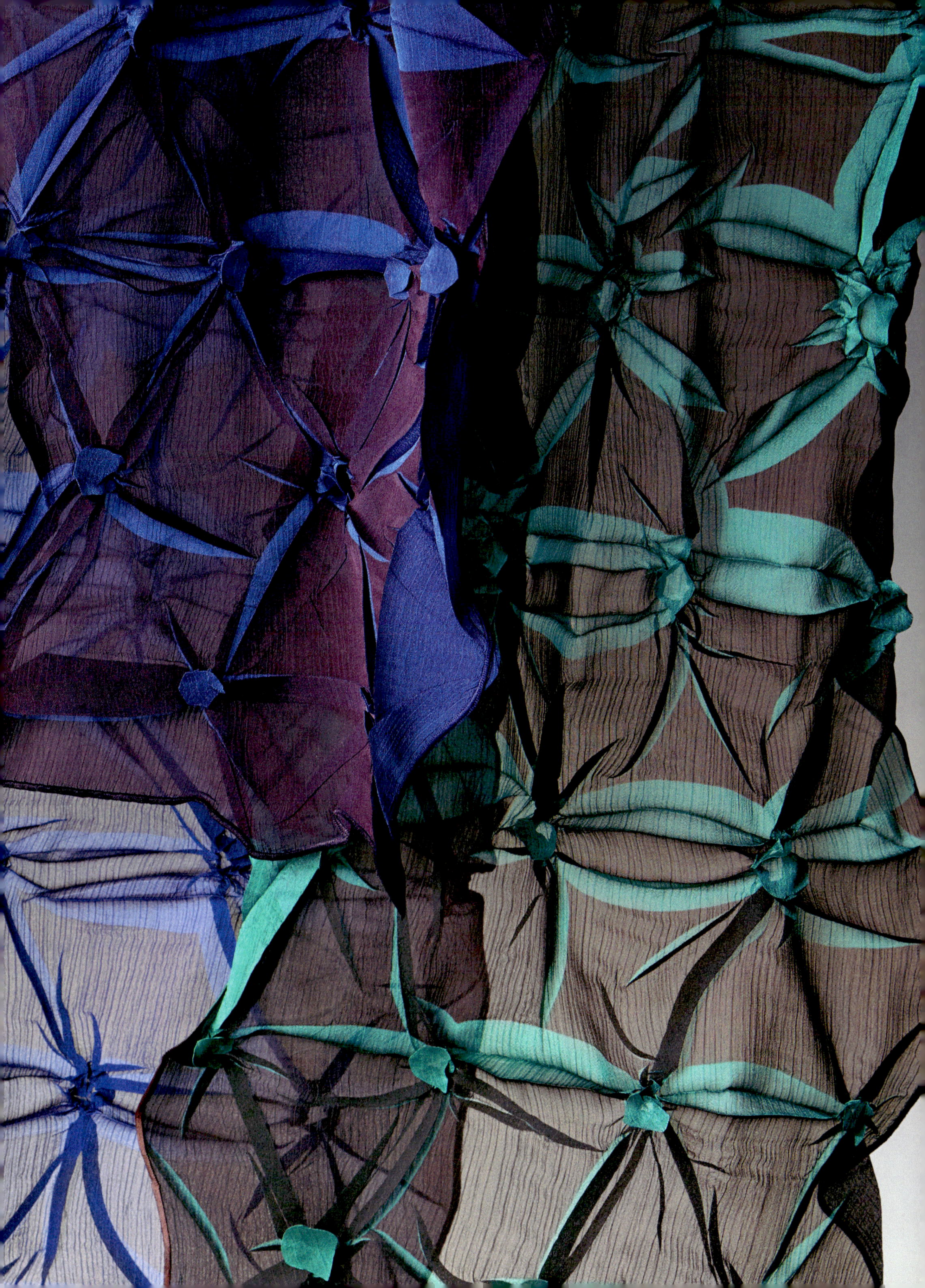

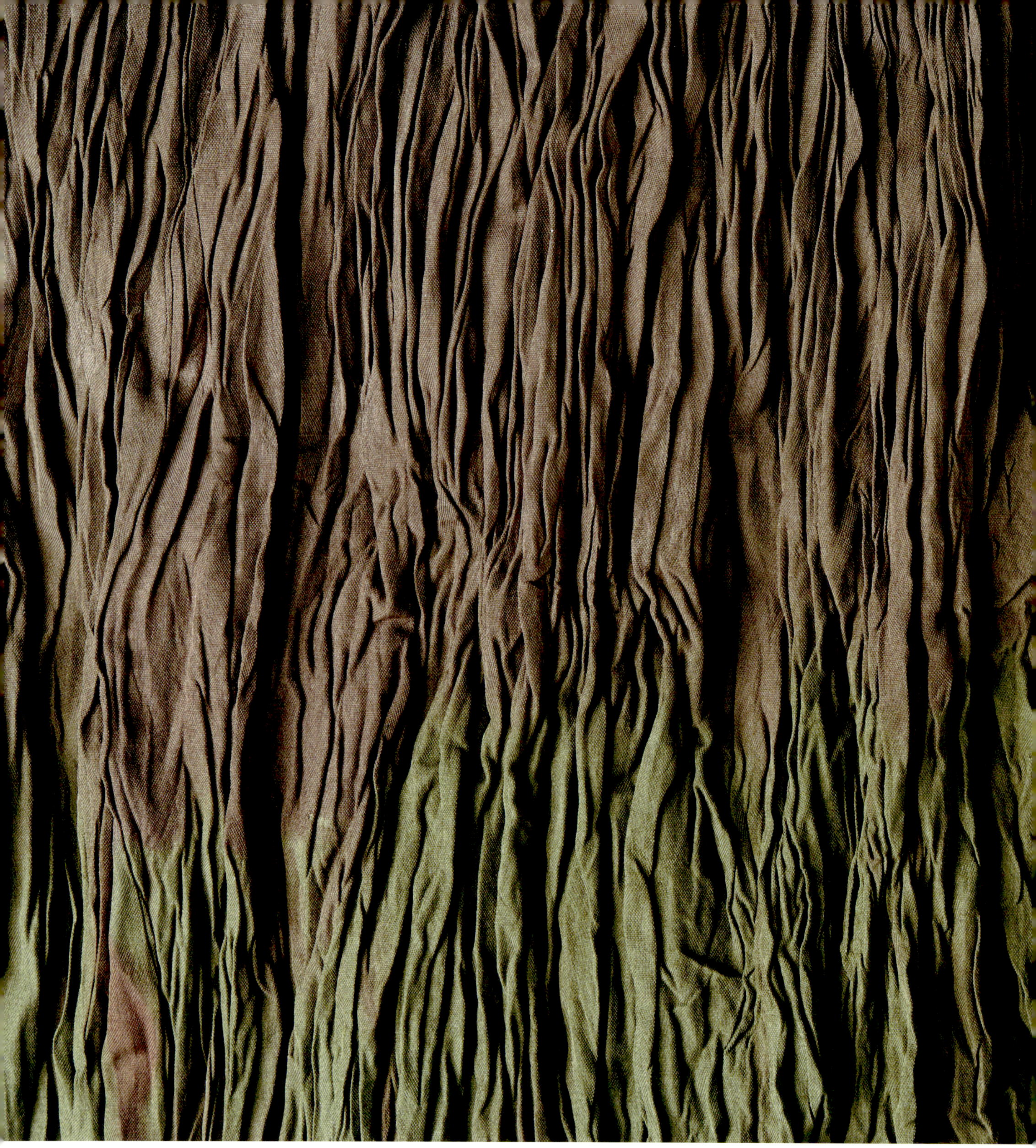

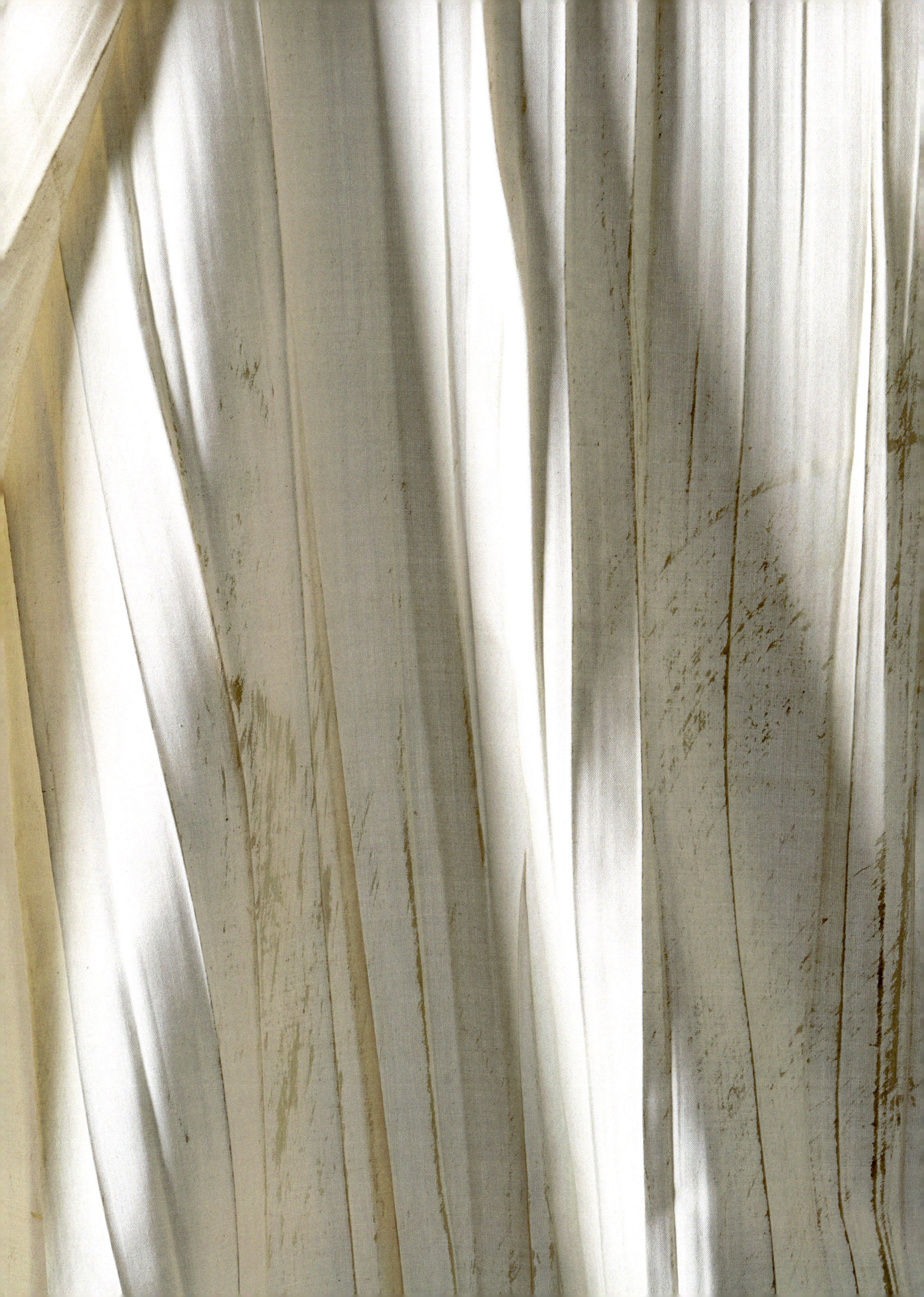

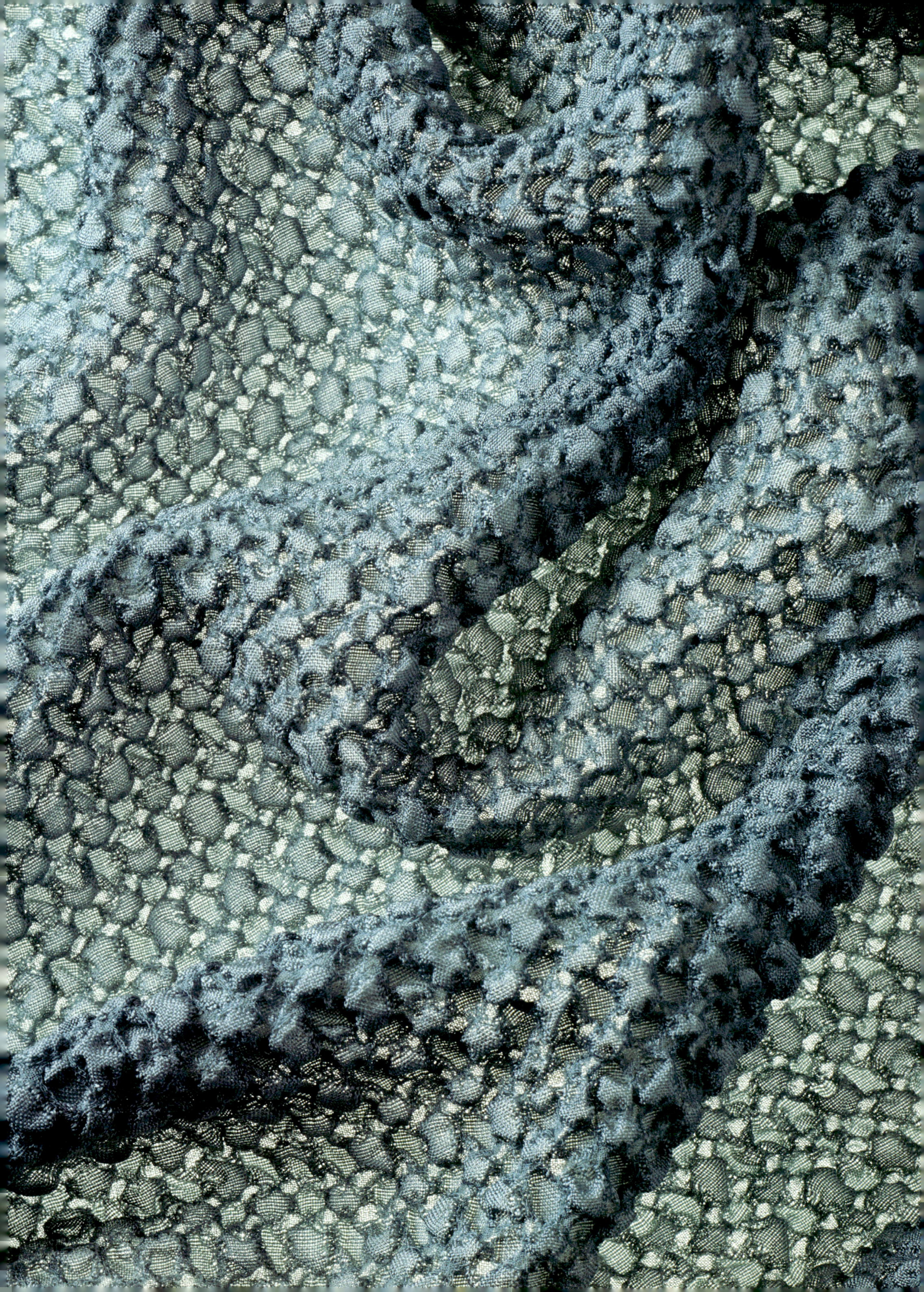

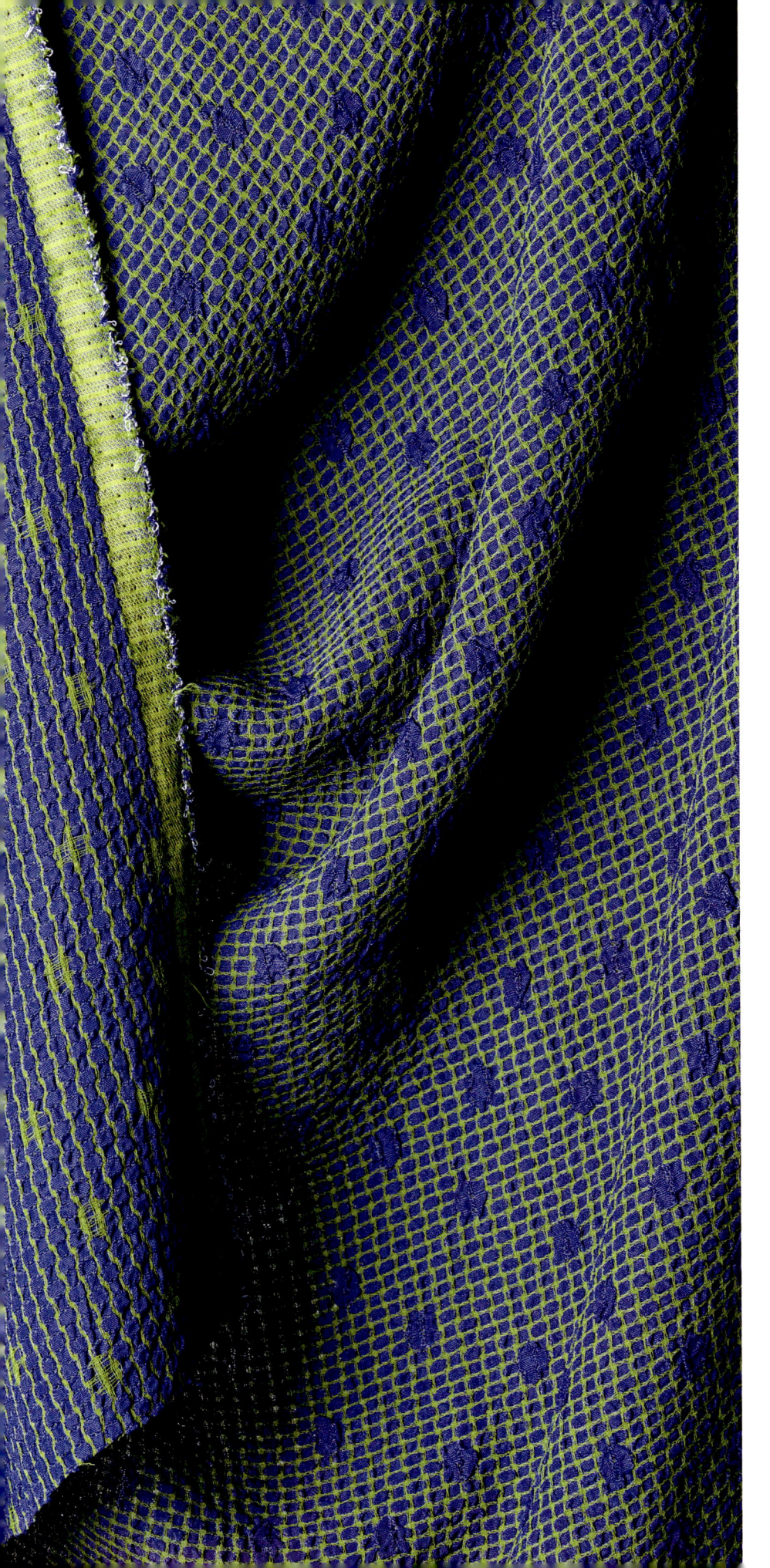

p. 92:
Osage-zome 'Braid-Transfer', 1993.
By Reiko Sudo.
Three lengths of polyester – dyed, but not dye-fixed, in three different colours – are braided together, then put under pressure so that the colours bleed in serendipitous shapes and colours.

p. 93:
Shigoki-zome 'Squeegee Wipe', 1993.
By Reiko Sudo.
A centuries-old *yuzen kimono* technique. Silk is spread on large boards, wiped with a paste dye, dried with a layer of sawdust, wrinkled and heat-pressed to produce crisply dyed folds.

opposite:
Imitation Hitta Kanoko, 1999.
By Reiko Sudo and Hiroko Kobayashi.
A 'deerskin' dappled fabric, traditionally made by laboriously tying one knot at a time, replicated in a silk dobby weave.

left:
Polka Dots, 2016.
By Reiko Sudo.
An array of dots adorns a ground woven from wood-based acetate cellulose and cotton linter-based cupra cellulose, the two fibres spun in twisted and untwisted threads, making for a soft volume.

SHIWA SHIWA

this page:
Embroidery Border, 1984.
By Reiko Sudo.
Embroidering soft and pliant cotton with stretch yarns, each with different contraction rates, makes the yarns and fabric bunch up in an unusual fashion.

opposite:
Coin, 2006.
By Reiko Sudo and Sayuri Shimoda.
A lightweight cotton lawn is embroidered with polyurethane core-spun yarn to create a built-up surface design.

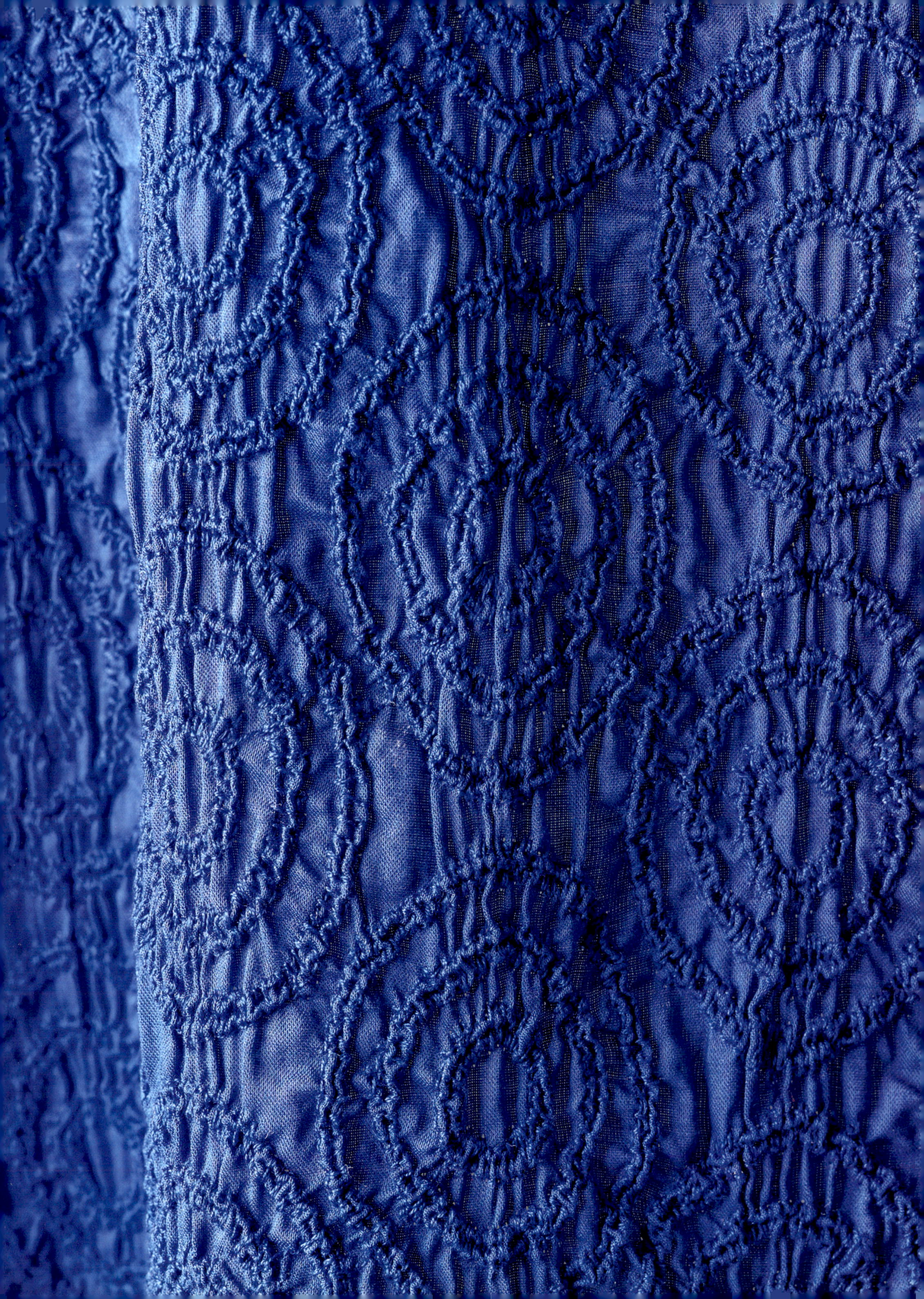

98

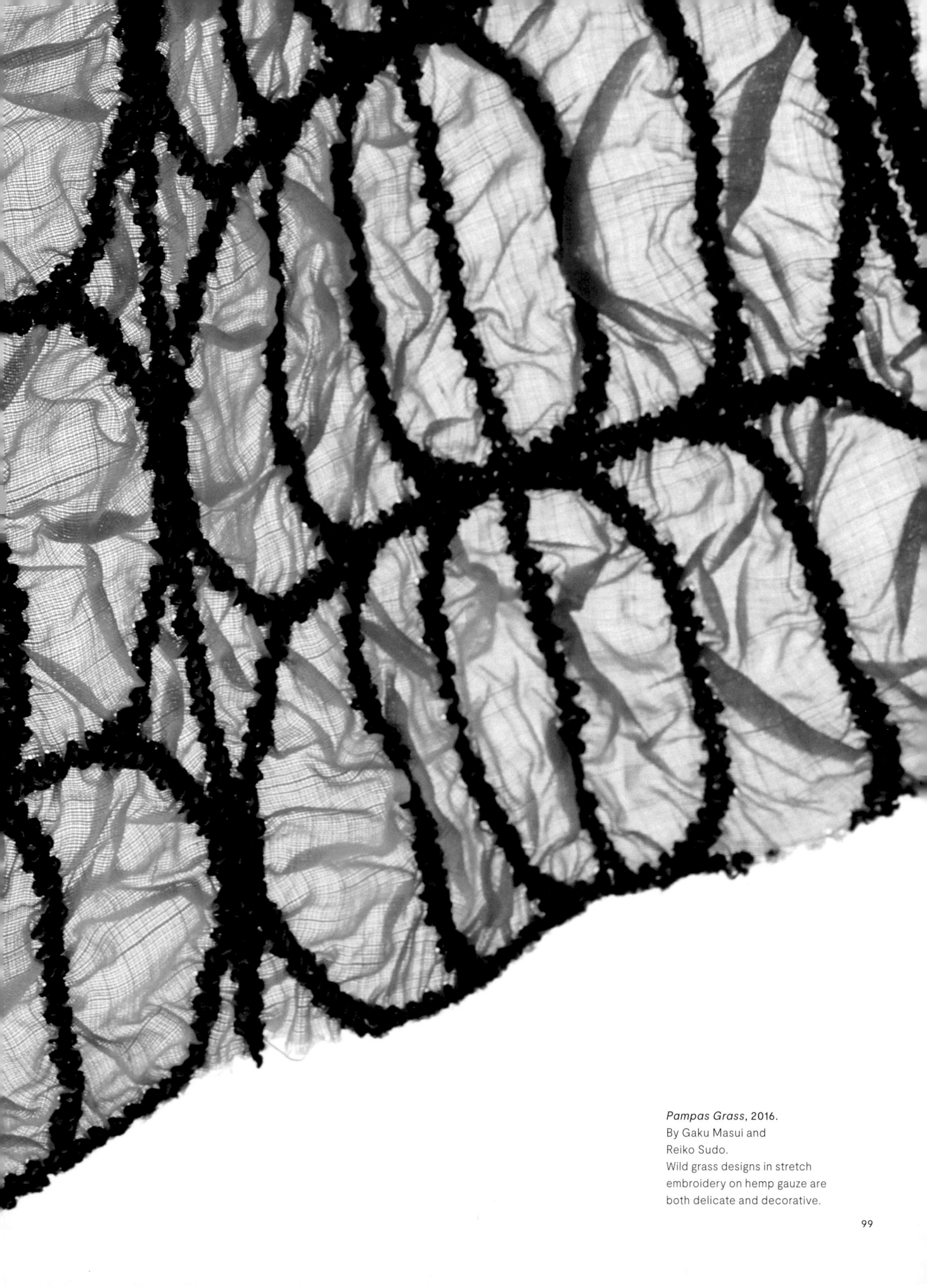

Pampas Grass, 2016.
By Gaku Masui and
Reiko Sudo.
Wild grass designs in stretch embroidery on hemp gauze are both delicate and decorative.

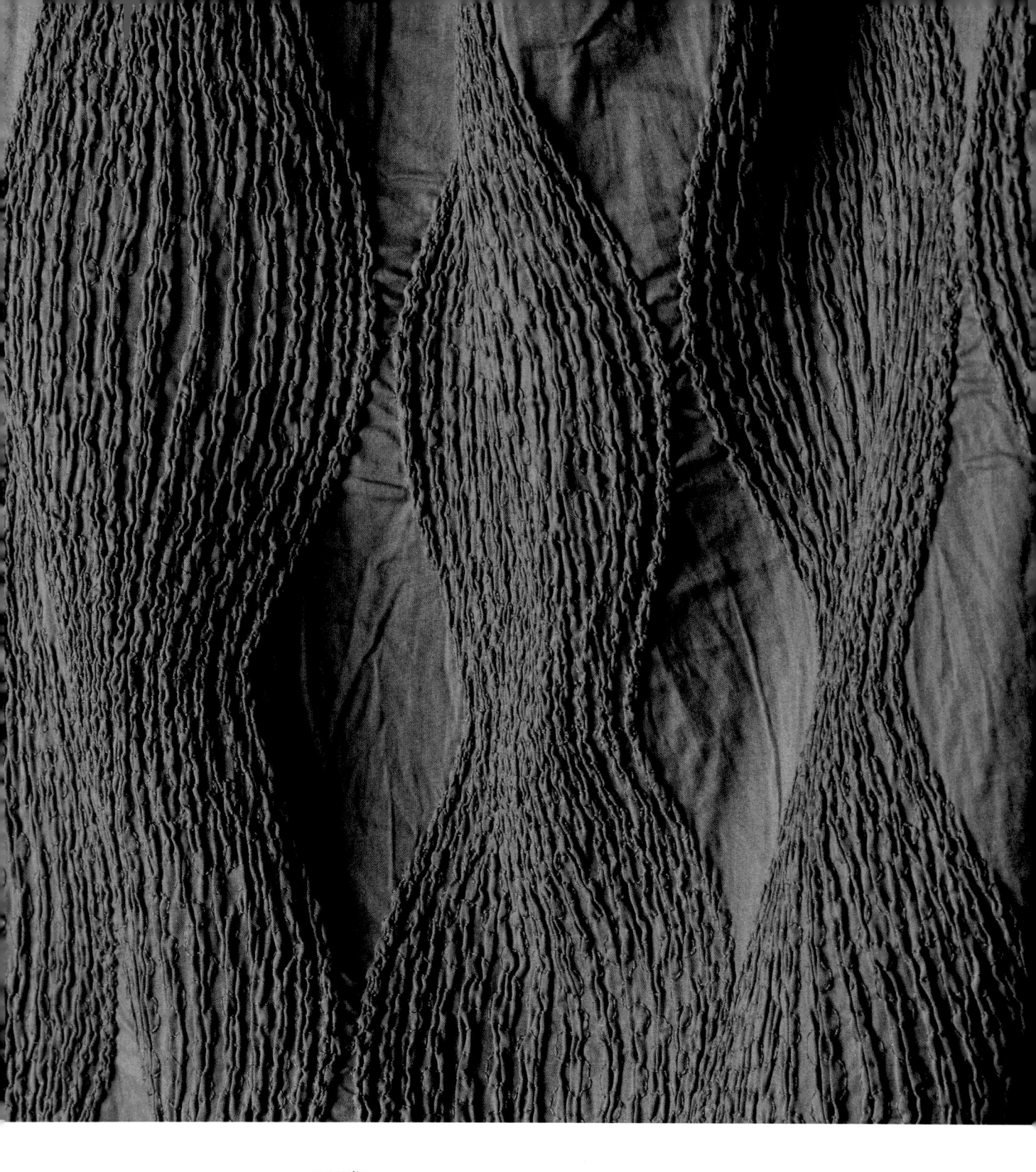

above:
Fisheye, 1997.
By Reiko Sudo.
Elastic embroidery thread makes the fabric bunch up, creating unexpected textural effects. Based on a sketch of a fisheye lens view, stitched repeats give it a wavy look.

opposite:
Embroidery Ajiro, 1992 (reissued 2010).
By Reiko Sudo.
A traditional *ajiro* basket-weave pattern, typically created using *akebi* vines, is embroidered in Spandex™ yarns on a rayon ground to create this stretchy fabric.

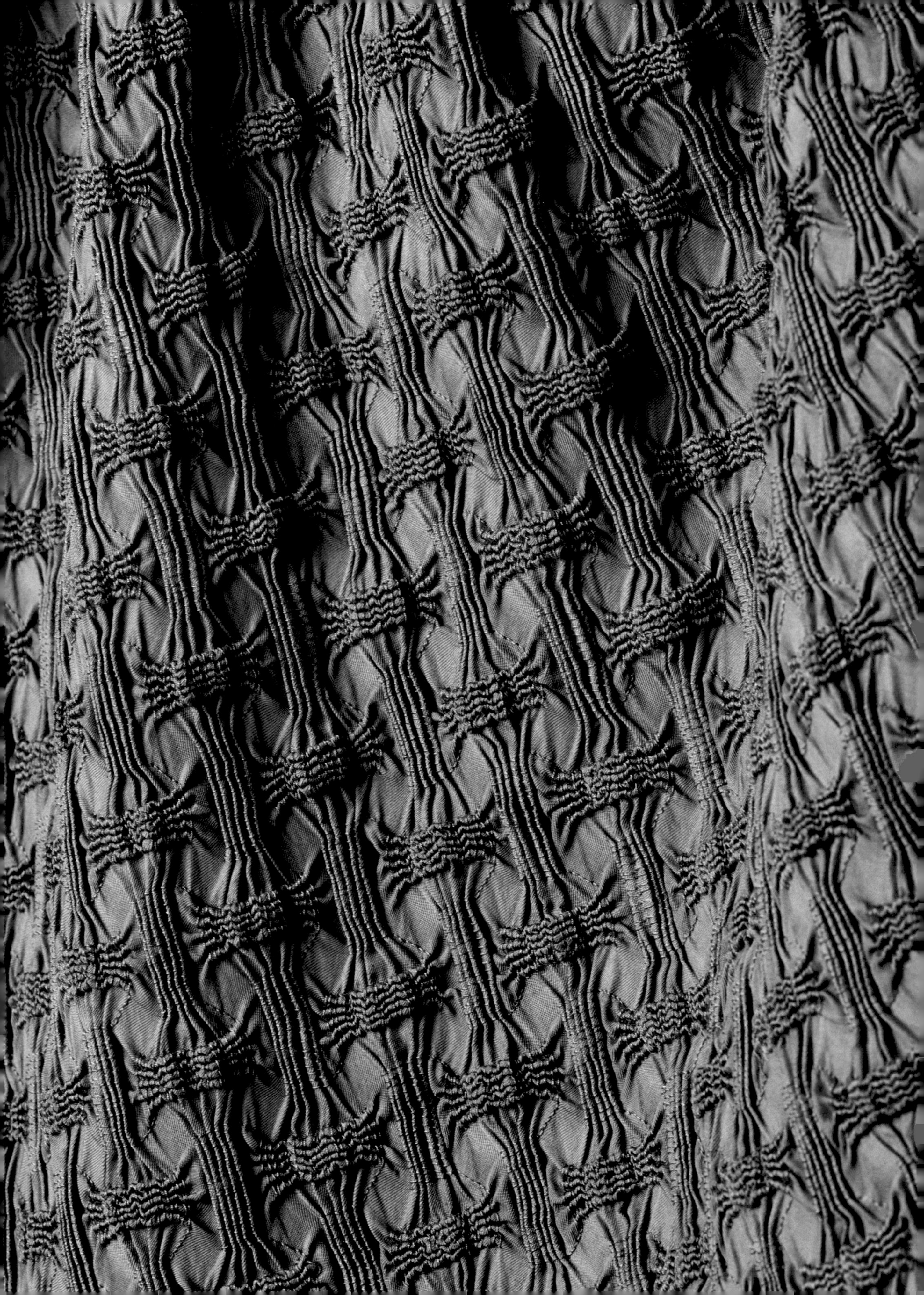

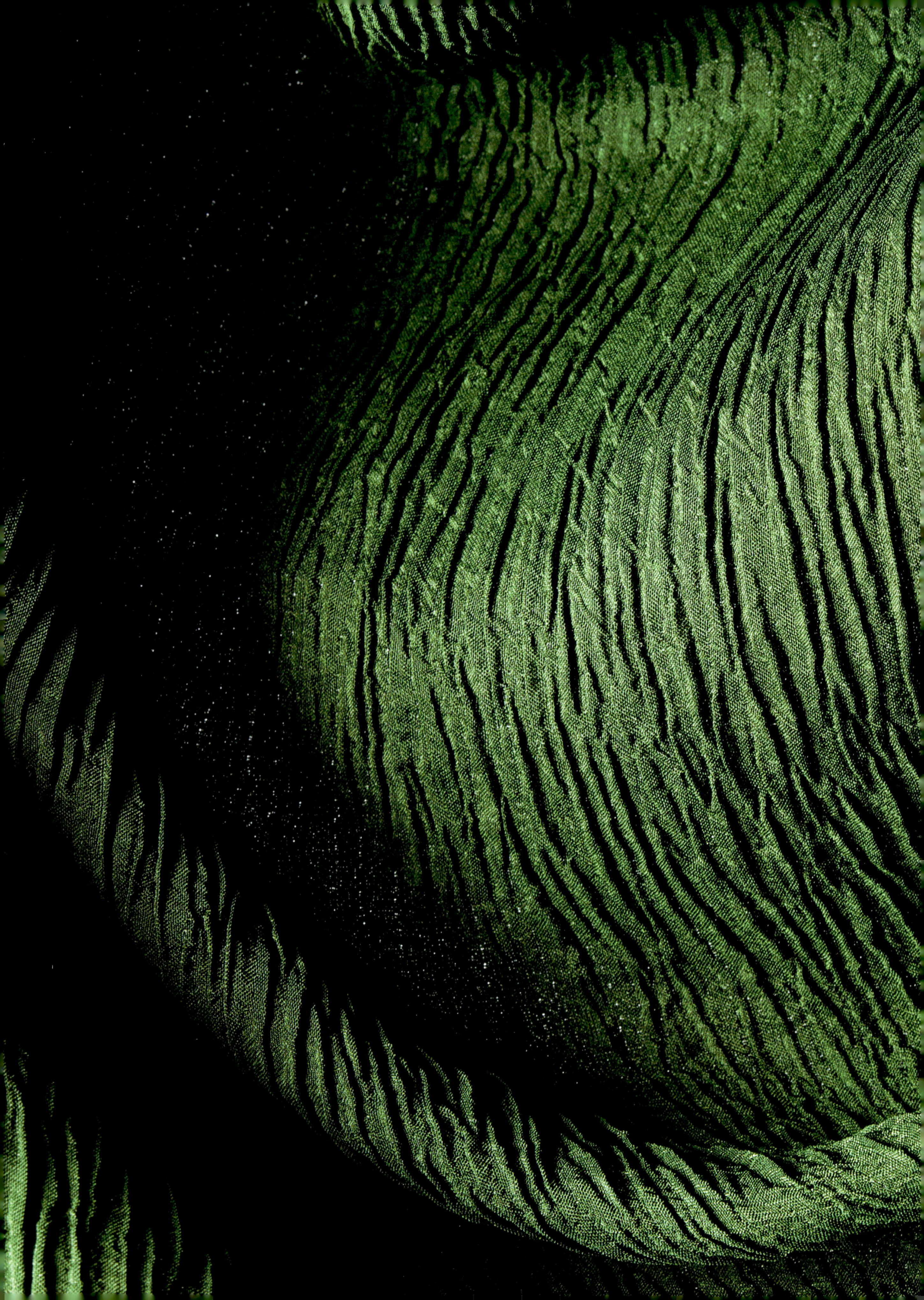

left:
Cedar Bark, 1986
(reissued 1993).
By Junichi Arai; reissued
by Reiko Sudo.
Elastic threads join the cotton
gauze on one side with the
shiny rayon on the other,
giving this double-weave its
distinctive rippled texture.

following page:
Origami Mosaic, 2015.
By Gaku Masui and
Reiko Sudo.
Experiments with our patented
'*origami* pleat' process finally
yielded this '*origami* weave'
technique that lets us weave
folded pleat patterns.

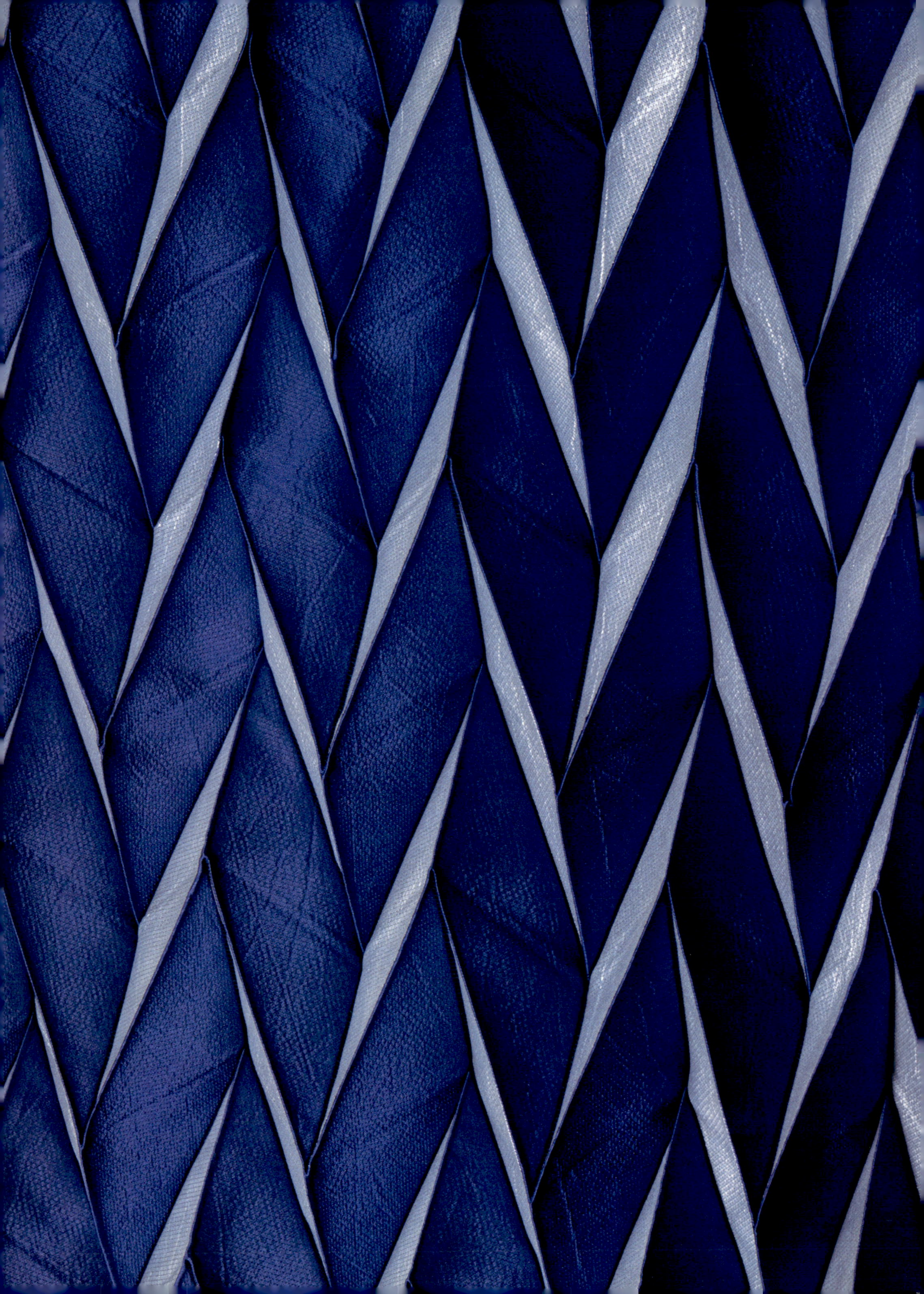

Portrait of a Textile: *Origami Weave*

Could the 'peak' and 'valley' folds characteristic of *origami* be recreated on the loom?

One of our NUNO team is very good at *origami*, the Japanese art of folding paper, especially simple repeated geometric shapes. Passing by her desk one day, I happened to see one of her folded abstract 'doodles' and thought, how could we make a fabric like that? Experimenting by trial and error, we developed a patented process in collaboration with the Gunma Prefectural Textile Research Insitute, whereby we lay fabric between two identically folded paper forms and heat-press to set the creases. Thirteen years and many *origami* textiles later, seeking to replicate the same results without all the laborious paper folding, we developed a loom that could create 'peak' and 'valley' folds mechanically, using alternating pin-tuck weaves to the back and front. We initially used elastic polyurethane-core threads, but this left the 'secret' behind the folding too plainly visible. Eventually, we hit upon heat-sensitive threads that allowed us to remove the elastic basting and keep the folds in place – just like magic!

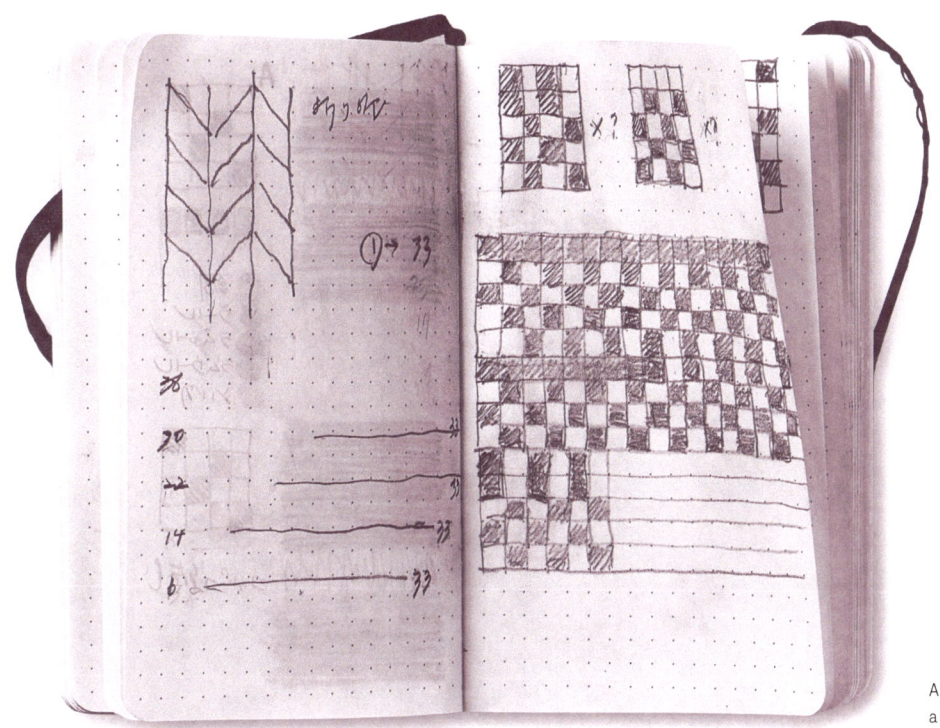

An *origami* diagram in a weaving draft notebook.

シワシワ

opposite and above
Polygami, 2010.
By Reiko Sudo and Hiroko Kobayashi.

below
The final shaping of *Origami Weave* is done by hand, after the heat-shrinking threads woven as supplementary wefts naturally form peak and valley folds when doused with hot water.

A three-legged race

Most textile design processes, from drafting patterns to cutting stencils to driving jacquard looms, can now be done on the computer, but the original idea still depends on human creativity. Even computer-controlled looming calls for artisan expertise to achieve the perfect finish. In other words, the effort requires both human reasoning and sensibility, with swift and accurate computers serving to bridge the gaps in between.

108

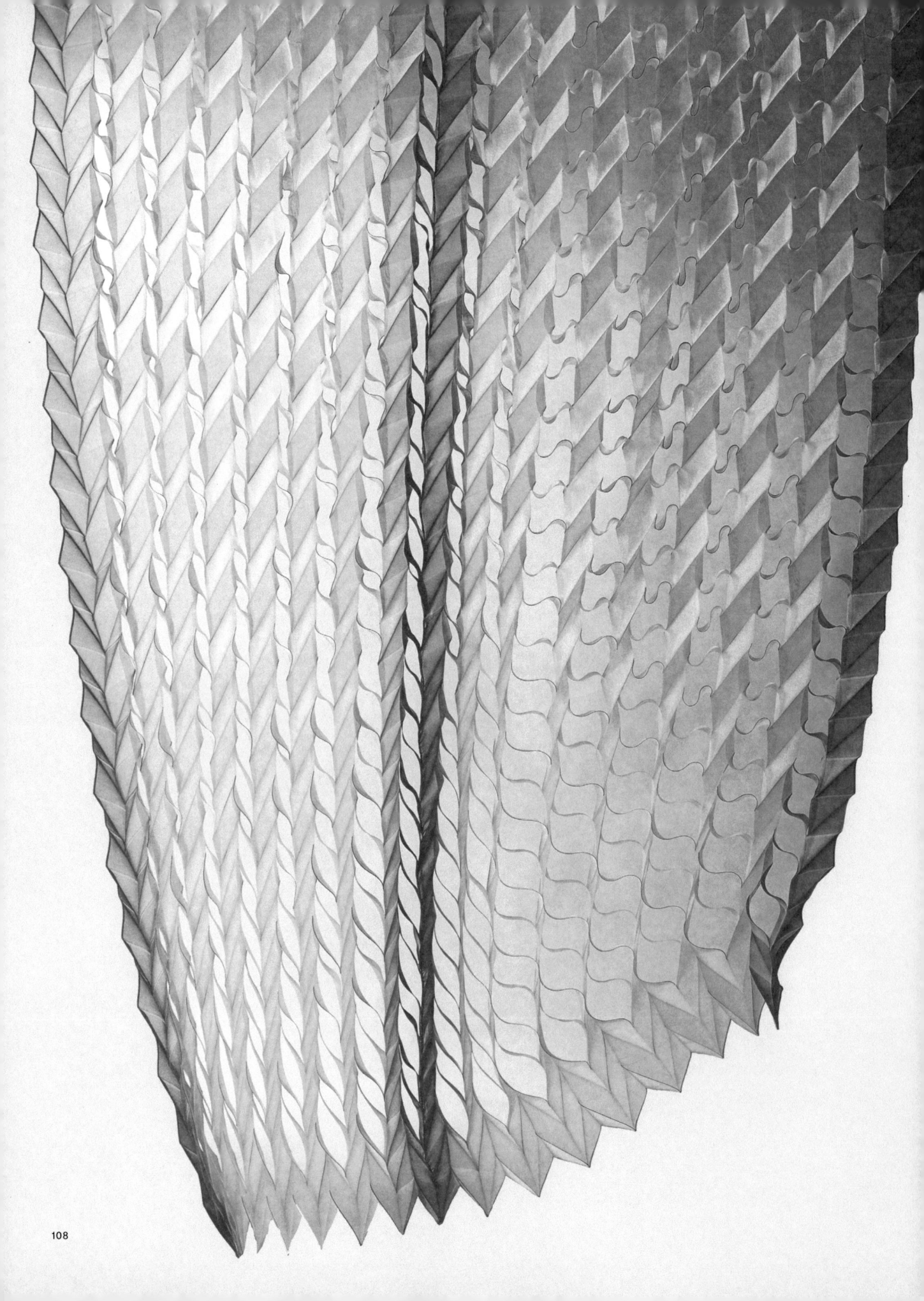

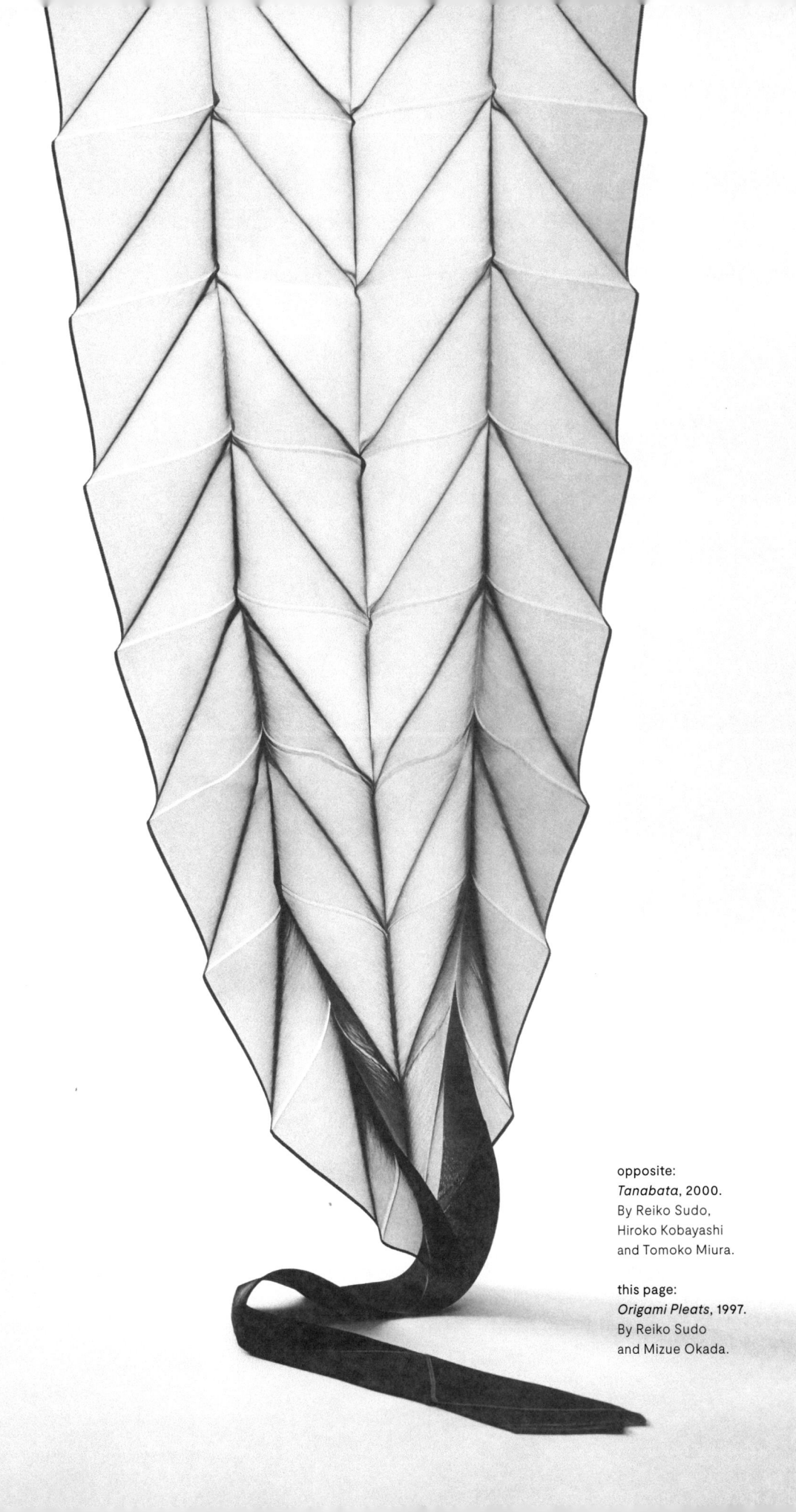

opposite:
Tanabata, 2000.
By Reiko Sudo,
Hiroko Kobayashi
and Tomoko Miura.

this page:
Origami Pleats, 1997.
By Reiko Sudo
and Mizue Okada.

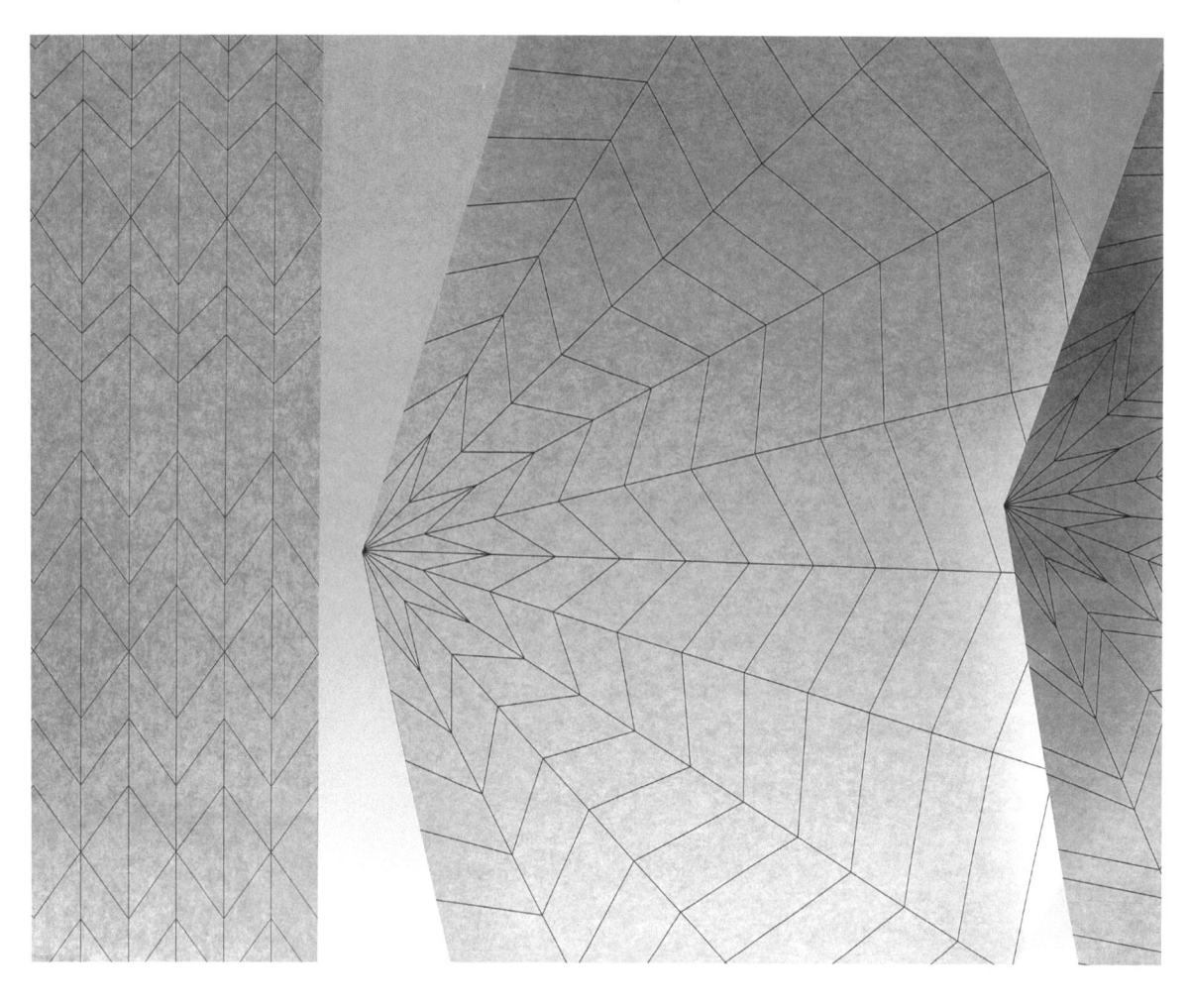

above
A paper pattern and diagram for *Origami Pleats*.

below
Inserting fabric into the paper pattern.

opposite
Origami Pleats heat-set in the paper pattern.

From *Origami Pleats* to *Origami Weave*

Heat-setting thermoplastic polyester between two folded sheets of recycled paper creates pleats. Simple, but clever enough to patent. Subsequently, it took another thirteen years of diligent trial and error to develop a method of weaving such pleats without paper patterns or heat-setting.

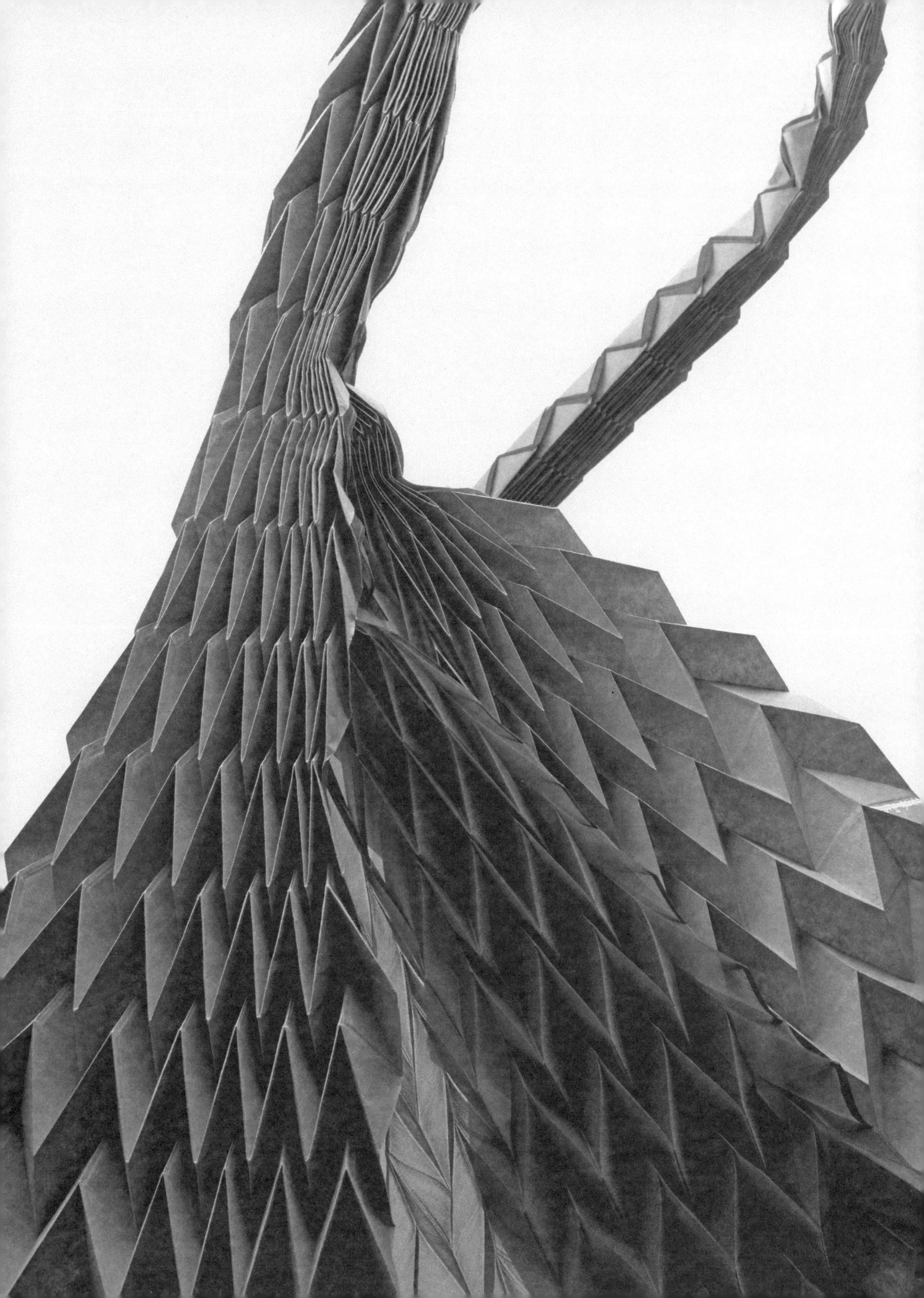

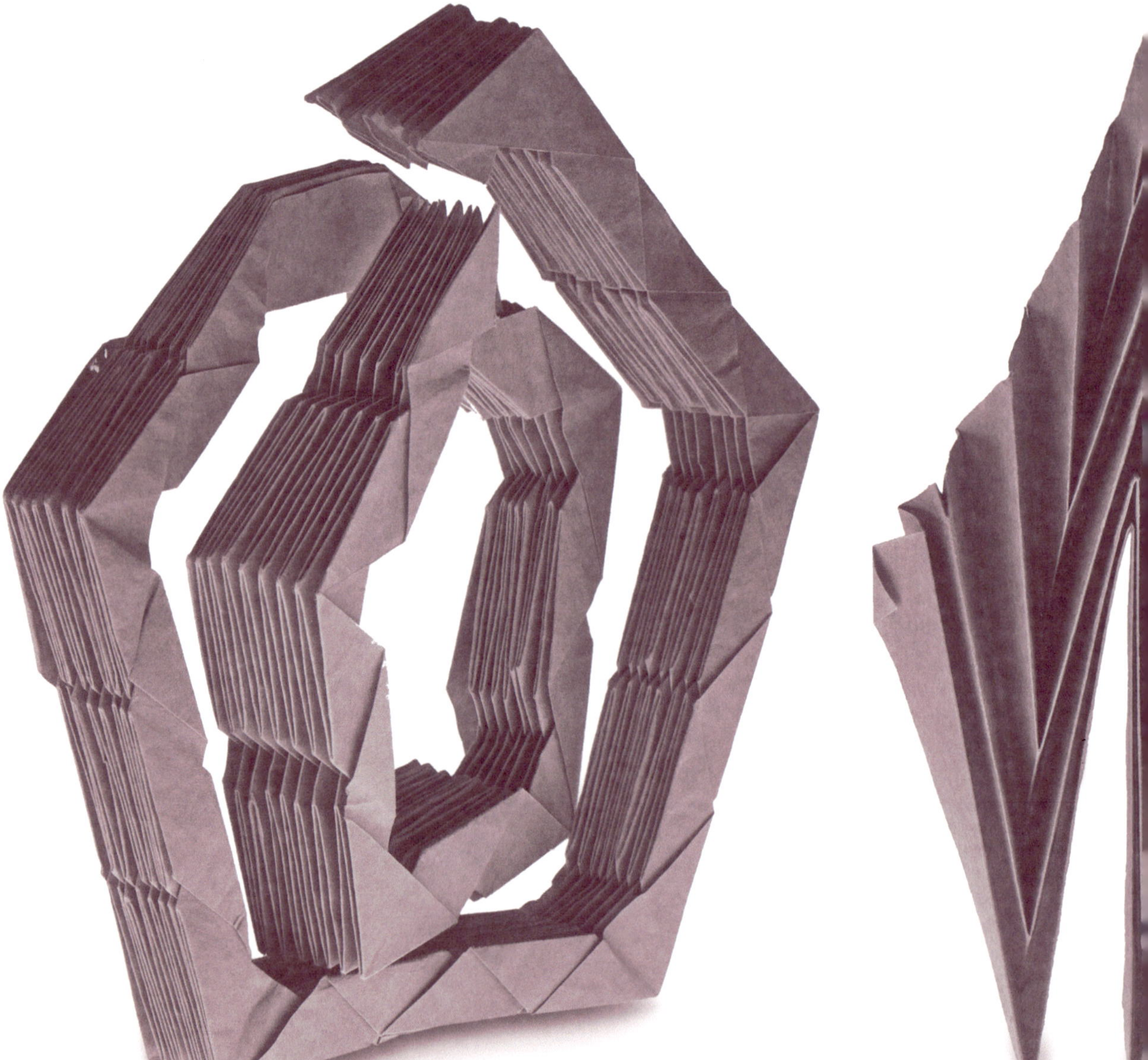

Continuing to experiment with paper folds.

SHIWA SHIWA

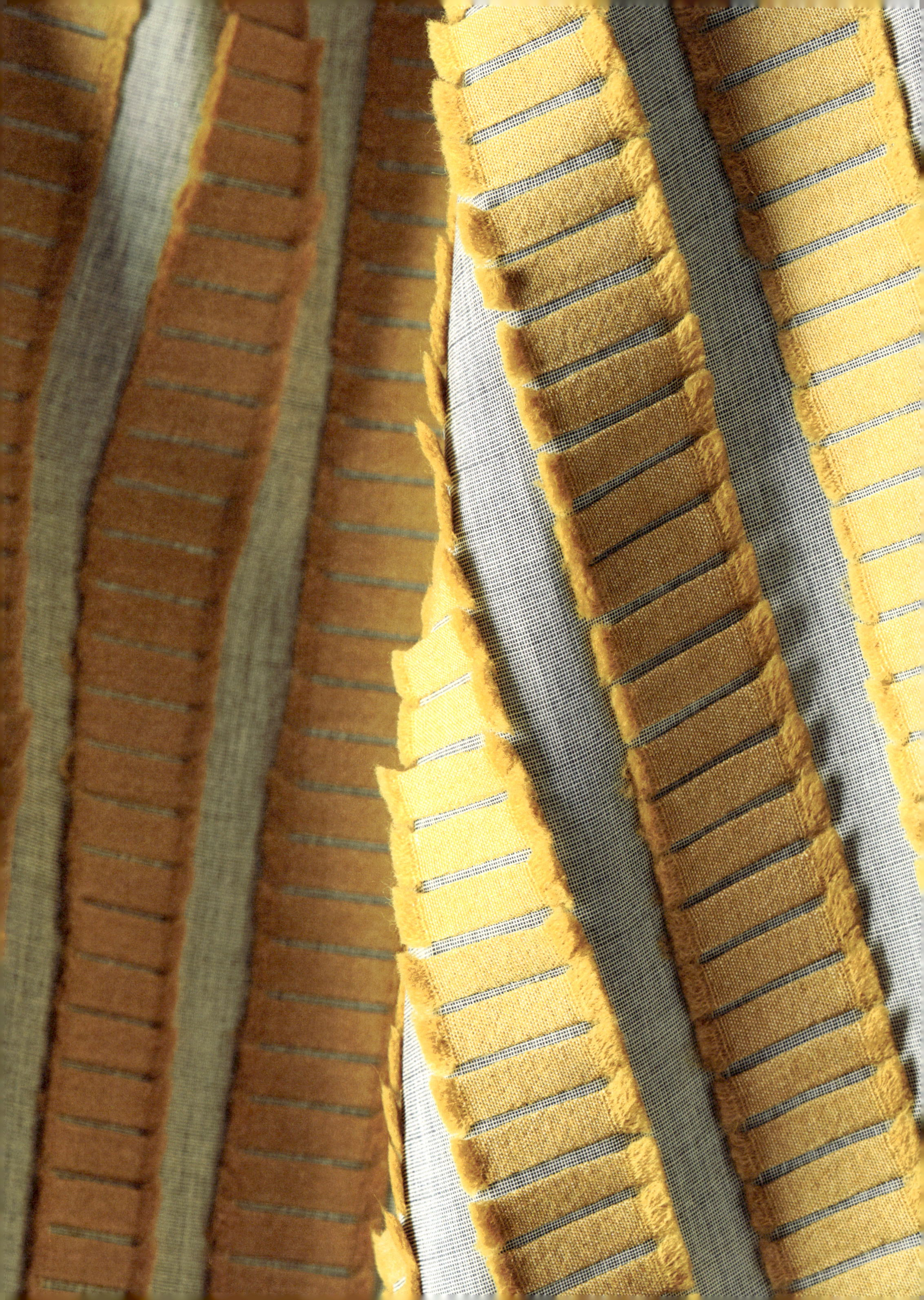

SHIMA SHIMA

shima shima (シマシマ)

1. Striped, banded, barred; patterned in bands, bars, stripes or strips
2. Lined, lineate, ruled; demarcated or measured with lines
3. Streaked, veined, grained, variegated; layered, striated
4. Wavy, sinewy, stroked (as in a painting)

|||||||||||||||||||||||||||||||||||||||||||||||||||||||||||||||||||||||||||||||||||||||||||||

The divisive code

Simple stripes used to spell trouble. In Japan, where people traditionally wrote right-to-left in vertical rows, something unorthodox, or someone with a contrary streak who went against the grain of social norms, was said to be *yoko-shima*, 'horizontally striped'. Likewise, in medieval Europe, highly visible stripes often equated to diabolical signs of heresy, scars of enslavement or criminal stigma, reminiscent of underworld tattoos, knife-cuts or brandings – which may explain why prison uniforms came to be striped.

But to textile professionals, such symbolism seems altogether loopy. Straight-line stripes are probably the most basic of any pattern that can be loomed with warps and wefts. Indeed, *shima shima* fabrics were so popular during Japan's pre-modern Edo period that stripes have since become virtually synonymous with folk weaving and dyeing. It's hard to imagine a *kimono* wardrobe without a few stripes.

In today's *shima shima* world, there's no shame in going striped. Stripes are everywhere, from flags and barcodes to bold fashions and fine art (think Bridget Riley or Daniel Buren). Stripes are truly international and multicultural, assuredly the most widely seen class of pattern on Earth. Universal yet individual, NUNO stripes go every which way.

p. 114:
Louvre Stripe, 1991.
By Reiko Sudo.
This double-weave utilizes two independent warp beams. One overtakes the other at regular intervals, causing one layer to pull back while the other distends to create accordion-fold pleats.

opposite:
Kibiso Suzushijima, 2009.
By Reiko Sudo.
Suzushi is a crisp, cool raw silk fabric, finished here with tonal stripes of *kibiso* cocoon roughage.

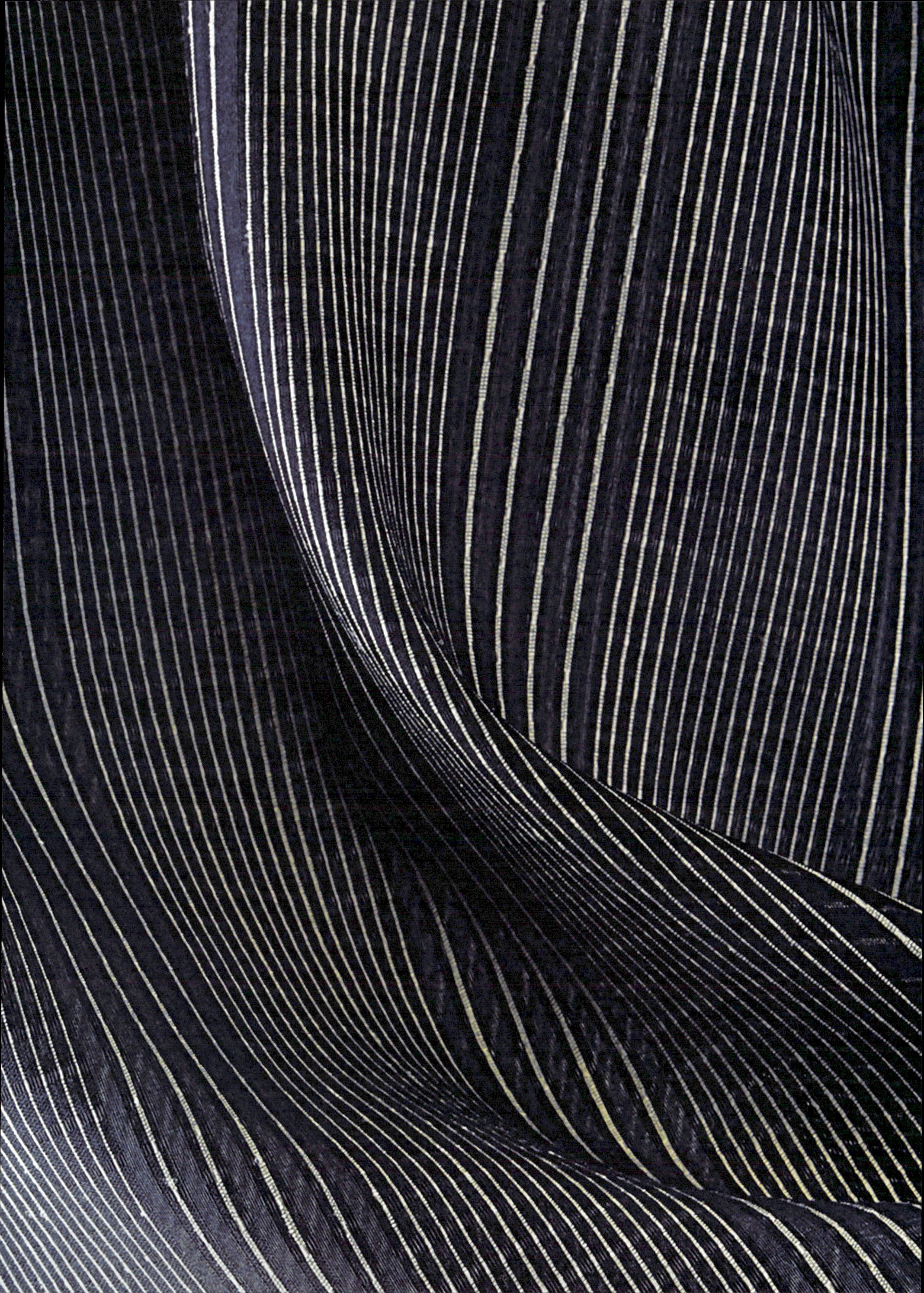

Stripes of all Colours

Brooke Hodge

Stripes conjure memories. Many memories. Memories of my mother admonishing me as a young girl to never wear stripes and plaid together. Or, almost worse, that horizontal stripes accentuate one's figure in ways that are not flattering. Over the years I've had, and loved, a number of pieces of striped clothing. A pair of striped trousers in fifth grade that seemed very cool at the time, not least because they reminded me of the groovy pair I dressed my Barbie doll in. A preppy Rugby shirt and pinstriped OshKosh B'Gosh overalls in high school. Blue and white stripes have been a perennial favourite of mine, from a Comme des Garçons Play long-sleeved top with its red heart appliqué, to a filmy striped Junya Watanabe dress with violet lace inserts. Stripes are still in heavy rotation in my wardrobe. My current favourites are a poncho – purchased on a recent trip to Marfa, Texas – with brilliant stripes of red, orange, fuchsia and teal, and a navy pinstriped shorts suit. The poncho's colourful stripes make me happy and remind me of time spent with good friends in one of my favourite places. The shorts suit was acquired on a recent summer trip to Lucca, Italy, and its subdued stripes make me feel elegant and sophisticated.

    No doubt that long-ago sartorial advice from my mother caused clothes to instantly come to mind when I first started thinking about stripes for this essay. But many of my fondest memories of travel, textiles, texture and time are visual, and stripes, because they form such a strong, bold pattern, are part of those memories. The marmalade stripes of a beloved cat departed too soon. Roberto Burle Marx's graceful, undulating paving pattern at Rio de Janeiro's Copacabana Beach, and the wonderful Gal Costa concert I saw there. The crisp stripes of seersucker mean summer and peach pies with woven lattice crusts. The striped awnings shading a room just in time for a post-*pranzo* siesta near the Mediterranean. Men immediately recognize the striped poles of barbershops no matter where they are in the world. The striped marble façades of churches and mosques rise upward to the heavens, giving worshippers the promise of an afterlife. The chalk stripes scrawled on sidewalks and in driveways for childhood games of hopscotch. That first kindergarten drawing of a landscape, with the sky represented by a simple blue stripe across the top of the page. The anticipation of waiting until Christmas morning to open a package beautifully wrapped in black-and-white striped paper criss-crossed with stripes of emerald green ribbon.

   Stripes can mean so many things. They are optimistic, representing speed and progress: the racing stripes of a fast car; the tyre tracks of burned rubber as it careens out of control; the twin tracks of cross-country skis gliding silently through freshly fallen snow; the contrails of a jet soaring towards the clouds; the streaking red tail-lights of cars on a Los Angeles freeway. Stripes also signify merit. In the military, stripes are a symbol of rank; 'earning one's stripes' is a phrase commonly used beyond its military association to signify success or advancement. When used metaphorically, stripes can refer to one's ideology, allegiance or opinion, as in 'revealing one's stripes', 'believers of all stripes' or 'political stripes'. In 1995, US Vice President Al Gore famously said of George W. Bush, 'we all know the leopard can't change his stripes'. Of course, we all know that it's spots that a leopard can't change, and that Gore was mixing metaphors and two majestic jungle cats.

   Flags and stripes go together – the vertical blue, white and red bands of the French flag, the red stripes of the Canadian flag bookending a red maple leaf on a white ground – perhaps because stripes as a graphic device communicate identity simply and boldly. The stars and stripes of the American flag symbolize freedom from generations of European rule. Its thirteen red-and-white horizontal stripes, designed by Francis Hopkinson in 1777, represent the

Breton stripes came to signify carefree summers sipping cocktails – many, many cocktails – in the south of France, and were worn by everyone from F. Scott Fitzgerald to Ernest Hemingway, and from Brigitte Bardot to James Dean to Andy Warhol.

thirteen colonies that became the first states in the Union by declaring independence from Great Britain. In 2001, the architect Rem Koolhaas imagined a new flag for the European Union. In his design, he lined up stripes, edge-to-edge, in the signature colours of the EU's member nations, their widths denoting the size of each nation.

When we think of Pablo Picasso we may think of his Cubist portraits of women or his Blue period; but when we picture Picasso himself, he is wearing a Breton striped t-shirt. In my favourite portrait of the artist, he is wearing a Breton t-shirt and holding a striped cat. Breton stripes came to signify carefree summers sipping cocktails – many, many cocktails – in the south of France, and were worn by everyone from F. Scott Fitzgerald to Ernest Hemingway, and from Brigitte Bardot to James Dean to Andy Warhol. Still in fashion today, Breton stripes evoke an effortless elegance.

One cannot think of Bridget Riley without imagining stripes. Her identity as an artist is completely tied up in stripes, from her 1960s black-and-white striped Op Art paintings to her later works, in which she painted stripes in vibrant colours next to each other, underscoring the physical identity of the individual colours but also creating a sublime sensory experience, as her colourful stripes interact with each other, moving and vibrating in new relationships.

Stripes are a surprisingly rich subject. From their use in language to the memories and symbols they evoke and the visual experiences they provide in nature, art and fashion, stripes are forward-thinking, uplifting and immediately recognizable. I've thrown that childhood admonition from my mother out of the window, and now I yearn to wear stripes and plaid together. And in case you were wondering what was in that beautifully wrapped Christmas gift? It was a painting, which I love even though it has no stripes.

Stripes are a surprisingly rich subject. From their use in language to the memories and symbols they evoke and the visual experiences they provide in nature, art and fashion, stripes are forward-thinking, uplifting and immediately recognizable.

Harmony Stripe, 2002.
By Reiko Sudo.
A rough 'homespun' fabric of thick silk threads woven with *konyaku* glutinous yam paste to irregular effect, creating colourful stripes that combine a warm heft with the lustre of silk.

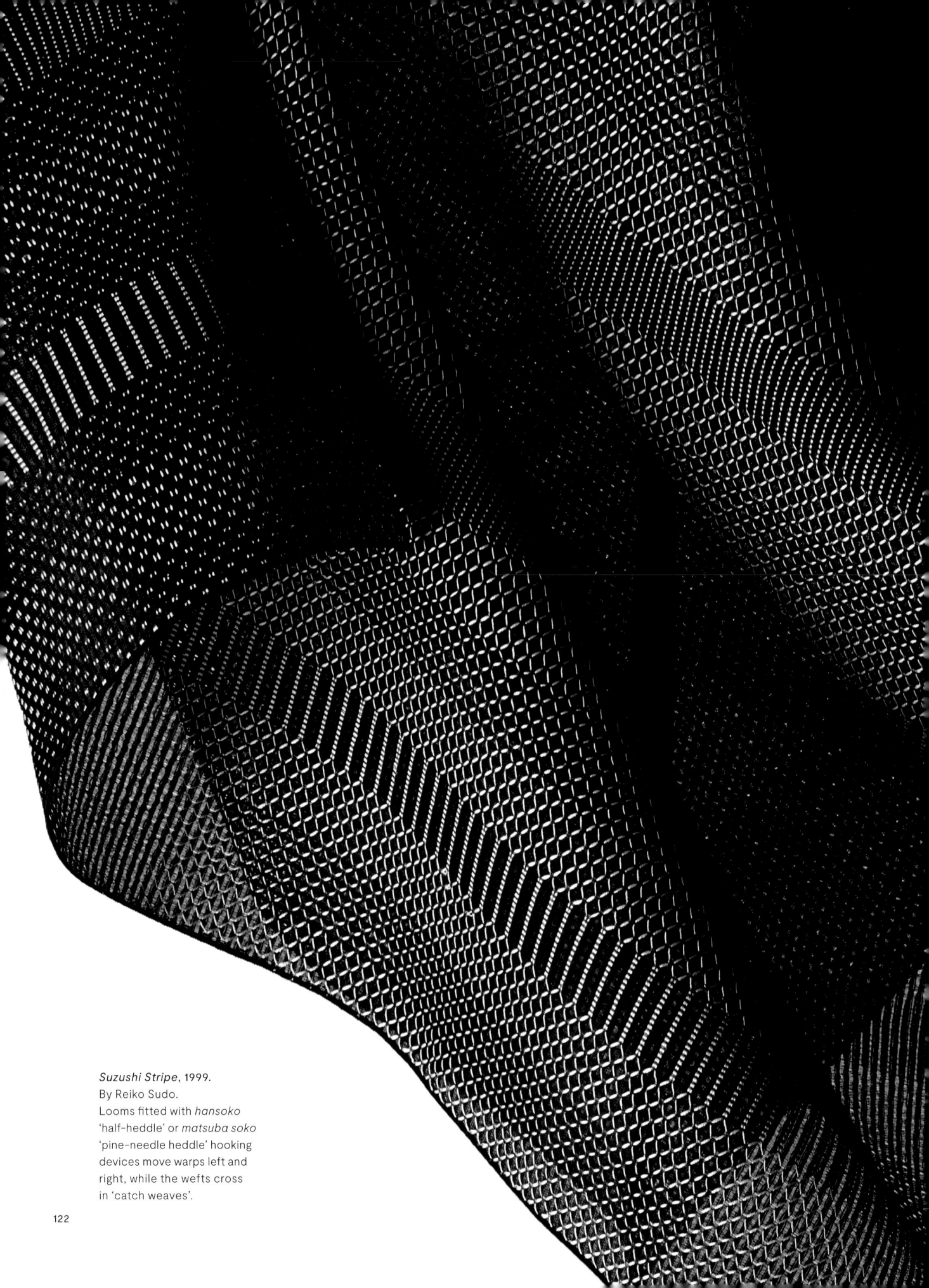

Suzushi Stripe, 1999.
By Reiko Sudo.
Looms fitted with *hansoko* 'half-heddle' or *matsuba soko* 'pine-needle heddle' hooking devices move warps left and right, while the wefts cross in 'catch weaves'.

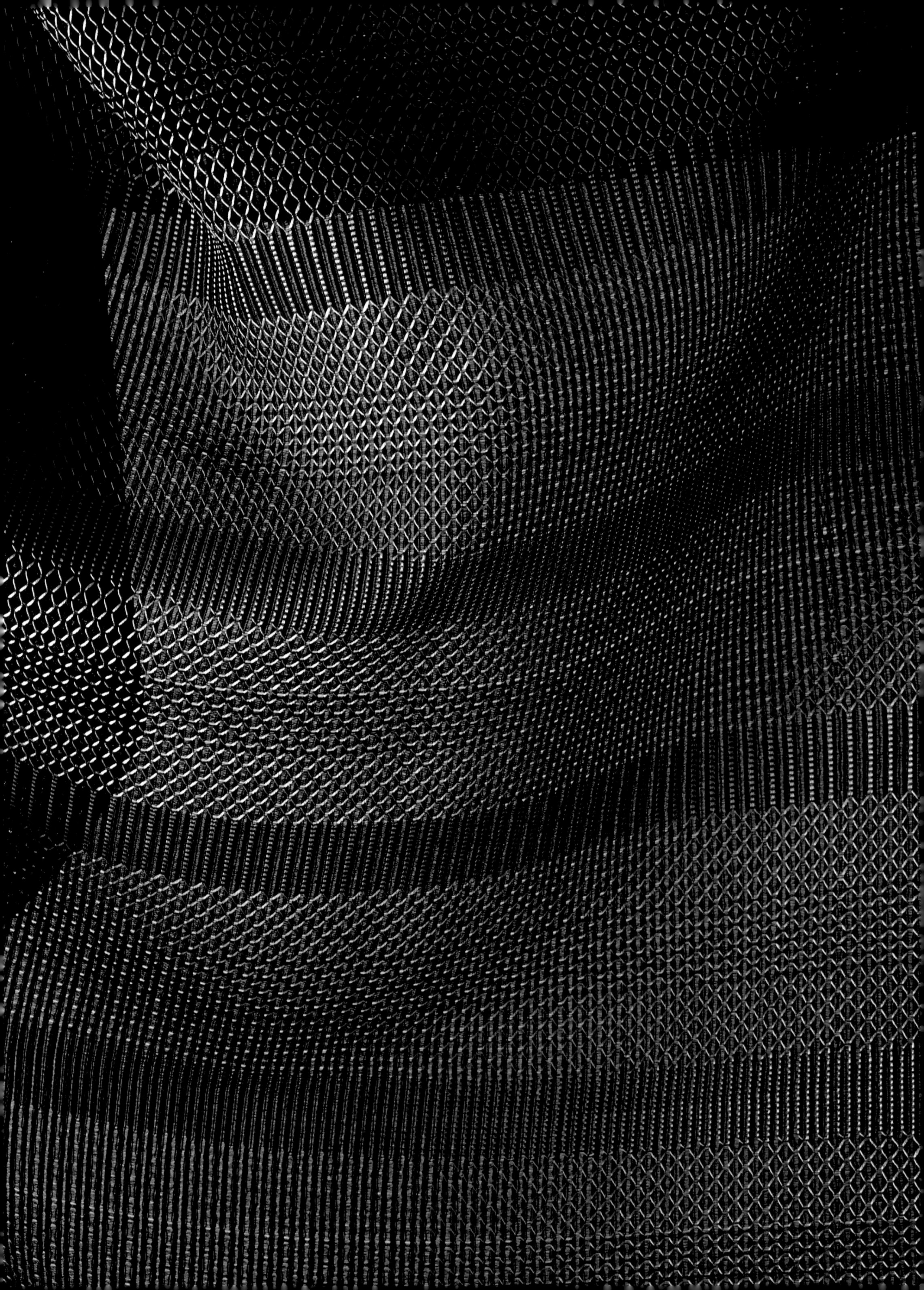

left:
Kibiso Handweaving Border, 2009.
By Reiko Sudo.
The *kibiso* shells of silk cocoons were considered too hard to weave and used for animal feed, but NUNO has found ways to use this high-performance material.

opposite:
Kibiso Futsu Crisscross, 2008.
By Reiko Sudo.
Horizontal and vertical stripes with overspun cotton warps create a fine, nubby surface that feels wonderful on the skin.

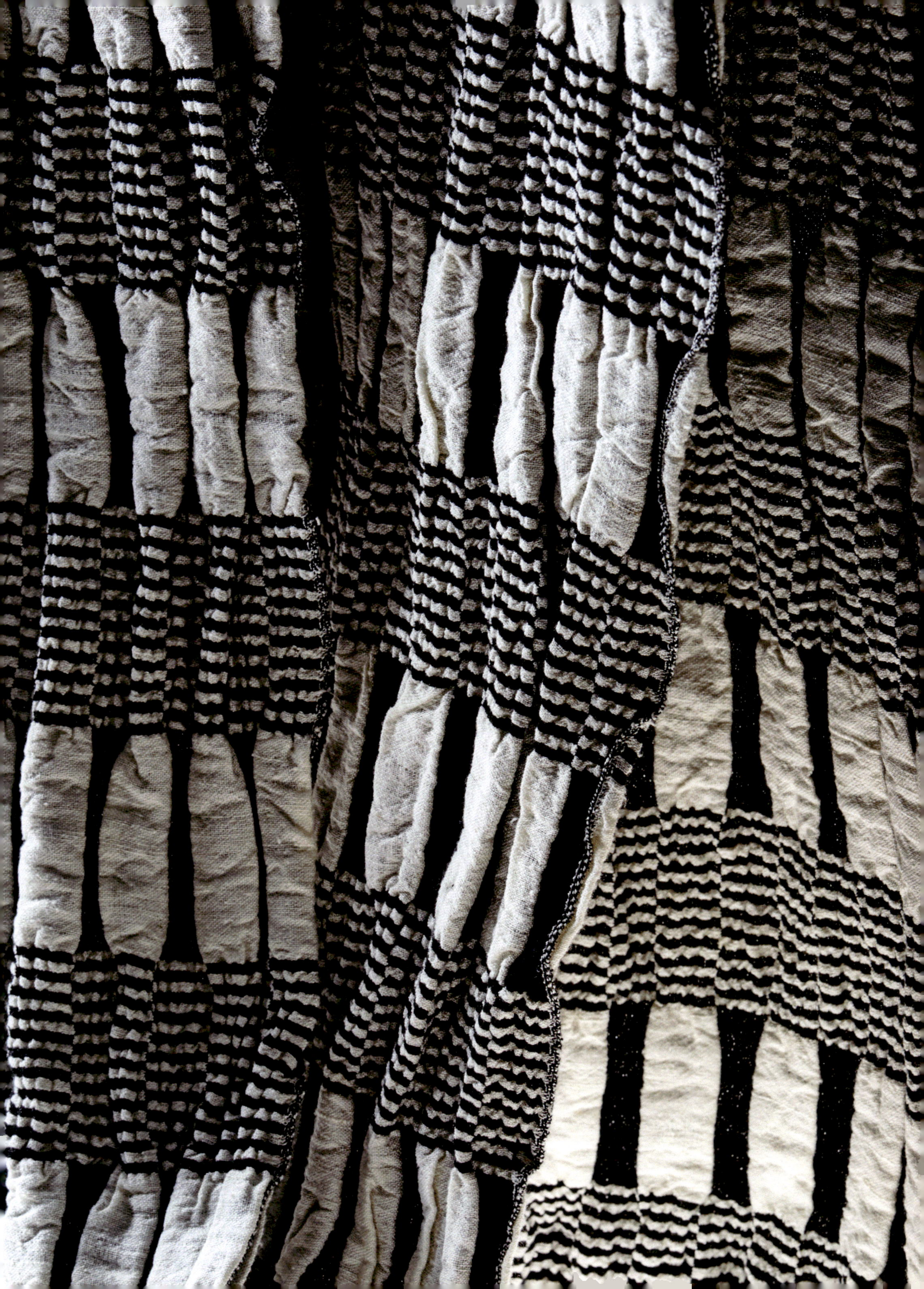

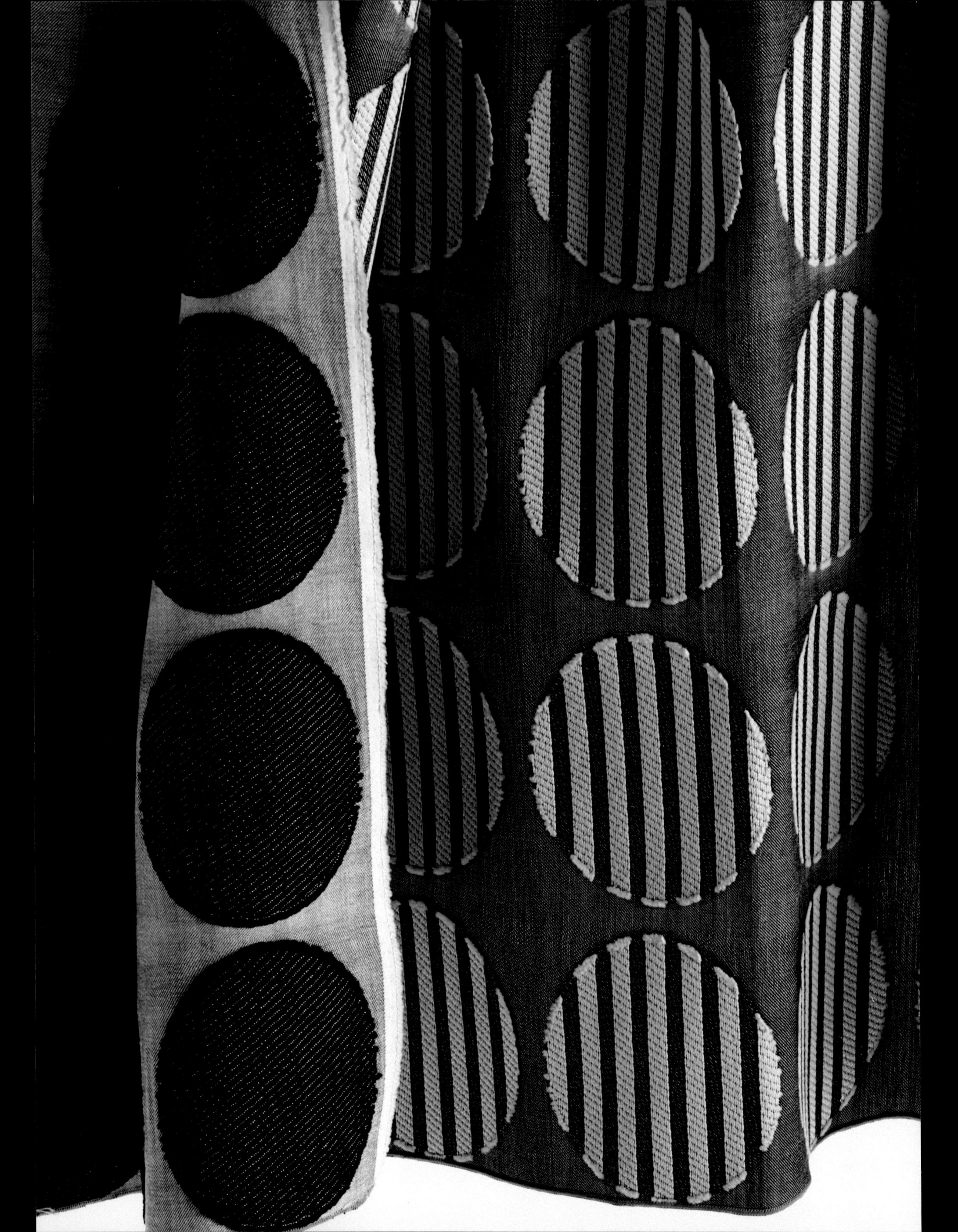

left:
Striped Rounds, 2004.
By Reiko Sudo.
A jacquard-loomed fabric with rows of striped circles, in which the ground, vertically striped circles and twill circles are each made in different weaves.

next page:
Film Pattern, 1984.
By Reiko Sudo.
A design homage to now-disused, pre-digital 35mm film, with its evenly spaced sprocket holes.

p. 93:
Cavex Stripe, 1999.
By Reiko Sudo.
A puckered silk organdy double-weave of Spandex™ and silk with concave and convex volumetric effects.

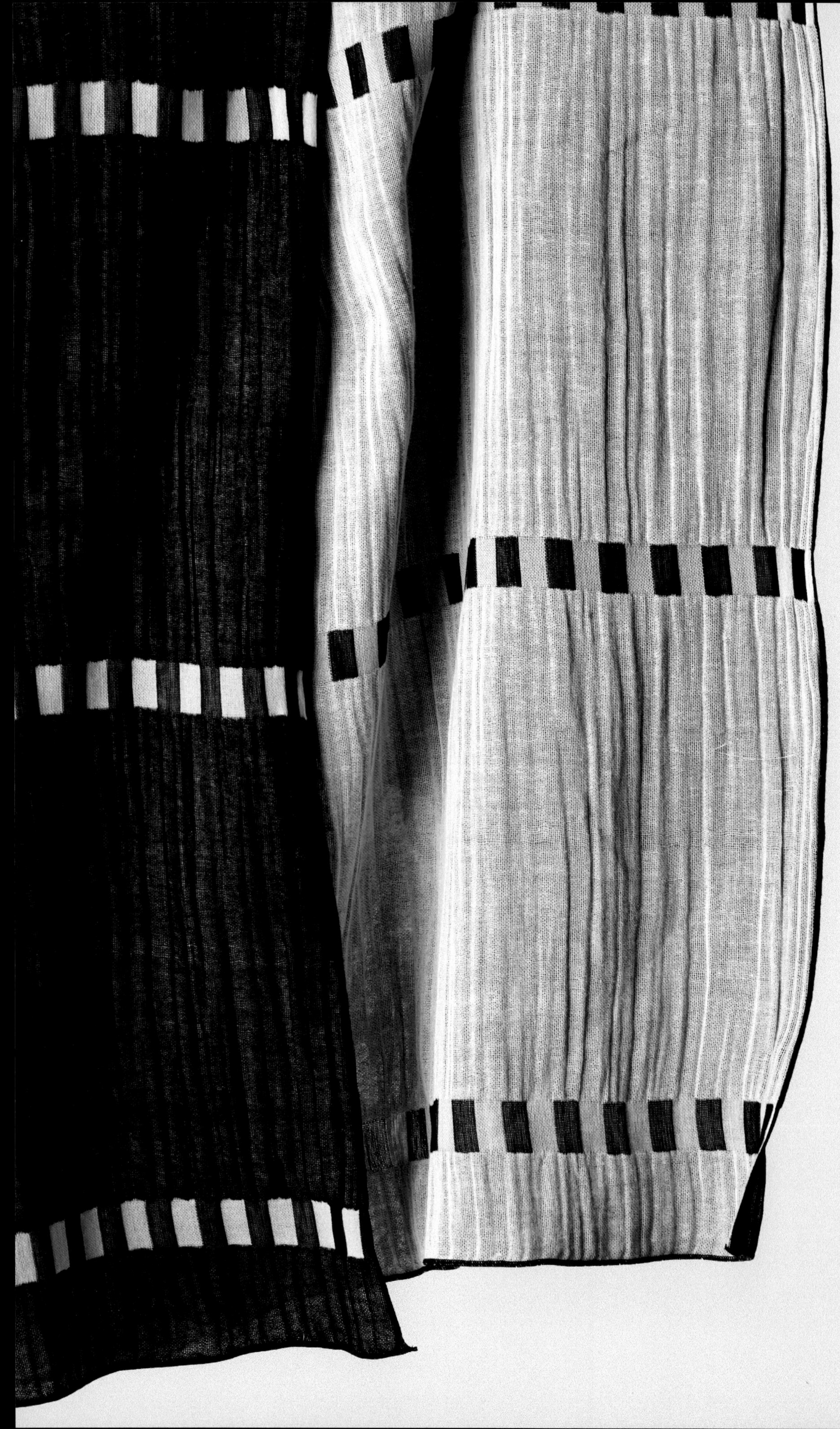

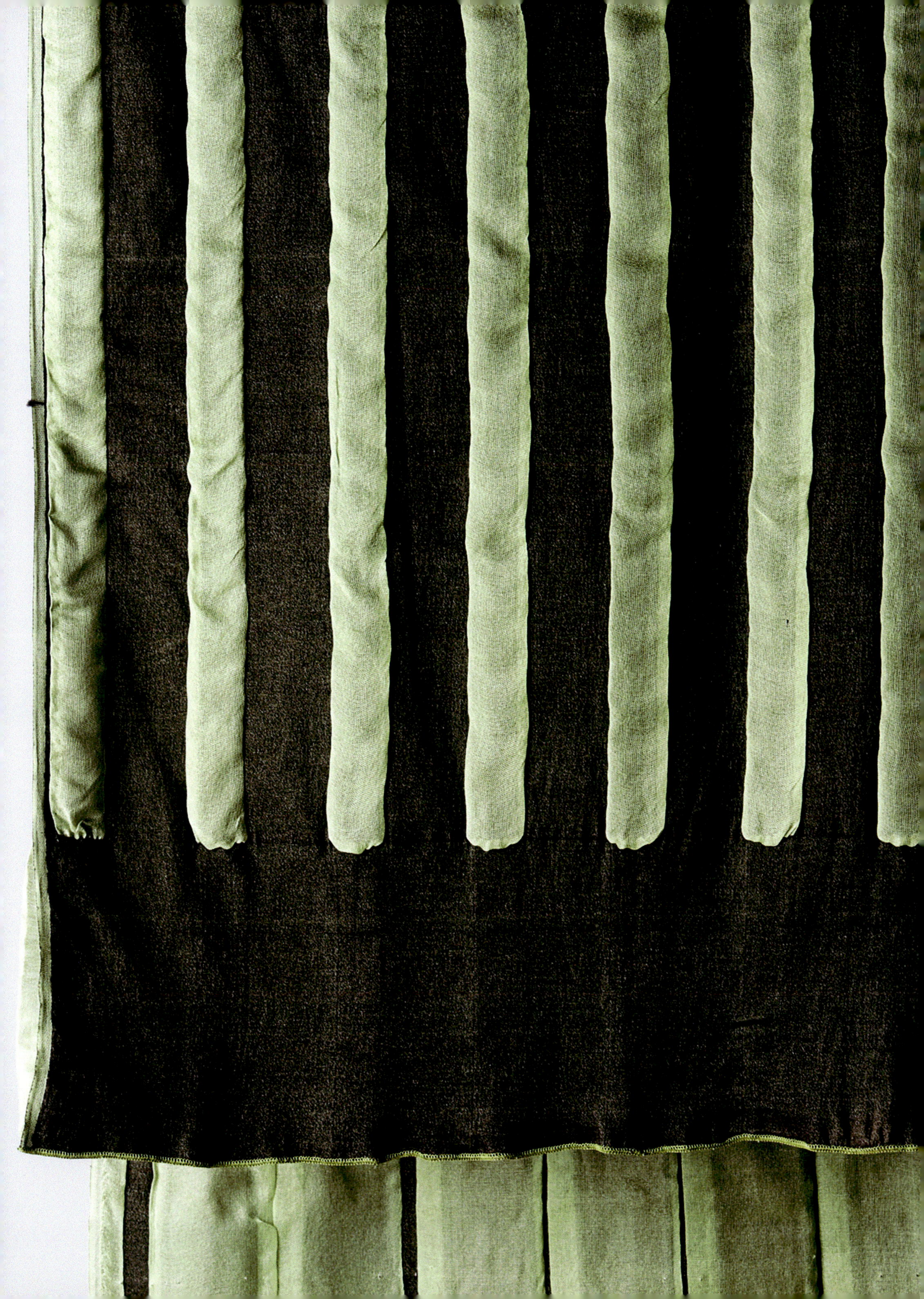

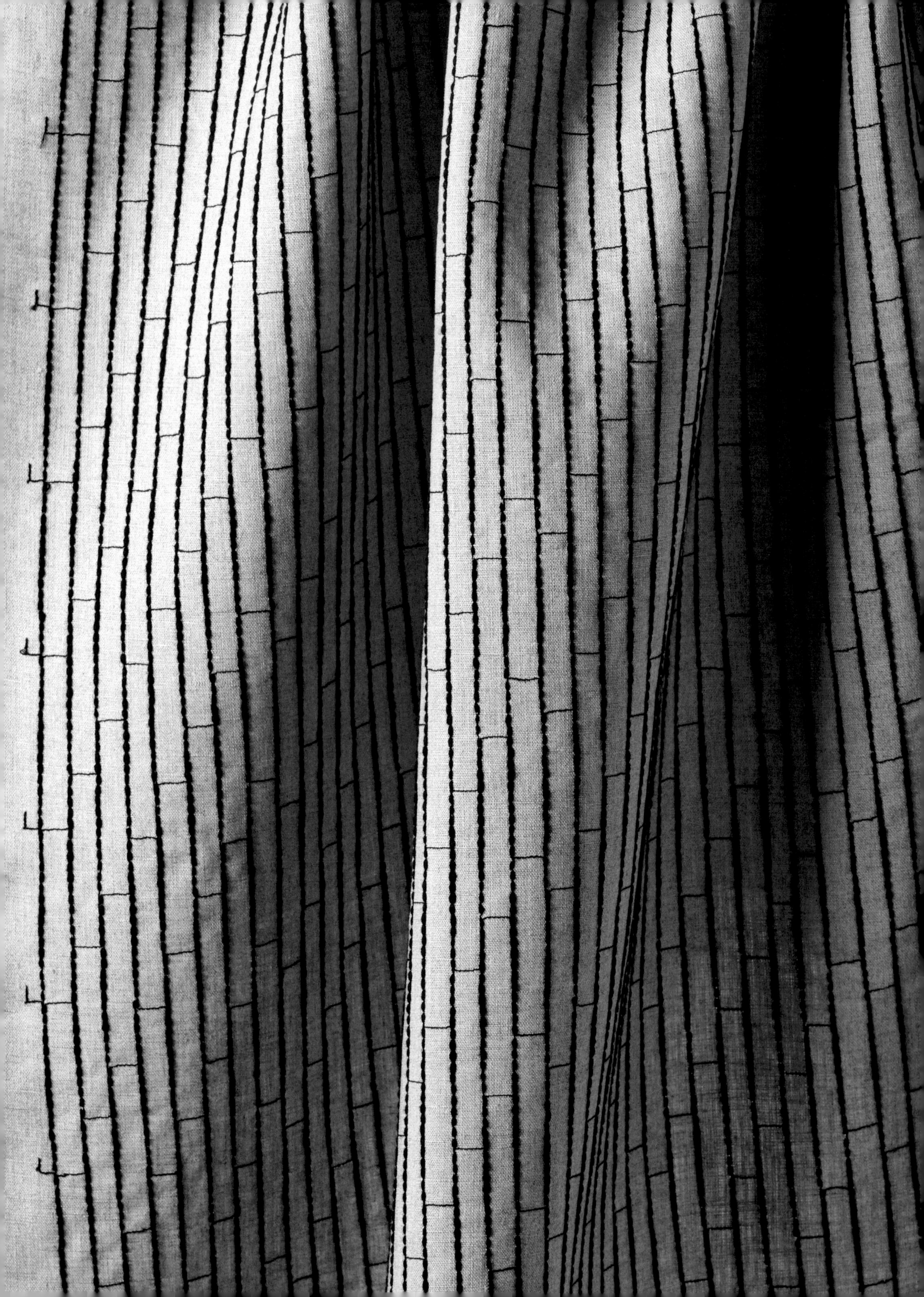

opposite:
Hariko Linen, 2019.
By Reiko Sudo.
A machine-embroidered *sashiko* in an old-fashioned design, reminiscent of the days when seamstresses were jokingly called *hariko*, 'needle jockeys'.

above:
Kibiso Itomaki, 2009.
By Reiko Sudo.
A sample book illustration of threads wound on *itomaki* spools gave us the idea for this fabric, only here they're all the same threadstuff and colour.

right:
Arrow Feathers, 2000.
By Reiko Sudo.
Warps in six colours intersect with four different colour wefts in this fine worsted merino yarn double-weave, to create intricate patterns of shifting tonal planes.

p. 134:
Stripe+Band series.
By Reiko Sudo.
Stripy Stripe (left), 2009.
This cotton double-weave scarf combines horizontal and vertical stripes, with stiff *kibiso* threads woven in between to create a crinkled texture.
Organ (right), 2019.
This crisp, springy cotton crepe woven with overspun wefts plays on a keyboard design.

p. 135:
Stripe Stop Stripe, 2019.
By Reiko Sudo.
As a rule, striped fabrics are made by varying warps. Here, however, both warps and wefts allow stripes to change midway to make for more modern, geometric variations.

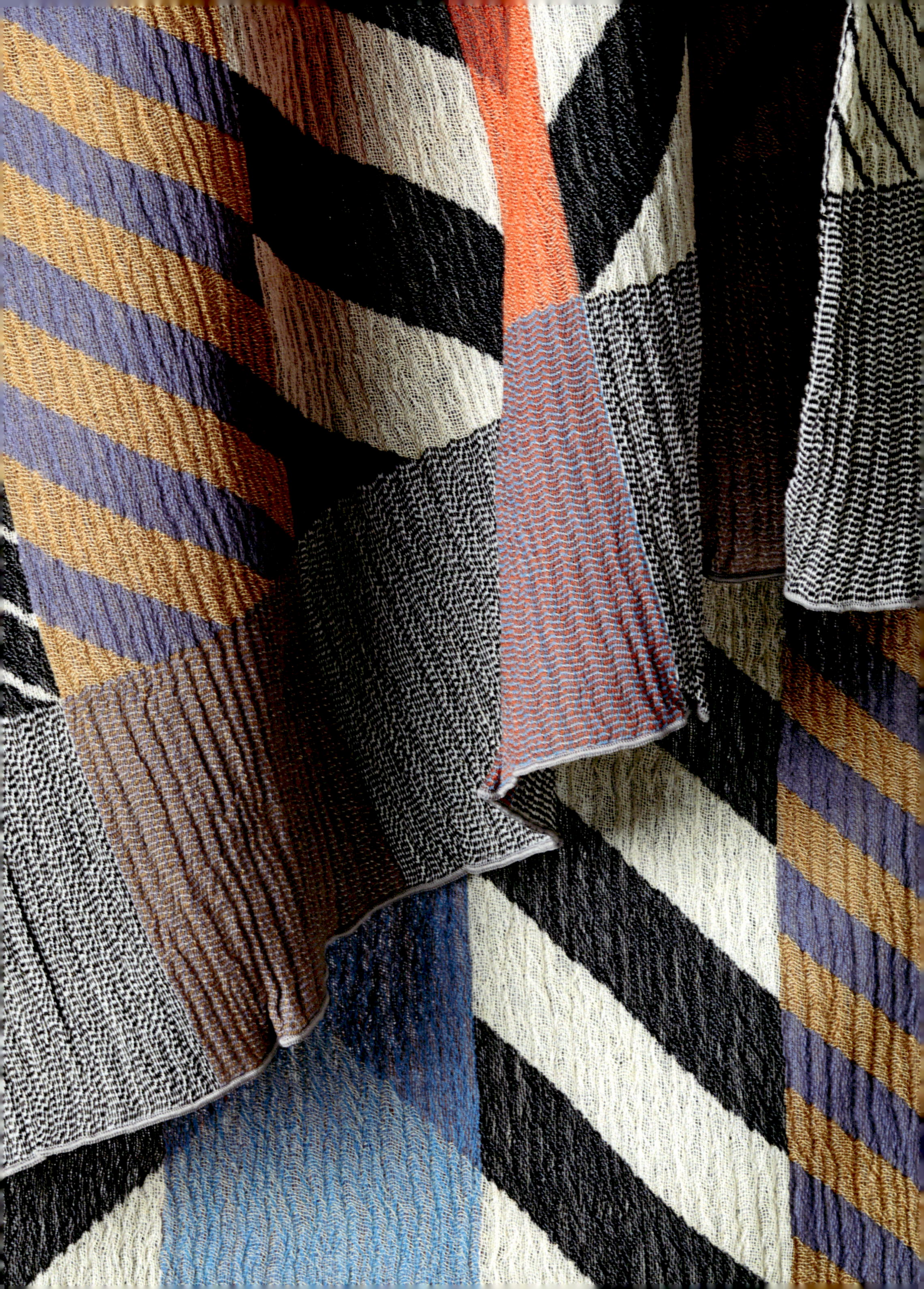

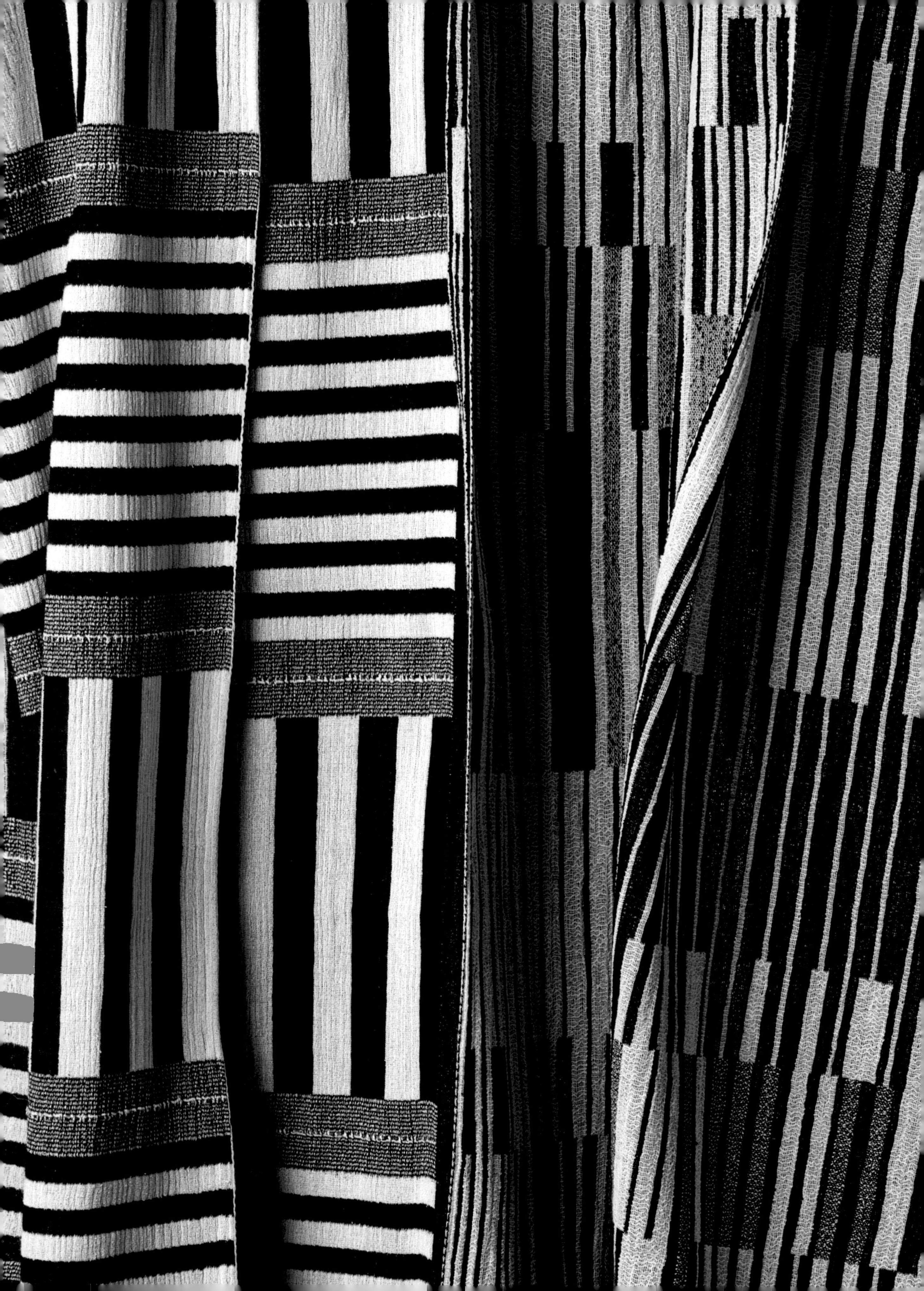

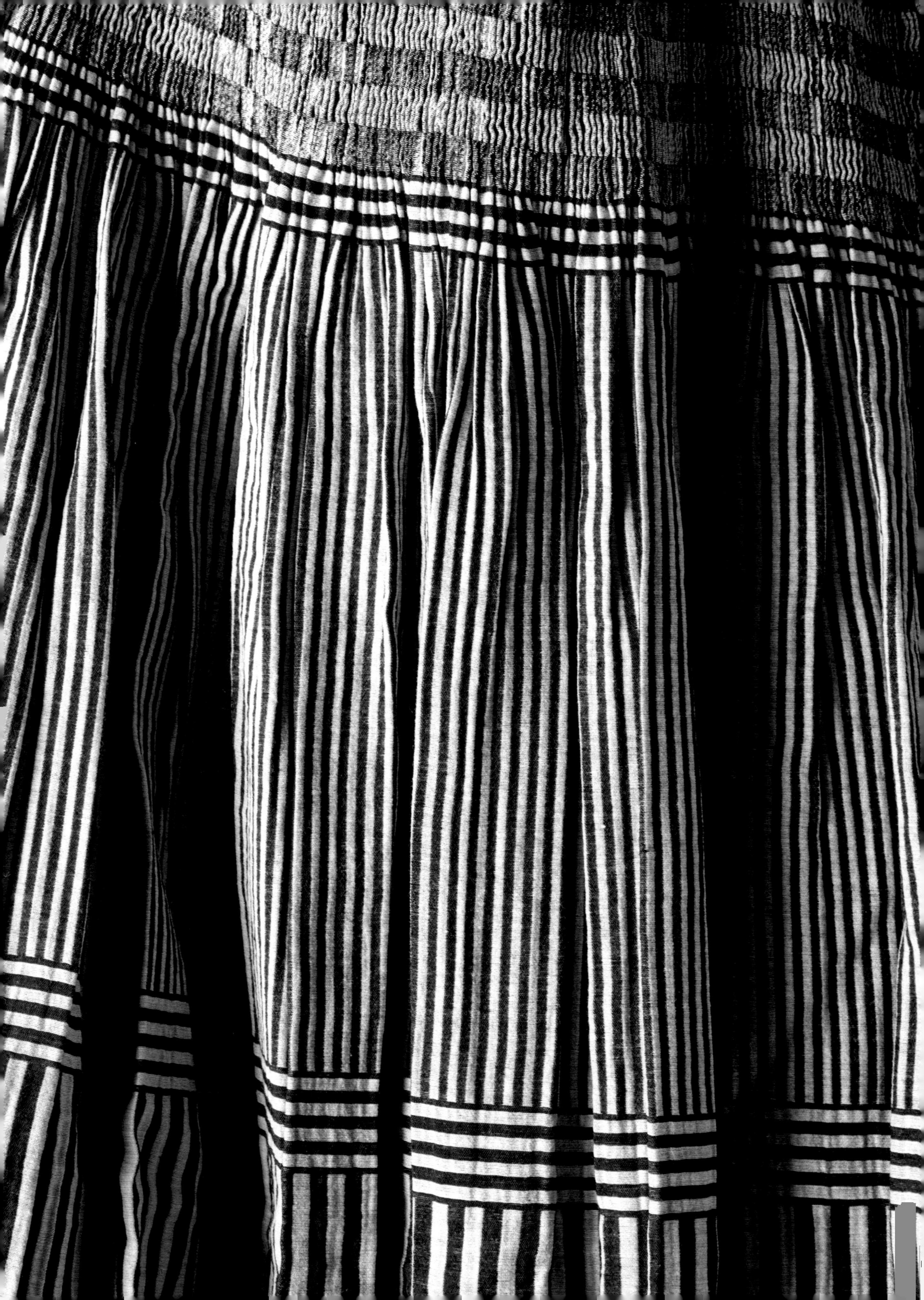

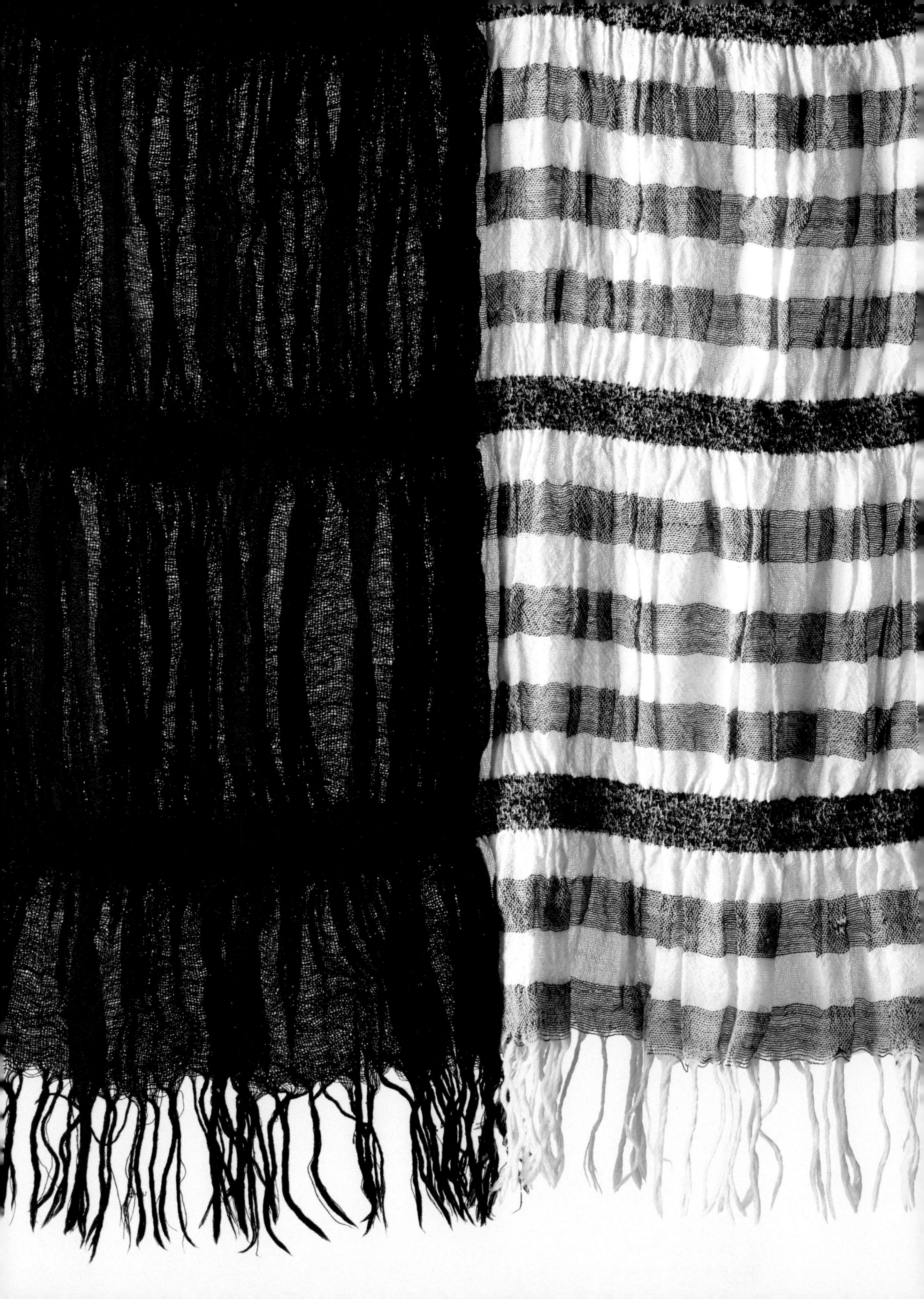

opposite:
Tubular Weave Border, 1989.
By Reiko Sudo.
This tube weave makes the most of the sleek lustre of merino wool and the fluffy softness of loop yarn, with rhythmic running designs along the borders.

above:
Kamaboko Stripes, 2013.
By Reiko Sudo.
A three-layer cotton jacquard weave featuring a pattern of half-rounds of *kamaboko* fishcake, richly textured front and back with twill 'shading'.

following page:
Hopscotch, 1999.
By Reiko Sudo.
Sashiko is a traditional baste-stitching technique for sewing together layers of cloth, recalled here in this jacquard-loomed mock-*sashiko*.

p. 139:
Chirimen Tazuna Stripes, 1984 (reissued 2008).
By Junichi Arai; reissued by Reiko Sudo.
Springy *chirimen* crepe is made by alternating right- and left-twisted overspun yarns, used here to create a striped pattern.

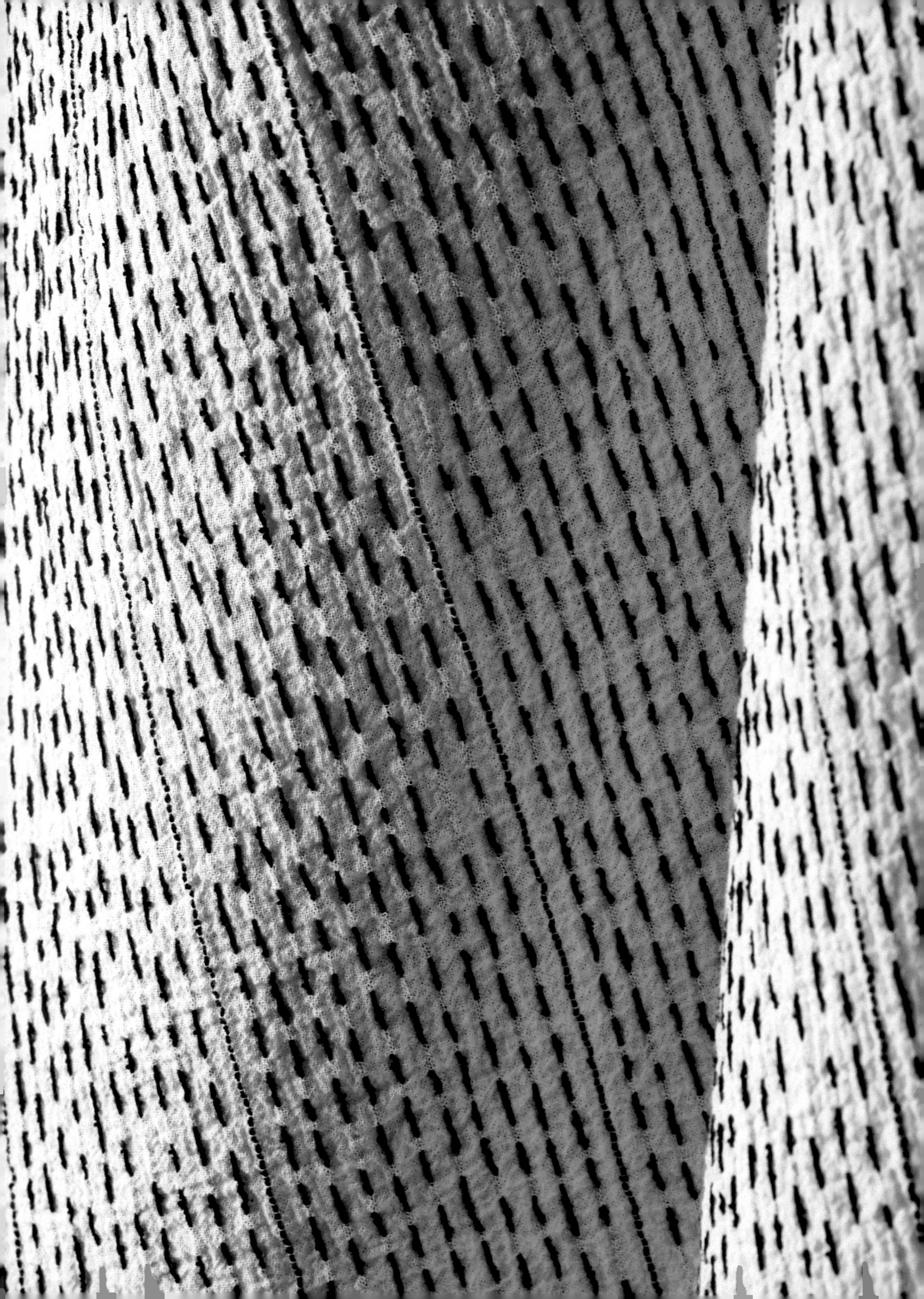

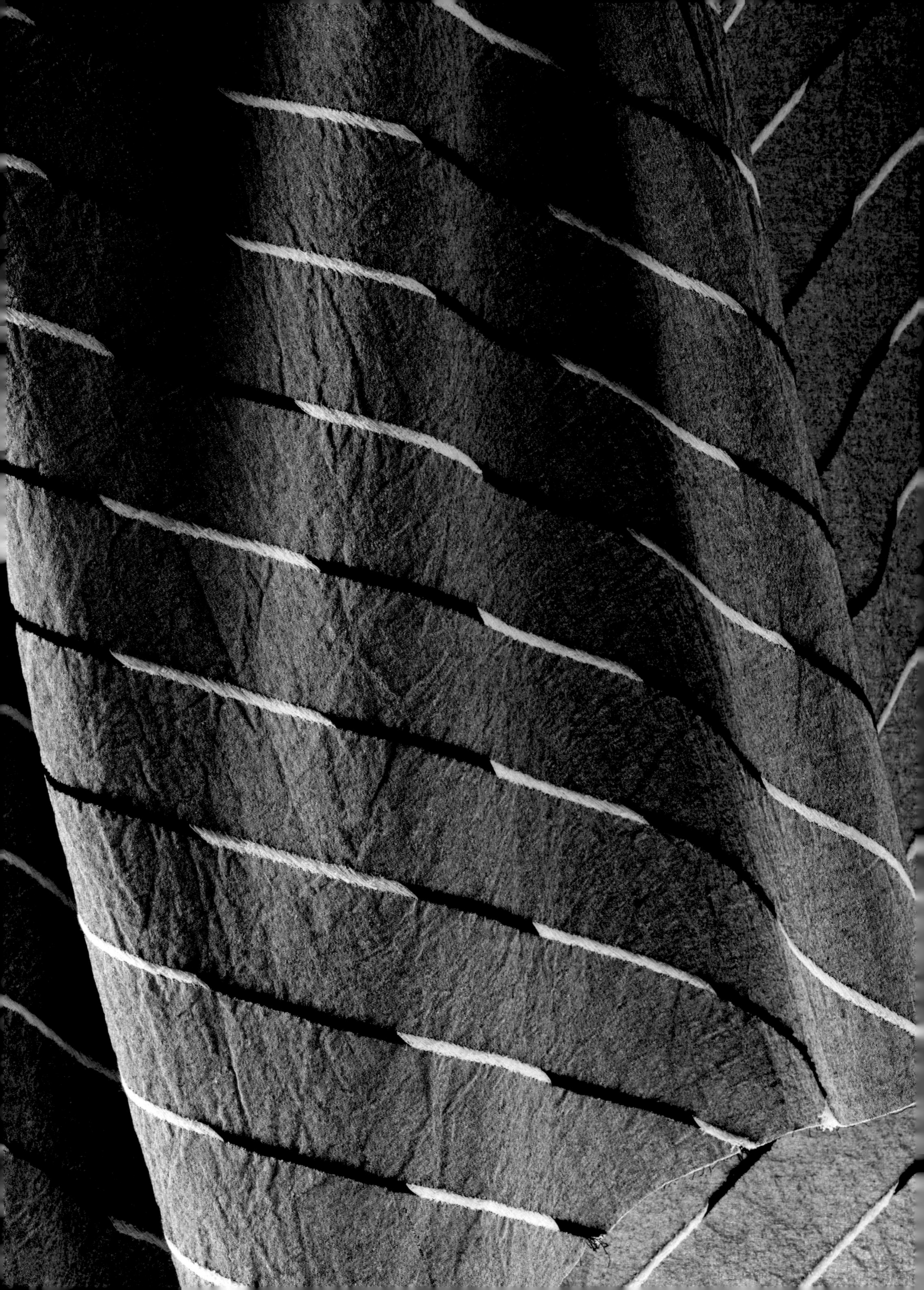

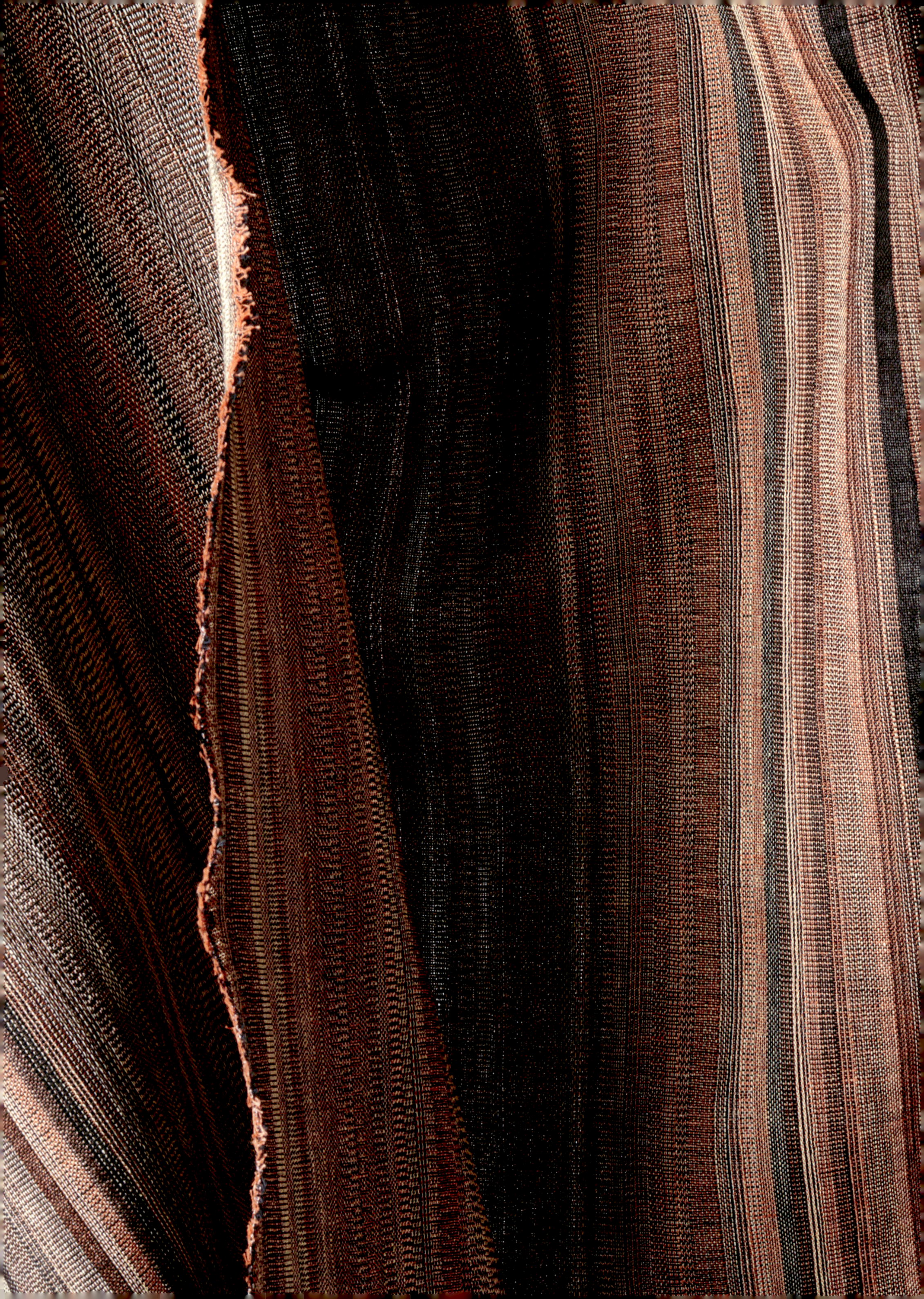

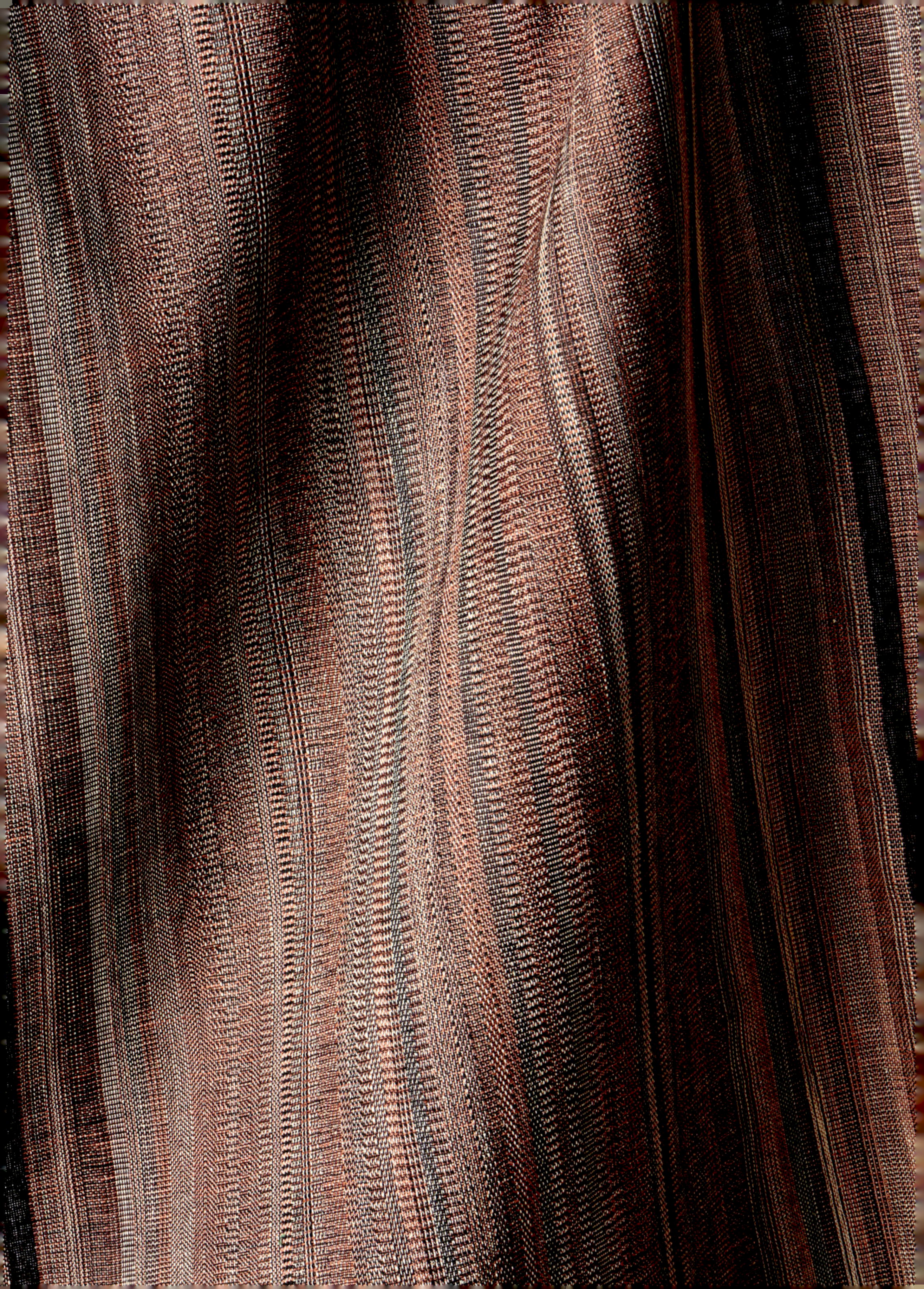

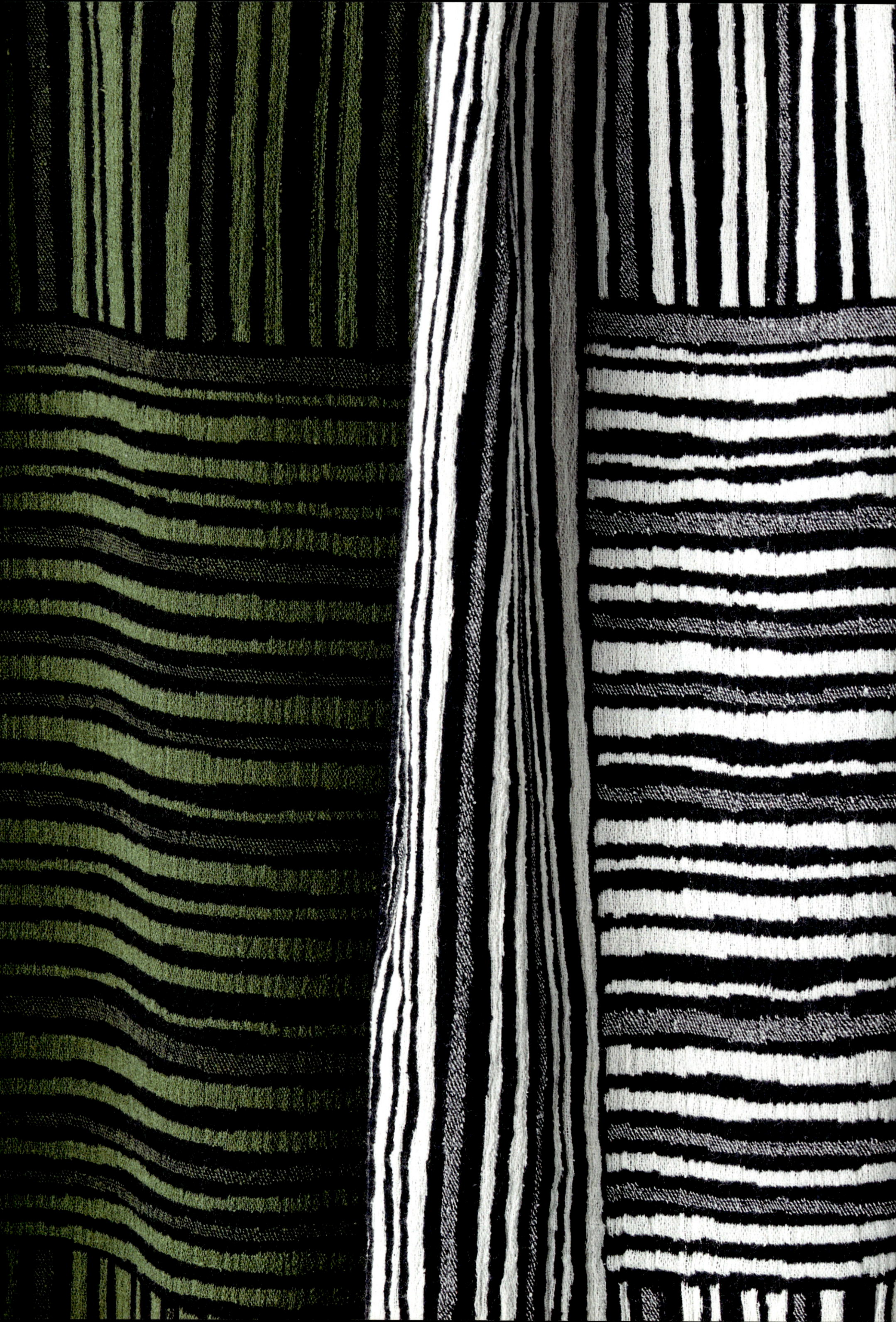

previous spread:
Bashofu 80 Stripes, 1984.
By Reiko Sudo.
Recycled *basho* plantain fibres make a texture like linen, but with a unique feel. Each of the eighty stripes is a different woven structure. Get out your magnifying glasses!

opposite:
Squared Stripes, 1993.
By Sayuri Shimoda and Reiko Sudo.
Overspun wefts add a springy texture to this jacquard weave, designed to look like a dithered copy of hand-drawn stripes.

below:
Sand Dunes, 1993.
By Reiko Sudo.
Vigorously overspun yarns curl and crinkle irregularly. Partially removing wefts here and there helps to accentuate the nubby texture.

following page:
Sandwich, 1999.
By Reiko Sudo.
A triple-weave with a cotton core sandwiched between silk layers. Stripes of the inner layer are burned out, creating an intentionally distressed effect.

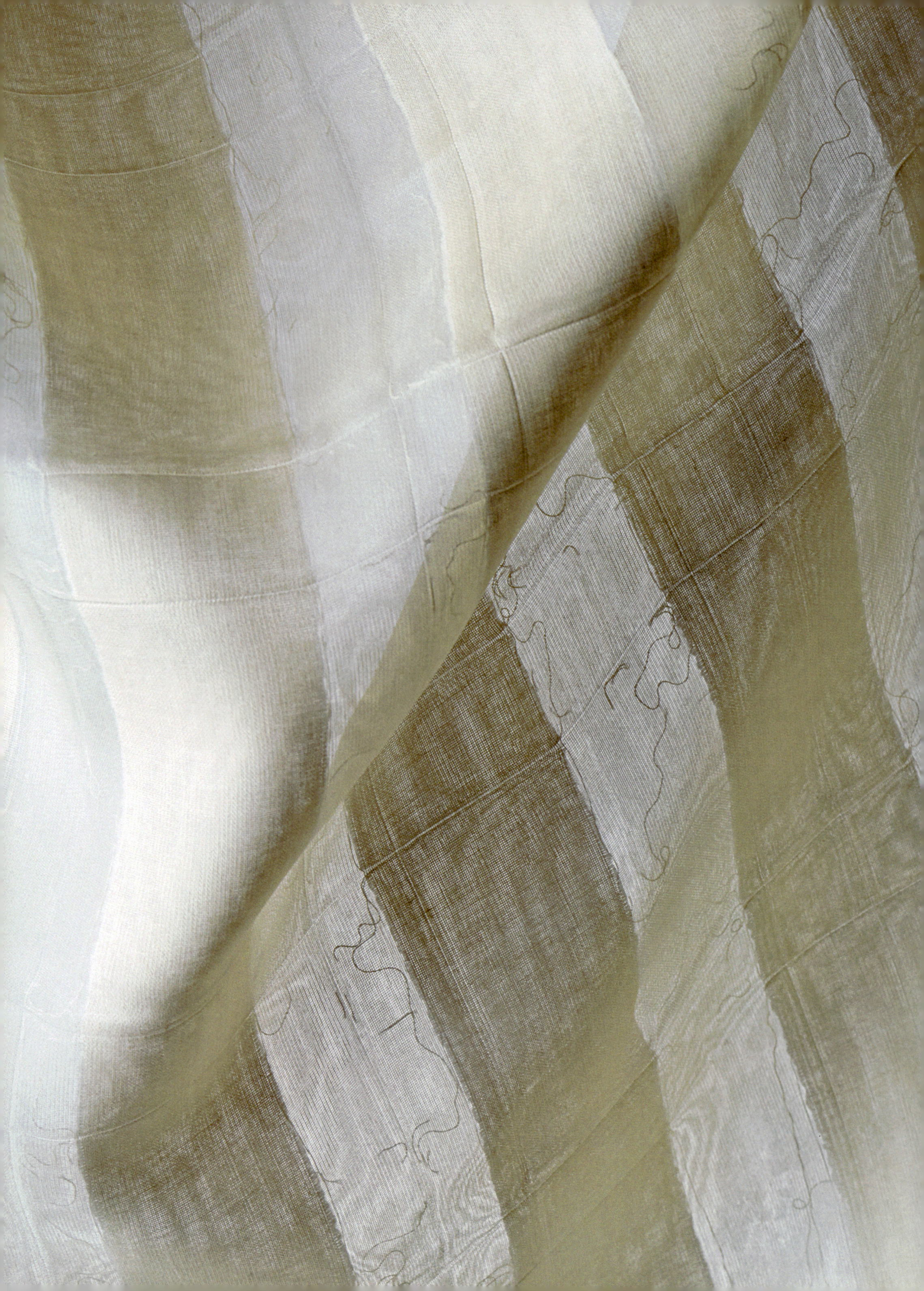

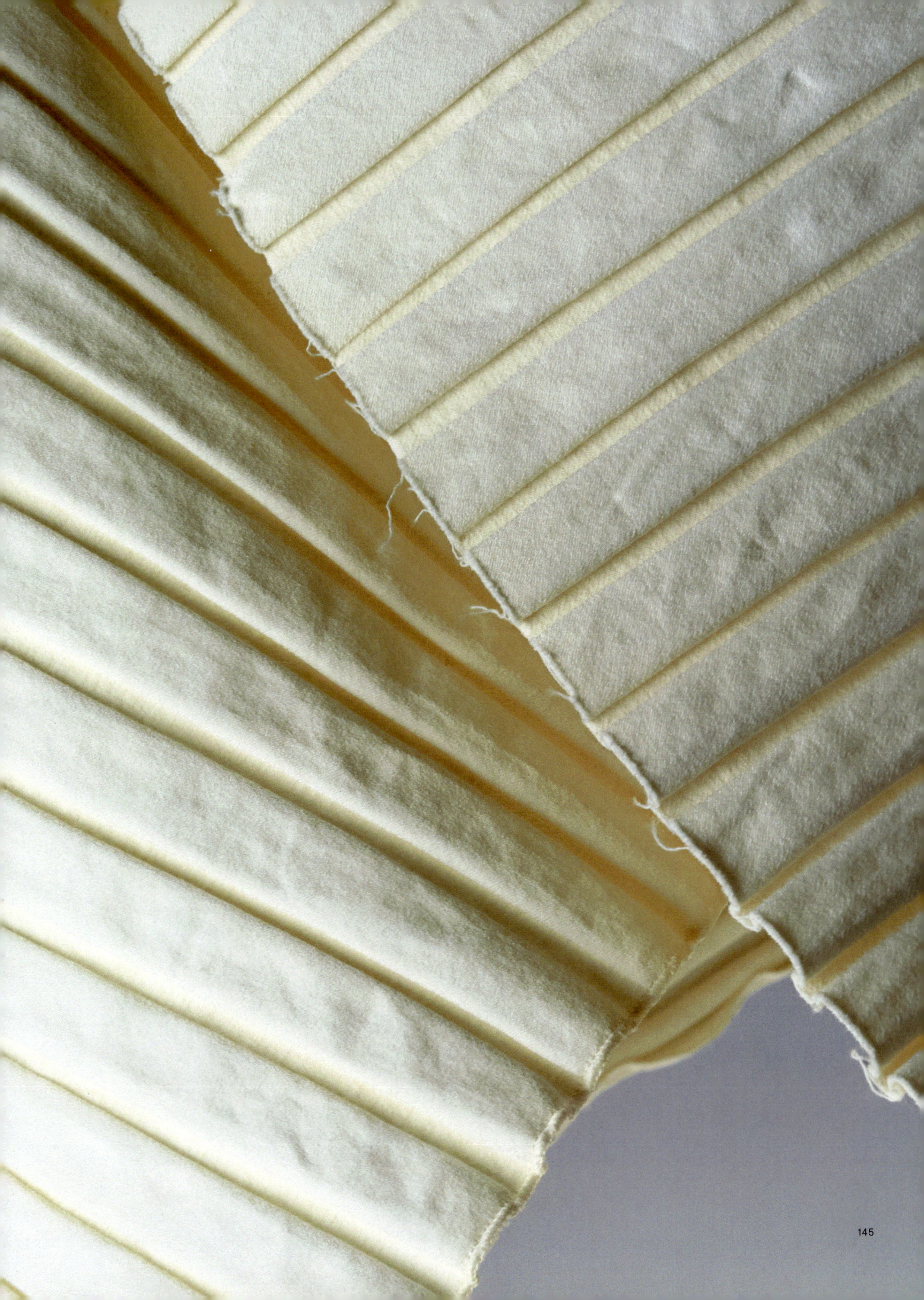

previous spread:
Biscuit, 1996.
By Reiko Sudo.
Machine looming with stretch warps was long thought impossible, but starching warps and wefts of Spandex™ wound in cotton, then rinsing after weaving lets them stretch in all directions.

Domino Stripe, 2004.
By Sayuri Shimoda
and Reiko Sudo.
Alternating colour warps determine vertical stripes; once strung on the loom, the stripes cannot be changed. Here, however, we finally succeeded in weaving horizontal weft stripes.

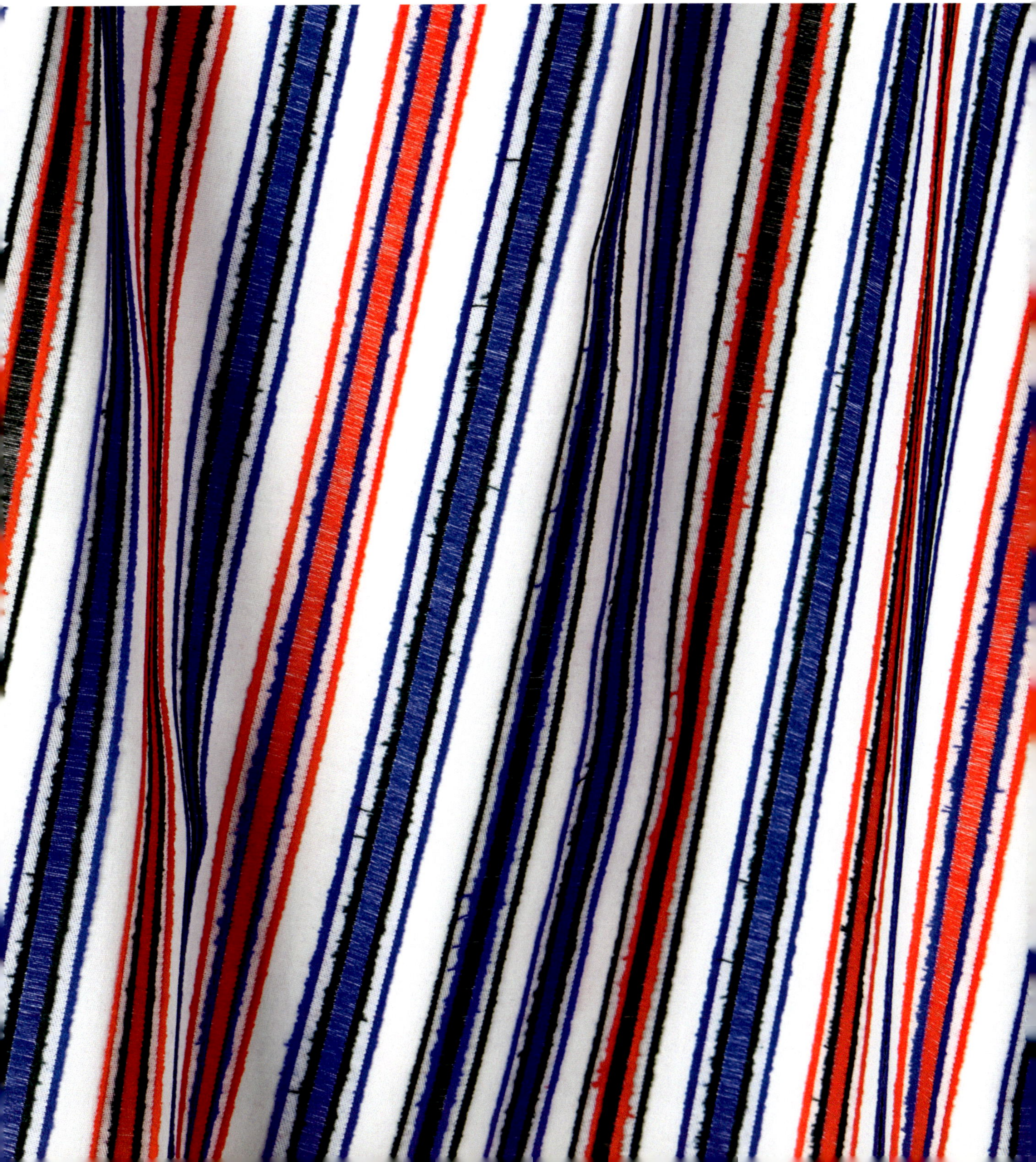

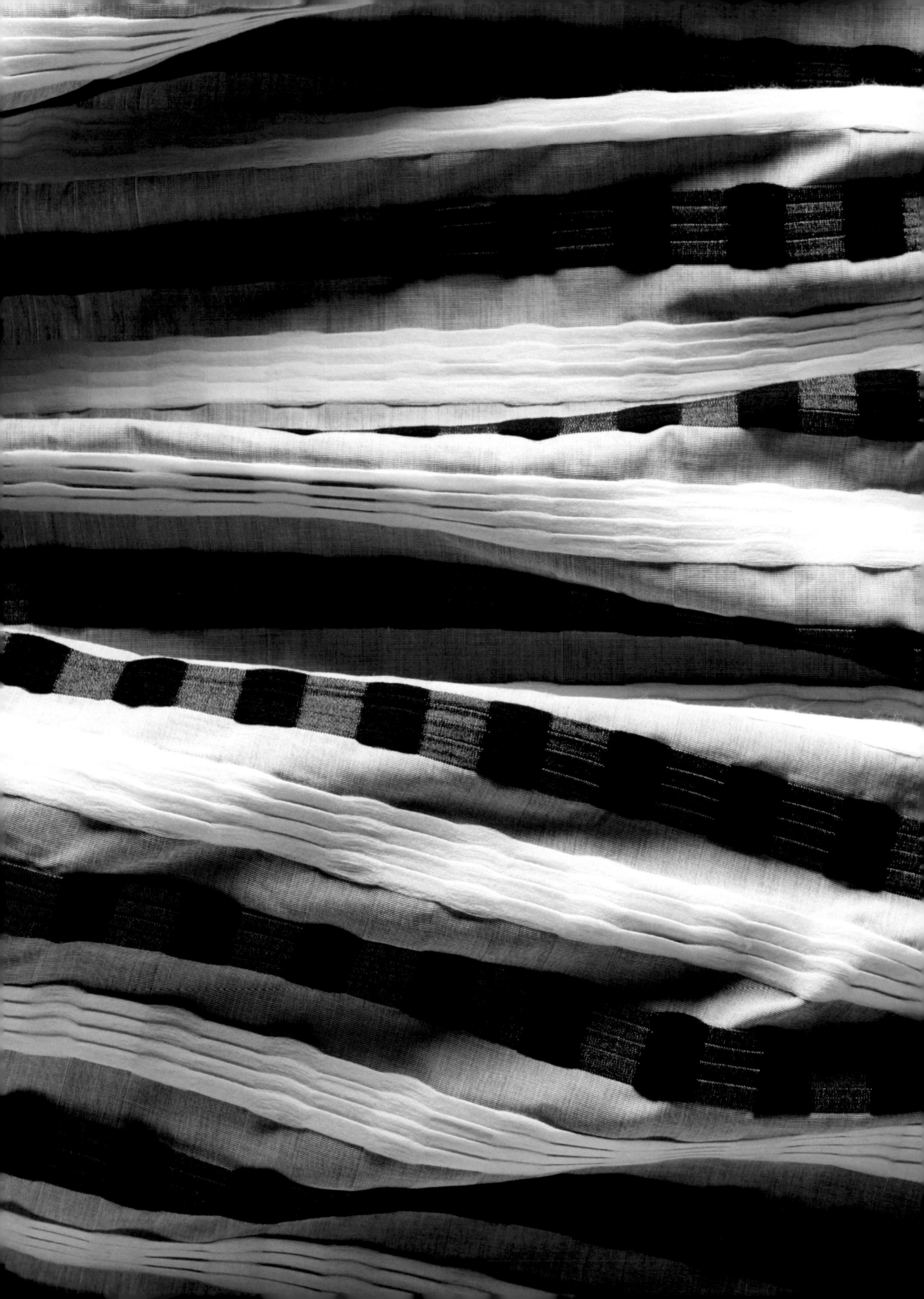

opposite:
Louvre Block, 1991.
By Reiko Sudo.
This very porous felt window louvre pattern can be further felted under heat and friction to achieve a tighter structure.

above:
Wavelets, 1997.
By Reiko Sudo.
Stretchy Spandex™ wefts interspersed with *washi* paper slit yarns create tiny waves.

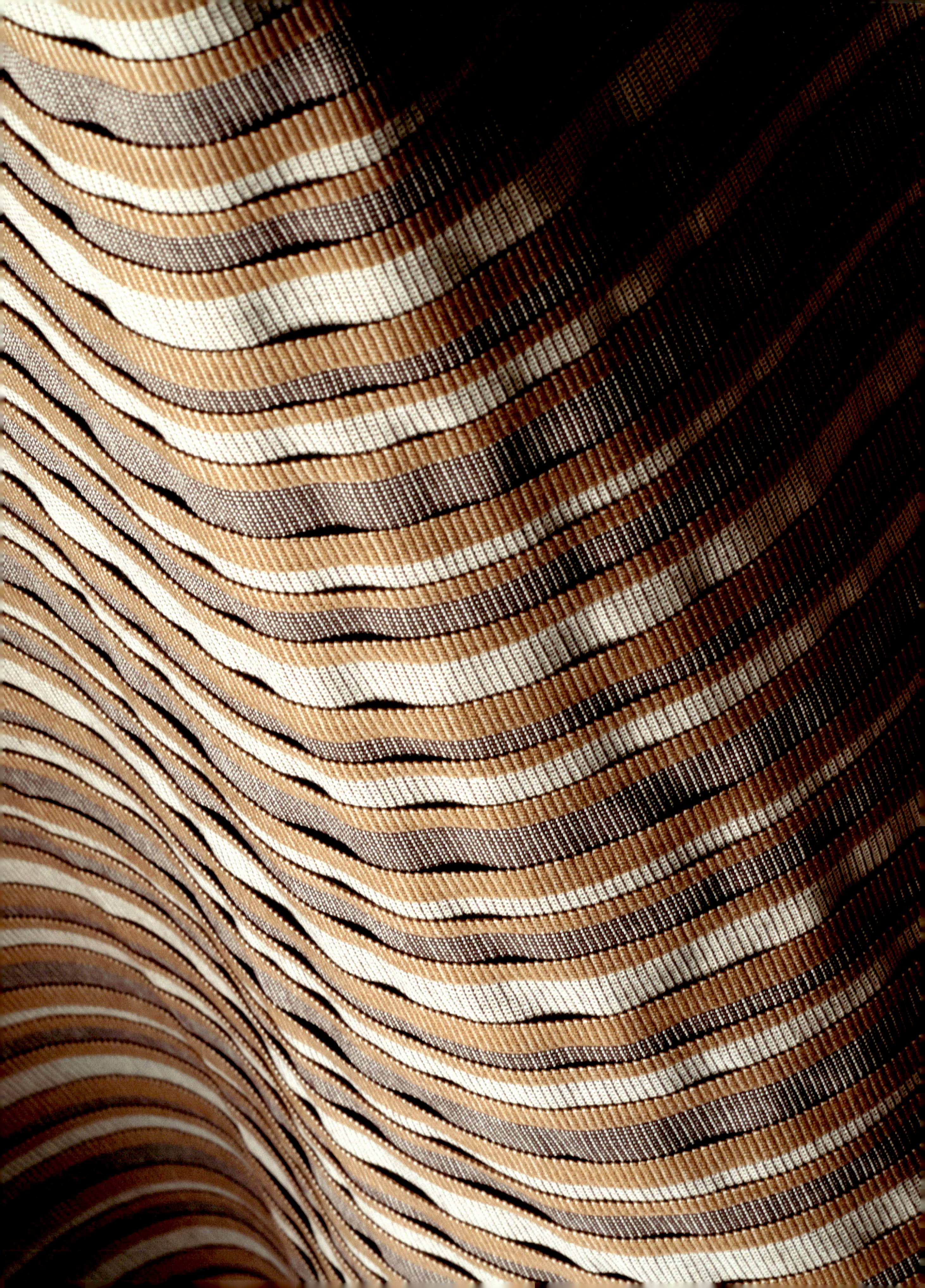

left:
Overhang, 1996.
By Reiko Sudo.
Varying back and forth between warps of two different tensions distorts the lay of threads, creating ribs and tucks or runs and pulls in the fabric for raised rhythmic effects.

following page:
Colour Plate, 1997.
By Reiko Sudo.
Planes of colour intersect to create patterns of shifting complexity.

SHIMA SHIMA

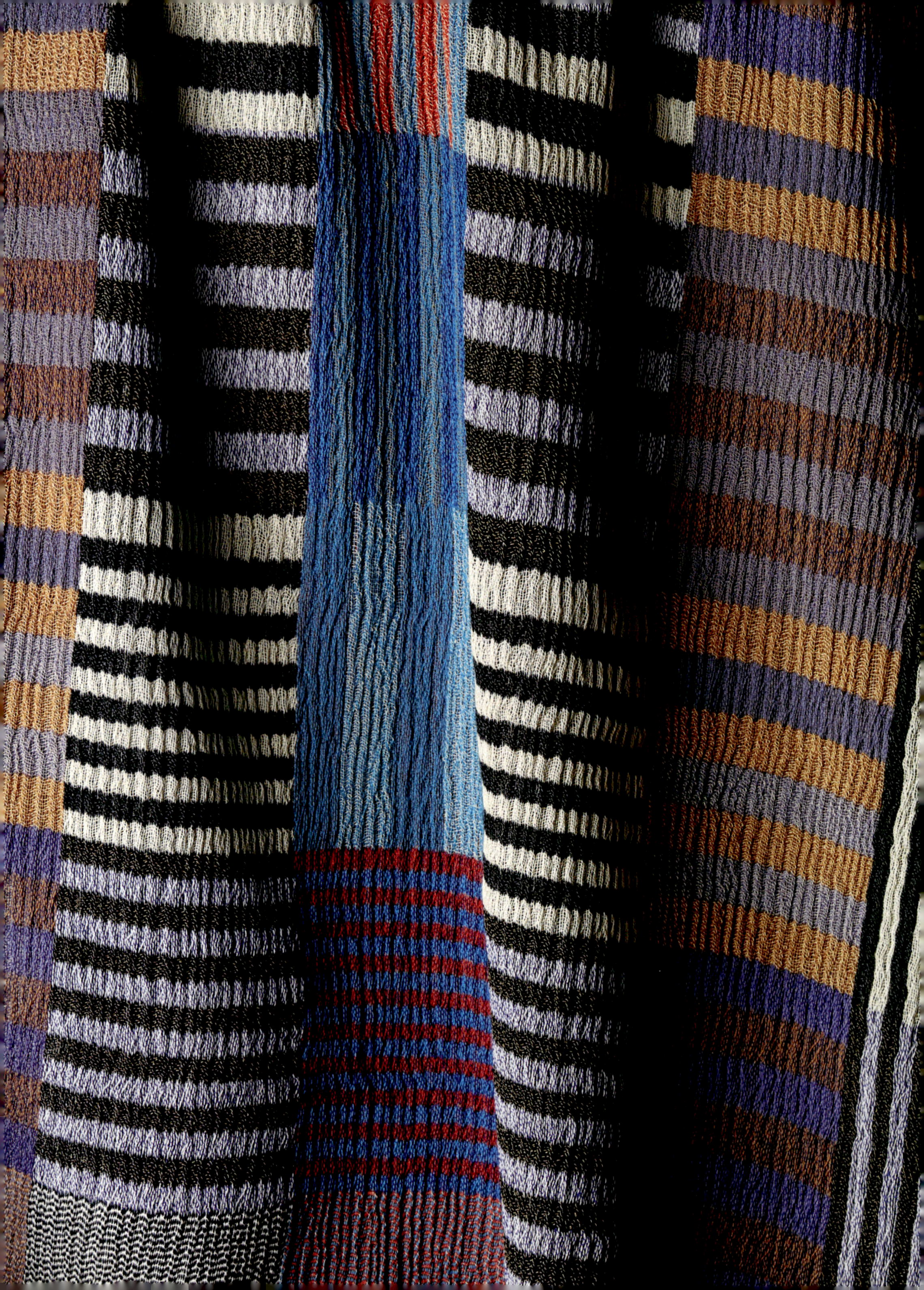

Portrait of a Textile: *Colour Plate*

How many different colours can be made by layering criss-crossed warps and wefts?

NUNO has had close ties with Kiryu, a major centre of Japan's textile industries, since it was founded in the city in 1983. With over 1,300 years of weaving and dyeing history, this 'Kyoto of Eastern Japan' is still very flexible and forward-looking, actively embracing new technologies in such diverse fields as interior design and automobile production. Like the town itself, NUNO draws upon the invaluable skills and expertise of artisans and technicians steeped in *kimono* traditions. Hyodo Orimono, specialists in gold and silver brocade sashes, have been trusted partners throughout our creative exploits. Their jacquard looms can weave incredibly detailed patterns up to 2,060 warps wide, with multiple layers and floated threads. Although accustomed to working with long-strand silk, they happily agreed to help realize our stretchy, crepe-like *Colour Plate*, in regular wool crossed with left- and right-twisted overspun wool yarns. Their four looms have created over 400 designs for us, and hopefully we will continue to work together for years to come.

A striped swatch book that Reiko Sudo made for fun.

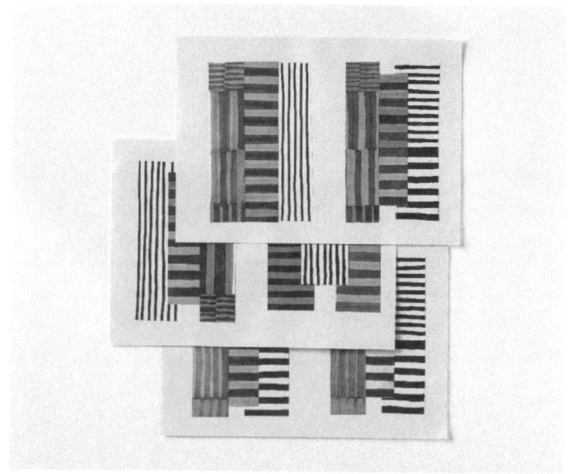

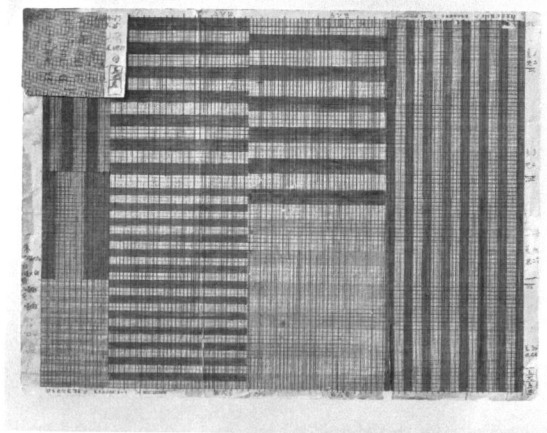

top left
Ideas sketchbook.

top right
Ideas sketched out in felt marker.

above left
The original design spattered on watercolour paper.

above right
The weaver makes a 'weaving draft'.

Multiweave colours

In 1804, the French merchant Joseph Marie Jacquard invented a loom that not only revolutionized weaving but contributed to the emergence of digital computing. The first jacquard looms were introduced to Japan in 1873, and likewise brought about a major transformation in the Nishijin weaving district of Kyoto, boosting the exquisite crafting of *obi kimono* sashes. NUNO uses these same period jacquard looms and artisan craftsmanship to create our multilayered scarves.

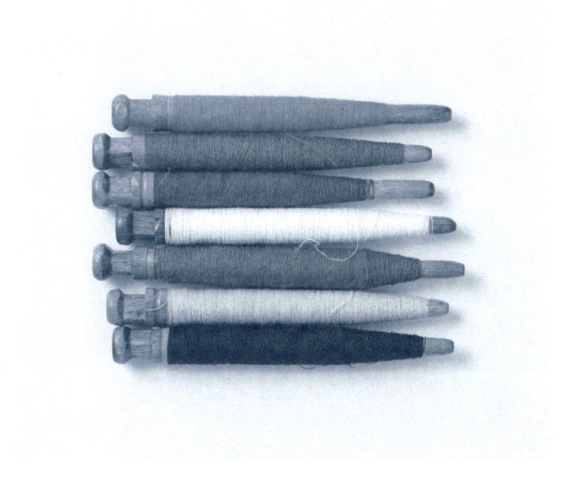

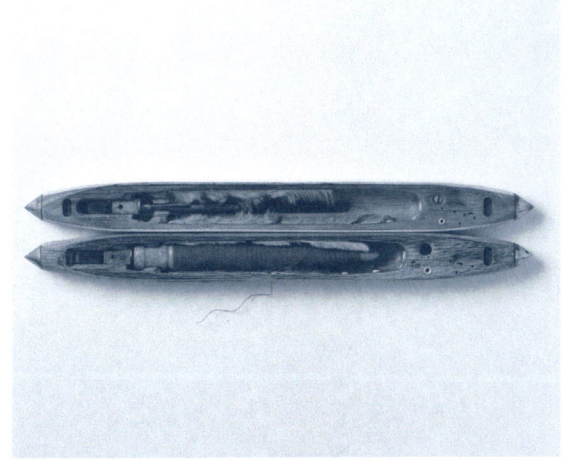

top left
Five spools wound with warp yarns in five colours.

top right
A warp tensioner ensures consistency of tension throughout the weaving process.

above left to right
Seven spools wound with wefts in seven colours, and weft spools and shuttles.

below left to right
Finishing shears; finishing crochet needles; darning needles.

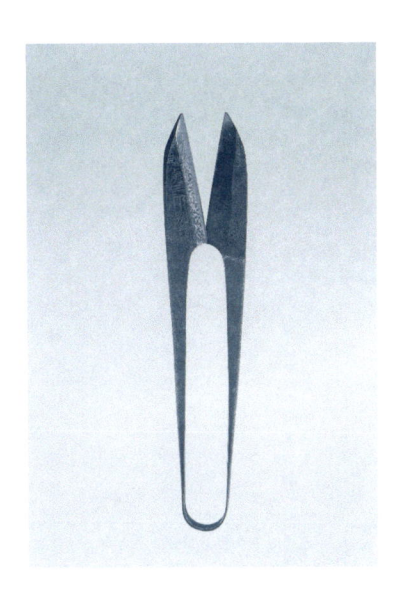

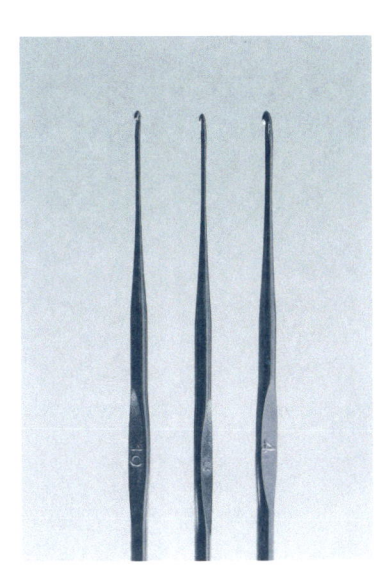

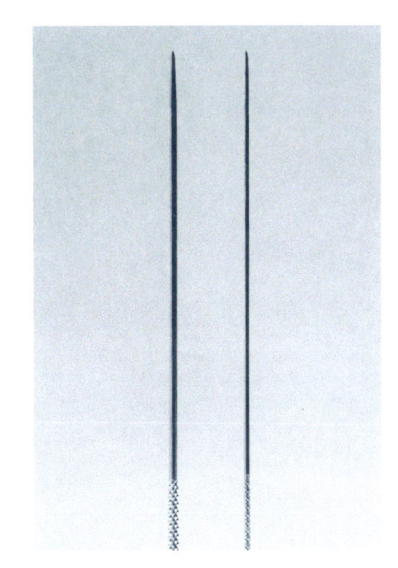

シマシマ

SHIMA SHIMA

シマシマ

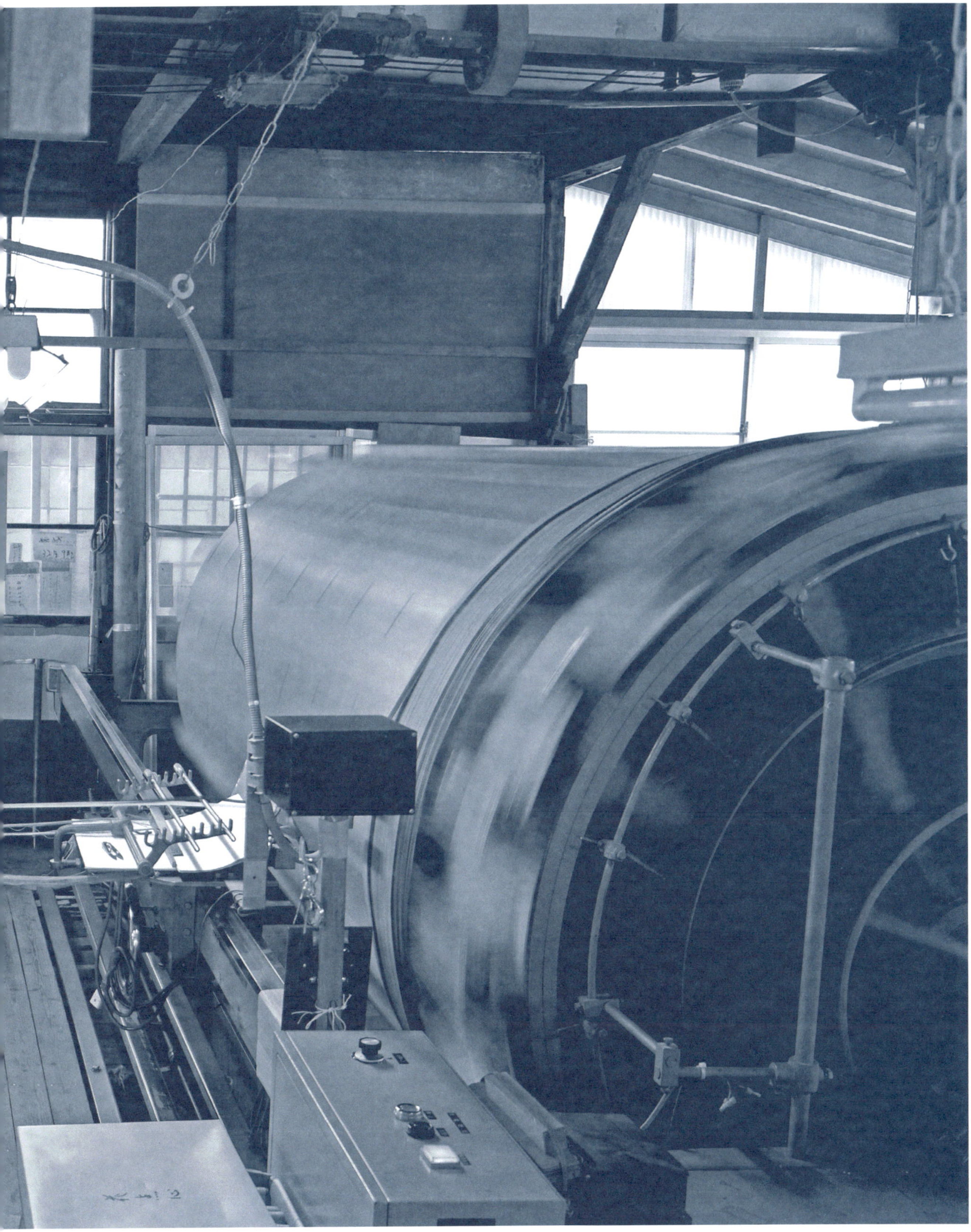

シアシア

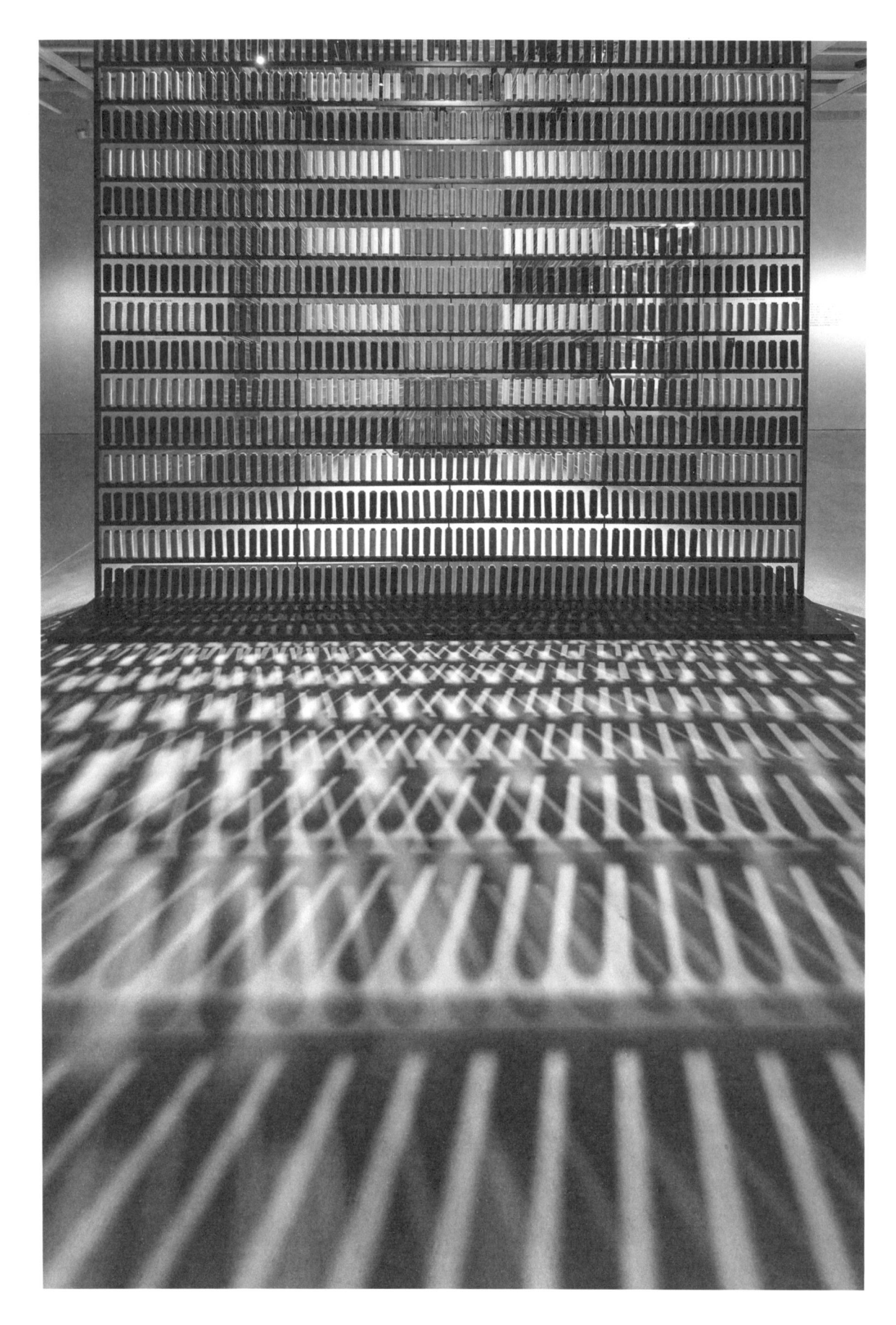

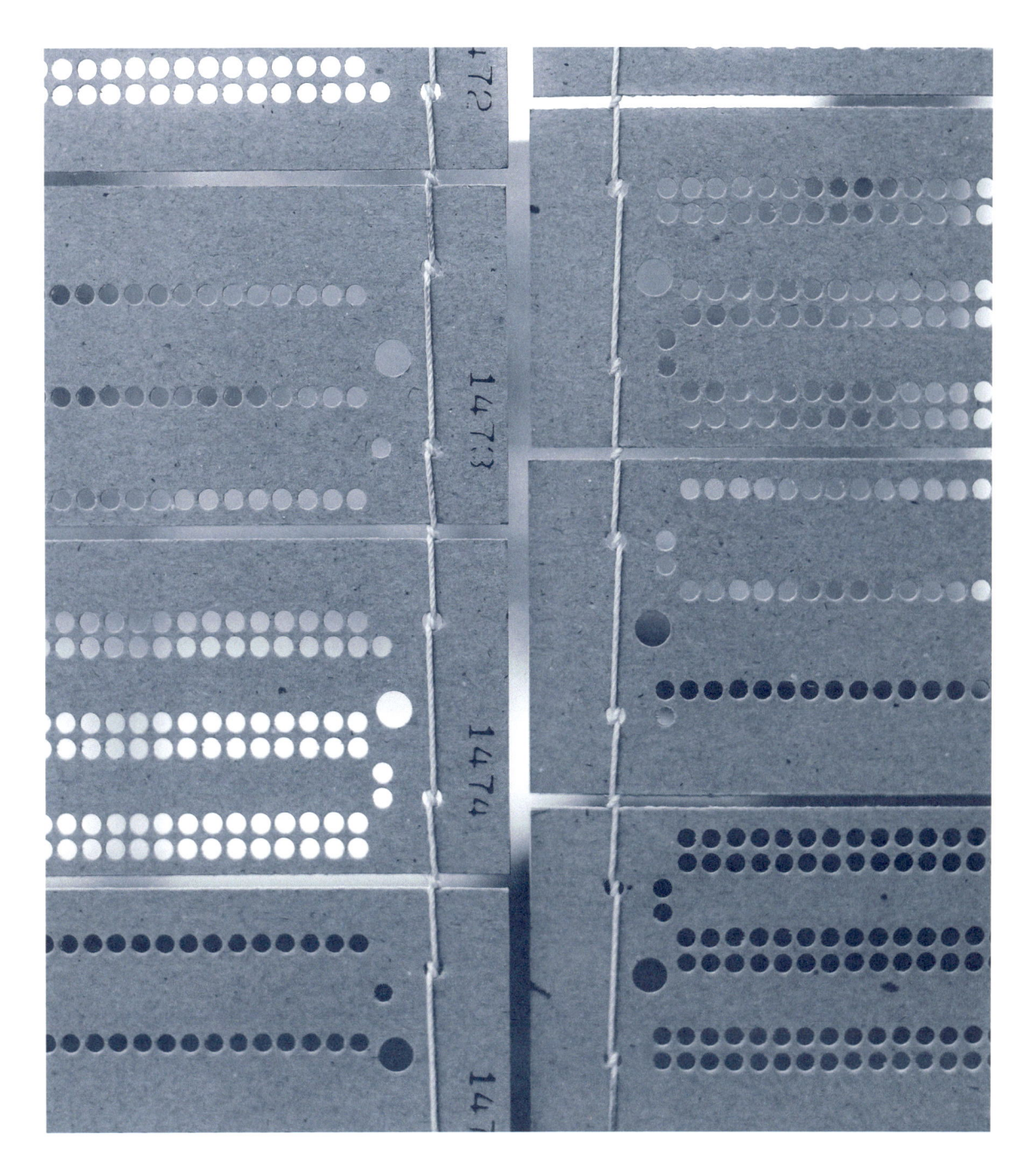

on pp. 156–57
The workshop previously produced woven *obi* sashes.

on pp. 158–59
A craftsperson prepares the warps.

opposite
Installation at the exhibition 'Sudo Reiko: Making NUNO Textiles', CHAT (Centre for Heritage, Arts and Textile), Hong Kong, 2019-20, which demonstrates the process of warping.

above
Thousands of punch cards, still used for controlling jacquard loom warps.

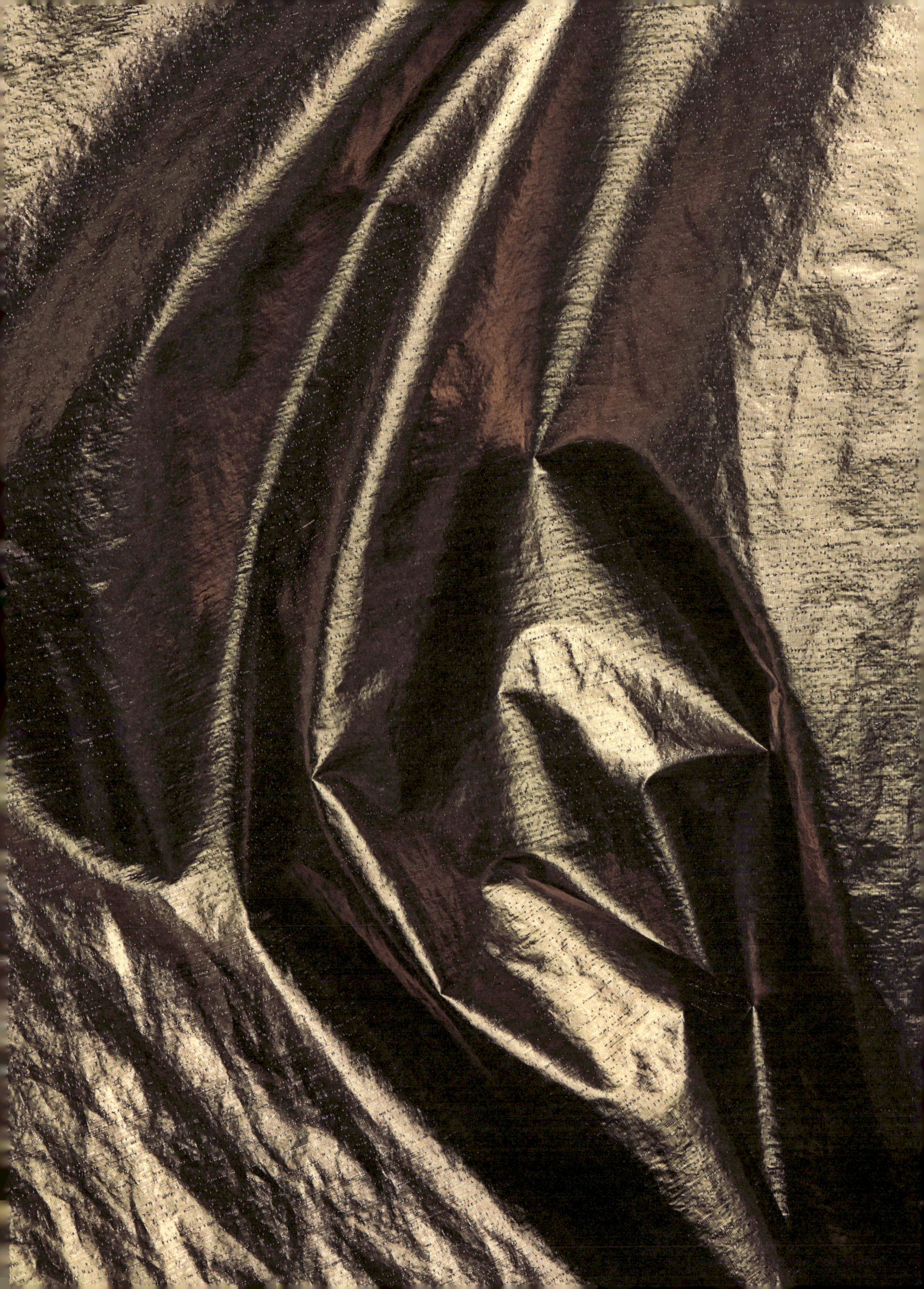

KIRA
KIRA

kira kira (キラキラ)

1. Glittering, glistening, glimmering, twinkling, sparkling, shiny
2. Dazzling, brilliant, bright
3. Resplendent, gala; gaily attired (cf. *kirabiyaka*, finely appointed)
4. Bedraggled, messy, untidy

All that glisters

Shining with aspiration, scintillating with achievement, sparkling with success – our eyes glow when we think of all that is beautiful. We are all glitterati; we all want to be stars or at least stand somewhere near the light. In olden times, feudal lords may have taxed the people into penury, but we still envied them the gleam of their gems; whereas today, in the age of brand-name goods, we might dismiss 'glitz' as the bad taste of the *nouveau riche*.

In a backhanded smear at the wealth we'll never have, we cynically tarnish what once reflected authority: *we hated those crass rhinestones anyway.* Patinated grapes. But let's not reject that lustre out of hand. There's more to metallics than Midas ever dreamed of. NUNO has created a portfolio of shimmering *kira kira* fabrics, each with its own subtle differences.

In our quest for textile brilliance (not to be modest) we've explored in improbable directions: industrial processes for bonding metal to synthetics, fine wires unbraided from telephone lines, audiotape coatings to ensure a smooth gloss; not to mention a repertoire of melt-off and burn-out techniques for dissolving fibres down to sheet opalescence. The results glint for themselves – iridescences and shimmers previously unknown to either royalty or commoner.

p. 162:
Bronze Aluminium Glitz, 1984.
By Reiko Sudo and Junichi Arai.
Coloured metal lamé from nylon slit yarn coated with aluminium. Compared to polyester, nylon provides a much greater range of possible colours.

right:
Copper Scarab, 1994.
By Reiko Sudo.
Dark earth tones shimmer iridescent copper-red in this mysterious fabric.

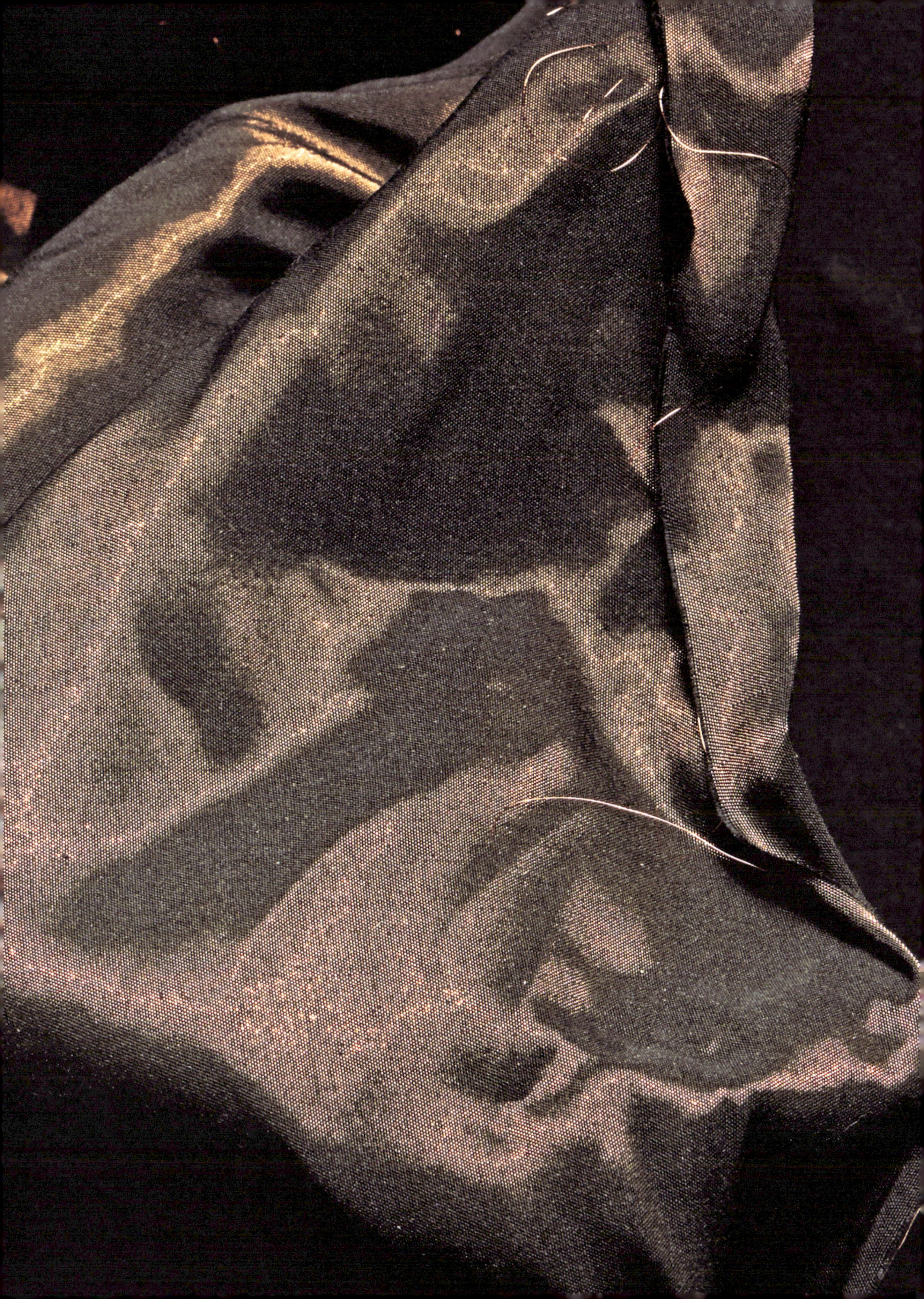

Shining Within

Akane Teshigahara

I used to have nightmares all the time when I was little. I'd dream someone was chasing me in a maze or shoving me into tiny, dice-sized boxes, so on nights when I simply couldn't get to sleep, I'd force my eyes shut and try to remember all the nice things I'd seen that day. The cake I'd had for a snack, a period drama on television that I'd watched with my grandmother, the ring glinting on my mother's slender fingers, grandfather's *ikebana* flower arrangement in the living room… yes, a large red and white-streaked camellia blossom in a petite celadon vase, bowed ever so slightly as if lost in thought. Just the thought of these little flower offerings that my grandfather loved so much always seemed to touch me deep inside and release a bright afterglow behind my eyes. Savouring that inner gleam, drowsiness would come over me before I knew it and bless me with a good sleep, safe from nightmares.

My deepest *kira kira* memories are thus not of the shimmering surface of the summer sea, nor of the gold and silver embroidery on my mother's *kimono*, nor of grandfather's well-honed flower scissors, but rather of those little specks of light behind my eyes.

As the middle of three sisters, I was positioned between the very sociable first-born four years my elder and the stubbornly independent last-born one year younger. From earliest childhood, I remember always coming in third. My father would try to console me by saying 'it's because you're so gentle'. In truth, I wasn't really gentle so much as lacking in self-confidence and awkward doing things in front of people.

When folding *origami* paper, my two sisters never hesitated to snatch up the shiny gold and silver papers, as well as the red and black for good measure. Which left me in third-choice position, ineffectually thumbing through all the other leftover colours. The same for divvying up snacks or jumping into a swimming pool: I was always the third. Although thanks to my father paying special attention and patiently teaching me the principles of swimming, I was the best swimmer.

As my father was a film director and my mother an actress, their circle included many leading artists and movie people, who often gathered at our home for drinks, loud talk and boisterous laughter. Sometimes the art talk would overheat into arguments. Big names, the likes of the wild painter Taro Okamoto, volatile actor Shintaro Katsu or experimental composer Toru Takemitsu, might conjure up glittering images of glamour and talent for most Japanese, but their oddball adult world just frightened me. Unlike my sisters, who joined in so easily, I invariably retreated to my room and prayed the party would end quickly.

I was twenty when unexpectedly my father became the Iemoto, or hereditary headmaster, of the Sogetsu Ikebana School of flower arranging, after his younger sister, the second-generation Iemoto, suddenly took ill and passed away within a year. Compared to the nearly six-hundred-year history of *ikebana* flower arranging, our Sogetsu tradition, which is less than a century old, is a relative newcomer with a somewhat more liberal ethos. Still, it must have been a major struggle for my father, someone accustomed to free expression in the arts and film, to assume the helm of a huge cultural organization with so many followers. Not that I gave much thought to his thinking at the time, or ever felt pressured by my parents to devote myself to *ikebana*. Fond of children, I basically remained as I was and became a kindergarten teacher.

But then in my fourth year of teaching at the kindergarten, my father suggested I take

My deepest kira kira memories are thus not of the shimmering surface of the summer sea, nor of the gold and silver embroidery on my mother's kimono, *nor of grandfather's well-honed flower scissors, but rather of those little specks of light behind my eyes.*

キラキラ

up *ikebana*-related work. I suppose it was his saying 'you don't even have to arrange flowers' that convinced me. But after doing secretarial jobs and public relations for the School, flower arranging grew on me little by little, to where I eventually became vice-chairperson and, later, after my father passed away, fourth-generation Iemoto. That was almost twenty years ago now.

Of course, I was surrounded by senior advisers and colleagues, who supported and encouraged me. But it was a different story when it came to arranging flowers. I alone had to forge my way.

The basic Sogetsu philosophy can be expressed in the simple phrase 'arranging flowers makes the person', meaning the arrangement of flowers is a direct expression of that person's spirit. In choosing which branches to cut or save, whether to tilt a blossom just-so or leave a slight *ma* of breathing space, one must never lose sight of that one important principle. Faced with decision upon decision, my relationship with flowers deepened little by little, and that profound connection bolstered my courage and self-confidence. Yes, now, I wouldn't hesitate to reach for that gold *origami* paper.

What I find most alluring about *ikebana* is the transition between when flowers are there and when they're gone; their presence lingers on in the room. That feeling suffuses the space and propels me to newer creations. Even with eyes closed, there's a *kira kira* afterglow of floral life that shines in the depths of the empty space. The tiny glimmer of a seed patiently waiting for a new arrangement to come forth. Inherited from my elders, this inner vitality of flowers continues to bloom in my heart. And someday I, too, will pass along this *kira kira* spirit of flowers to someone new.

opposite:
Contour Line, 1988.
By Reiko Sudo.
Strong alkali solutions can 'melt' aluminium-nylon slit yarns from lamé fabrics, leaving openwork patterns such as these topographical contours.

following spread:
Copper Mocha, 1993.
By Reiko Sudo.
Warps synthesized from milk casein and acrylonitrile create a deliciously draping blend of cream and copper.

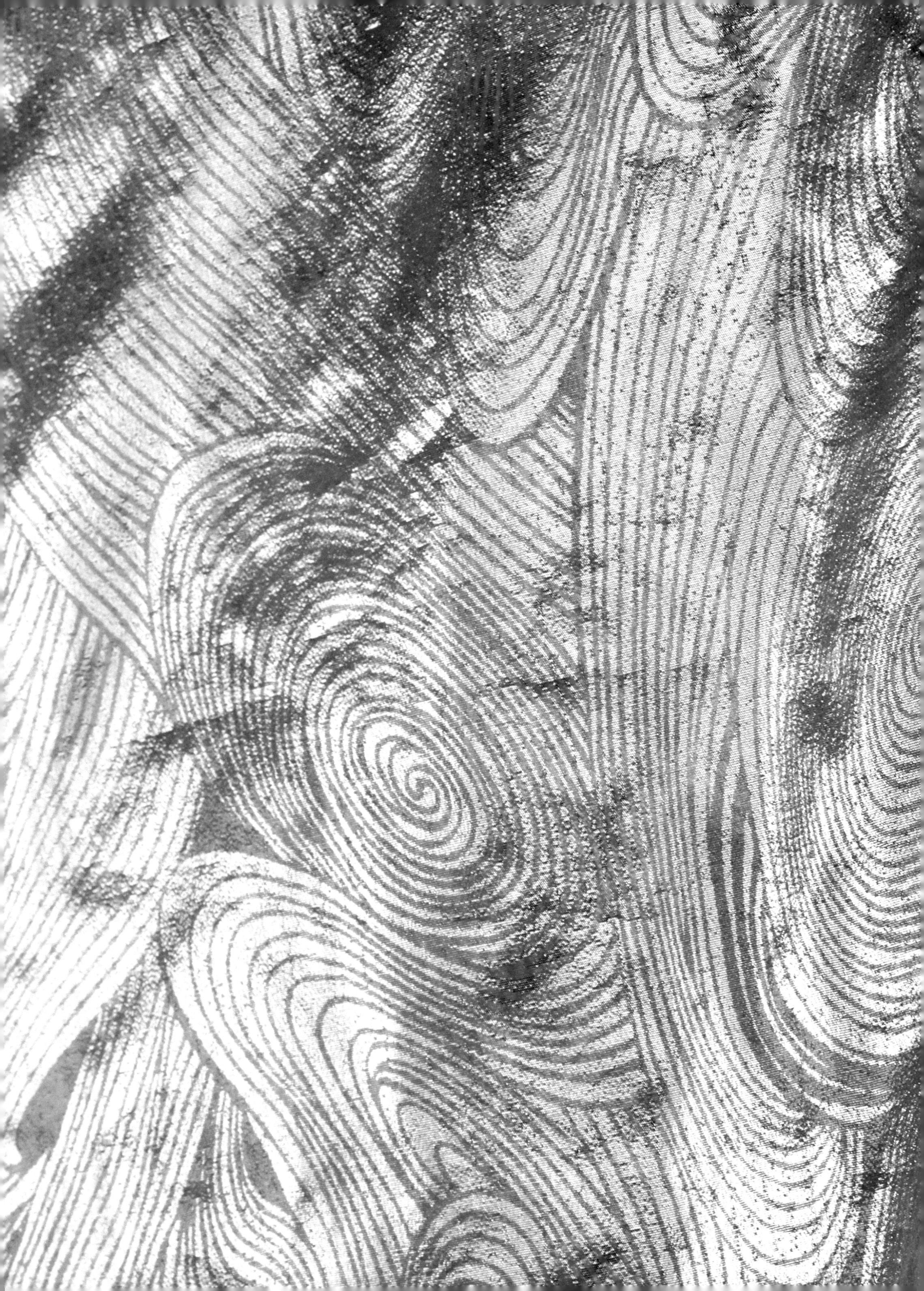

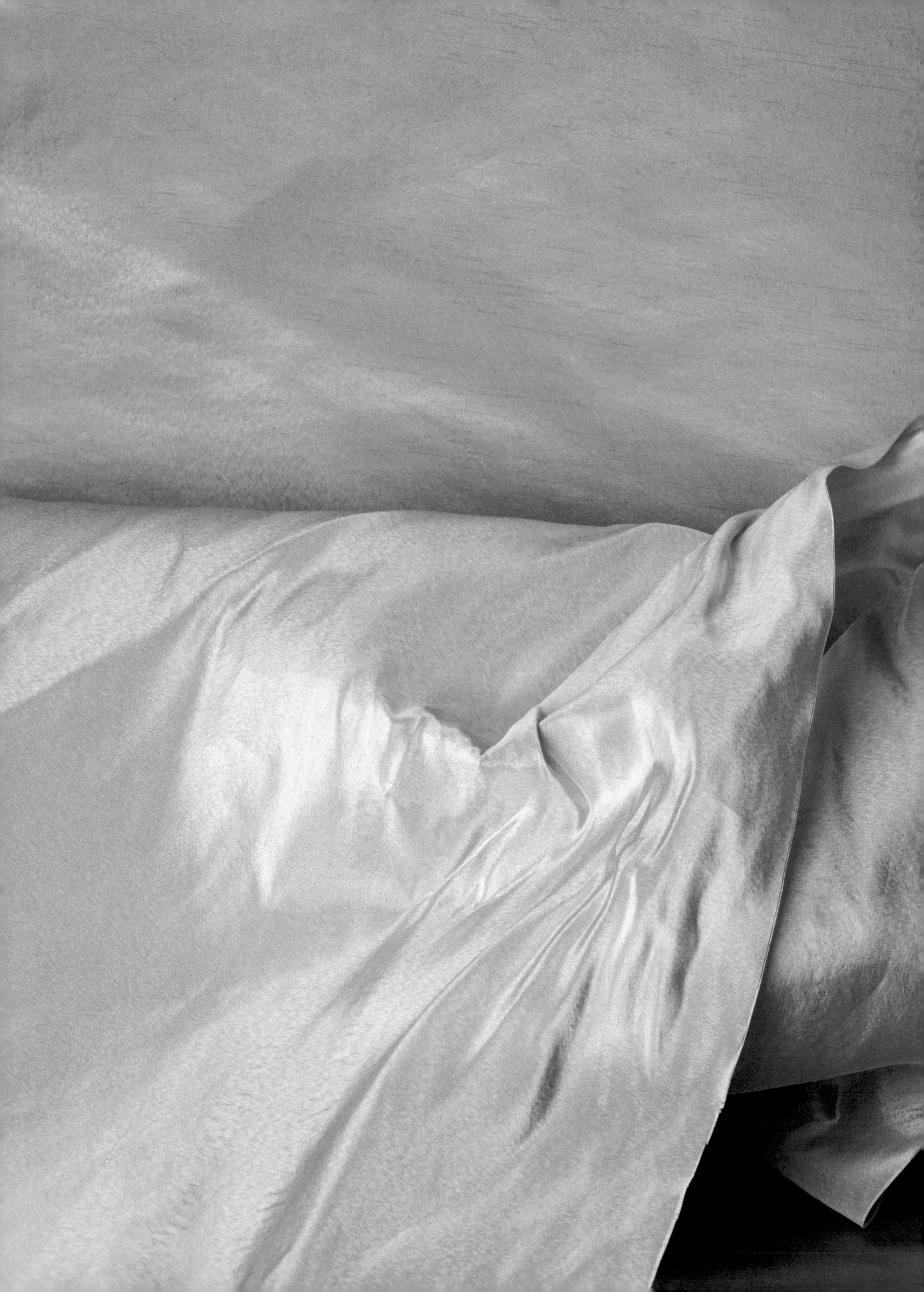

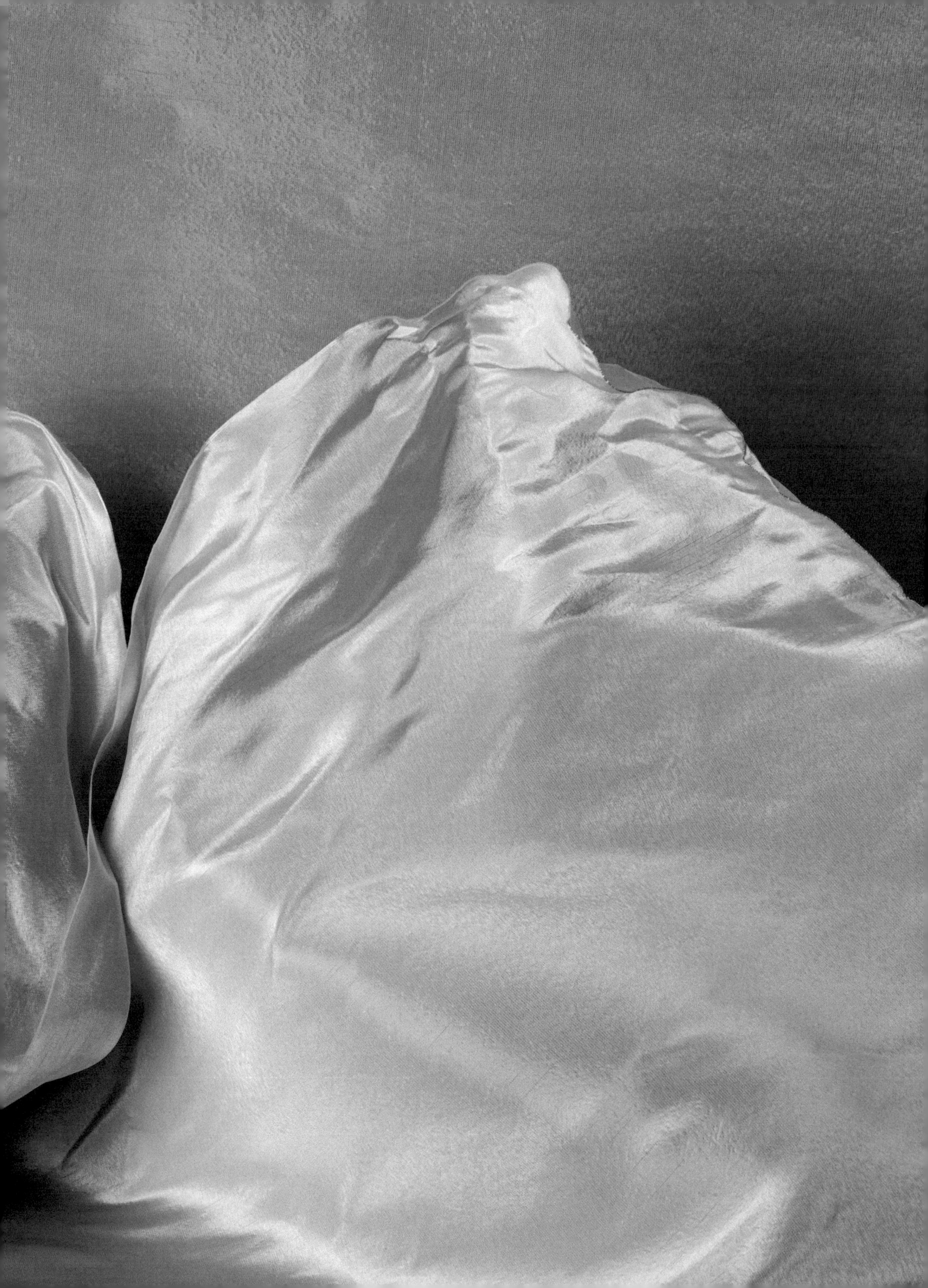

below:
Suzushi, 1999.
By Reiko Sudo.
A weave made on specially modified looms with hooking devices that divert warps left and right, over and under the wefts.

opposite:
Southern Cross, 1999.
By Ryoko Sugiura and Reiko Sudo.
The famous constellation of the southern sky is rendered here in tiny glass beads affixed with industrial glue.

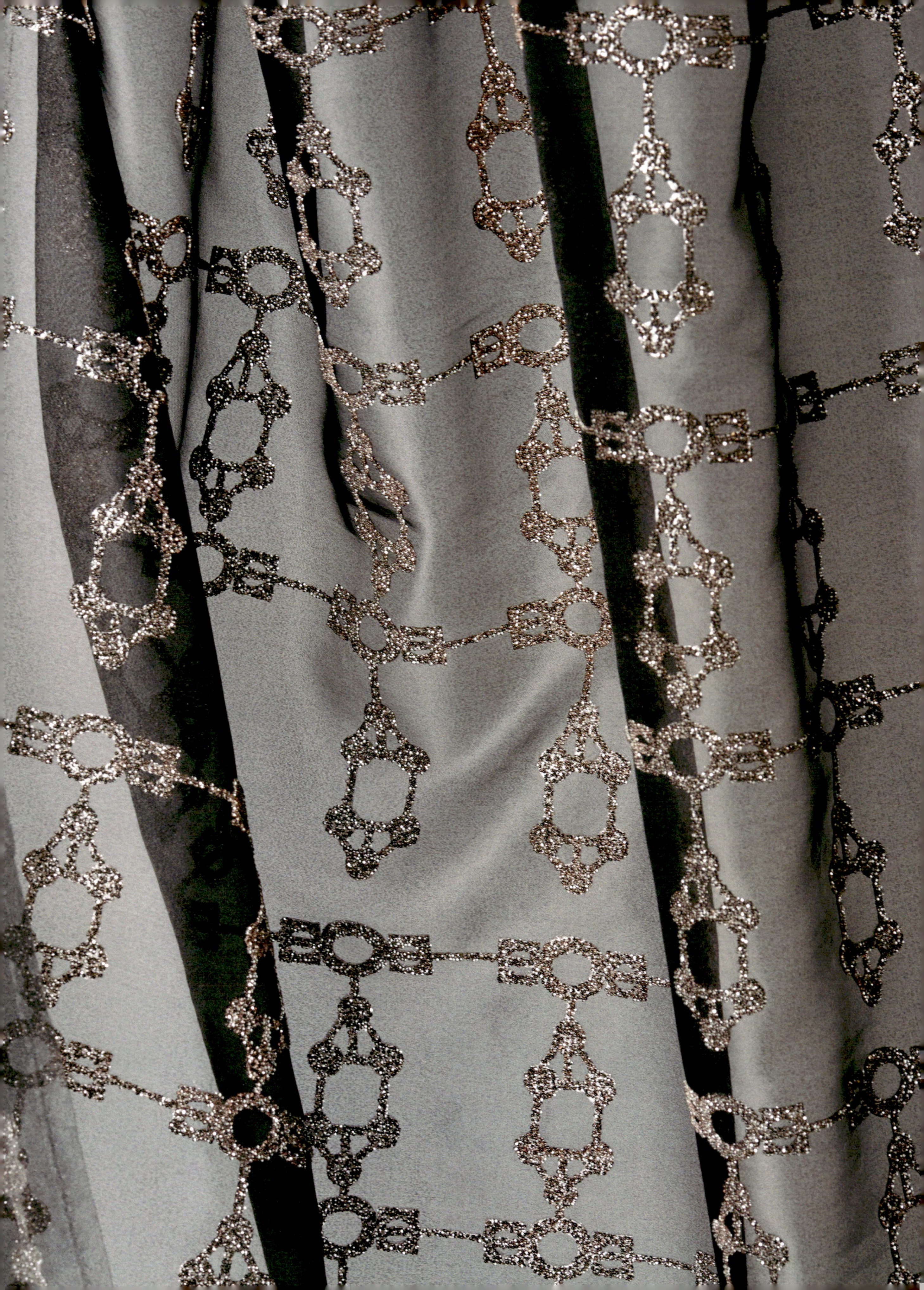

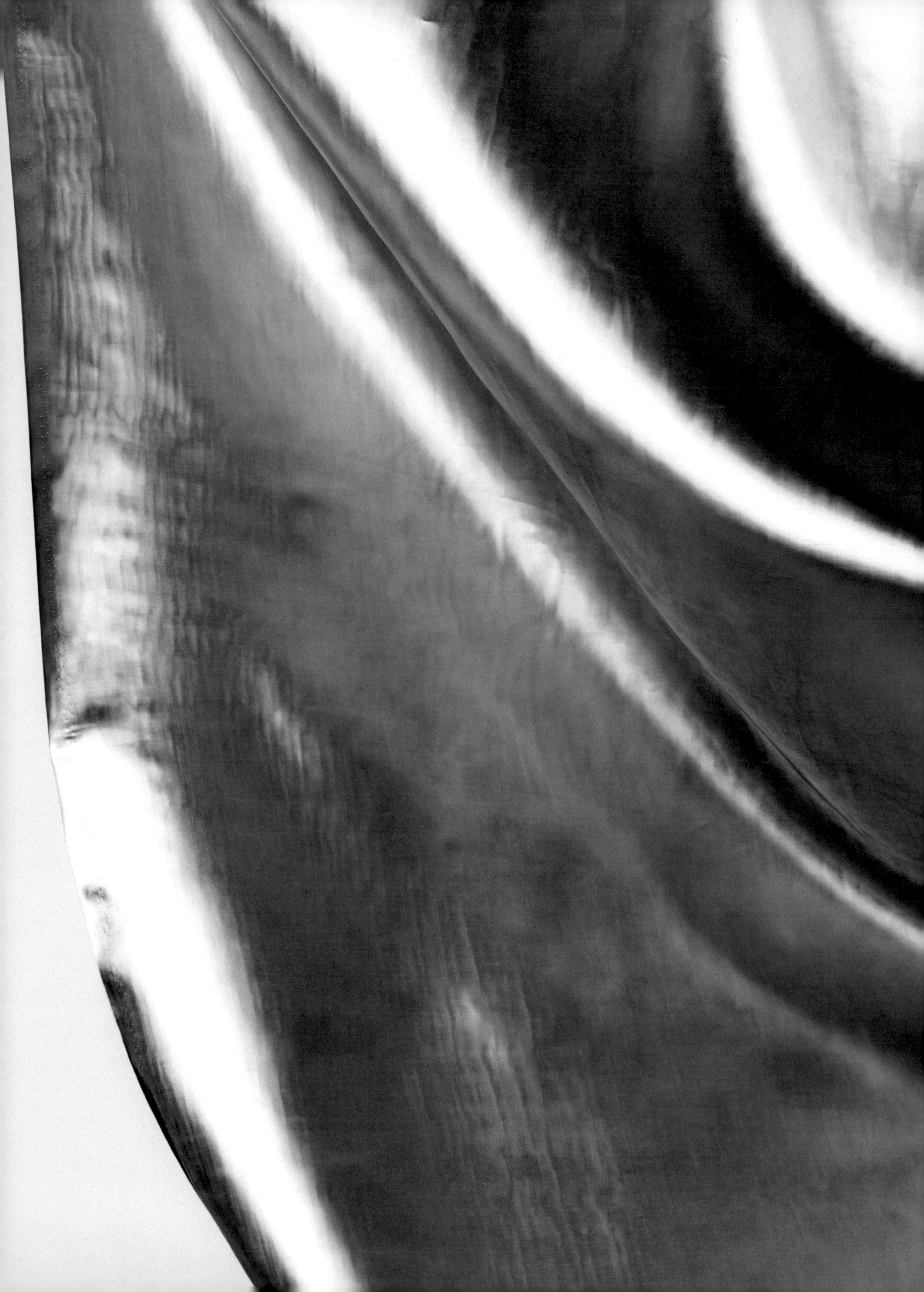

Sputtered Gloss, 1990
(reissued 1994).
By Reiko Sudo.
A polyester plain-weave is calendered mirror-smooth, then microstructured chrome, nickel and iron – alloy elements for stainless steel – are 'spatter-deposited' to a shiny finish.

Mercury, 1997.
By Reiko Sudo and Keiji Otani.
A double-layered silk organdy with aluminium foil appliqué and an acrylic resin binder to give an added *repoussé* build-up.

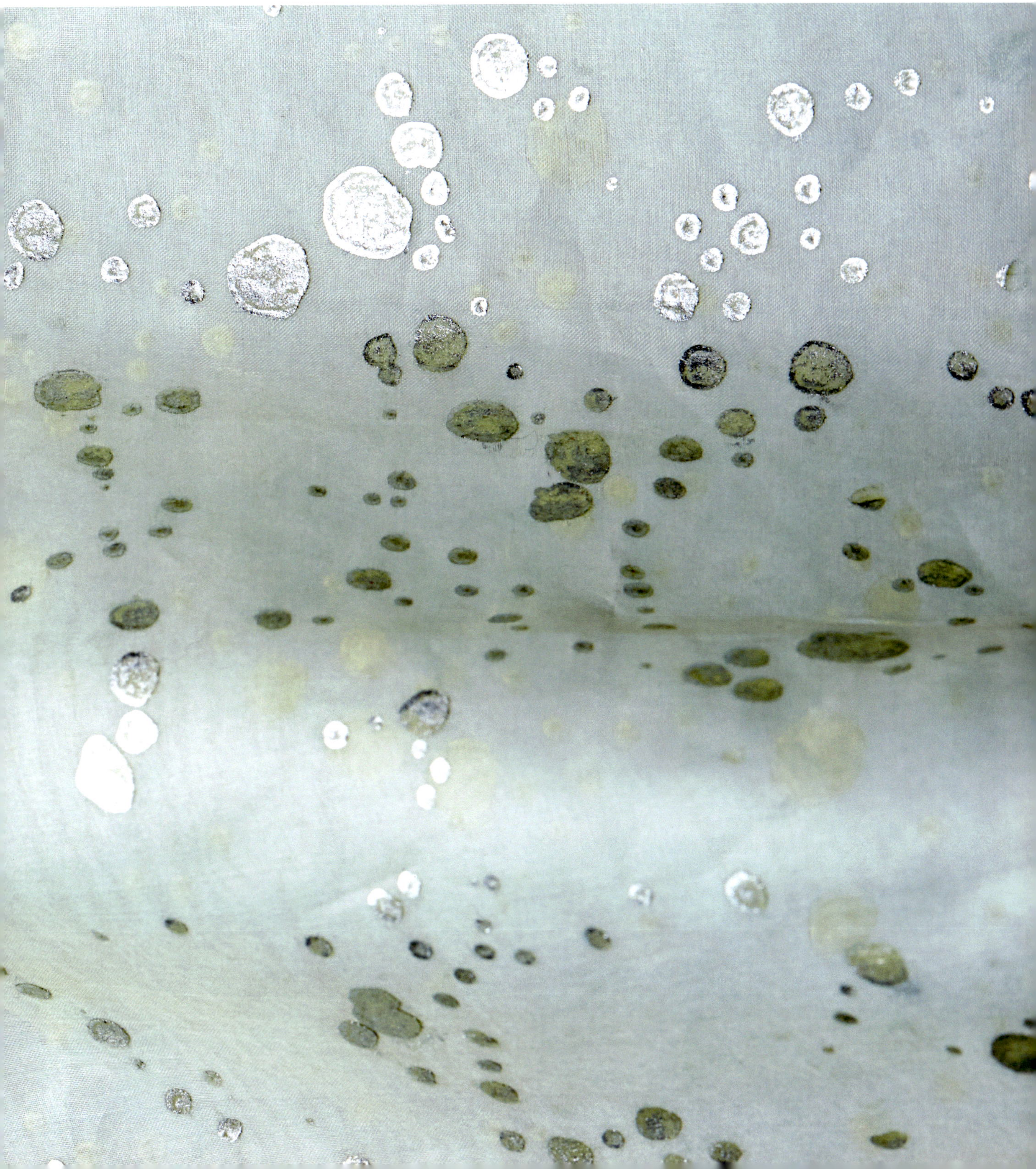

above:
Satin Snow, 2009.
By Reiko Sudo.
Monofilament fishing line and wool yarns give sheen and softness to this full, draping vision of powdery snowdrifts.

opposite:
Bamboo Flower, 1994.
By Reiko Sudo.
Velvet is hand-screened with an acid paste in bamboo flower patterns, which selectively burns out rayon fibres to expose the transparent polyester base.

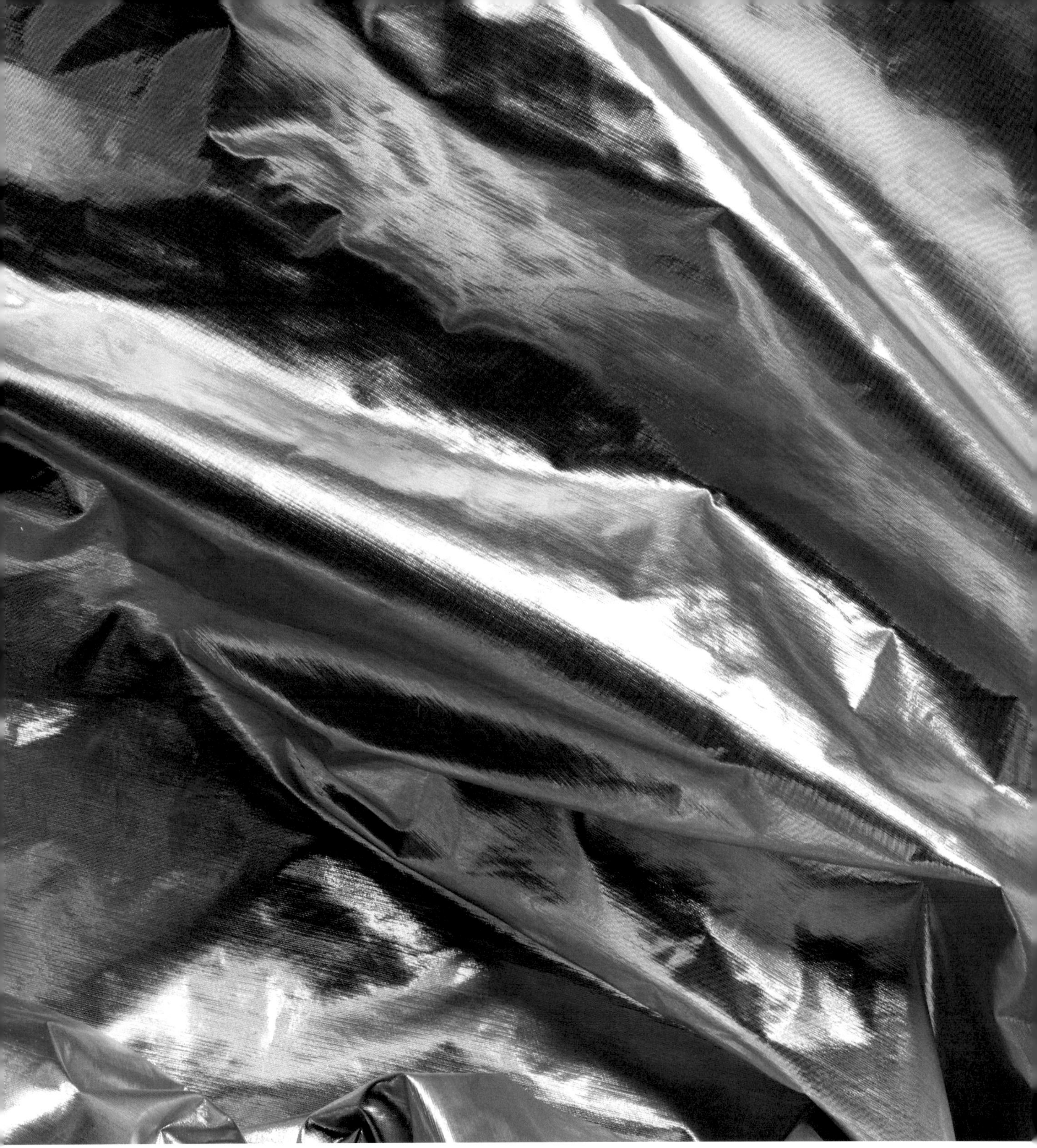

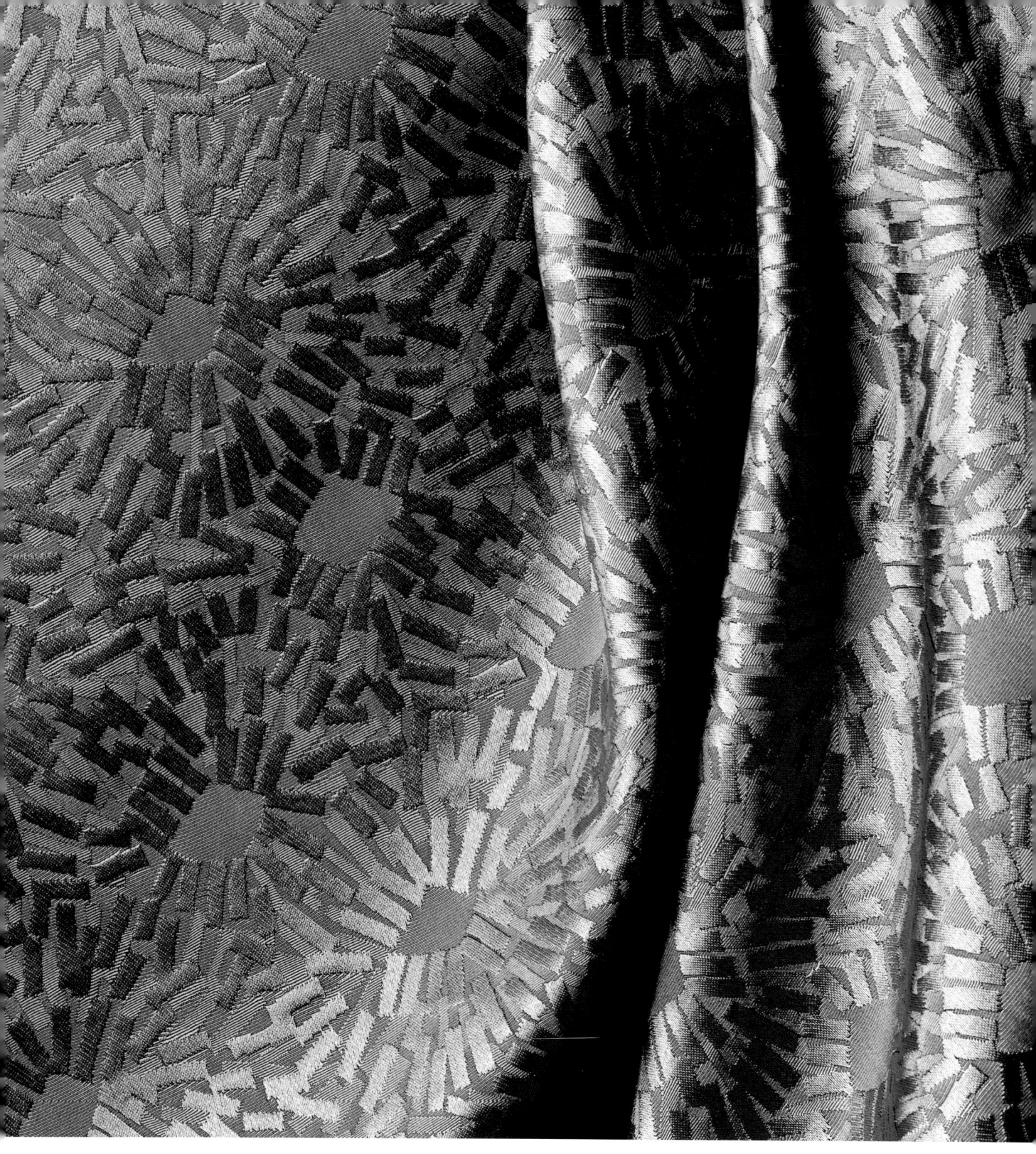

p. 180:
Stainless Sparklers, 1998.
By Reiko Sudo.
Stainless steel spun into complex long-fibre yarns combines cloth softness with the hardness of metal. As stretch yarns, the resultant fabric sparkles and reshapes with every move of the body.

p. 181:
Space Suit, 1994
(reissued 2007).
By Reiko Sudo and Junichi Arai.
Aluminium-coated polyester warps suppress static when woven with polyester filament wefts, leaving this sheer, space-age fabric.

opposite:
Kapanese Thistle, 2007.
By Kazuhiro Ueno and Reiko Sudo.
Inner padding adds heft under the calendered high-gloss enamelled surface in this evocation of the wild mountain thistle.

below:
Mayumi, 2016.
By Reiko Sudo.
Matelassé meets cut velvet in this jacquard weave patterned after the deciduous *mayumi* 'spindle bush', with its tiny four-petal flowers.

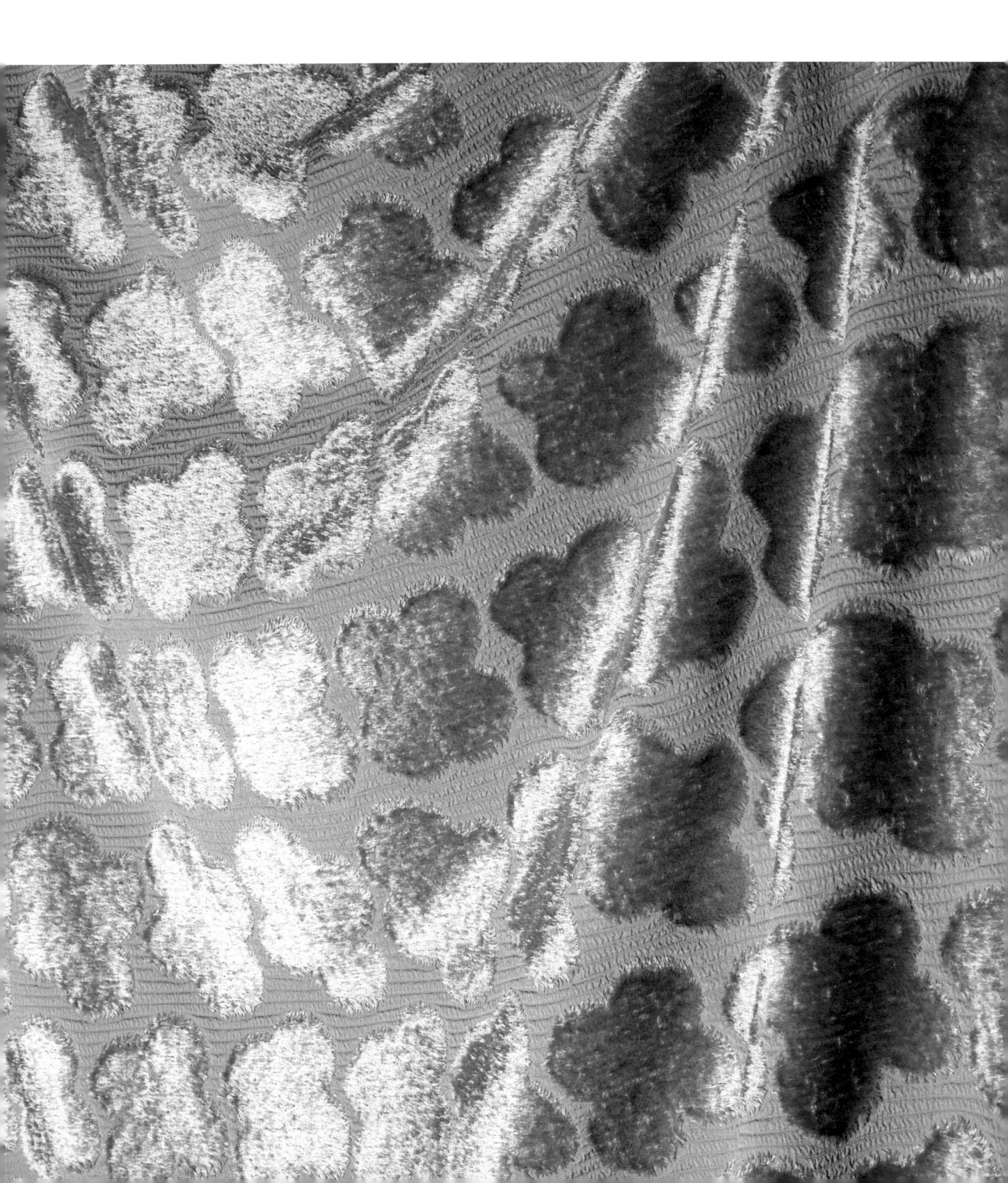

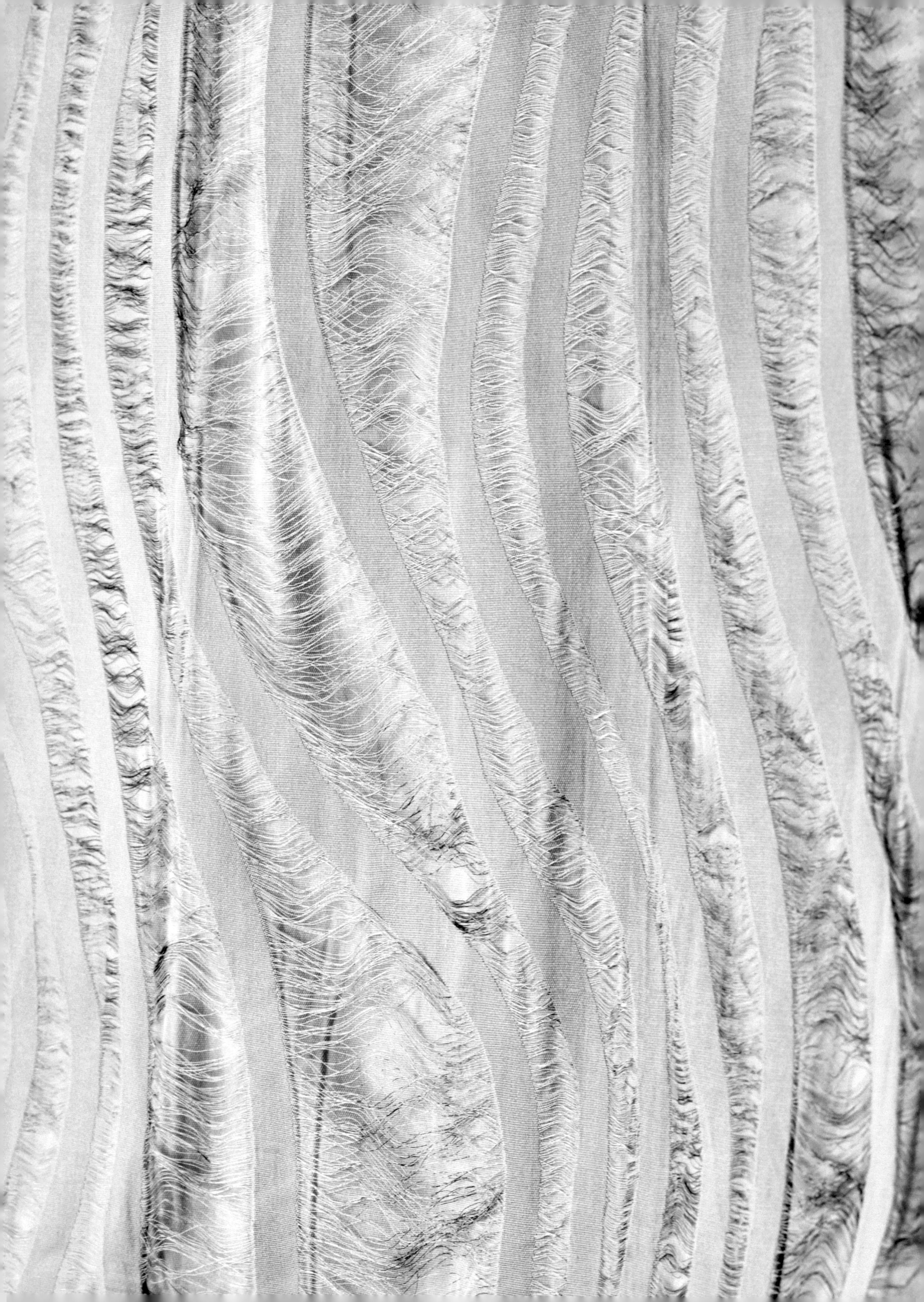

opposite:
See the Sea, 2003.
By Reiko Sudo.
Lines of copper wire
form waves on an open
sea of cotton.

this page:
Copper Scarab, 1994.
By Reiko Sudo.
Coating copper telephone
wires in polyurethane to
shield against electric shock
and signal noise also prevents
'greening' and brittleness,
making ideal warp threads.
The cloth is woven in both
black and white.

following spread:
Stainless Cloth, 1993.
By Reiko Sudo.
Extremely fine steel wire
for filter screens and sieves
gives a subdued metallic
sheen when woven together
with soft cotton warps.

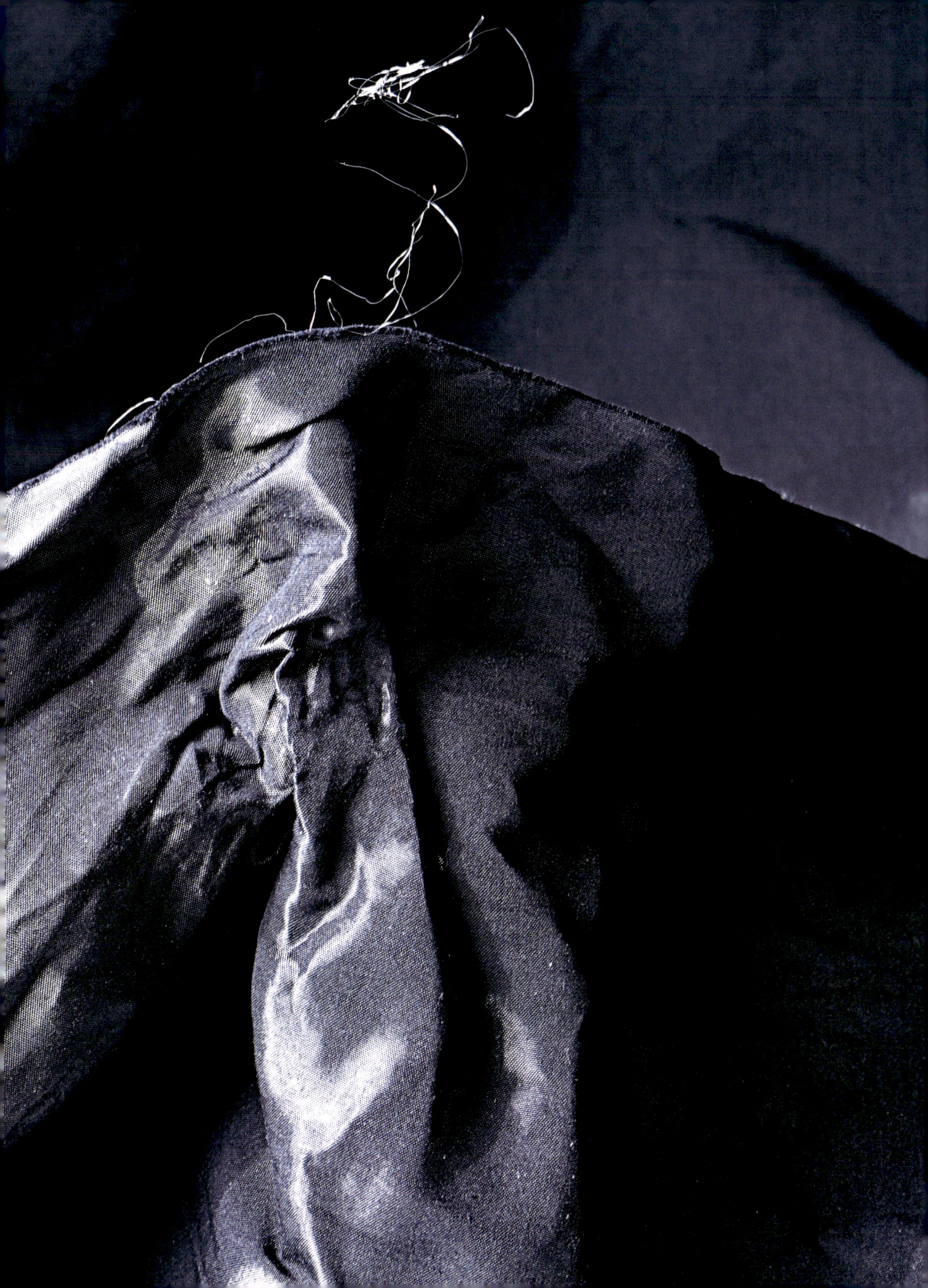

above:
Brass Cloth, 1994.
By Reiko Sudo.
Fine brass wires used as disposable cutting edges are recycled into yarn and wefted with cotton warps to create this soft fabric with a light metallic sheen.

opposite:
Coin Roll Crepe, 2020.
By Reiko Sudo and Bruce Li. Wool and cotton threads connect the wool gauze on one side to the polyester aluminium lamé on the other, giving this double-weave its distinctive rippled texture.

following spread:
Satin Stripes, 2009.
By Reiko Sudo.
Monofilament fishing line and wool yarns give sheen and softness to this full draping fabric.

pp. 192–93:
Leopard Spots, 1992.
By Reiko Sudo.
Heraldic beasts and flowers woven on ancient Turkish velvets inspired this dense jacquard weave, calendered to a high lustre.

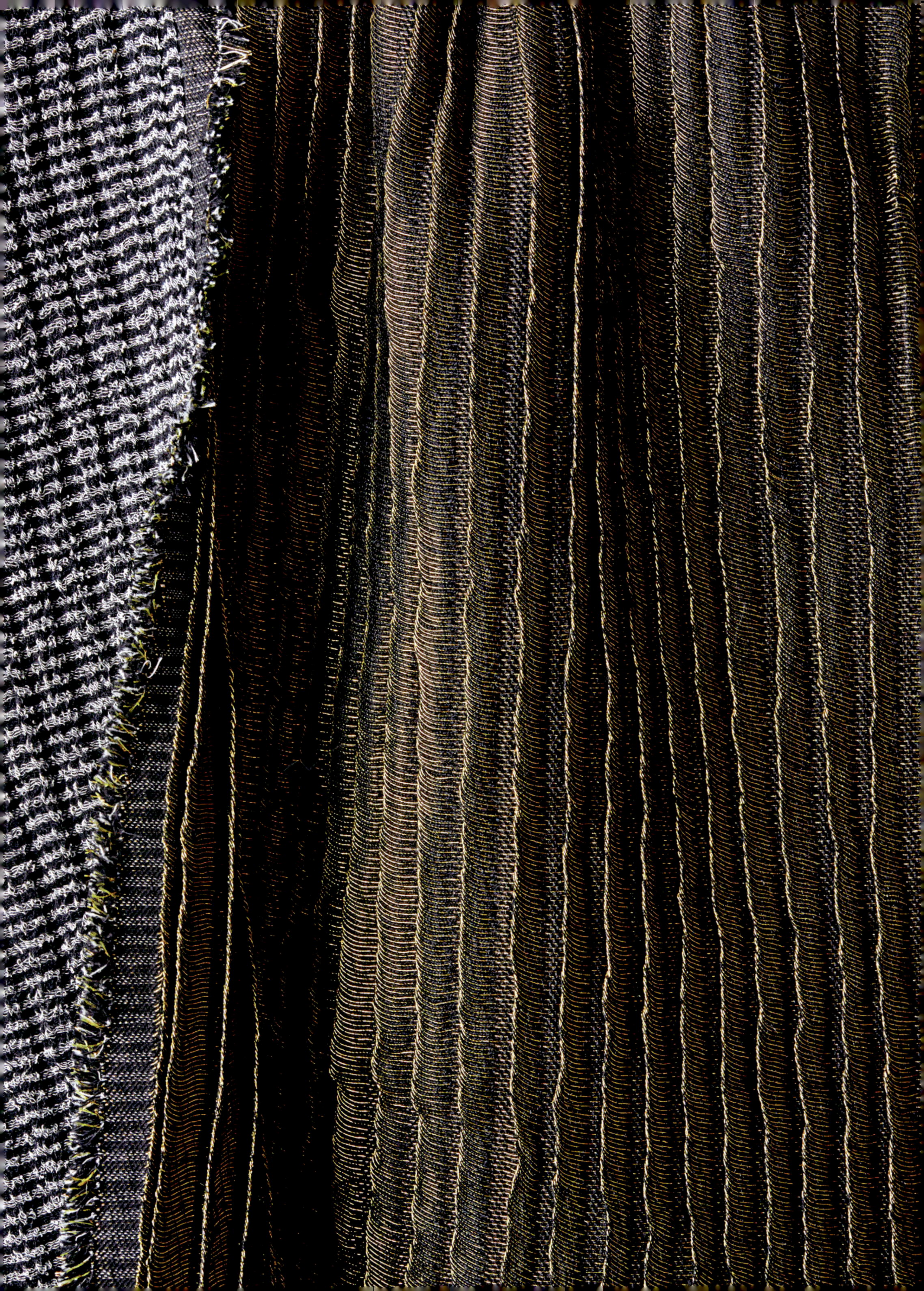

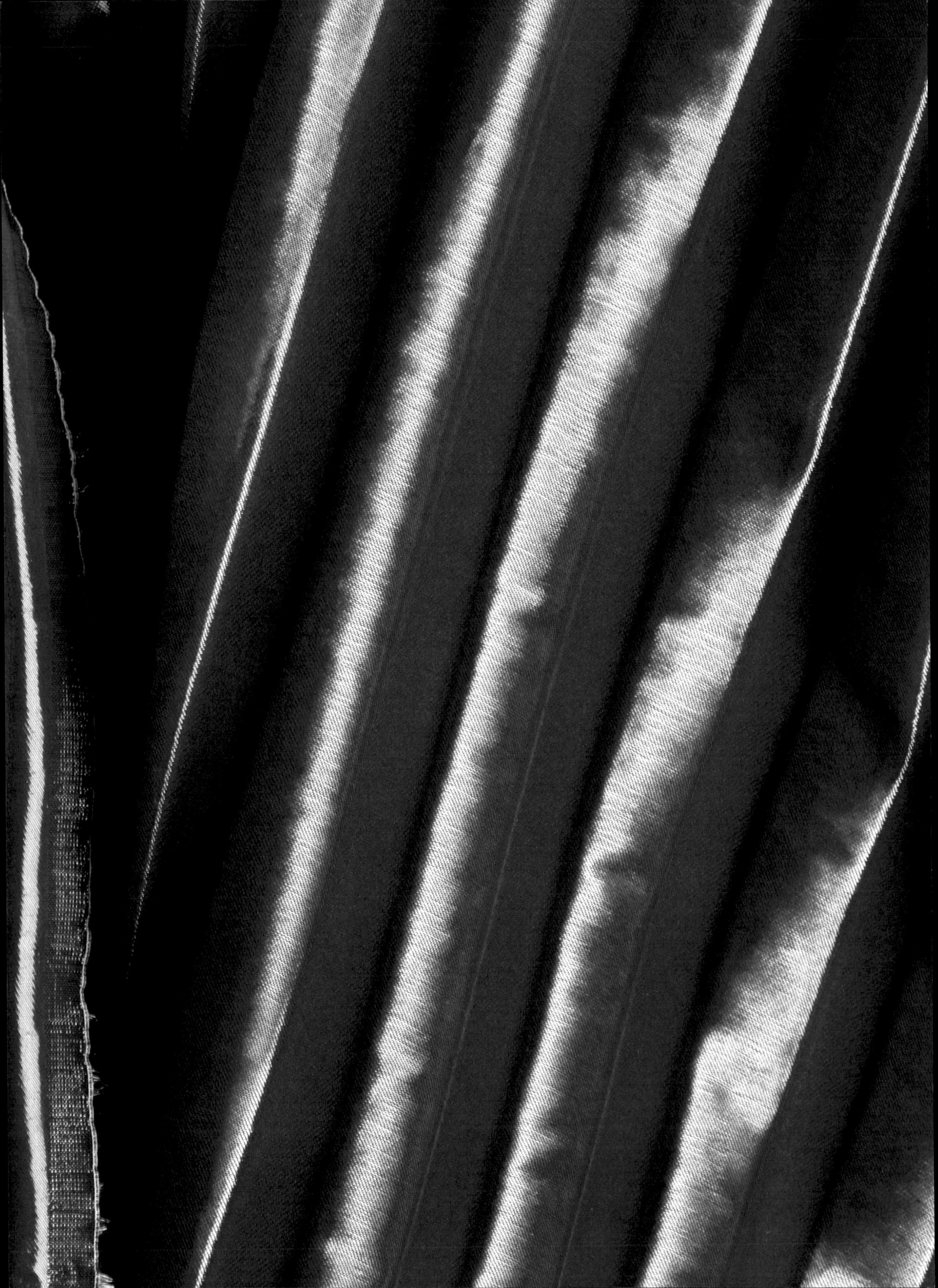

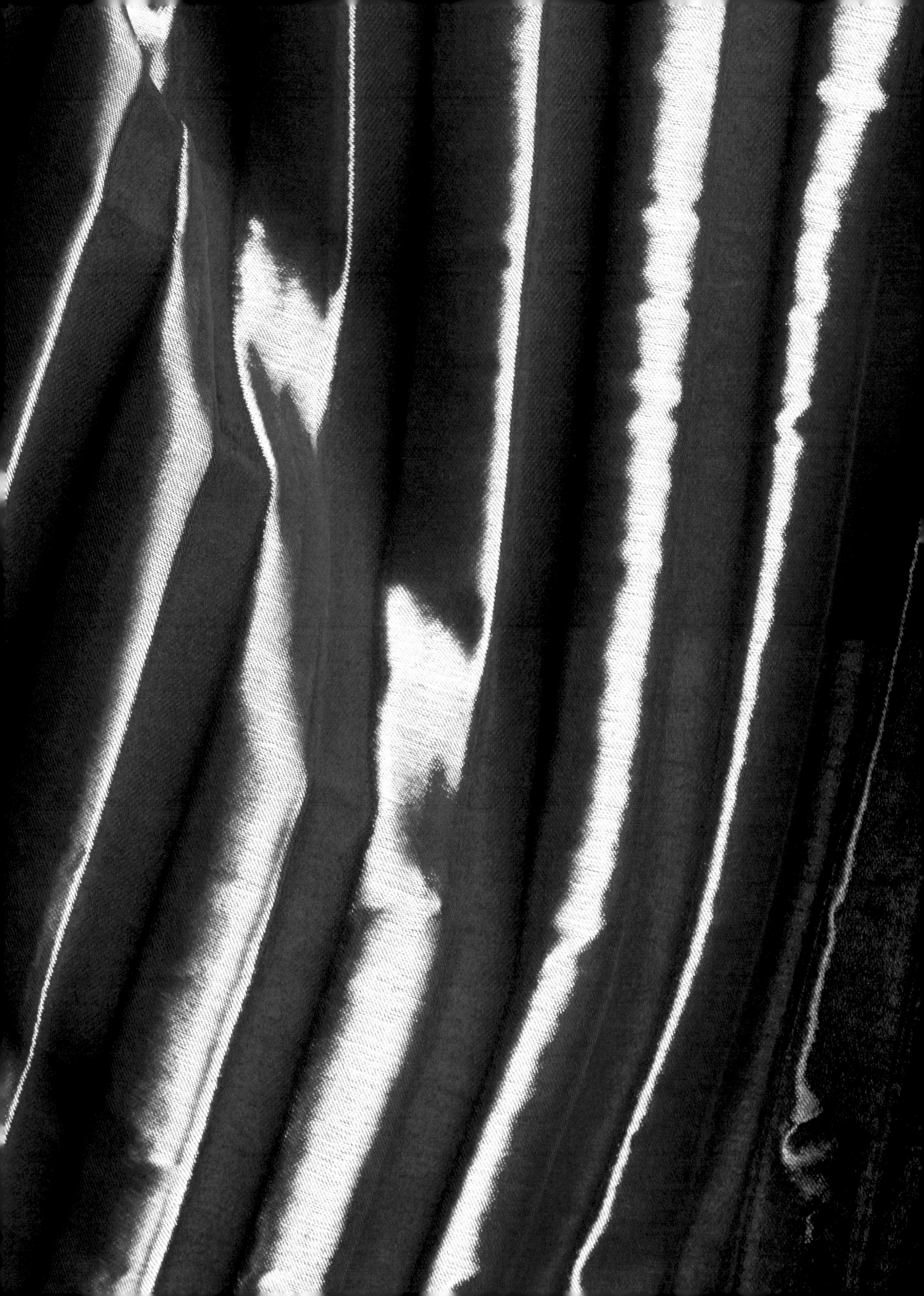

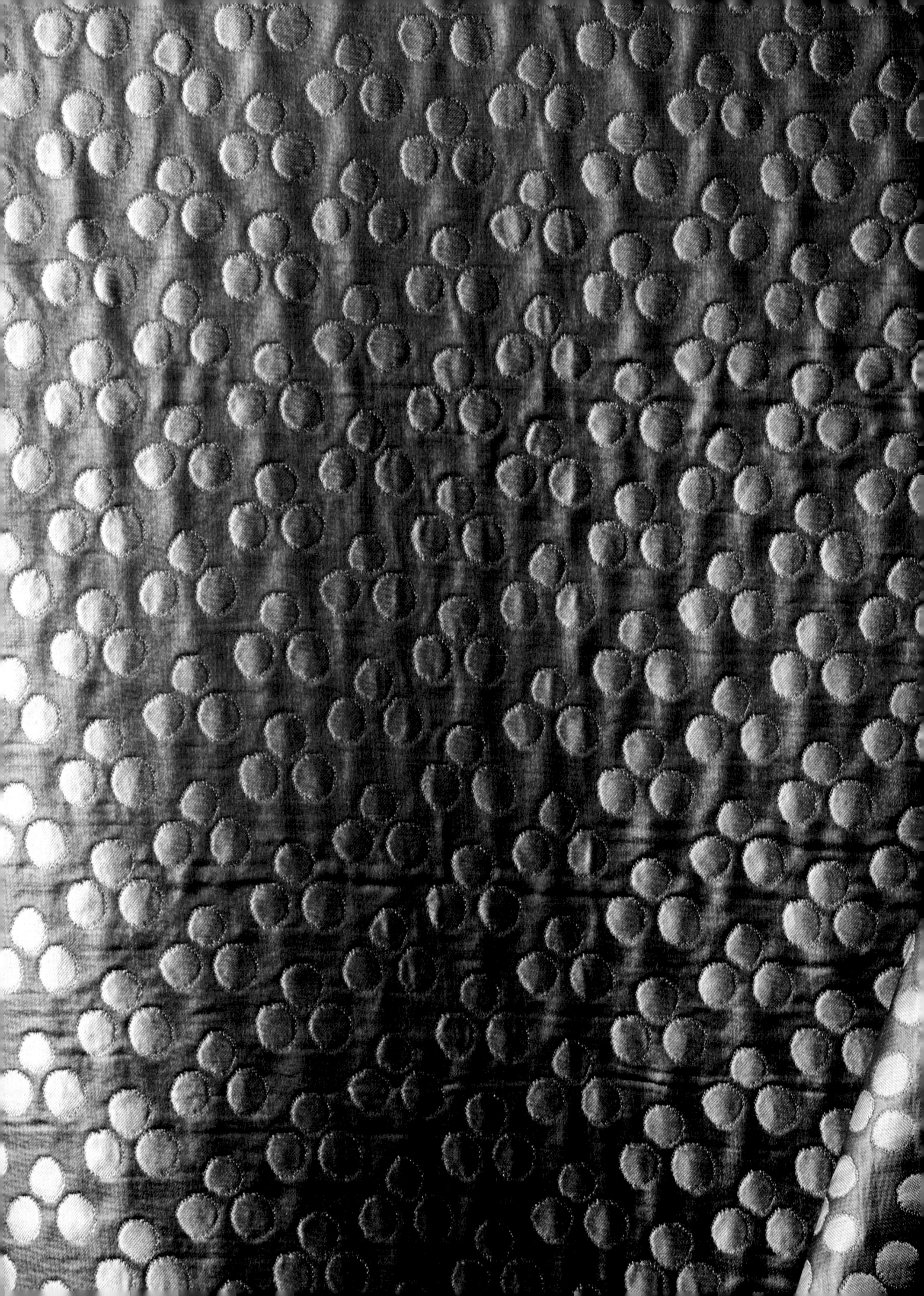

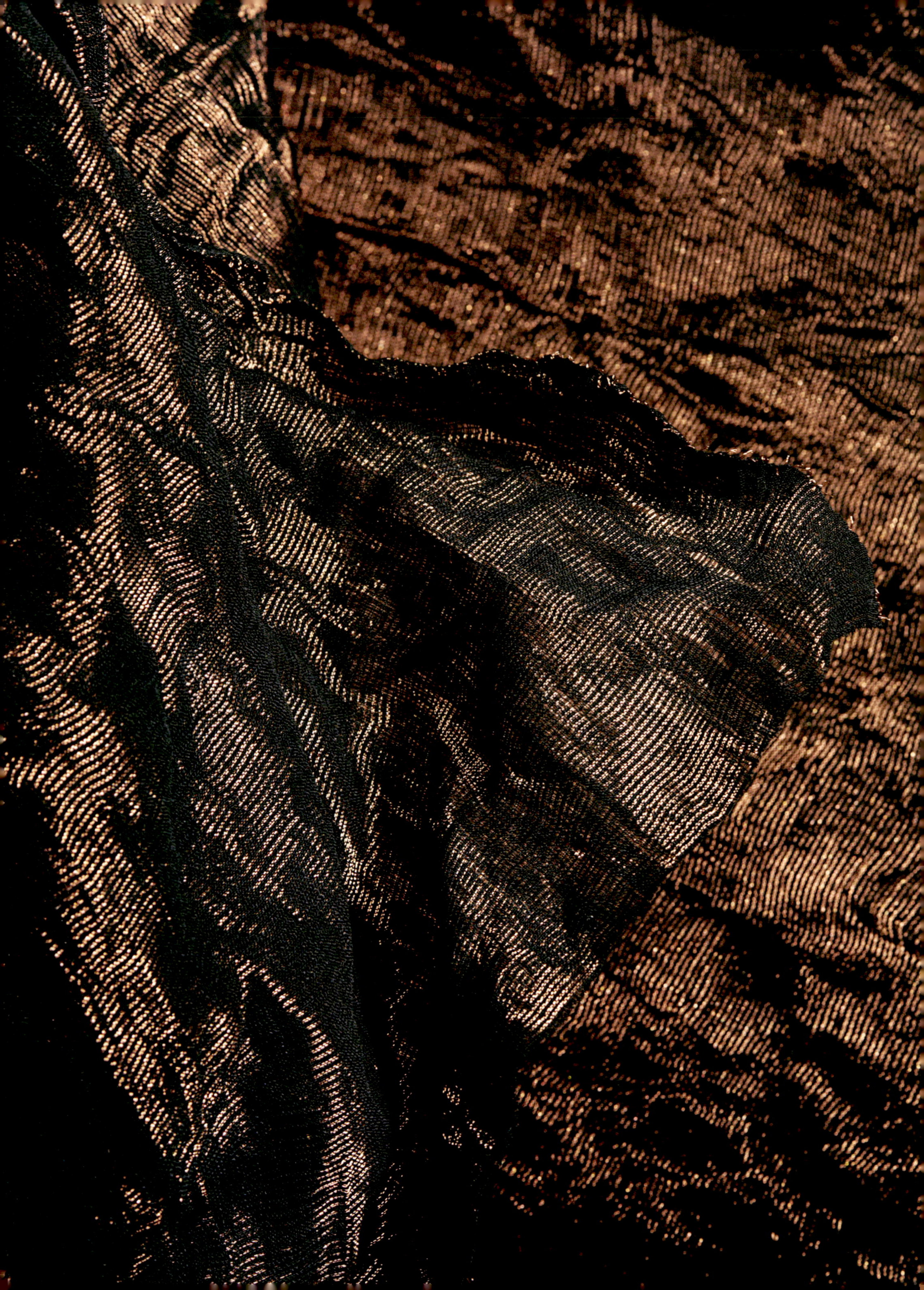

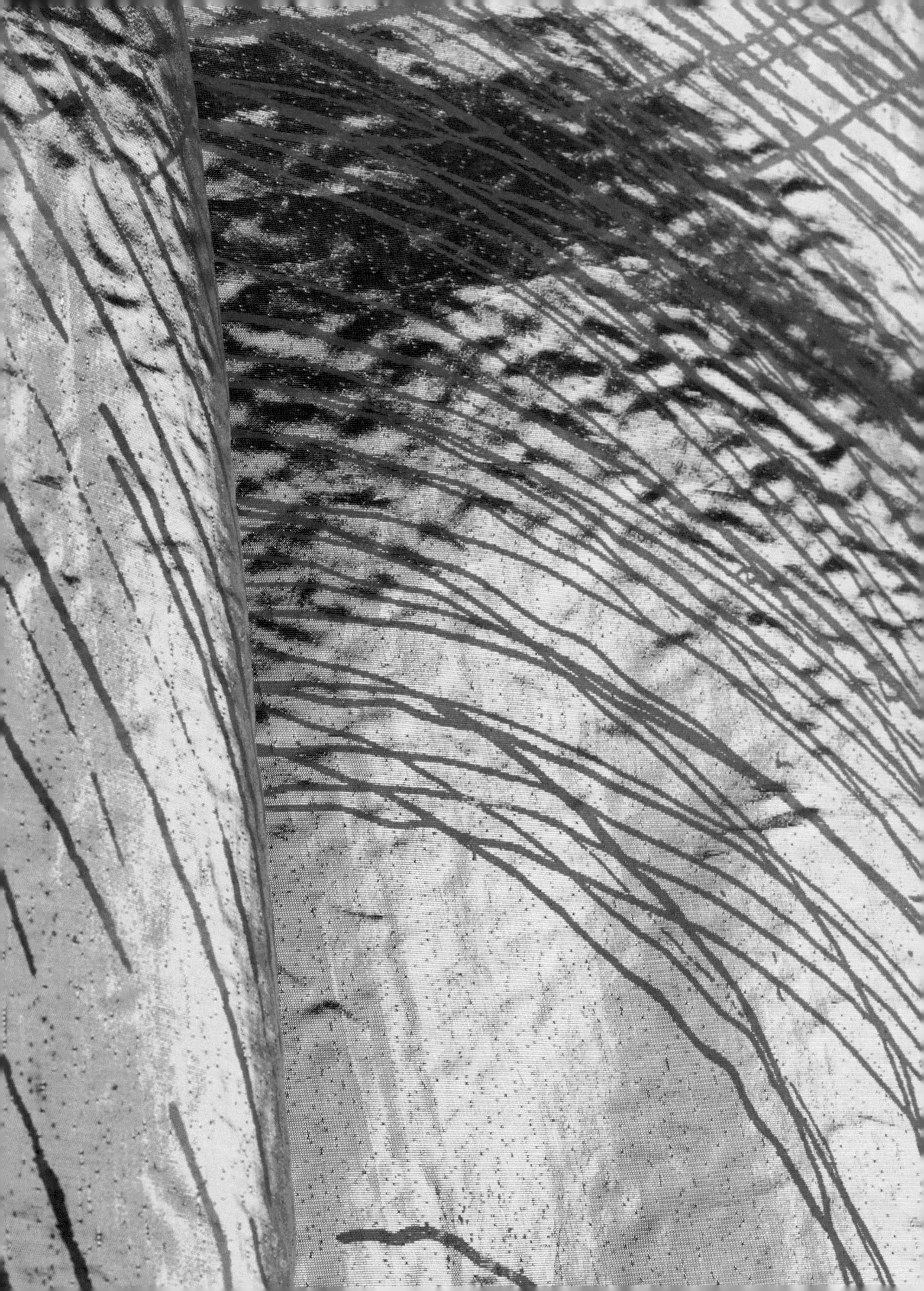

p. 194:
Copper Comb, 1994.
By Reiko Sudo.
Antibacterial and hypoallergenic copper thread is used for disposable surgical masks. Polyurethane coating keeps it from 'greening' and makes it easier to loom.

p. 195:
Cloud Chamber, 1997.
By Keiji Otani and Reiko Sudo.
Aluminium may not be radioactive, but when printed onto a polyester–nylon base the resulting arc-trace filigree seems positively energized.

below:
Kernels, 2003.
By Reiko Sudo.
Taking a hint from seed grain, each fleck on this cotton double-weave is ringed with shiny touches of aluminium lamé.

following spread:
Silver Leaf, 2016.
By Reiko Sudo and Kyoji Tamiya. 'Burnt' silver foil on *washi* paper, oxidized with sulphur, was traditionally used to give a metallic finish to fabrics, a technique requiring consummate craftsmanship.

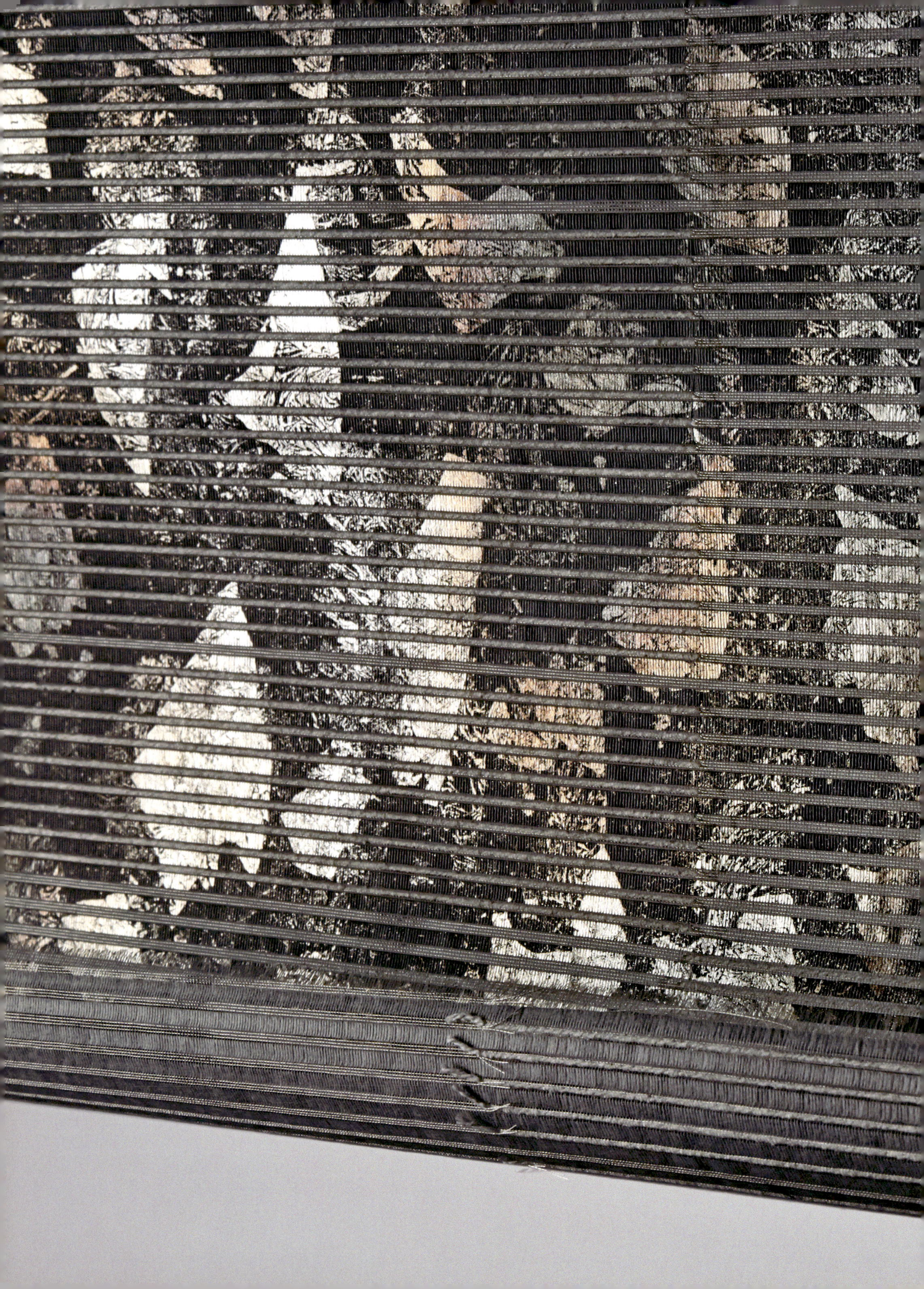

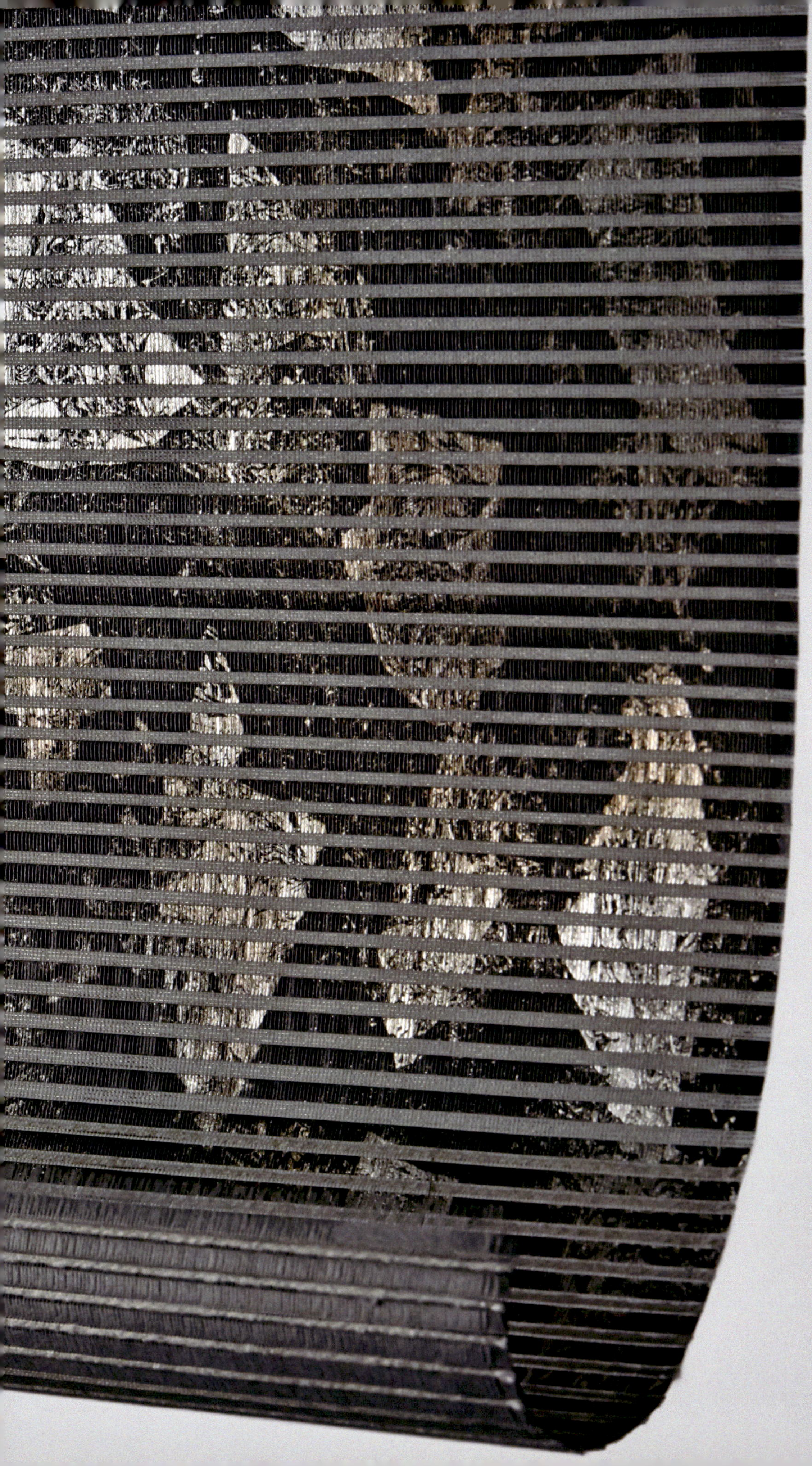

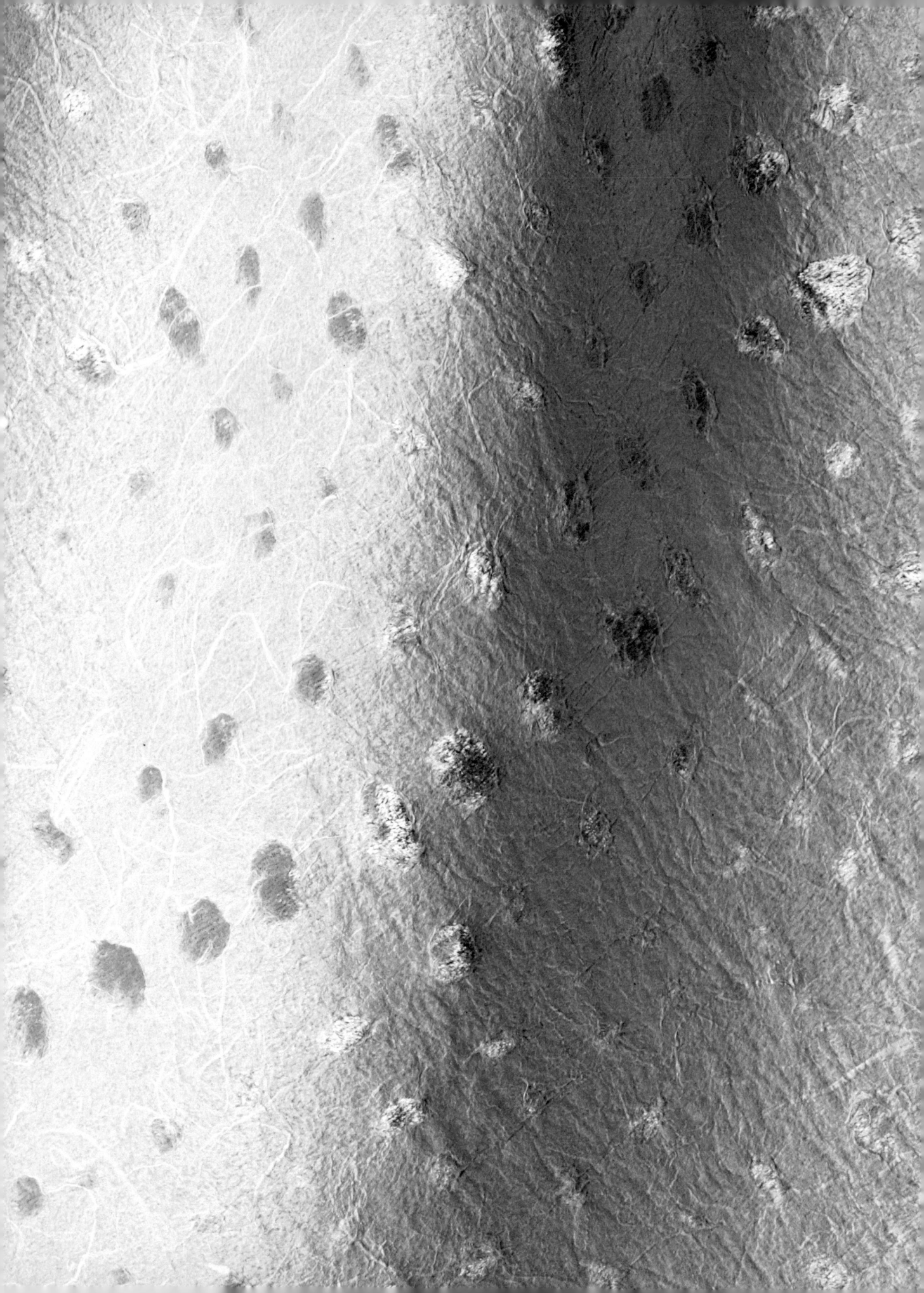

Portrait of a Textile: *Amate*

Woven and pounded into sheets, can tree bark become textile?

Japanese *washi* papers, whose long history traces back to the eighth century, are still widely used today in crafts and for papering *fusuma* sliding doors and translucent *shoji* window screens. The plasticity of *kozo*, *mitsumata* and *gampi* plant fibres makes it possible to create thin, strong papers of unparalleled quality. Much rougher though no less appealing, *amate* 'bark cloth', made by indigenous Otomí artisans in central Mexico, is the product of traditions harking back to pre-Columbian times. Fashioned by cross-laying strips of *jonote* tree bark into grid-like sheets, its earthy texture is unlike anything in Japan. So why not celebrate the contrast of textures as a textile design statement? We cross-laid thick sheets of *kozo* paper, and metal-leafing experts at Kimura Senko Dye Works affixed them to a lustrous velvet, backed with old newsprint tear sheets for added texture. We ourselves were surprised at how leathery our *Amate* looks.

opposite:
Amate, 2000.
By Reiko Sudo.
The indigenous Otomí of central Mexico make *amate* paper by cross-laying strips of tree bark. Here, we affix Japanese *washi* paper onto coloured velvet in a similar rough grid pattern.

left
Mexican *amate* bark paper.

キラキラ

KIRA KIRA

opposite
Original image drawing for *Amate* (ink and bleach on Kent paper).

above
Tapa cloth from the Pacific Islands is also made from paper mulberry.

below
Kozo, or paper mulberry sticks.

bottom
Kozo with its outer bark stripped away for paper-making.

Weaving around the mulberry bush

The deciduous shrub *kozo*, also known as paper mulberry, has long bark fibres that have been used for paper-making since ancient times. We use it because it makes extremely strong yet light *washi* paper, perfect for our bark-like *Amate* textile.

203

恵那和紙（岐阜）

越前もの紙（福井）

越前和紙（福井）

宇和和紙（愛媛）

大洲和紙（愛媛）

因州和紙（鳥取）

市川和紙（山梨）

土佐和紙（高知）

伊予和紙（愛媛）

土佐和紙（高知）

因州和紙（鳥取）

opposite
Samples of handmade *washi* paper from all over Japan.

above
A trial printing of *washi* paper onto velvet.

right
Washi smoothing brush.

following page, top
Removing the impurities and knots from *kozo* fibres by hand.

following page, bottom
Making paper by shaking and spreading materials with water on a 'boat'.

on p. 207, top
Washi paper is removed from the drier for finishing.

on p. 207, bottom
Washi paper is affixed onto velvet, then silkscreened with adhesive in the *Amate* pattern.

キラキラ

KIRA KIRA

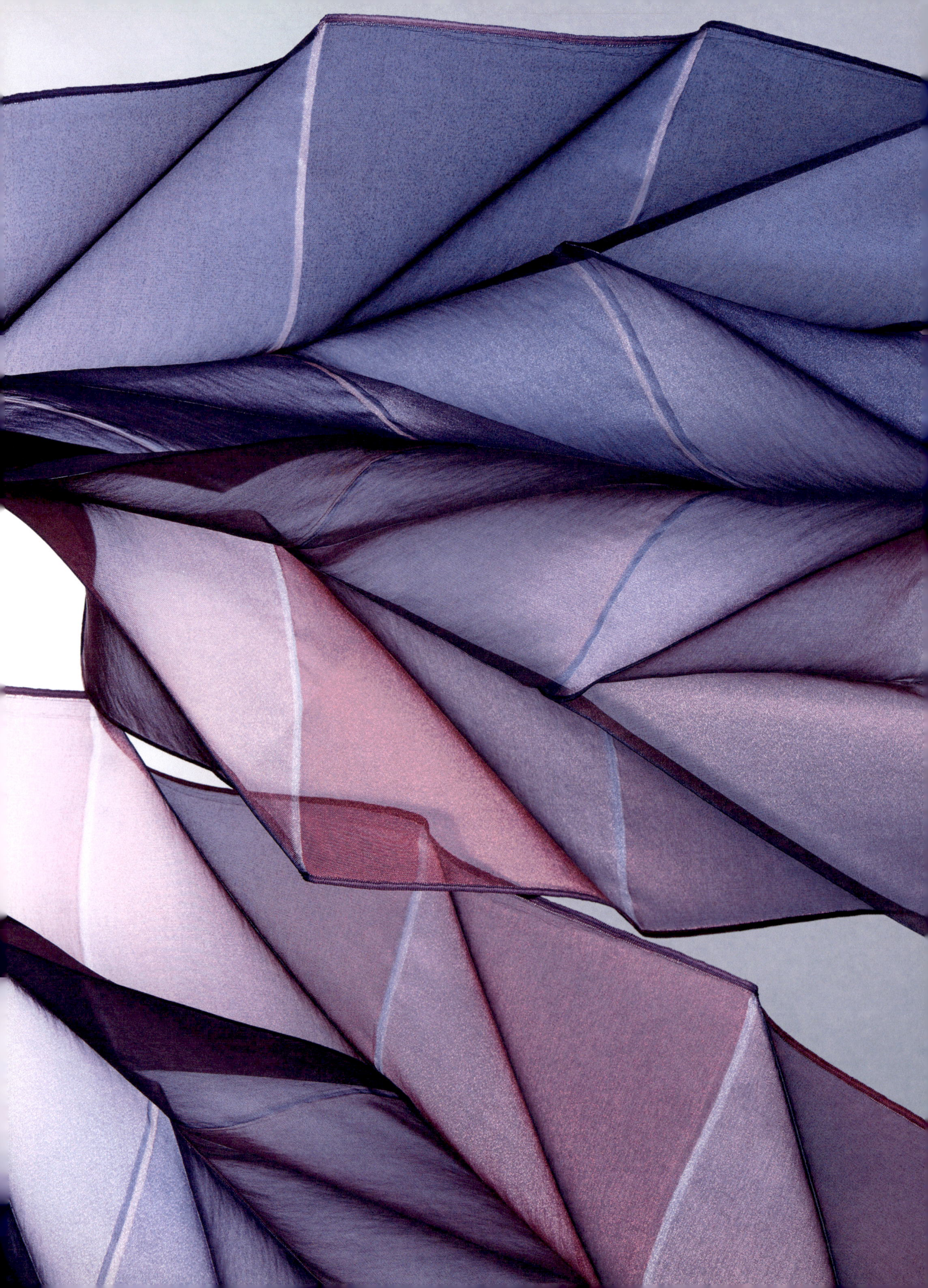

SUKE SUKE

suke suke (スケスケ)

1. Revealing, allowing the other side (inside) to show through
2. Sheer, gossamer, diaphanous, translucent
3. Flimsy; so thin as to present no barrier

The Emperor's new textiles

Ultra-sheer, filmy wisps of transparency, by definition *suke suke* fabrics all have see-through qualities. One might imagine that this makes them easier to appreciate! But with *suke suke* fabrics, what you see is not what you get – only a small part of it.

Long before virtual reality, dematerialization represented the ultimate challenge: how to weave down to nothingness? An undertaking fraught with difficulty, this ambivalence of craft, erasing itself yet keeping traces of its own negation in spidery threads of pure idea, appeals to both the most transcendent spiritual aspirations and the most sensual desires. Angelic robes of gossamer or revealing libertine nightgowns, with hardly a stitch of hesitation between.

Surprisingly complex in conception and execution, NUNO's 'little nothings' all differ in unseen ways, often involving revolutionary new materials and techniques. Whether buoyed with air pockets or folded with feathers, physical lightness should 'hold up to the light'. Clarity and translucency must be structured unobtrusively, invisibly. All of which calls for more technical sophistication than meets the eye. Like the 'Emperor's New Clothes', if you can appreciate the beauty that's almost not there, then aren't you clever!

p. 208:
Origami Pleats, 1997.
By Reiko Sudo and Mizue Okada.
Polyester is folded repeatedly at sharp angles and dyed in three separate hues, then permanently pressed in abstract patterns that suggest innumerable puzzle shapes.

right:
Tube, 2006.
By Reiko Sudo.
Warps of continuous monofilaments and short fibre-spun threads, woven at expertly controlled tensions, are finished by hand-cutting and cropping by machine.

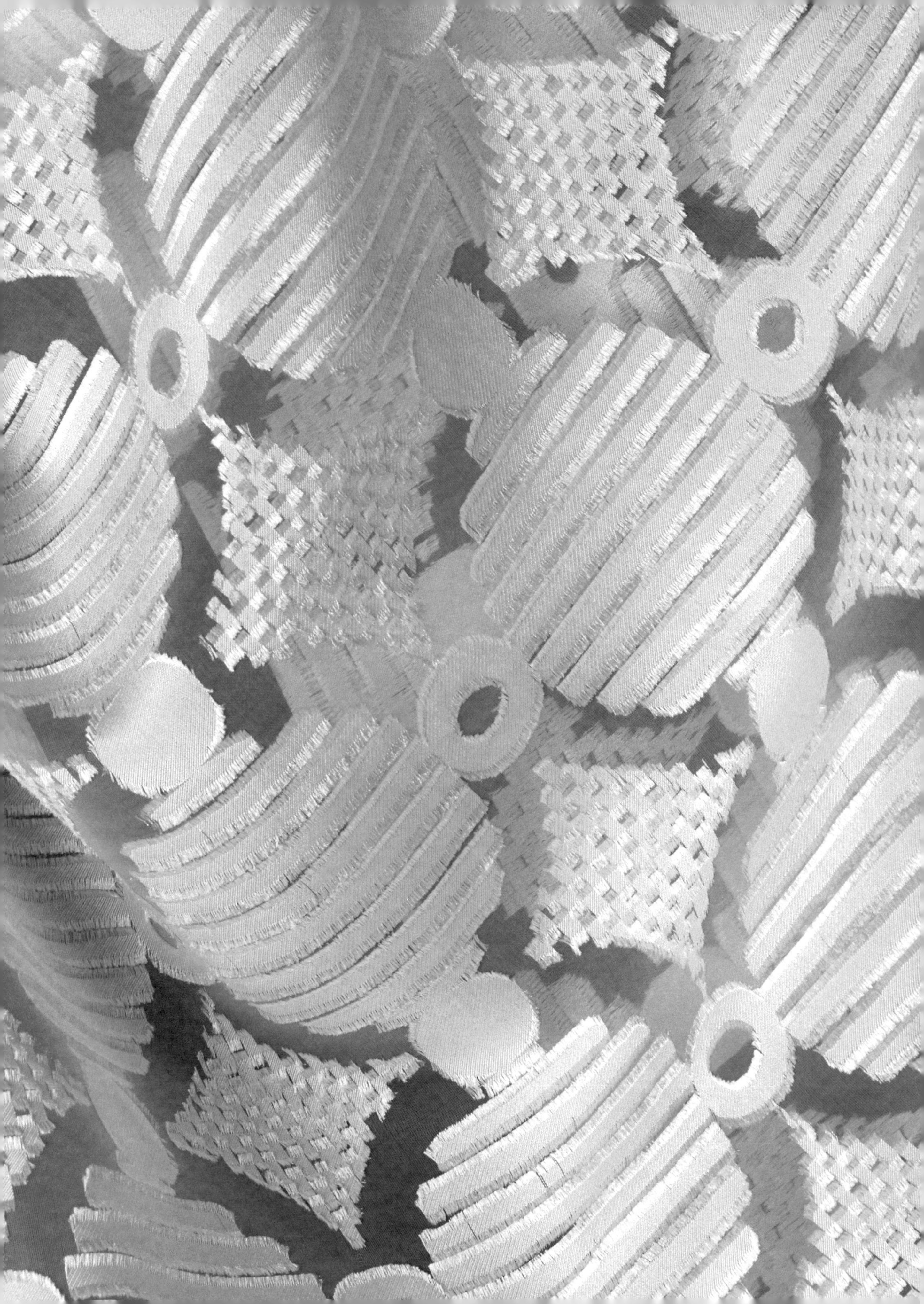

Three Transparencies

Toyo Ito

1. Fluid Transparency

To stand before a giant fish tank at the aquarium is to experience the curious sensation of being in two places at once. With only a clear wall in between, 'here' on this side one is on dry land surrounded by air, while 'over there' on the other opens an aquatic world. Not so long ago, aquarium tanks were relatively small affairs, peered at through window-like openings in the wall. Today's aquariums, however, have impossibly huge tanks, where staggering volumes of water press at us with awesome force through layers of acrylic tens of centimetres thick.

 To see through walls like this represents a major paradigm shift, as different as architectural elevations and cross-sections. When looking through a window, the view beyond is inviolate, self-contained. Not so with a transparent wall: an environment that ought to permeate everywhere suddenly cuts off at an invisible boundary, leaving its sheared face fully exposed. A visit to the aquarium in days gone by was like going to the circus; now, one is immersed in the experience.

 Thanks to these new aquariums, we now have a clearer image of aquatic life. The underwater plants and animals move in ways unimaginable above ground, particularly in deeper, previously inaccessible waters, where the increased water pressure makes the deep-sea swimmers lethargic, the swaying fronds heavy. Like the subdued dramatics of Noh theatre, all is continuous movement caught in a slow-motion time warp, each cell and body part suspended at half-speed.

 The reduced transparency of water shows everything as if through a silk curtain. A gauze-like diffusion that sets the reality of things off at a fixed distance. One loses the vital physicality; we see glazed fruits floating in a gelatine universe.

In one project, my initial image was of an aquatic scene. Sited in the very heart of the city, facing onto an avenue lined with large, beautiful cedars, a transparent cubic volume rises seven storeys from a fifty by fifty-metre square ground plan. Seven thin floor layers are supported by thirteen tube-like structures, each irregular, non-geometric tube resembling a tree root, thicker towards the top as it nears the soil surface, splaying and bending slightly. These hollow tubes are sheathed in a basketry of plaited steel piping, mostly covered in frosted glass. The effect is that of hollow translucent candles.

But why the aquatic image for a building on solid ground? For one thing, water is the primal shape-giver, the source to which all lifeforms trace back.

In the margin beside my first sketch for these tubes, I wrote: *Columns like seaweed*. I had imagined soft tubes slowly swaying underwater, in a tank-like volume filled with fluid. Without resorting to the typical wall-with-windows – no glass façade dividing the building from the street, no clear acrylic plate out of a massive fish tank – I wanted to express the cut face to another world.

But why the aquatic image for a building on solid ground? For one thing, water is the primal shape-giver, the source to which all lifeforms trace back. Trees, for example, as they branch out recursively from trunk to twig to leaf-tip, resemble nothing so much as rivers that gather tributary streams and empty into the sea. The thick opacity of the trunk dividing into ever-finer branches, gradually forming an intricate membrane and finally attaining the near-transparency of the leaves – the very image of fluidity.

If this is true of a tree above ground, how much more fluid, then, are those plants and animals that exist underwater? Their very forms embody such movement. As with fish fins, those parts that suggest movement grow more transparent further out towards the tips. Motion and form meet in fluidity, and fluidity is always translucent-to-transparent.

2. Erotic Transparency

Translucent objects always seem to be in transition from opaque to transparent. I am reminded of insect metamorphosis: the transparent larvae just out of their hard pupae are covered with a milky liquid; then, in an instant, contact with the air turns them into adult insects with hard, clear wings. A half-formed translucent gel-state stirs transformative imaginings; the moment it turns transparent and solid and fixed, that ambiguous fascination is lost.

Certain architecture, such as the early works of Mies van der Rohe, almost attains such gelatinous, near-fluid translucency. Known as the creator of transparent glass-and-steel twentieth-century architecture, at the beginning of his career Mies built with opaque materials – brick and stone. Then, suddenly, in the 1920s, his architecture underwent a metamorphosis. In sketches for 'Glass Skyscrapers' and his Barcelona Pavilion interior, fluid, translucent spaces truly come to life.

The Barcelona Pavilion, the German pavilion at the 1921 Barcelona World's Fair, was steel in structure, but it was stone and glass that gave it flamboyant dynamism. The stone mosaic covering the abstract planar formation of the walls describes a boldly fluid wave pattern. Poised between these stone-faced walls, greenish frosted-glass screens give the impression of tanks filled with water. The various planes play across at right angles, but never actually intersect. Rather, they overlap with the shallow outdoor pool surfaces to create a fluid space: the very image of solid form slowly melting away to a liquid state. A most erotic space.

Similarly, the Japanese designer Shiro Kuramata was keenly attuned to such transparency in contemporary society, and actively, intuitively pursued it in his creative work, at times playing the 'villain' of bad taste.

From the start of his career in the 1960s, he frequently used clear acrylic in his furniture designs. In one such acrylic chair, the furniture-object virtually disappears, leaving only the 'primitive' act of sitting. His clear wardrobes and bureau-dressers were even more powerful in this regard – the reason being that storage, the act of putting things away, is essentially one of hiding objects in opaque, unseen places. But here, far from hiding them, the clothes on hangers and folded garments are displayed floating in space. The material box-forms vanish and only the act of storage remains – in an erotically charged space, might we add. The effect of his transparent touch was not unlike trespassing in some forbidden room, catching a glimpse of what one is not supposed to see.

Three years before his death, one particular Kuramata design made direct gesture to the eroticism of the transparent. The clear acrylic chair 'Miss Blanche' (1988) achieved a heightened transparency by scattering artificial roses through its 'empty' interior. The red petals float this way and that, as if drifting in a stream; floral patterns released from the heavy upholstery fabrics of old and turned into real flowers suspended in clear, liquid space.

Where making things transparent seemingly ought to have been the most abstract of acts, a divesting of form into pure space, suddenly there appears an all-too-real, even seductive presence. This polarity, these startling reversals, this real-unreal ambiguity are distinctly transparent tastes.

3. Opaque Transparency

Transparency, however, is not always so light and clear. We Japanese have willingly surrendered any opacity of self so as to blend into today's society. We live see-through lives, undistinguished from anyone else in an extremely streamlined regulatory system. Urban Japan has become a convenience store peopled by instant snack foods wrapped in plastic and lined up on a shelf. We are mere signs, wholly transparent, devoid of any scale of value. What's more, this mediocre transparent existence is entirely comfortable. And yet, as the individual in contemporary society turns ever more transparent, architecture and the city are becoming conversely more opaque.

One major characteristic of the contemporary city is that each space is utterly cut off from the next. Interiors partitioned room from room, walls everywhere. Such, perhaps, is the destiny of social control: a vast, homogenized cityscape is fragmented into places with almost no spatial interrelationships. This is especially true in commercial spaces, where divorcing the interior from the external environment facilitates dramatically 'staging' the premises. Spaces thick with shining product are clearly set up, when seen from a slight remove, on the basis of their uniformity and particularity; spaces seemingly so idiosyncratic are merely the accumulation of introspectively inflated fragments of homogeneity. This is today's city.

Walking through Shinjuku or Shibuya Station, two of the most complex spatial configurations in central Tokyo, is a very strange experience. All the criss-crossed levels of communication, intersecting train and subway lines, the three-dimensional knots of interlinking pedestrian passageways between, commercial spaces surrounding and interpenetrating and surmounting this maze, everything is designed to make us lose our way inside a viewless world almost entirely cut off from the outside. All we have to go on are signs and verbalized cues. While we are in the midst of this complicated spatial experience, it is all we can do to create a correspondingly abstract and semioticized mental space.

What is demanded of today's architect is to discover 'relationships' between such hermetic, fragmented spaces; to seek opaque-yet-transparent connections between multilayered spaces. In a project commissioned by one Japanese city, a Fire Department completed in 1995, I tried to realize an 'opaque transparency'. Almost all functional aspects of the building were raised on rows of columns to the upper storey. This so-called 'pilotis' structure allowed the ground floor to maintain a continuity with the street in the form of a park-like space left open and accessible to all. The only provision is that a dozen or more fire trucks and ambulances and various pieces of training equipment be kept there as well. In the middle of a turfed area, two tower structures, large and small, are strung with climbing ropes and a long rope bridge between for the fire brigade's daily exercises. There is also a drowning-rescue practice pool and a small gym. The townsfolk can drop by and watch the firefighters go through their paces; meanwhile, the corridors connecting the

What is demanded of today's architect is to discover 'relationships' between such hermetic, fragmented spaces; to seek opaque-yet-transparent connections between multilayered spaces.

individual rooms on the upper storey look down onto whatever is going on below. There are even lightwells through the upper-storey floor to allow communication between all levels. All this is designed to give the fire brigade a 'face' in the daily life of the town, not just in the event of emergency.

The building is not by any means glassed-in or transparent. However, openings here and there in the floor make for a certain dynamic between levels above and below – what I call 'opaque transparency'. Glass buildings aren't the only way to achieve transparency; no, the task on hand today is how to forge relations between otherwise walled-off spaces.

In *The Mathematics of the Ideal Villa and Other Essays* (1976), Colin Rowe terms such relations 'phenomenal transparency' as opposed to 'literal transparency'. In the title essay, he cites by way of 'phenomenal' example the early works of Le Corbusier or the paintings of Ferdinand Léger; and for 'literal', the Bauhaus architecture of Walter Gropius and the artworks of László Moholy-Nagy. In other words, while the latter is merely composed of transparent elements, the former layers non-transparent 'blind' elements so as to create transparent interrelationships. Take, for instance, Le Corbusier's famous early work, the 'Villa Stein' at Garches (1927), and its abstract layering of overlapping vertical and horizontal planes. The effect is such that despite the actual volume of the physical building, the composition becomes a Cubist painting, with planes of no visual depth advancing and receding in non-Euclidian space.

Now more than ever, architecture must deliver such spatial relationships. For despite our apparent transparency, like all-too-colourless products lined up in a convenience store, we continue to build ever more solid barriers between us. Not that we should return to the world-without-walls collective existence of times past – even if we could. The key lies in introducing new openings through the walls we have already built.

Feather Flurries, 1993.
By Reiko Sudo.
Goose, peacock and guinea fowl feathers, individually inserted by hand, are showcased in rectangular pockets between translucent silk organdy layers, to optimum 'weightless' effect.

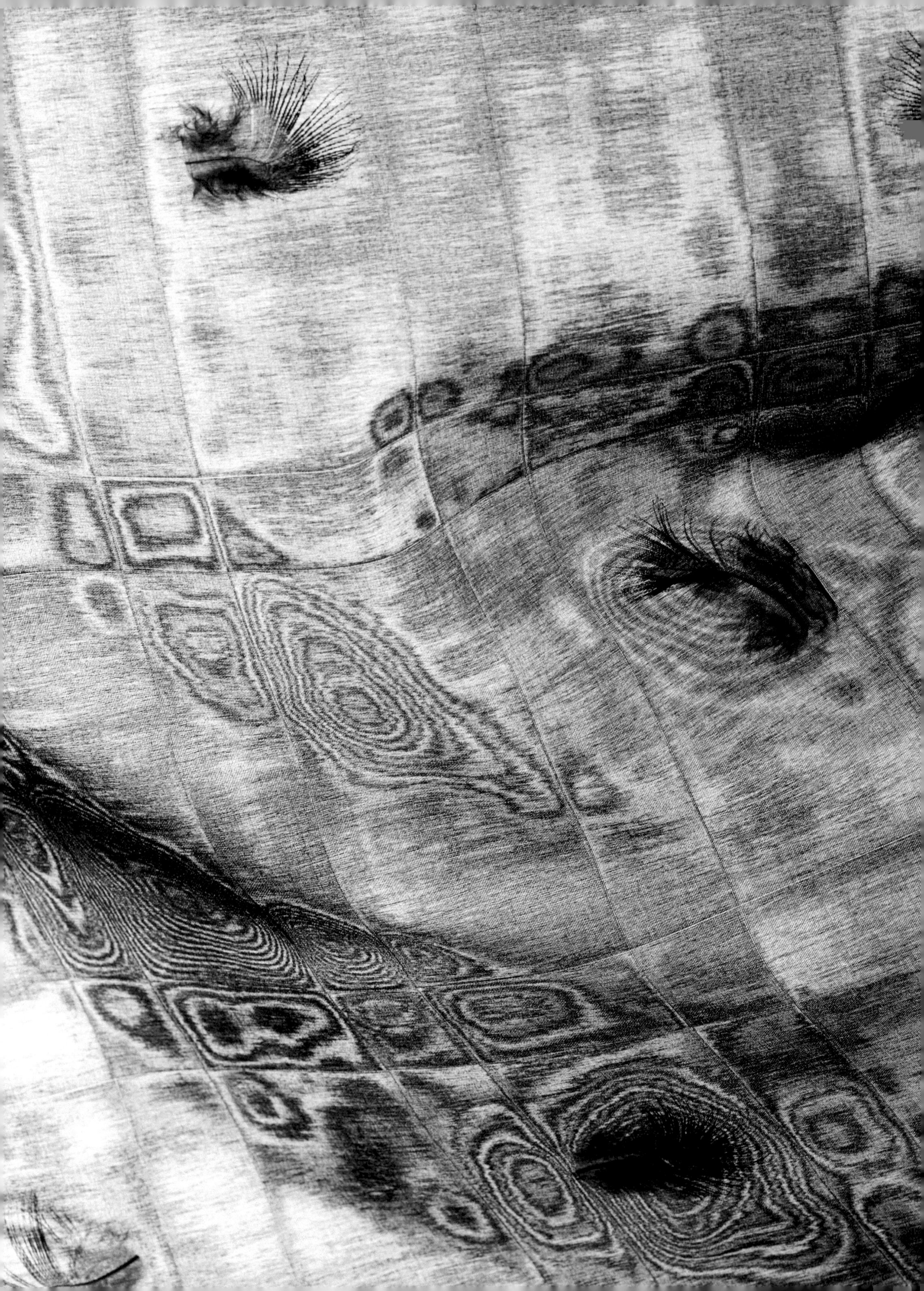

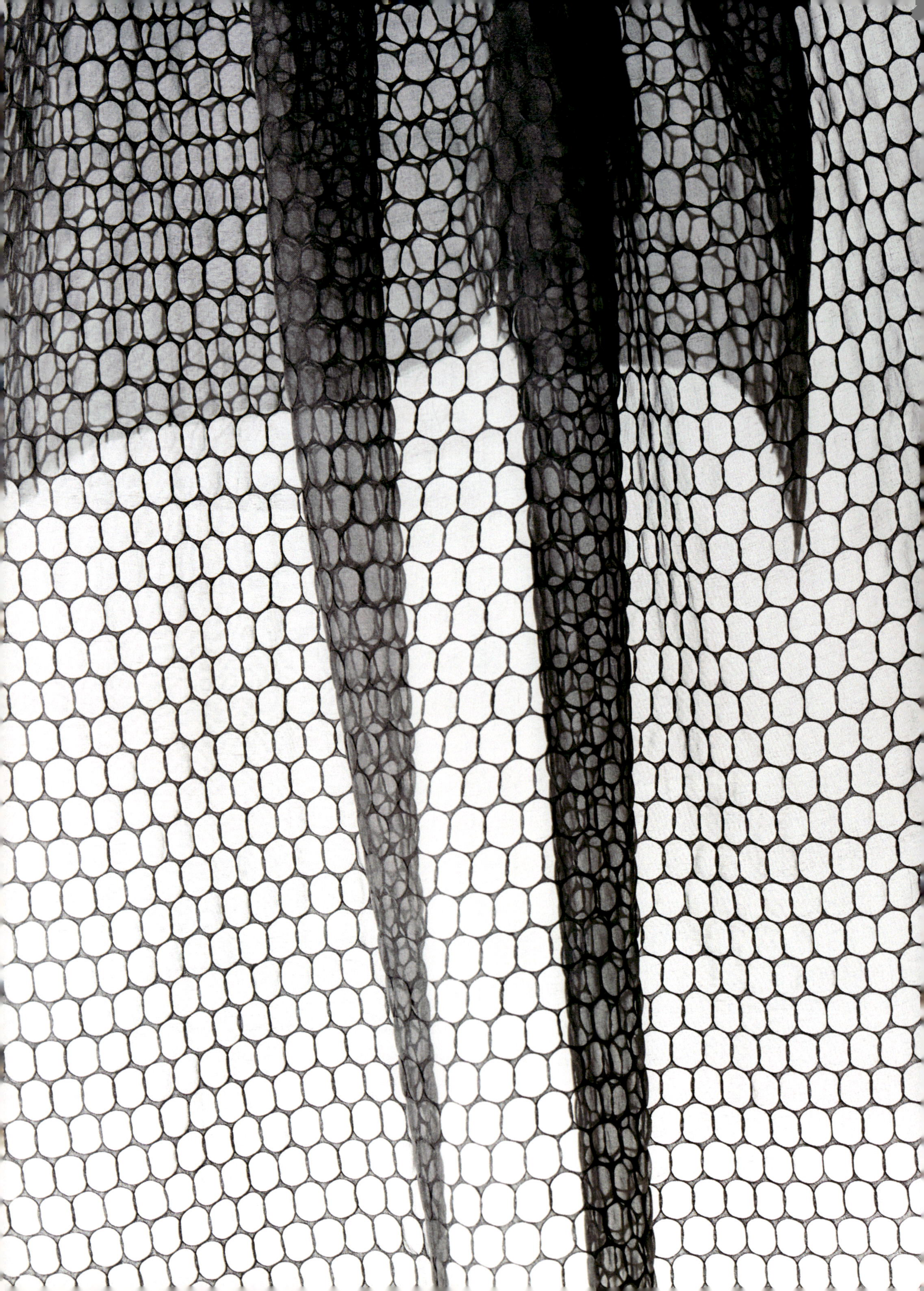

Bubble Pack, 1994.
By Reiko Sudo.
Pure silk and 100% humour, inspired by today's ubiquitous plastic packing material. Silk organdy is printed with dye-resist dots, then chemically shrunk to leave 'inflated' bubbles.

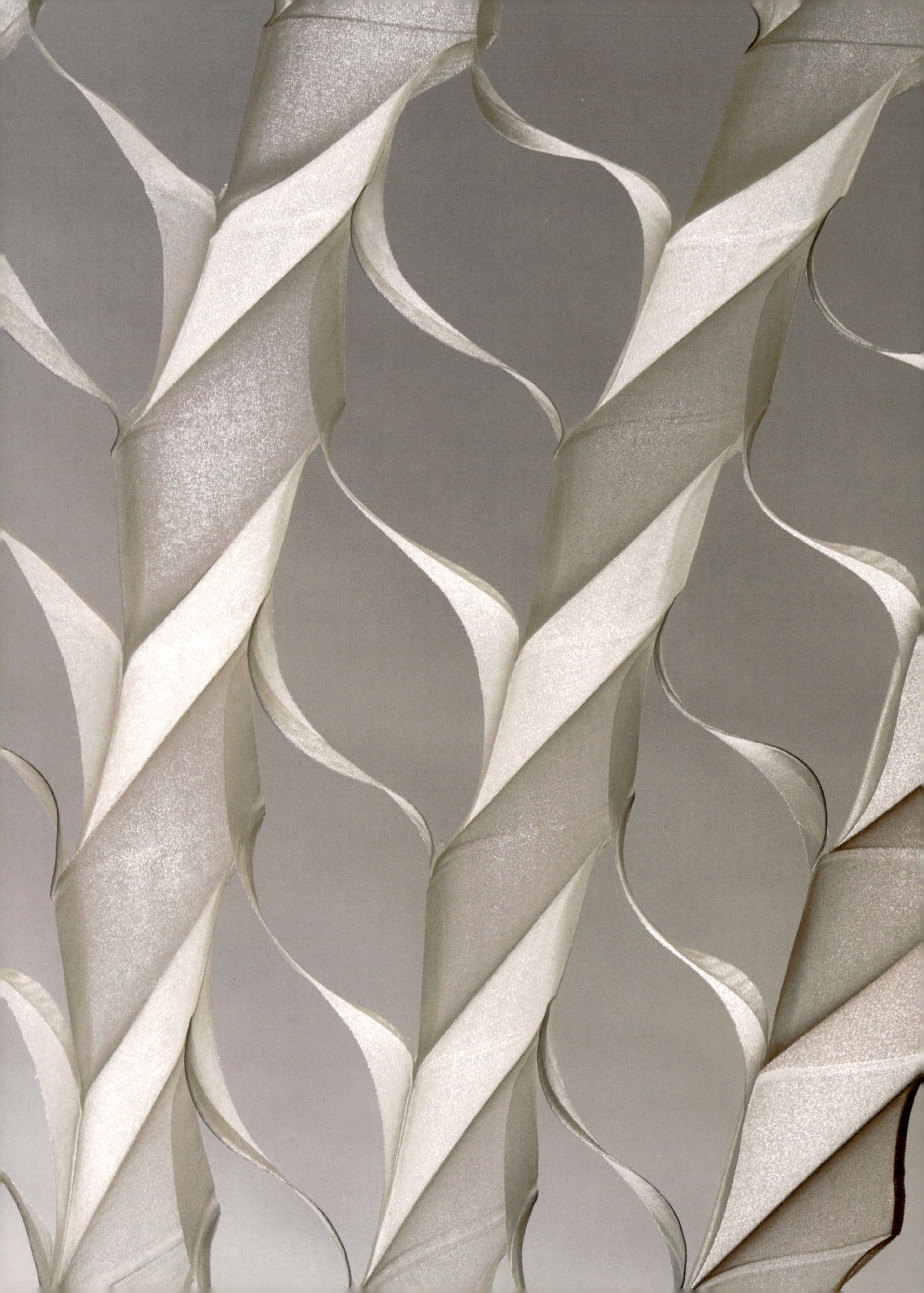

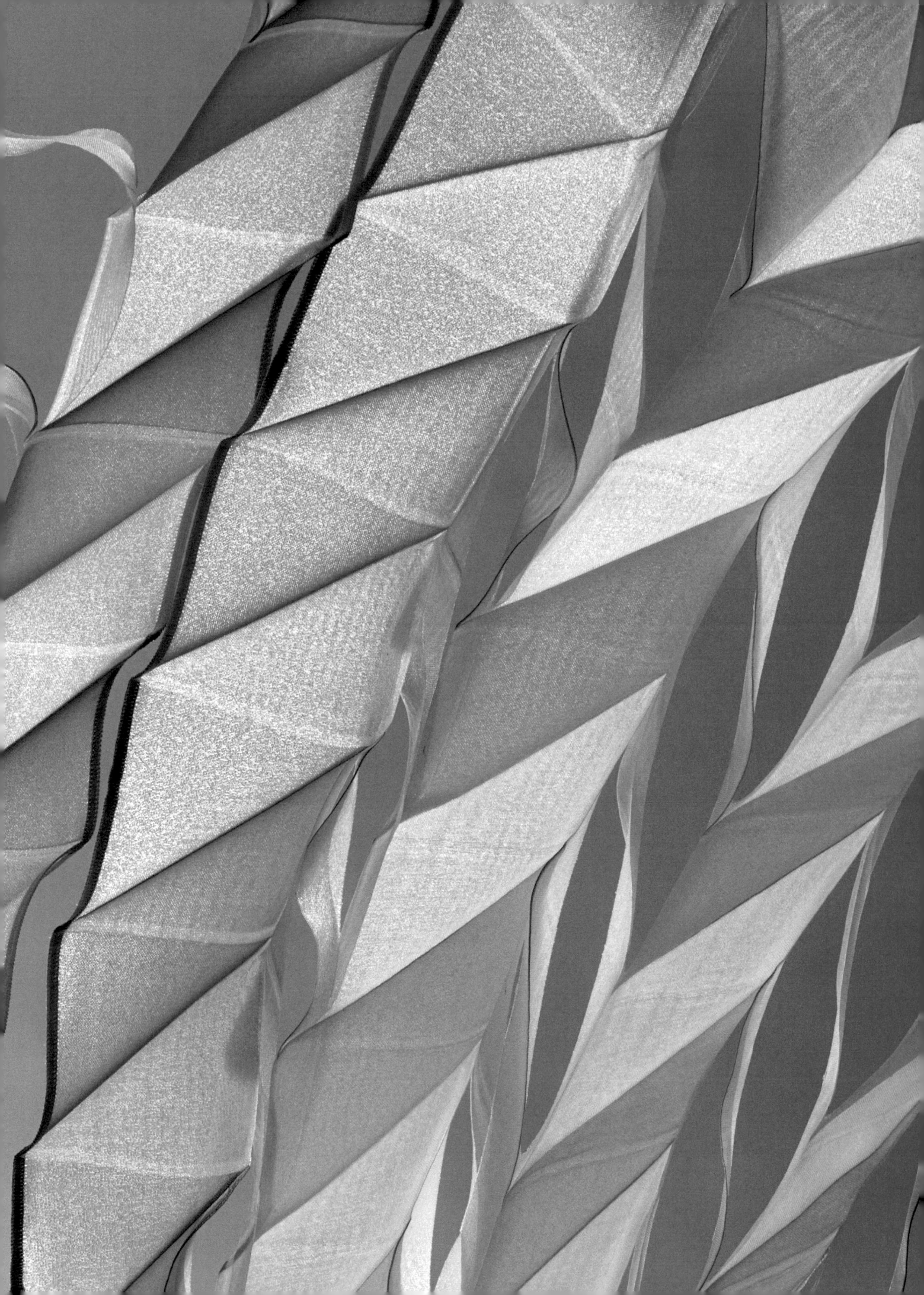

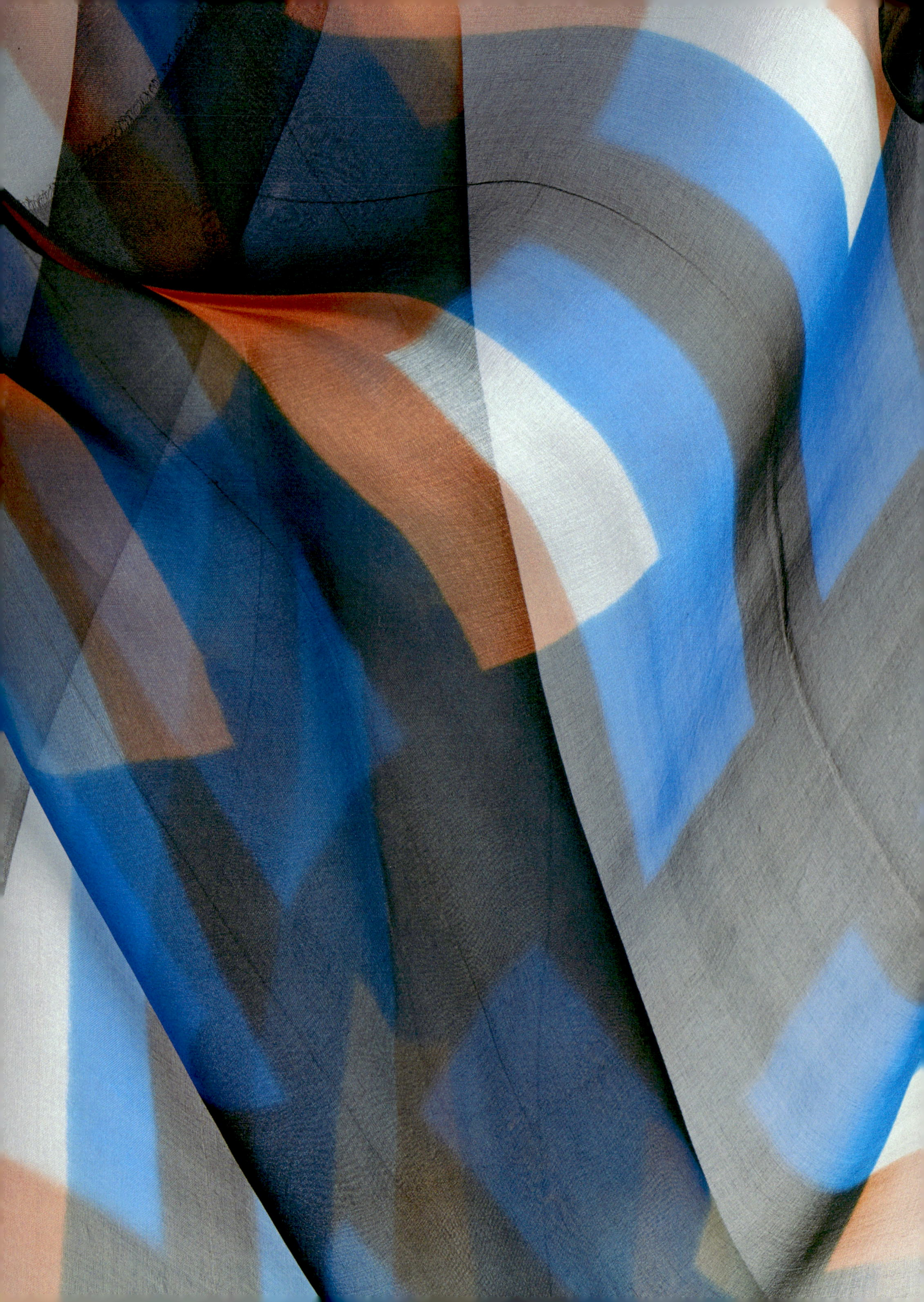

previous spread:
Tanabata, 2000.
By Reiko Sudo and
Tomoko Iida.
Fabric is pressed into fanciful *origami* shapes, then heat-cut in slits along the folds to resemble paper charms fluttering on bamboo at the Japanese summer festival of the weaver-girl constellation.

Itajime Rectangle, 2002.
By Reiko Sudo and Tomoko Iida.
Minutely folded fabric is pressed tight between boards and then dyed, the compression acting as a resist. This variation on *shibori* 'clamp-dyeing' has been used in Japan for over a millennium.

スケスケ

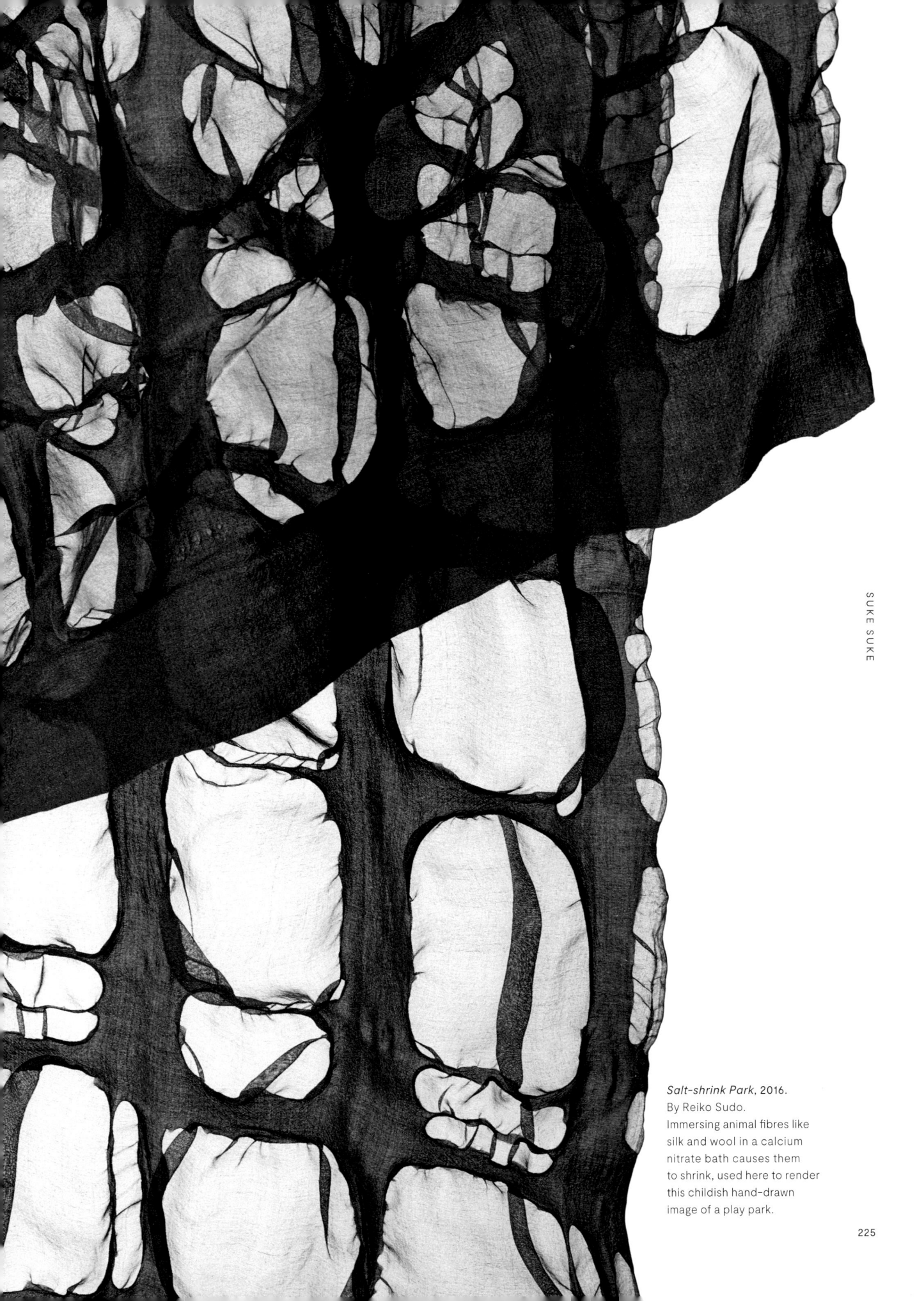

Salt-shrink Park, 2016.
By Reiko Sudo.
Immersing animal fibres like silk and wool in a calcium nitrate bath causes them to shrink, used here to render this childish hand-drawn image of a play park.

below:
Ice Floes, 1995.
By Reiko Sudo.
Flat rayon threads tightly woven into large squares on a background of silk organdy are connected by unwoven rayon threads, suggesting floating icebergs.

opposite:
Mica, 1996 (reissued 2006).
By Reiko Sudo.
Polyester can be permanently moulded or pleated under heat by hand or machine, resulting here in a glittering, multilayered fabric.

following spread:
Flyaway, 2006.
By Reiko Sudo and Yuka Taniguchi.
8mm (5/16 in.)-wide strips of polyester taffeta stitched onto organdy create a slightly raised lace.

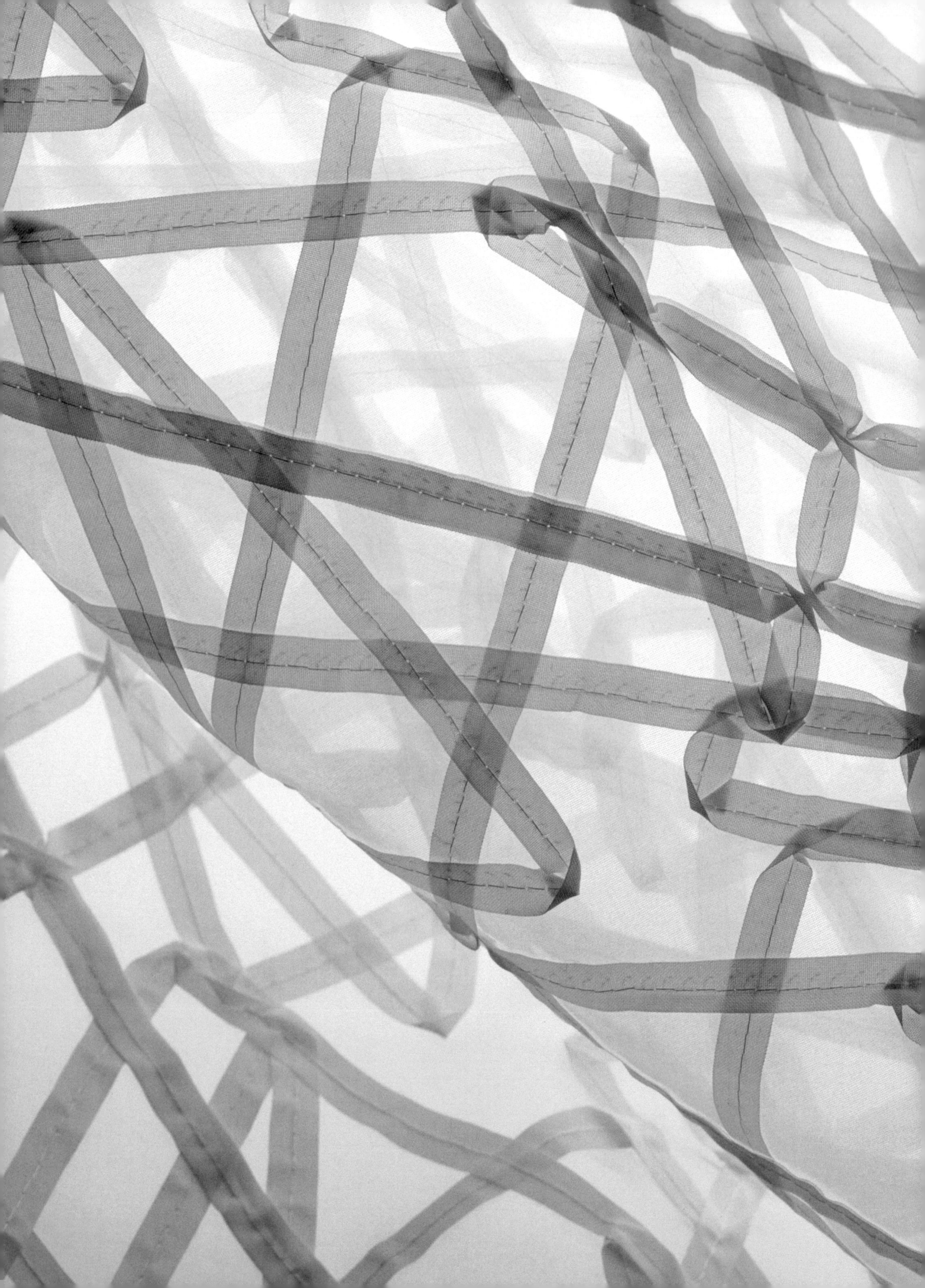

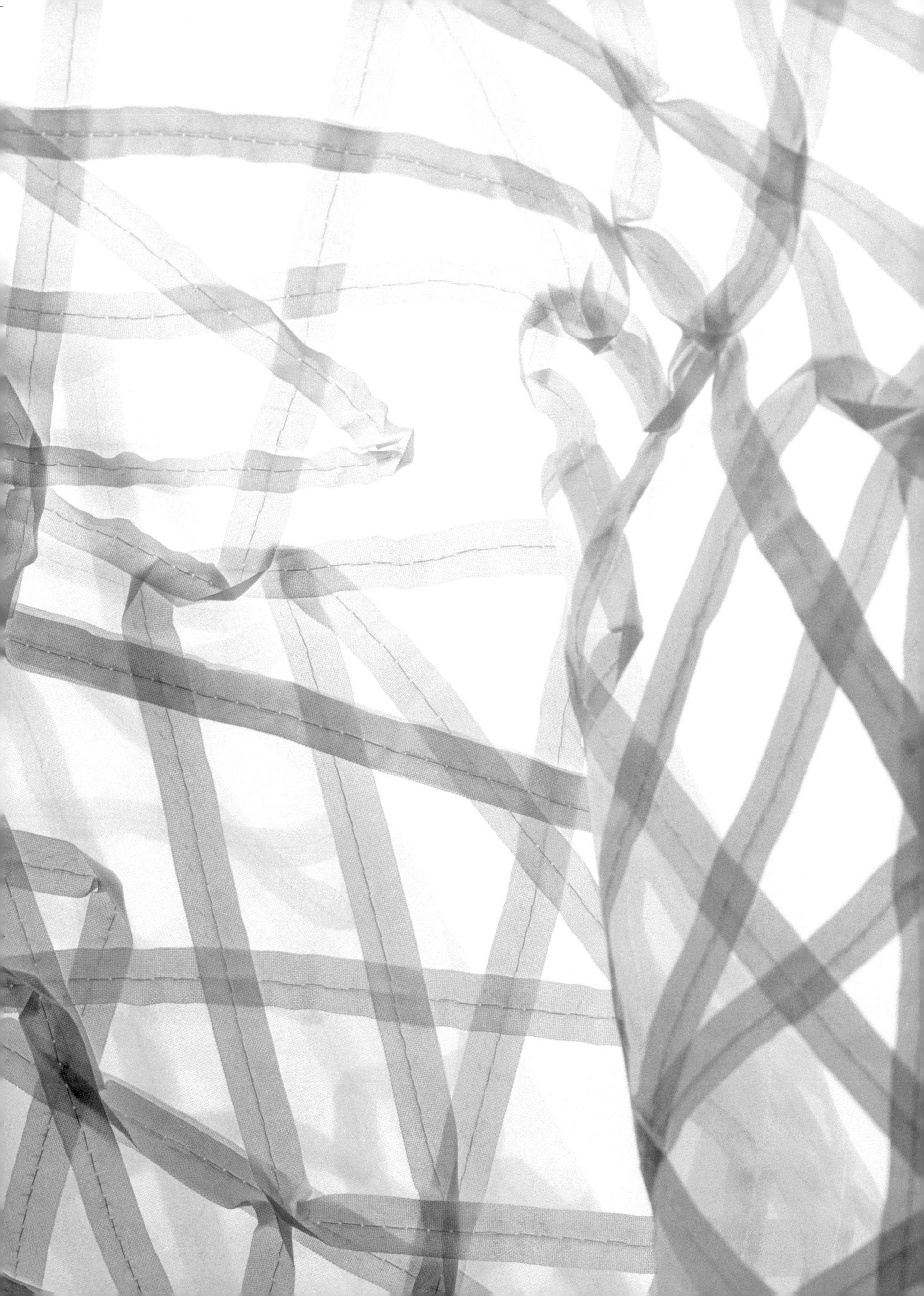

above and opposite:
Combed Paper, 1997.
By Reiko Sudo.
Finely slit Mino *washi* paper woven into a sheer polyester organdy base. A foil brocade specialist ensures the paper strips lie uniformly flat, to give a soft lustre to the final fabric.

following spread:
Reed Ripple, 1996.
By Reiko Sudo.
Most *osa* loom reeds are flat, but rippled reeds were used for lilting wave patterns in summer *kimono*. Few artisans can still do this work; fewer still can craft the rippled reeds.

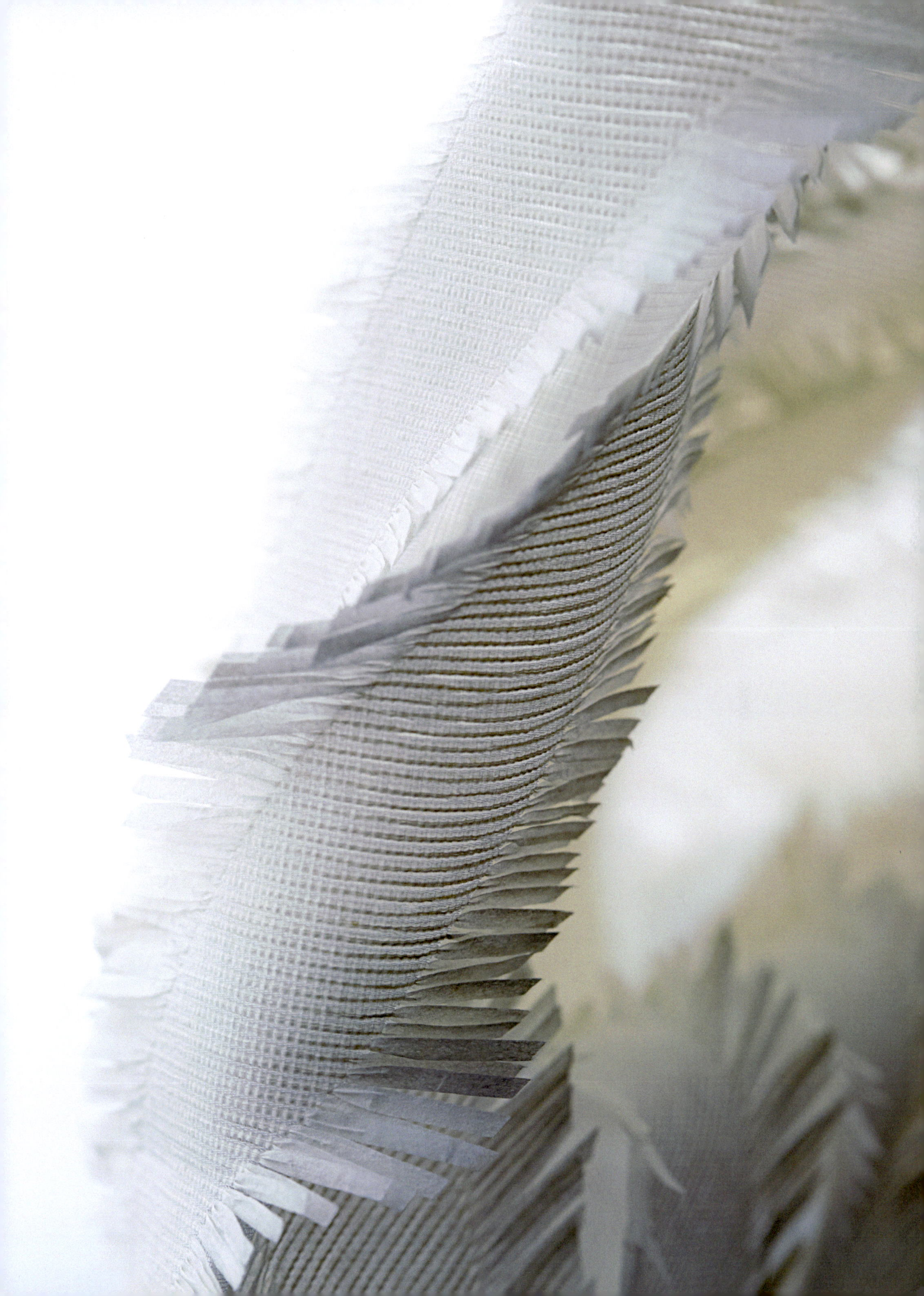

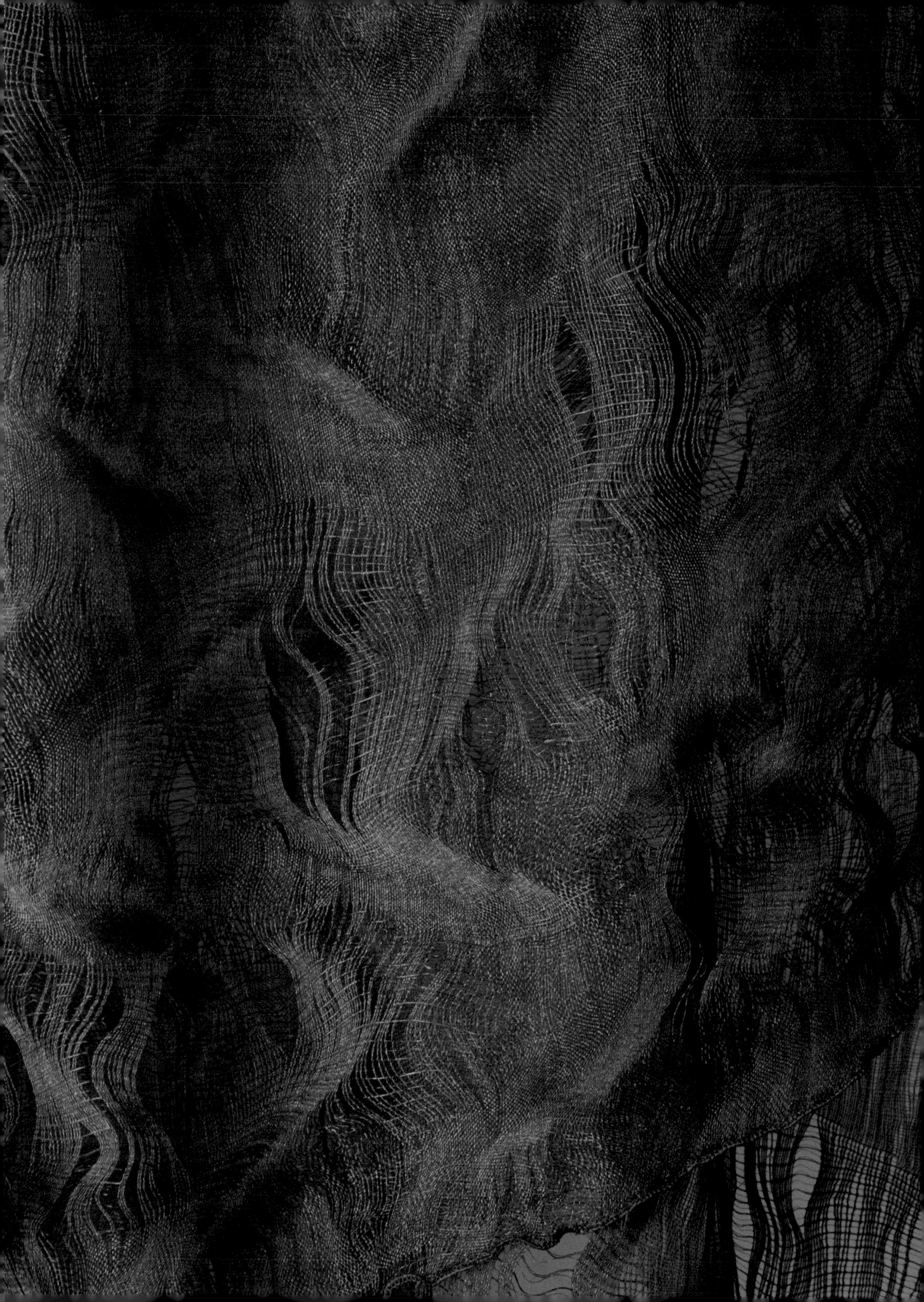

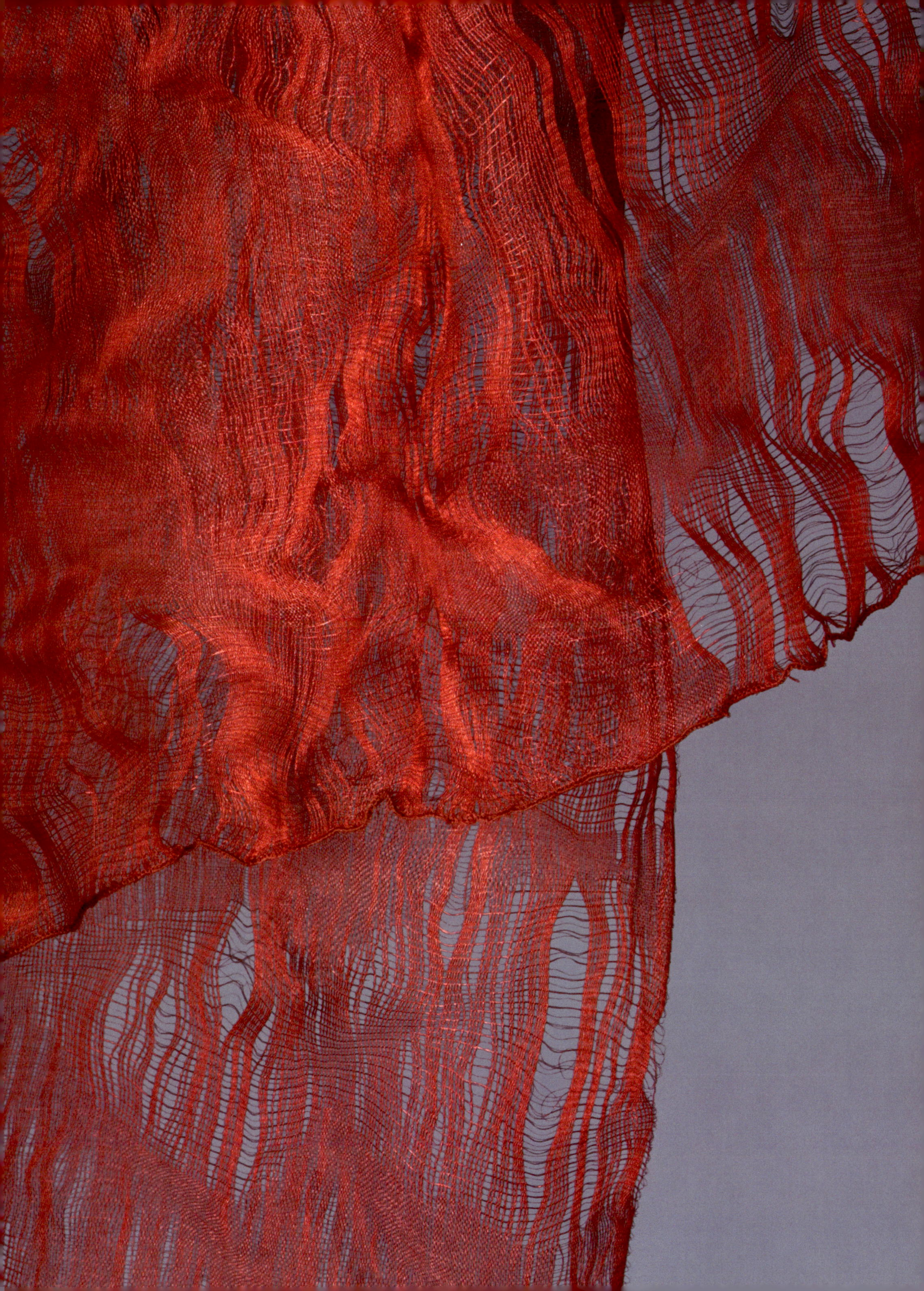

below and opposite:
Slipstream, 1994.
By Reiko Sudo.
Durable Mino *washi* handmade mulberry paper was traditionally used for making *shifu* paper cloth. Thin strips between layers of silk organdy create patterns reminiscent of flowing water.

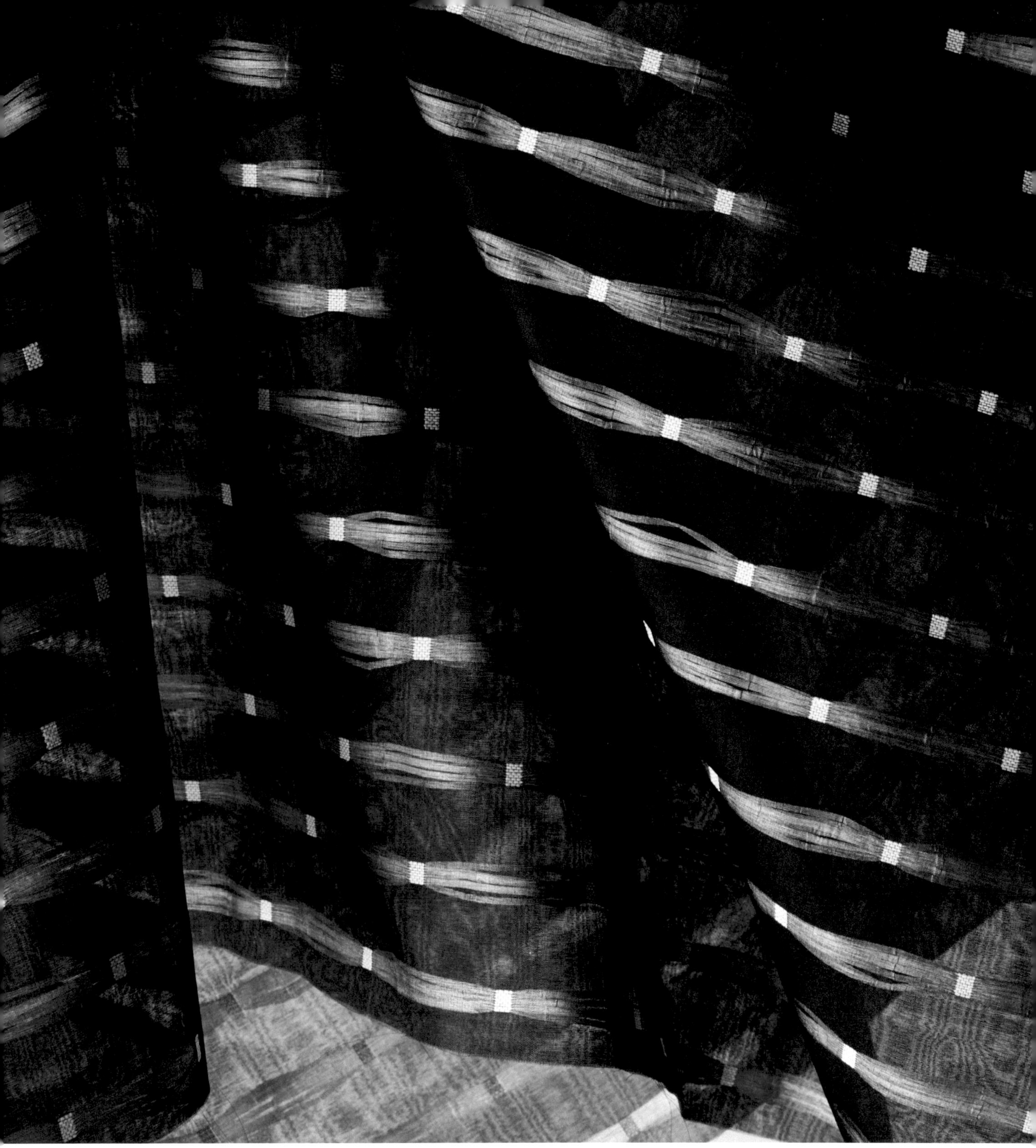

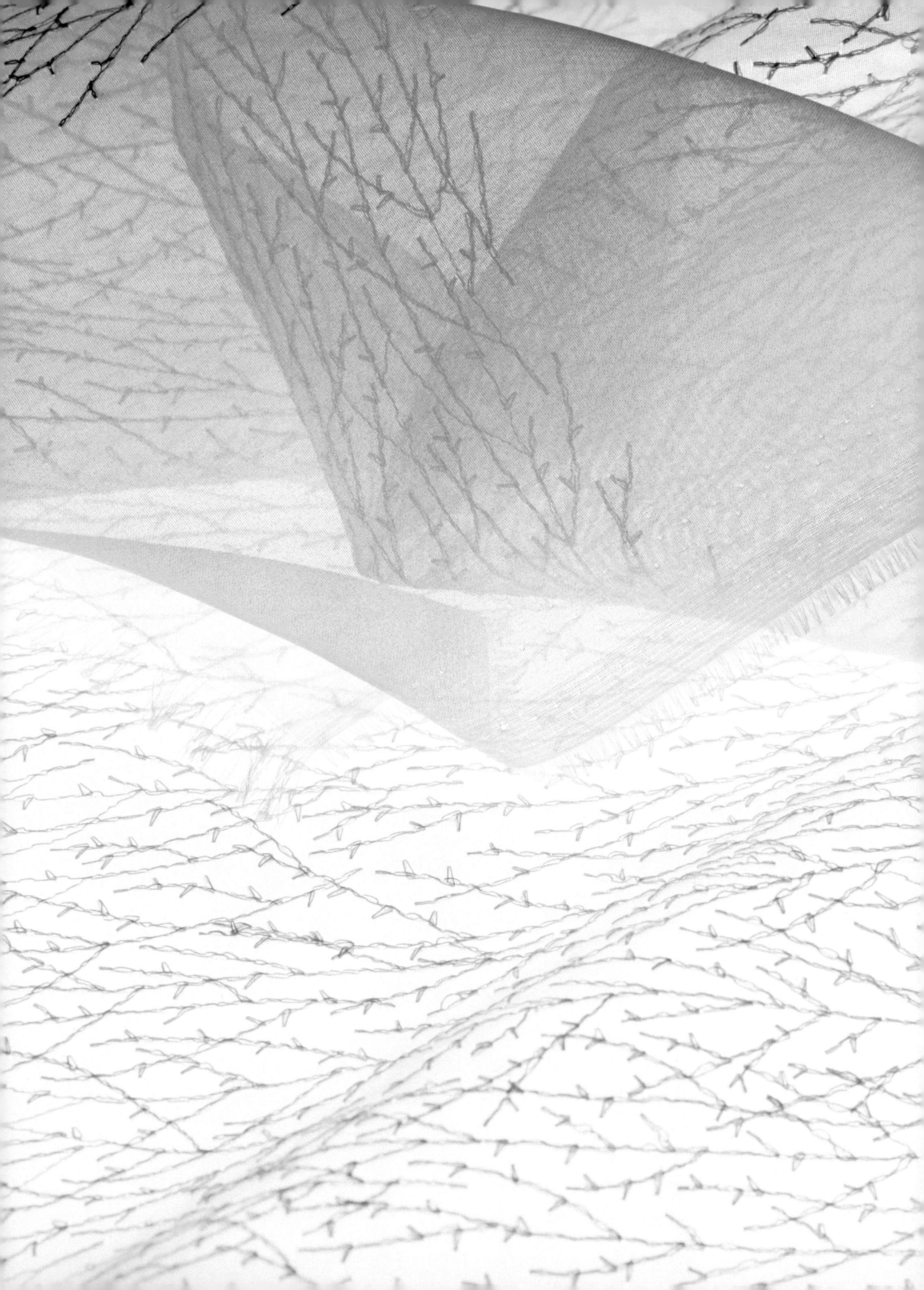

Snowy Branches, 2011.
By Reiko Sudo.
A casement fabric with
a sketch of snowy branches
intricately embroidered
on polyester organdy.

スケスケ

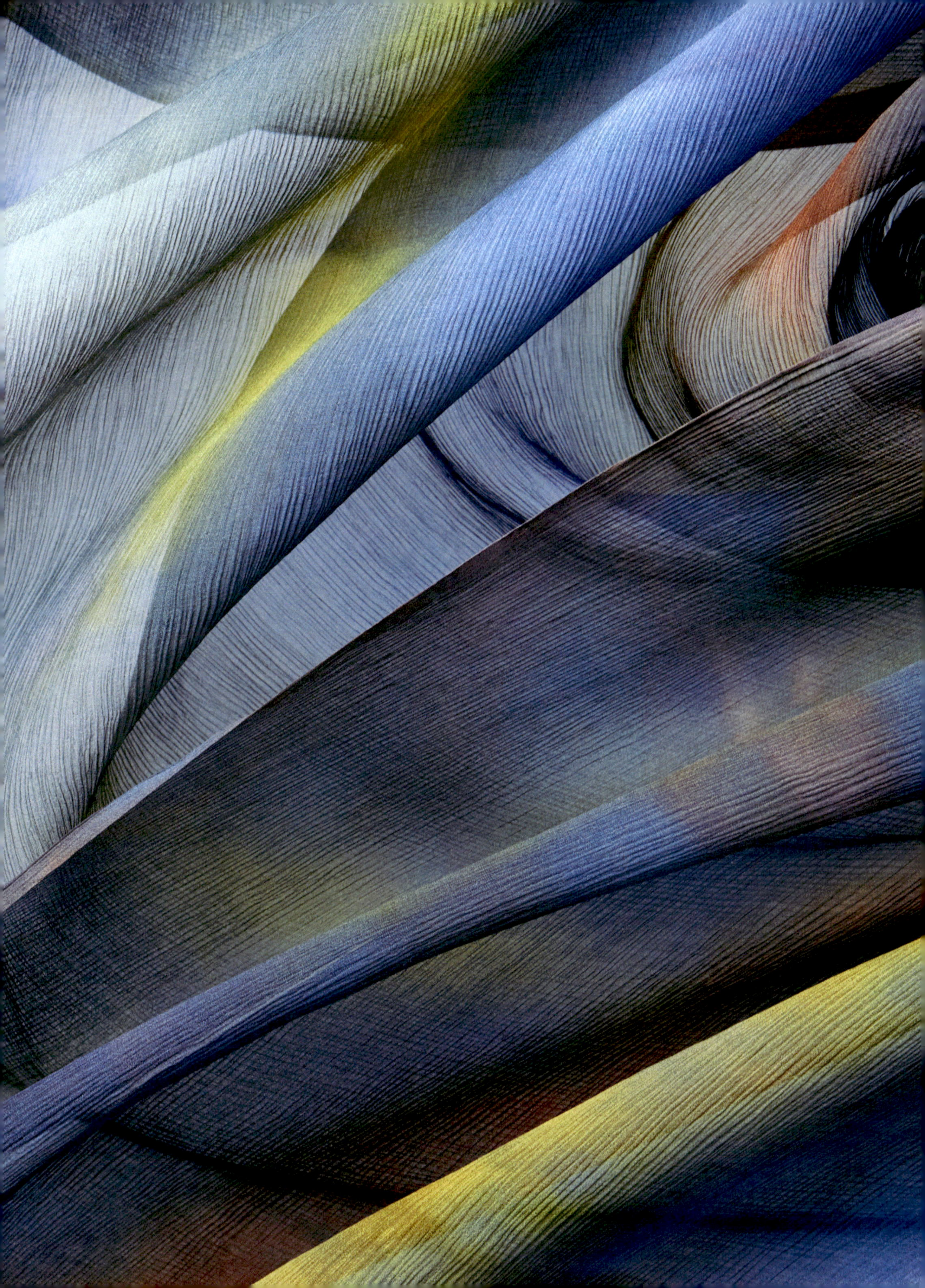

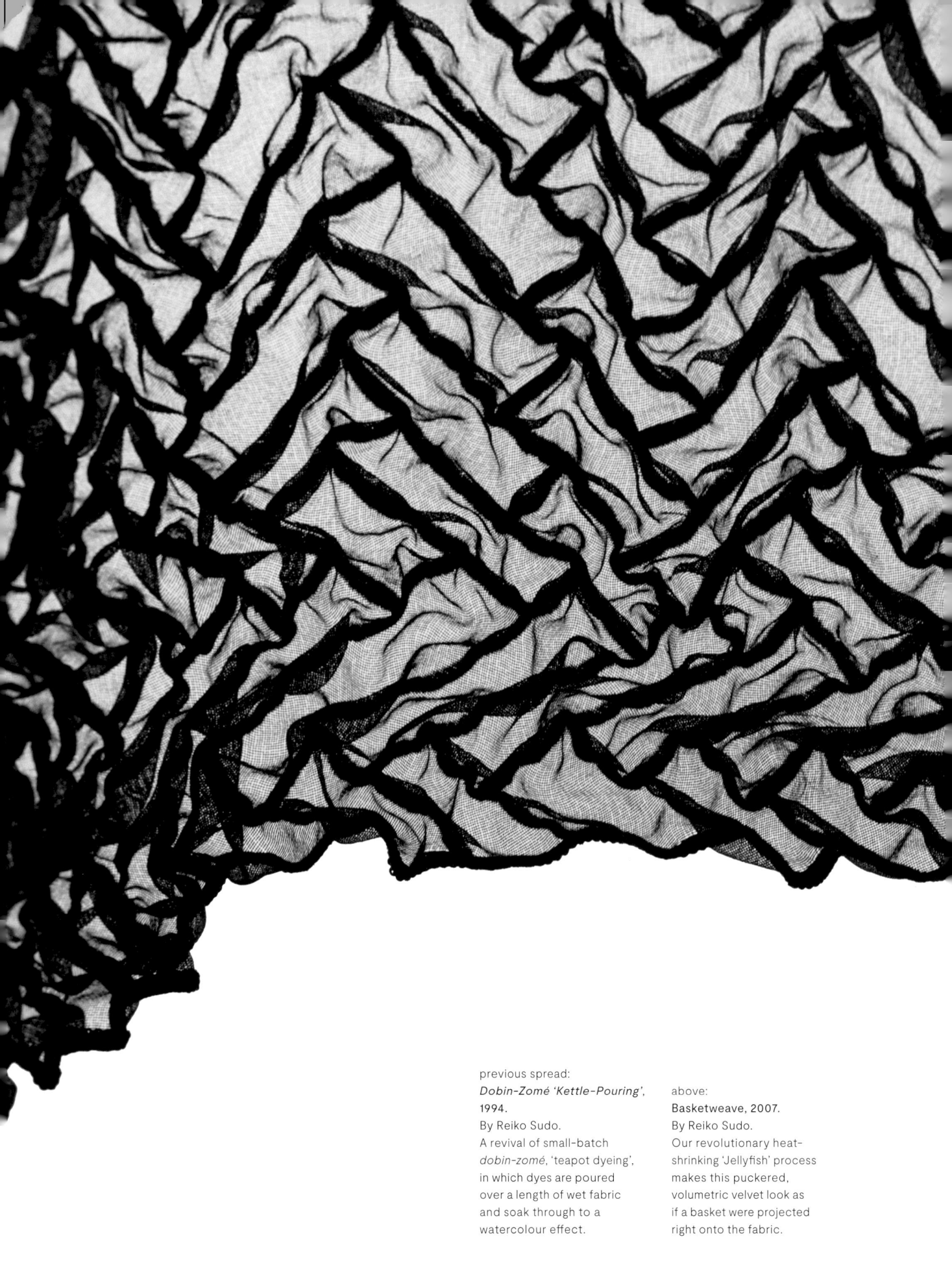

previous spread:
Dobin-Zomé 'Kettle-Pouring', 1994.
By Reiko Sudo.
A revival of small-batch *dobin-zomé*, 'teapot dyeing', in which dyes are poured over a length of wet fabric and soak through to a watercolour effect.

above:
Basketweave, 2007.
By Reiko Sudo.
Our revolutionary heat-shrinking 'Jellyfish' process makes this puckered, volumetric velvet look as if a basket were projected right onto the fabric.

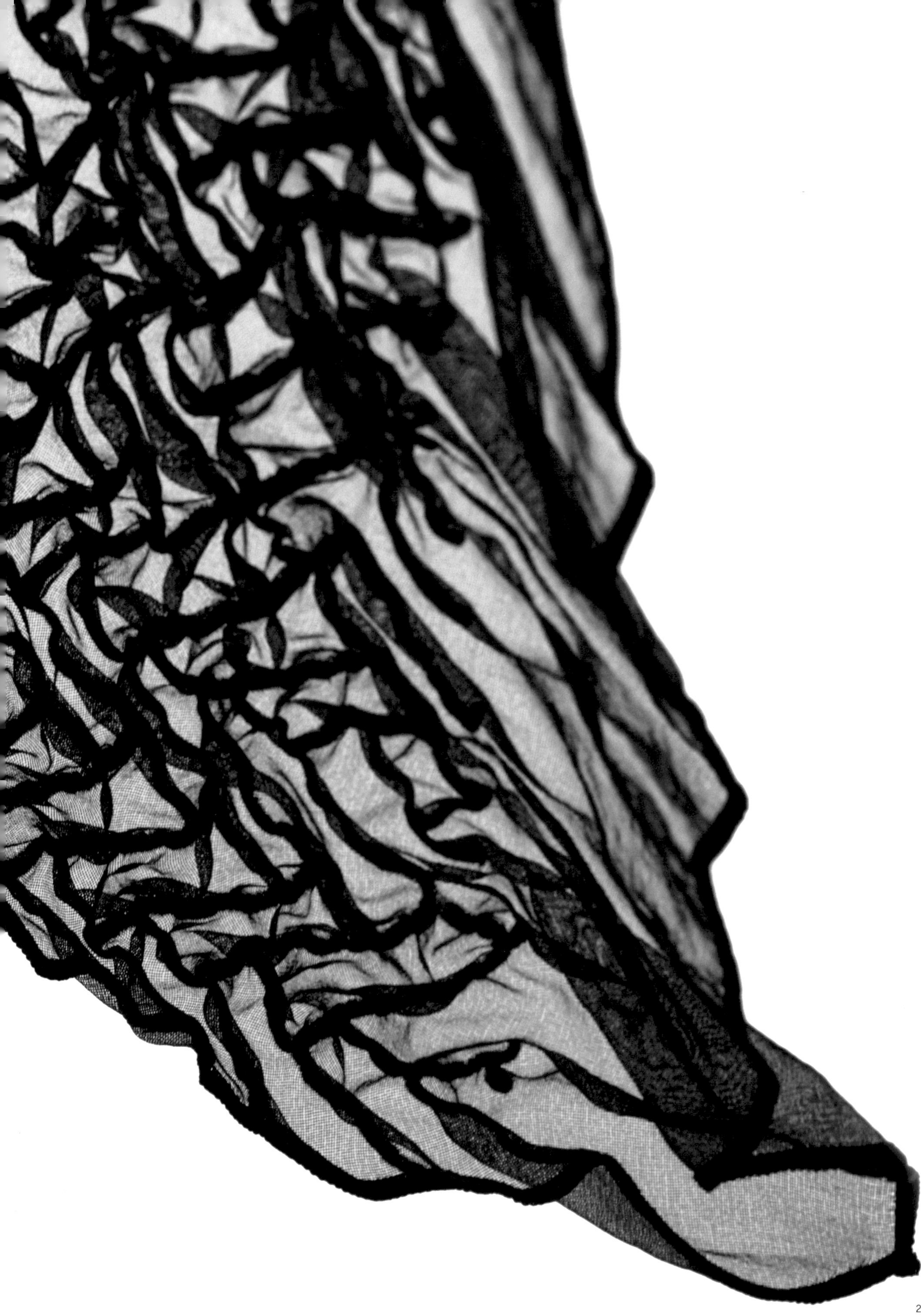

above:
Nimbus, 1992.
By Reiko Sudo and Yuka Taniguchi.
This silk organdy is hand-painted with a starch resist, then immersed in calcium nitrate, causing the exposed areas to contract into opaque knots while leaving the coated areas transparent.

opposite:
Stratus, 1992.
By Reiko Sudo and Yuka Taniguchi.
Enshuku, 'salt-shrinking', causes silk or wool animal fibres to contract in a calcium chloride or calcium nitrate. The stronger the chemical solution, the more intense the shrinkage.

following spread:
Kinugasa Mushroom, 2006.
By Reiko Sudo.
A charming 'forest sprite' mushroom motif is created using a 'chemical lace' embroidery technique.

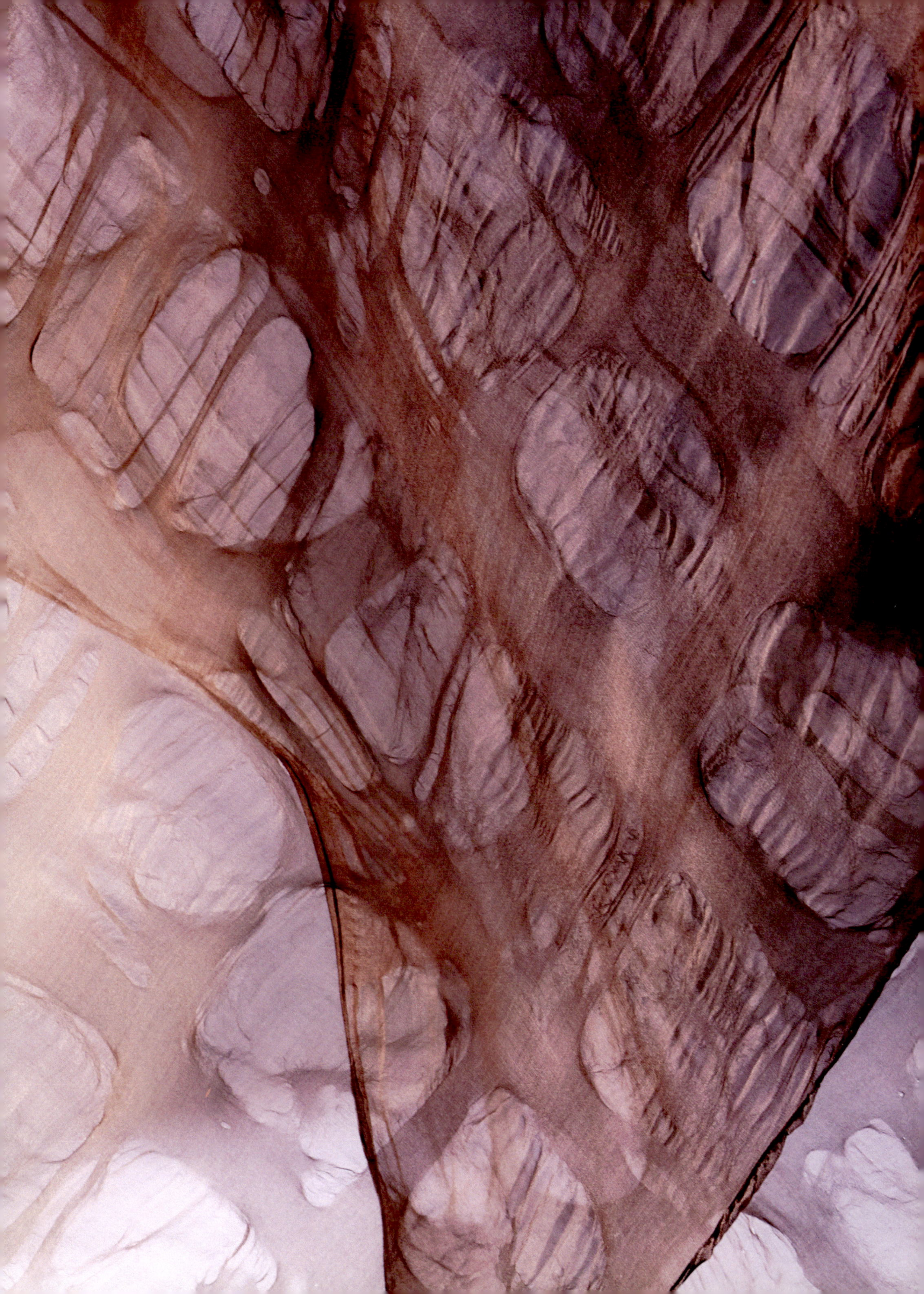

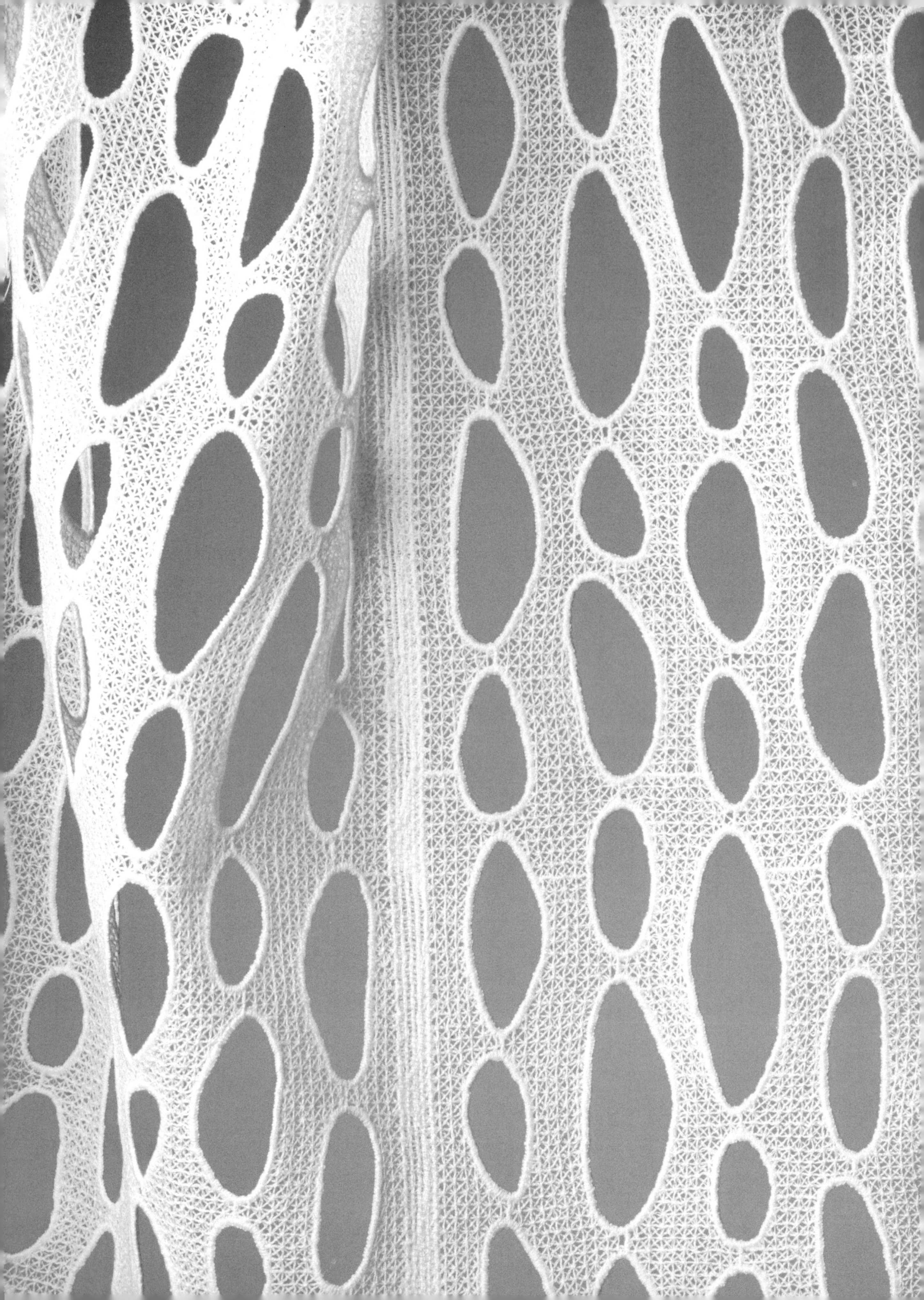

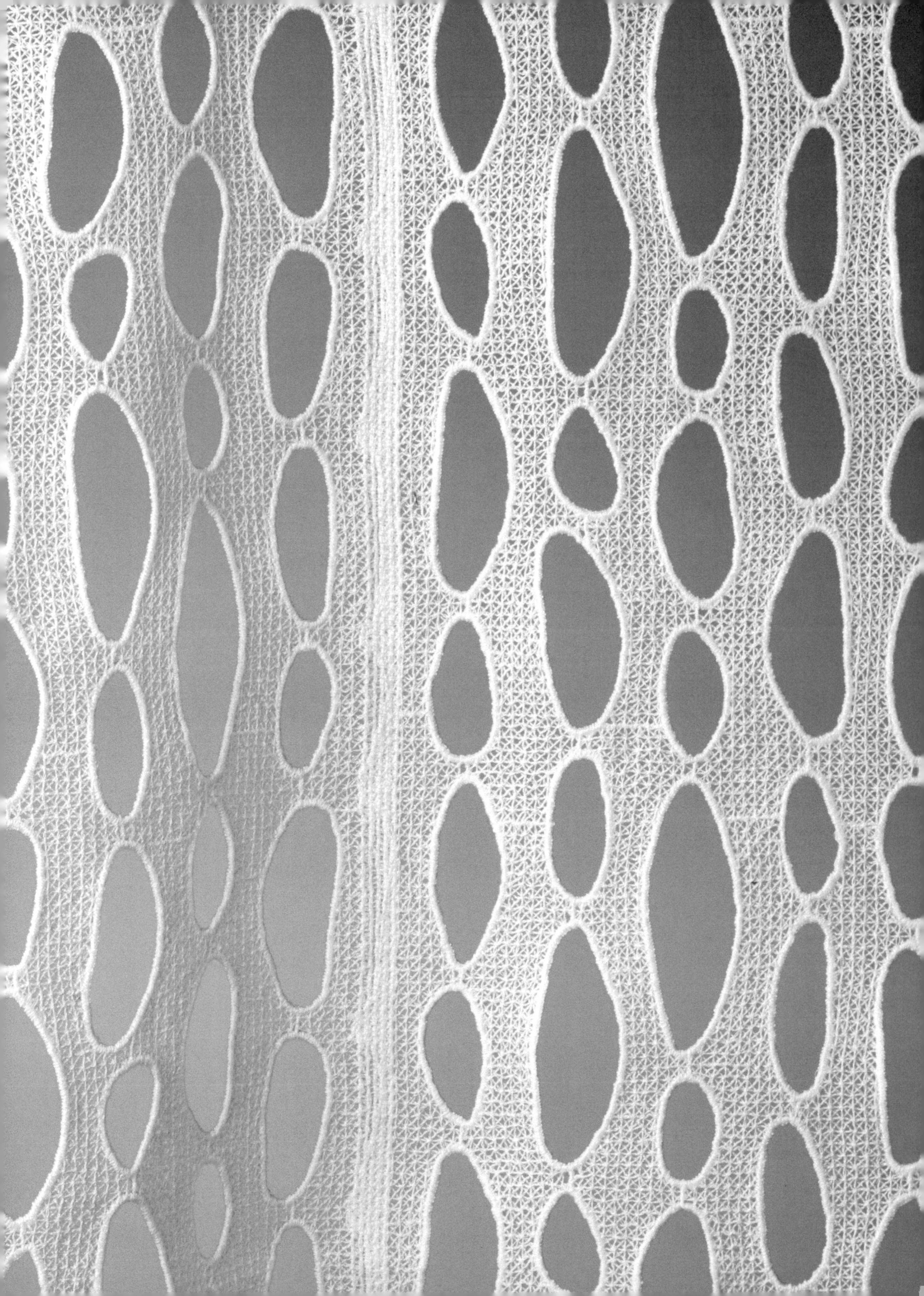

Itajime Round, 2002.
By Reiko Sudo and Yoko Kaneichi.
An adaptation of ancient *kyo-kechi* 'clamp-dyeing', tiny folds of fabric are secured at both ends with round boards, then twisted tightly and dyed, the pressure acting as a resist.

247

Turkish Wall, 1995.
By Reiko Sudo.
A cheap T-shirt printing process combined with electrostatic flocking renders textural depth in this fabric, a study of light and shadow on a limestone terrace in Turkey.

Portrait of a Textile: *Turkish Wall*

How might the humble glory of graffiti, rubbish and pottery shards be translated to a textile?

On my first visit to Turkey in 1980, I was amazed to see the gigantic travertine 'castles' built up so very white and layered in texture by the thermal waters of Pamukkale. When I got back to Tokyo, I tried to translate my memories into a new textile by experimenting with different white pigments – *gofun*-shell powder, lead white, titanium oxide, magnesium chloride, as well as flocked rayon microfibres, foaming polymers, even fluorescent paint – sometimes printing two or three different agents together on a single piece of fabric, only to find that multilayered effects failed to add much depth. Not one to give up, I then tried colourants on the front and back of the fabric and ultimately settled on electro-steaming rayon flocking onto a polyester ground, followed by titanium oxide pigment on the reverse side. Very labour intensive and nowhere near as magnificent as those travertine deposits, but the process was a momentous discovery for NUNO.

The original design artwork, in gouache on *washi* paper.

スケスケ

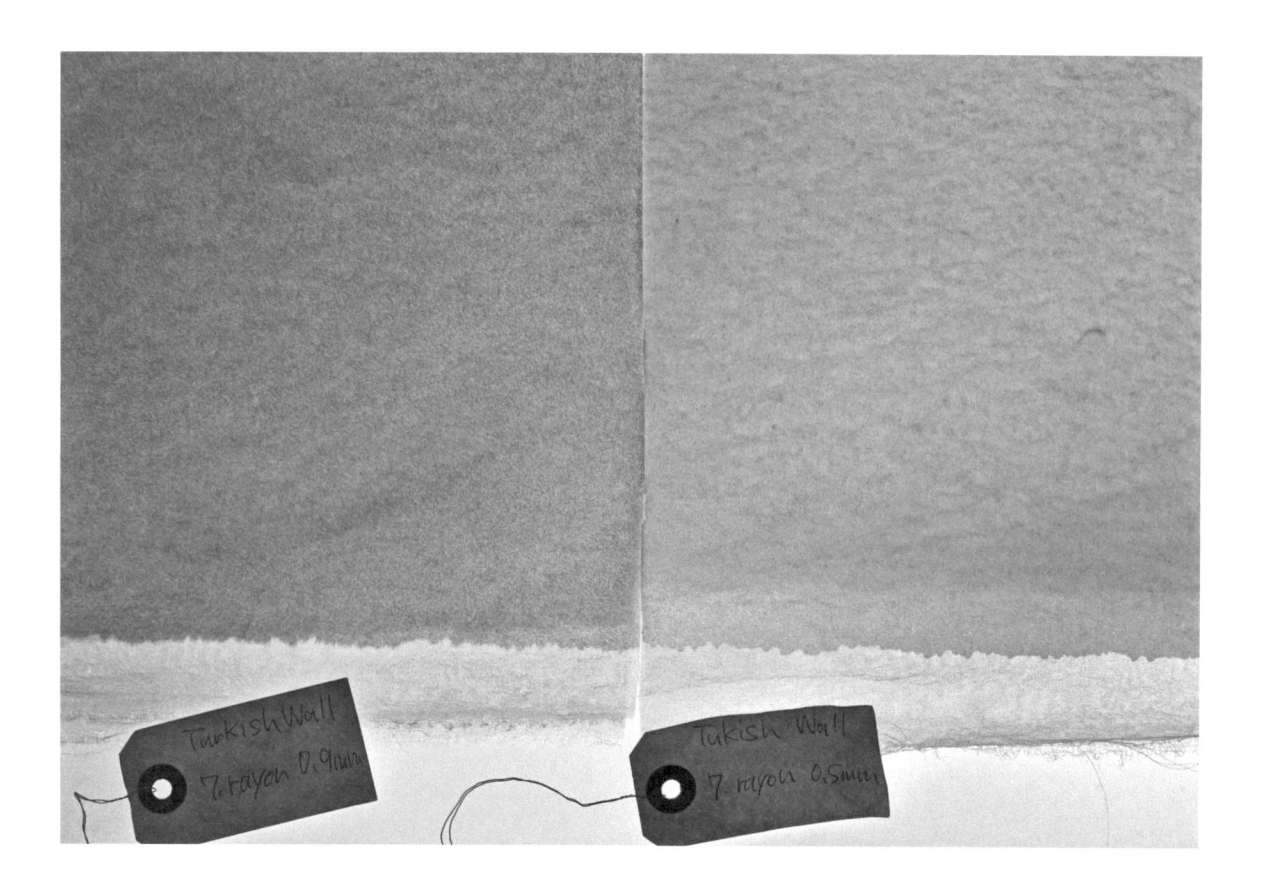

above
Trial flock printing: 9mm (3/8 in.) rayon fibres and 5mm (3/16 in.) rayon fibres.

below
Sea shell and corals, both traditionally ground to make *gofun*-shell white pigment.

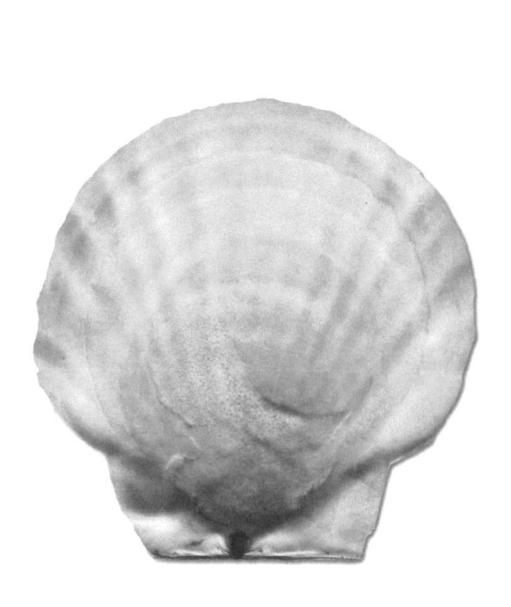

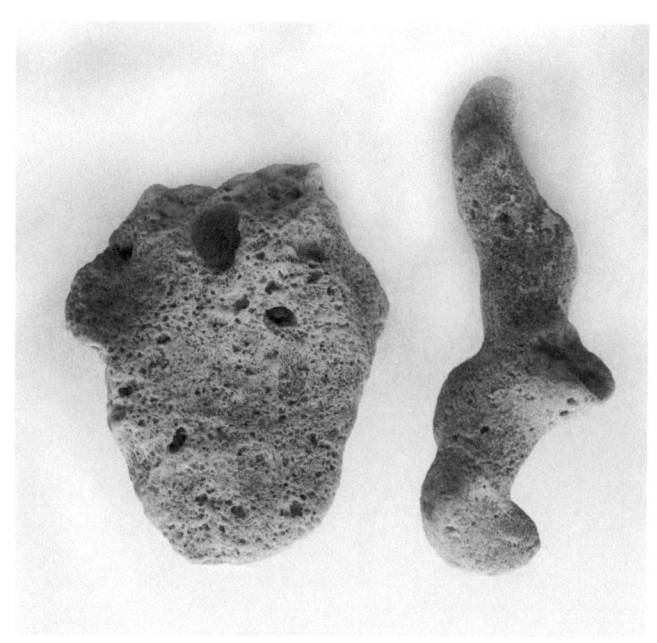

250

The dyer's touch

NUNO favours hand-drawn shading, stippling and dots for making bold, dynamic design statements, often bringing together intentionally mismatched elements to create a dizzying sense of counterpoint and unexpected effects.

above and left
Travel sketches made with seawater.

following spread:
White pigment tests: two coats of *gofun*, three coats of *gofun*, five coats of *gofun*, titanium white, pearl white.

p. 252:
Trial titanium white print.

p. 253:
Original design artwork, in gouache on *washi* paper.

スケスケ

SUKE SUKE

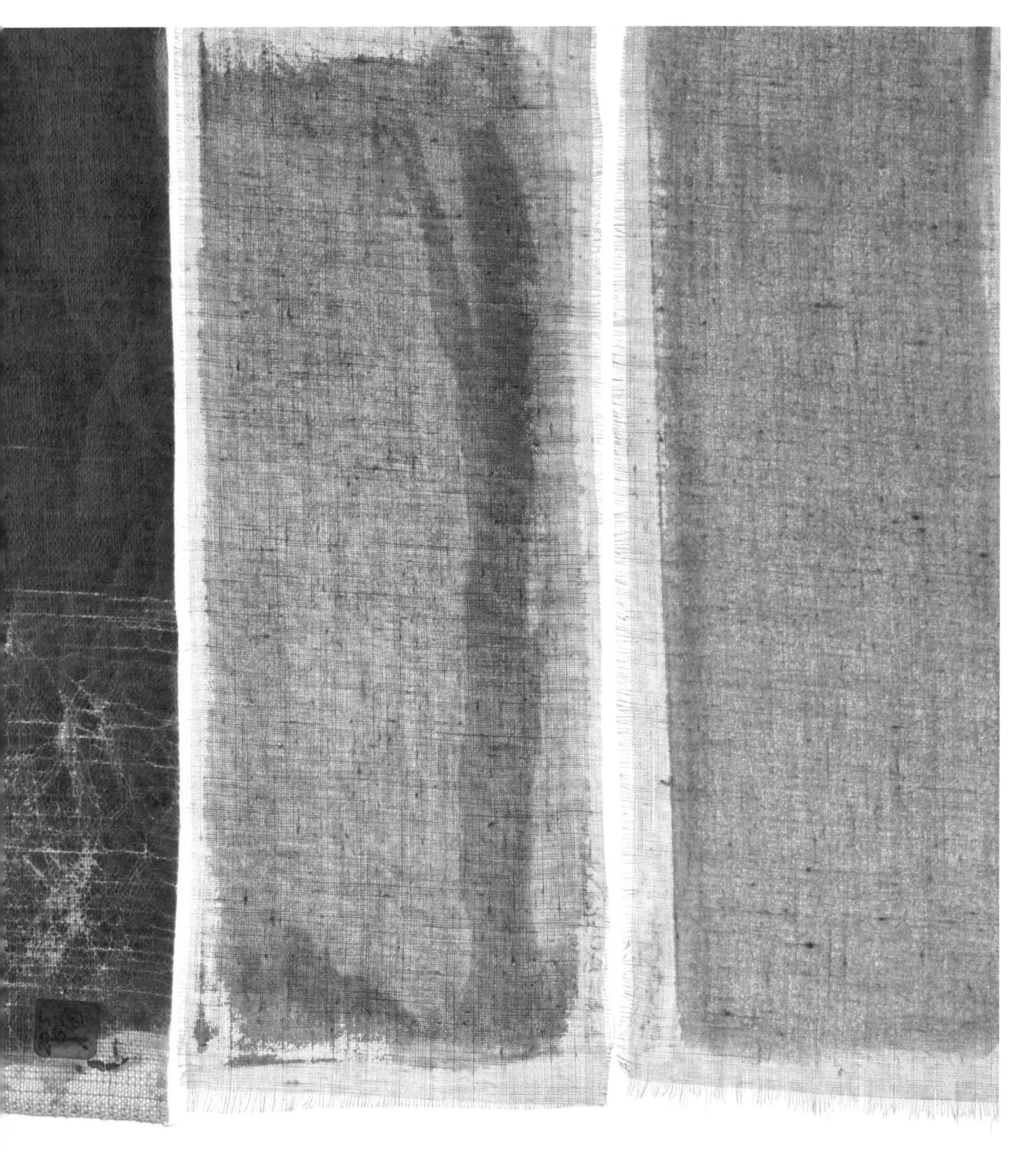

P-122T
C/#0F
10M

following page
After printing in titanium white, a flocking device electrostatically applies 5mm (³⁄₁₆ in.) rayon fibres onto an adhesive pattern, moving side to side to ensure evenness and brush off excess fibres.

p. 257, top
Manipulating metal electrode rods to conduct power to the flocking machine.

p. 257, bottom
Fabric is brushed after flock printing to align the fibres, then heat-treated.

スケスケ

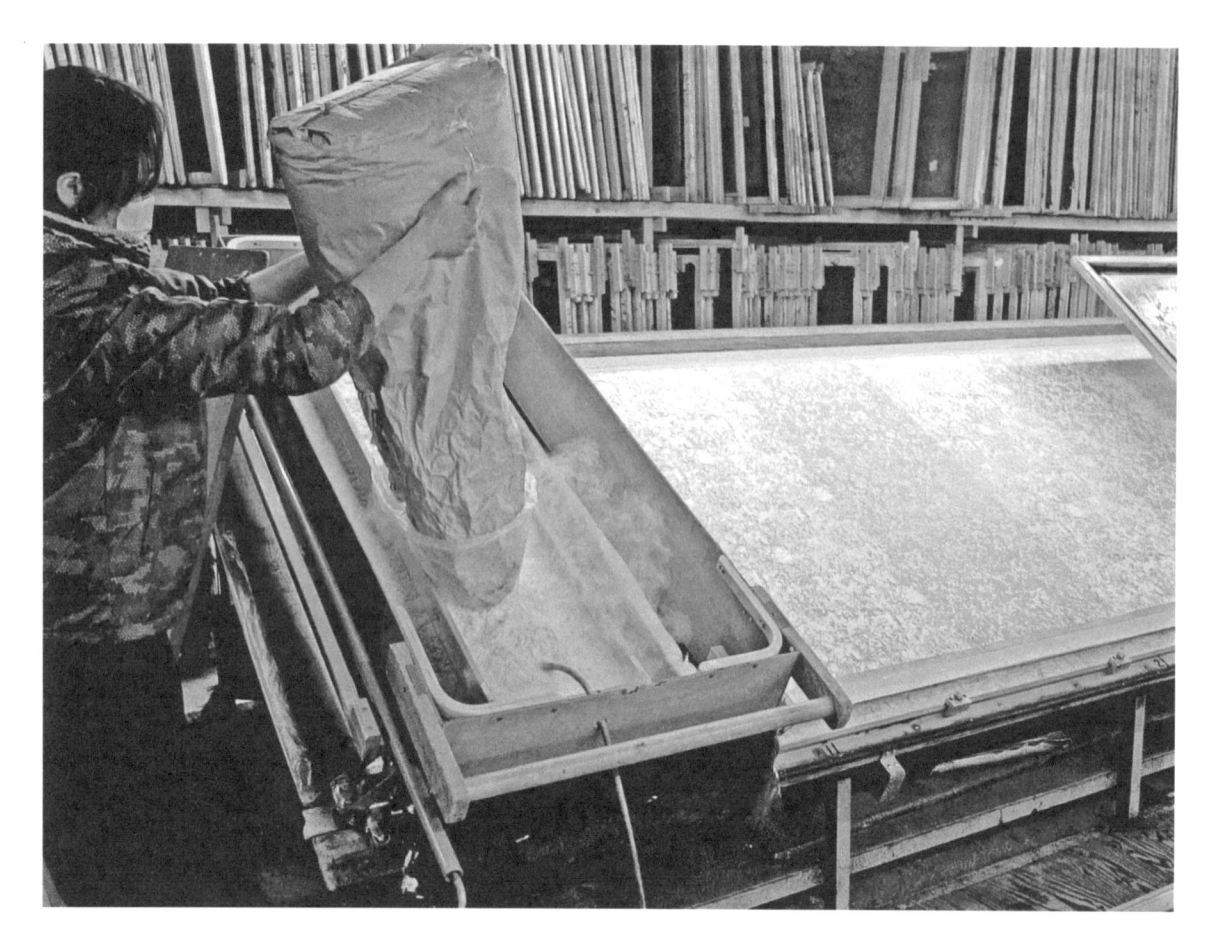

SUKE SUKE

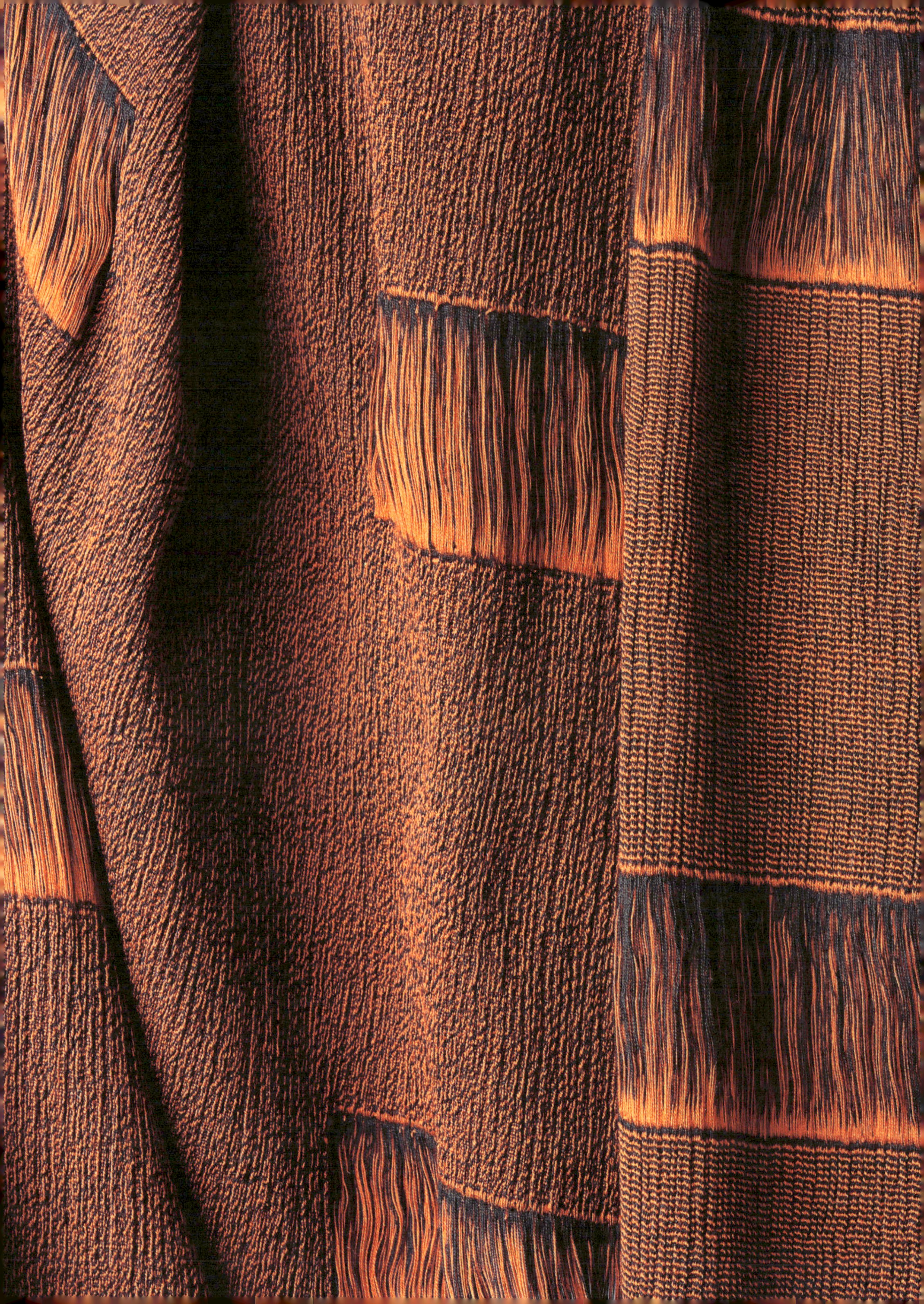

ZAWA
ZAWA

zawa zawa (ザワザワ)

1. Noisy, clamorous, buzzing, humming, assonant, making a din
2. Teeming, bustling, astir, agitated, alive (with activity)
3. Busy, frenetic, lively; hyper(active) [slang]
4. Intense, densely marked or figured

The rumble of the unknown

What's that noise? Unnervingly unidentifiable, far off amid the bustle of the city or deep in the dense darkness of the forest, we hear something. Almost immediately we feel a palpable distress and expectation. Whether the rumblings of faceless urban crowds or the rustling of creatures through the underbrush, *zawa zawa* sounds set us on edge. In the movies, such sounds signal the appearance of some fantastic ghoul or axe murderer with bloodshot eyes. On a street corner, an ominous buzz of voices makes us look around for a commotion in the making. In paintings and collages, excessive details seem to chatter with nervous glee, a nightmare of obsessive pattern recognition.

Zawa zawa is the bump of things in the night, indistinct yet laden with tonal nuances that scratch at the back of the mind. These *zawa zawa* textiles are a mixed bag of diverse styles and tastes. Like the murmurs of manifold phenomena from everywhere and nowhere, they arrest us with their sheer irreducibility and power to suggest. Swathed in restless visual and textual noise, sending ripples of excited disquiet through the otherwise normal everyday, your look may not be 'loud', but people will certainly 'hear' you coming.

p. 258:
Skyscraper, 1995.
By Reiko Sudo.
Jacquard-loomed cotton rises ten storeys, with wefts cut at regular intervals into 'windows'.

right:
Karéha, 1998.
By Reiko Sudo and Yoko Ando.
A 'chemical lace' openwork embroidery pattern renders *karéha*, autumn leaf skeletons.

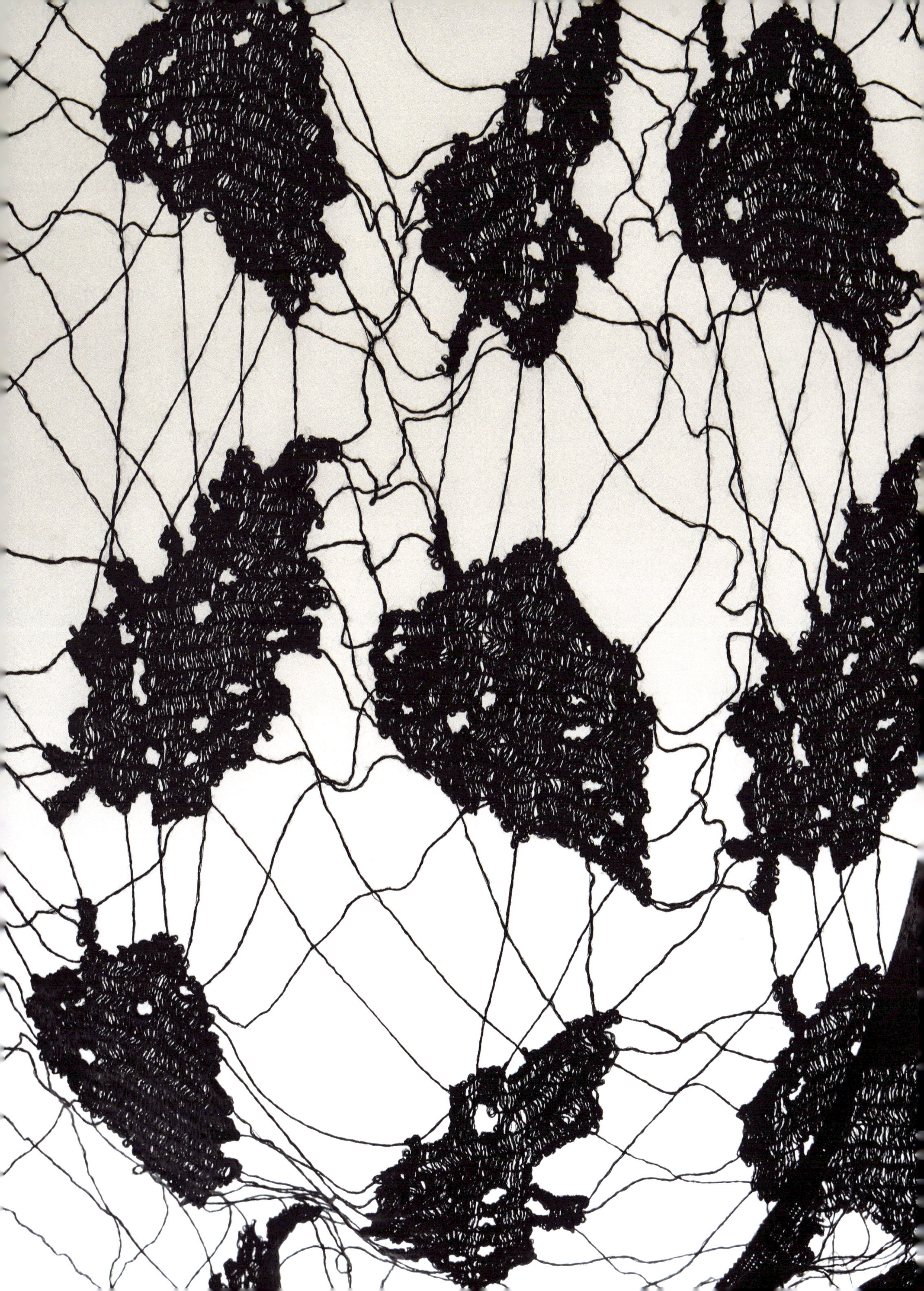

Four Poems

Arto Lindsay

ALMOST APHORISTIC

Why don't we say the rain is noisy?

Volume is different than noise

Rudeness is like a quick jolt of volume

We say clothes are too loud

Static is warm

Noise is unsuited to horror

Great music is a series of decisions about noise

Sound like the wind in
Sound like the wind out

Noise is to touch as, well,
not the first thought.

Noise of hair on skin

Unconscious noise

Applying lipstick

Lower frequencies from on high

The tragic all across the sky: noise

Noise can be sentimental too

The law of the title:
Everything recalls its opposite

IN LIEU OF OBJECTIVITY

What is this thing called noise music?
The sum of all musics, their essence

Dissonance being an object, and behaving like one
Leading harmony to be perceived as transparent

Dissonance should more properly be a cliché
of ecstasy than of anguish

Major to minor over the cliff hit the wall hit the glass

Fascination as a kinder surrender
to the primacy of electrical instruments over man
Electrical or even mechanical excess
is a nice fractal eye-view of pleasure
Feedback is a metaphor no more,
a creature of the same inexpressible
seduced to a halt

Whatever it is, all at one time
Noise is closer to a simple melody
then to elaborate harmony
But noise is also the next step beyond complexity

Noise is made of the same stuff as silence

NOISE SONG

If you arrive when it is raining
you have to leave before the rain stops
A day between seasons
was all she could offer
Dark patches caught in a tree at night
And then you know it will snow and it does

Into the room with water on your shoulders
A turning point where you can see it
say stay still as the noise gets closer
And then you know it will snow and it does

ANOTHER NOISE DRAMA

hundreds of extras
each shaking a leaf
hundreds of pairs
of lips like blades of grass
under a helicopter

head thrown back
for throat sounds and throat singing
what you take to be your full height
exaggerate the need

Nuno Tataki, 2012.
By Reiko Sudo and Hiroko Kobayashi.
A patchwork of our print fabrics arranged on an organdy base, then worked together by needle-punching. Cute designs, cruel treatment – but then *tataki* does mean 'beating'.

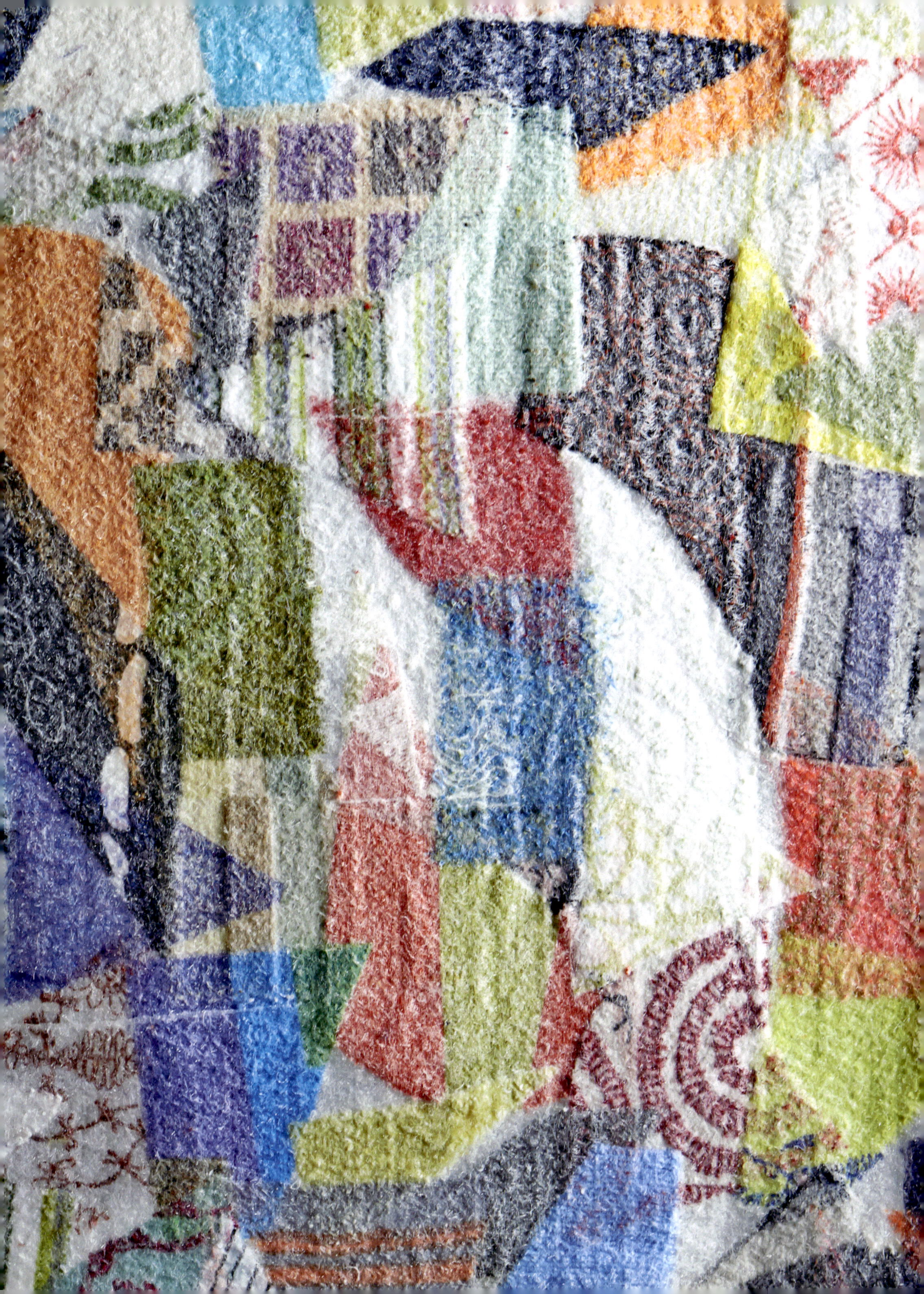

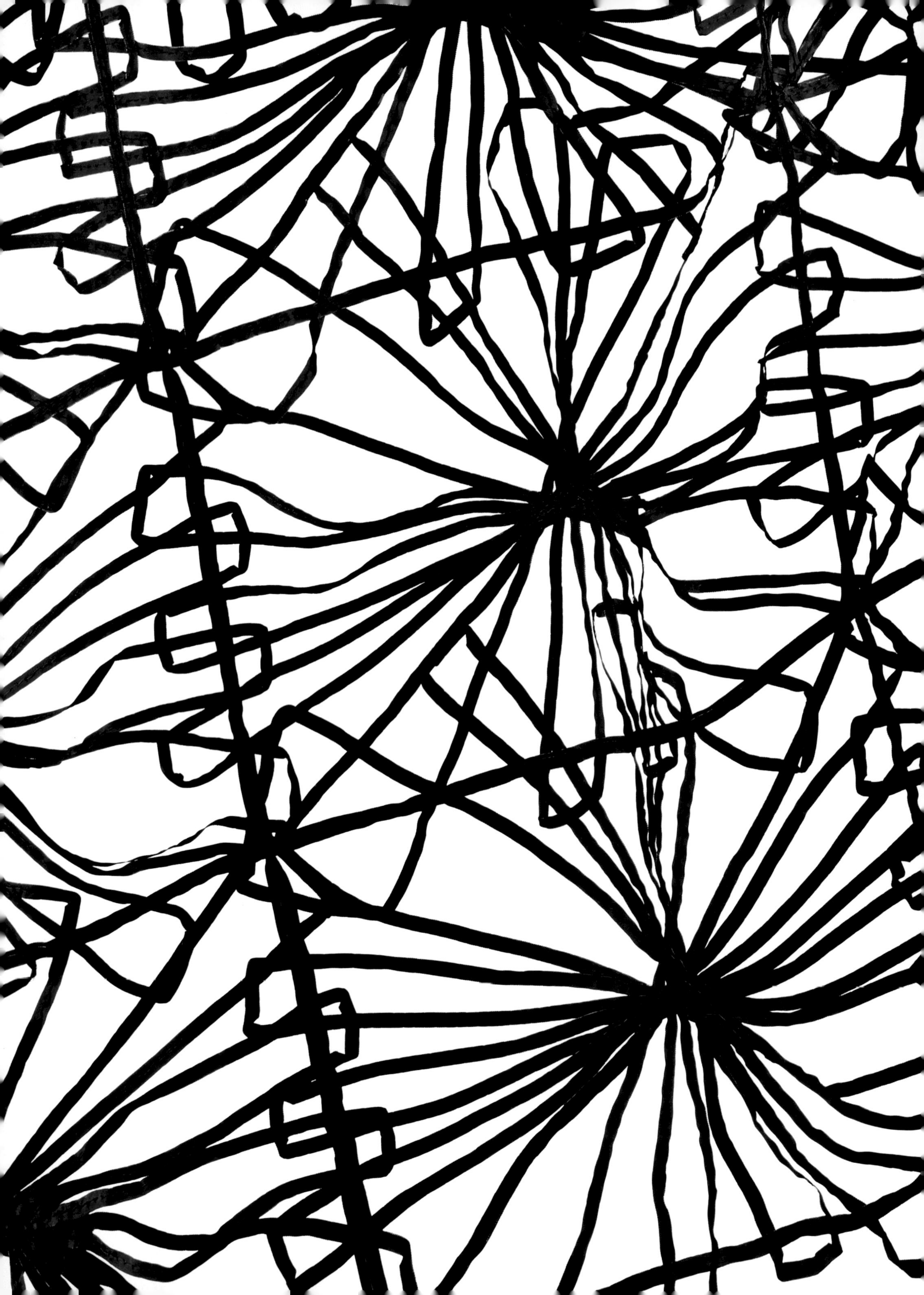

Stalagmite, 2005.
By Kazuhiro Ueno.
Embroidered on a special steering-wheel embroidery machine typically used for *uchikake* wedding *kimono*, this design emulates calcified rock formations.

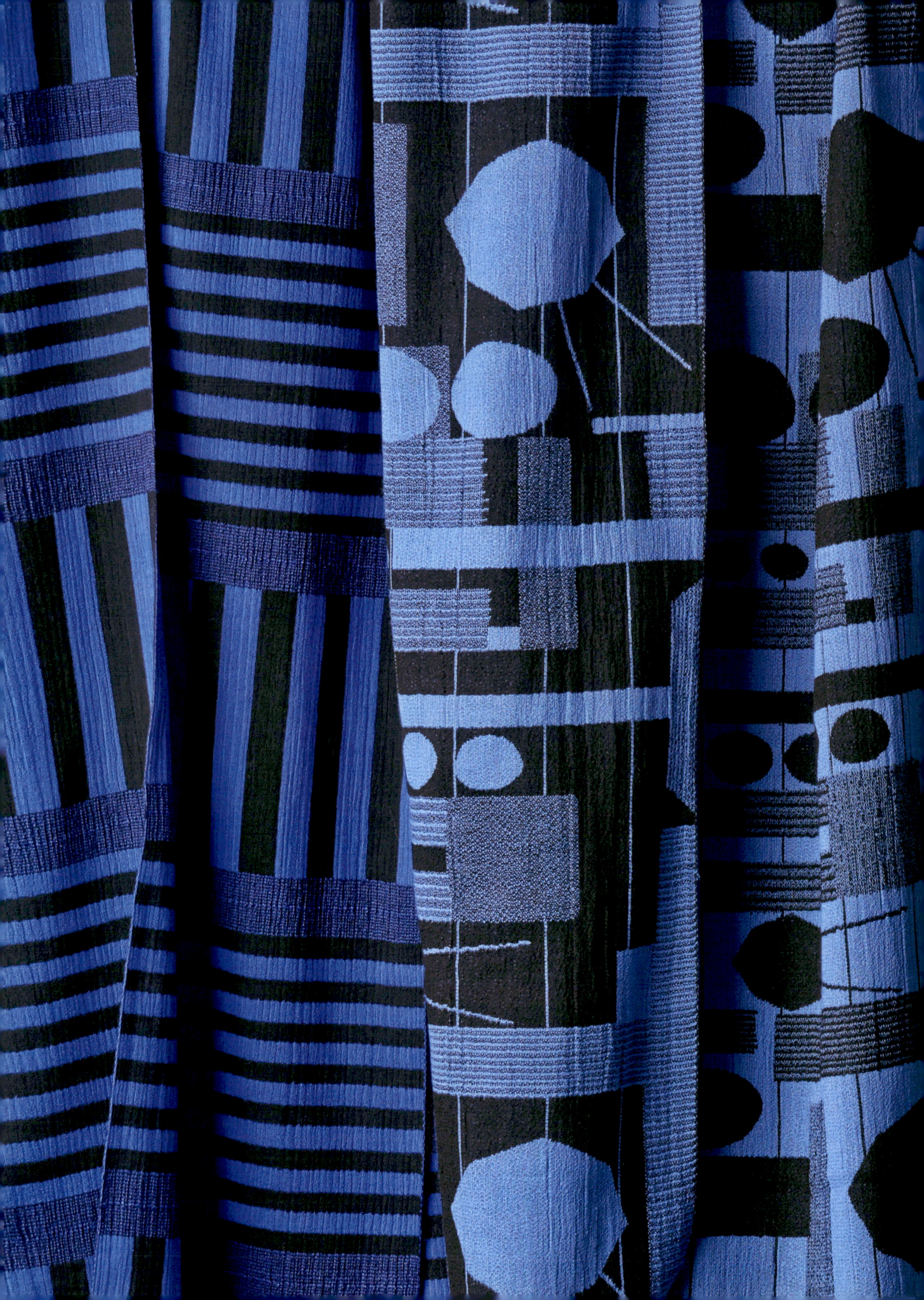

ZAWA ZAWA

Multilayer Weave series.
left to right:
Stripy Stripe, 2009.
By Reiko Sudo.
This cotton double-weave scarf combines horizontal and vertical stripes, with stiff *kibiso* threads woven in between to create a crinkled texture.
Kite, 2018.
By Reiko Sudo.
An overspun cotton jacquard double-weave imagines kites cut loose to drift freely with you.
Warps and Wefts, 2018.
By Reiko Sudo.
A freehand ink drawing of warp and weft threads reproduced in a double-weave, with various weave structures to create subtle tonalities.
Big Ring, 2013.
By Kazuhiro Ueno.
Our signature stretchy cotton crepe patterned with sun and moon rounds together with stripes.

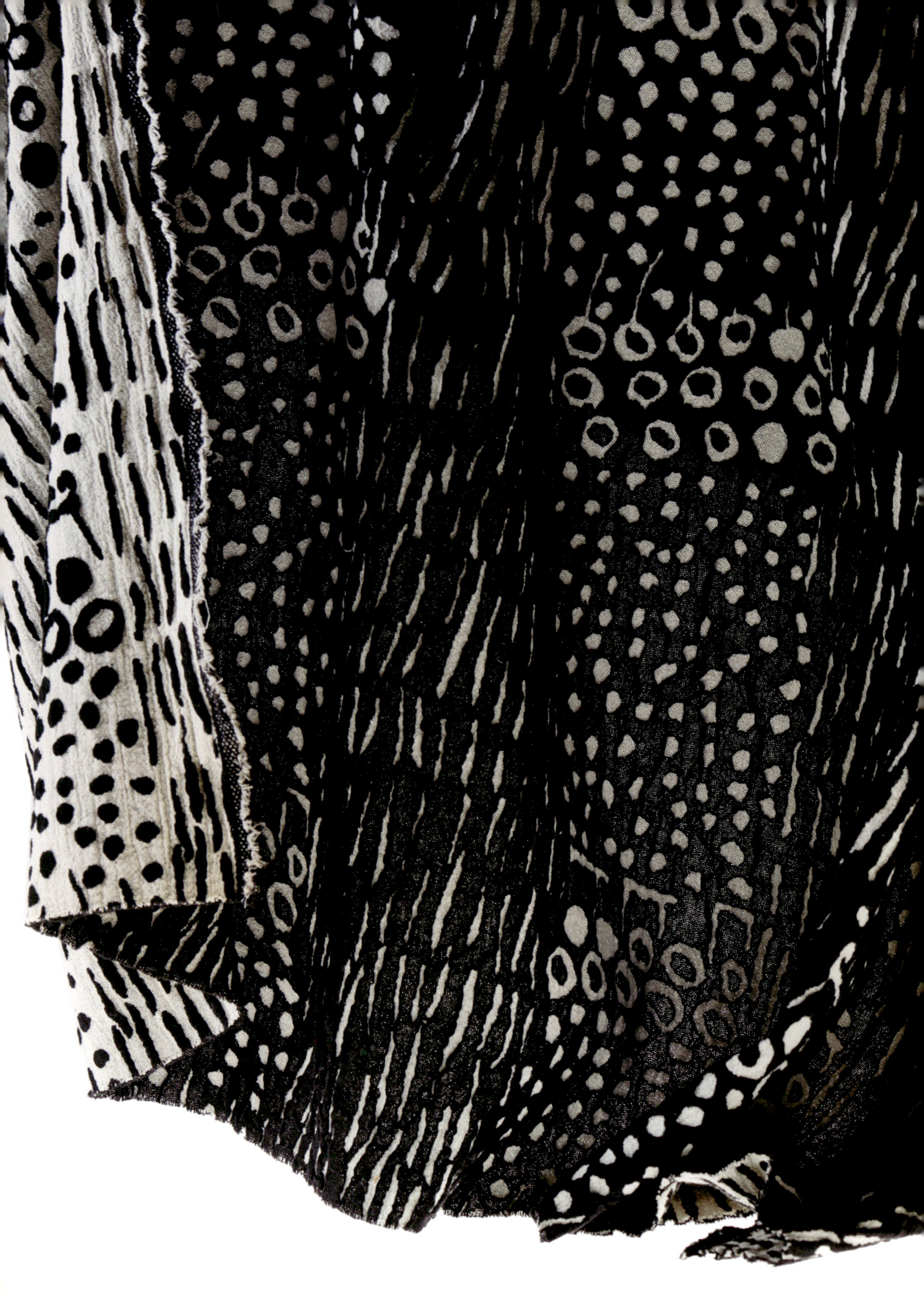

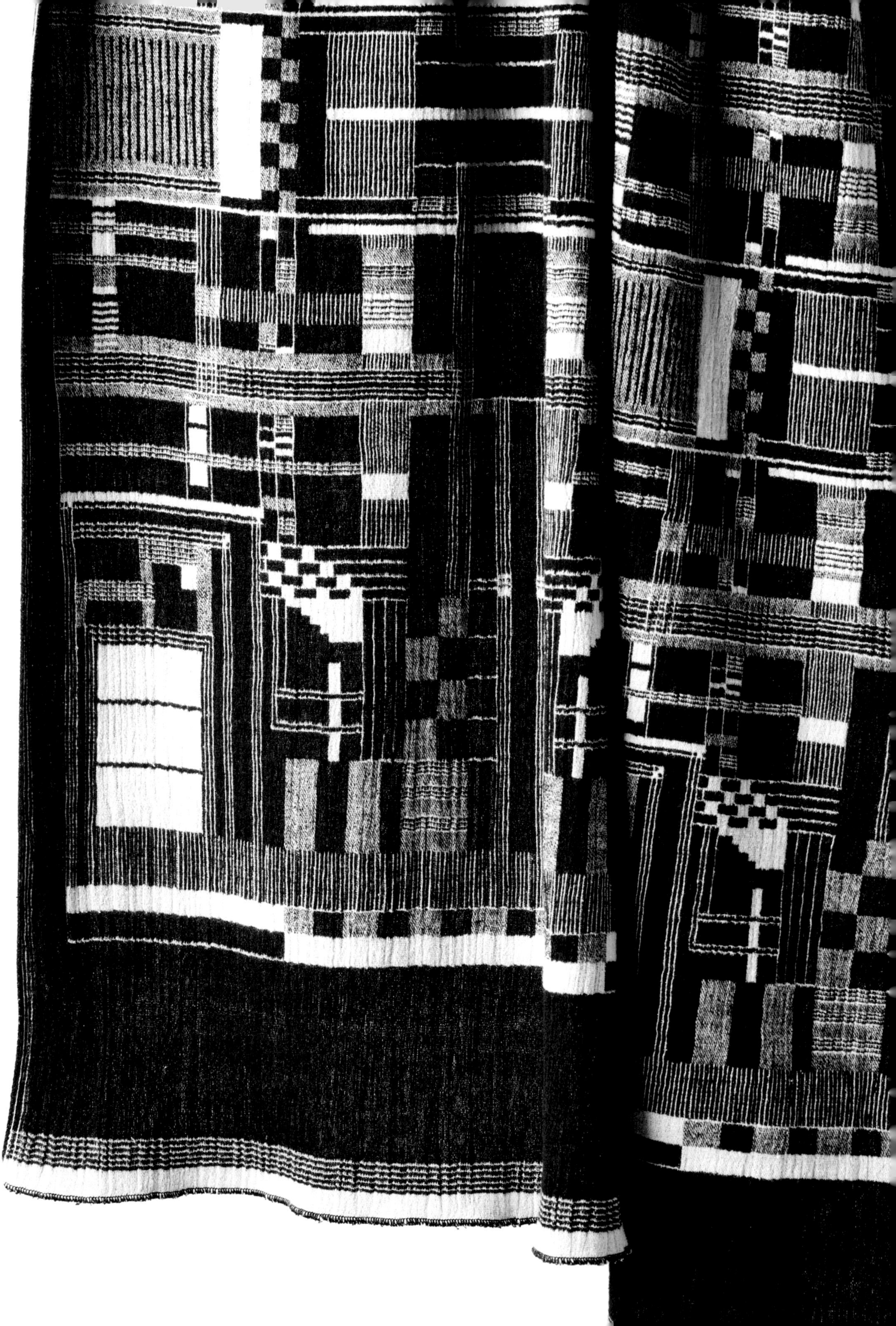

p. 270:
Rice Hulls, 1995.
By Reiko Sudo.
A jacquard double-weave inspired by the lively natural patterns drawn on bark cloth by the indigenous Mbuti people of Zaire.

previous page:
Computer Chip, 1996.
By Reiko Sudo.
The precise detailing and brilliant colours of an enlarged IC chip describe a breathtaking geometry unnoticed by machines, but sheer inspiration to the human eye.

below:
Fuse, 1991.
By Reiko Sudo.
This pin-tuck fabric utilizes two independent warp beams with alternating wefts of different colours that distort in fascinating ways.

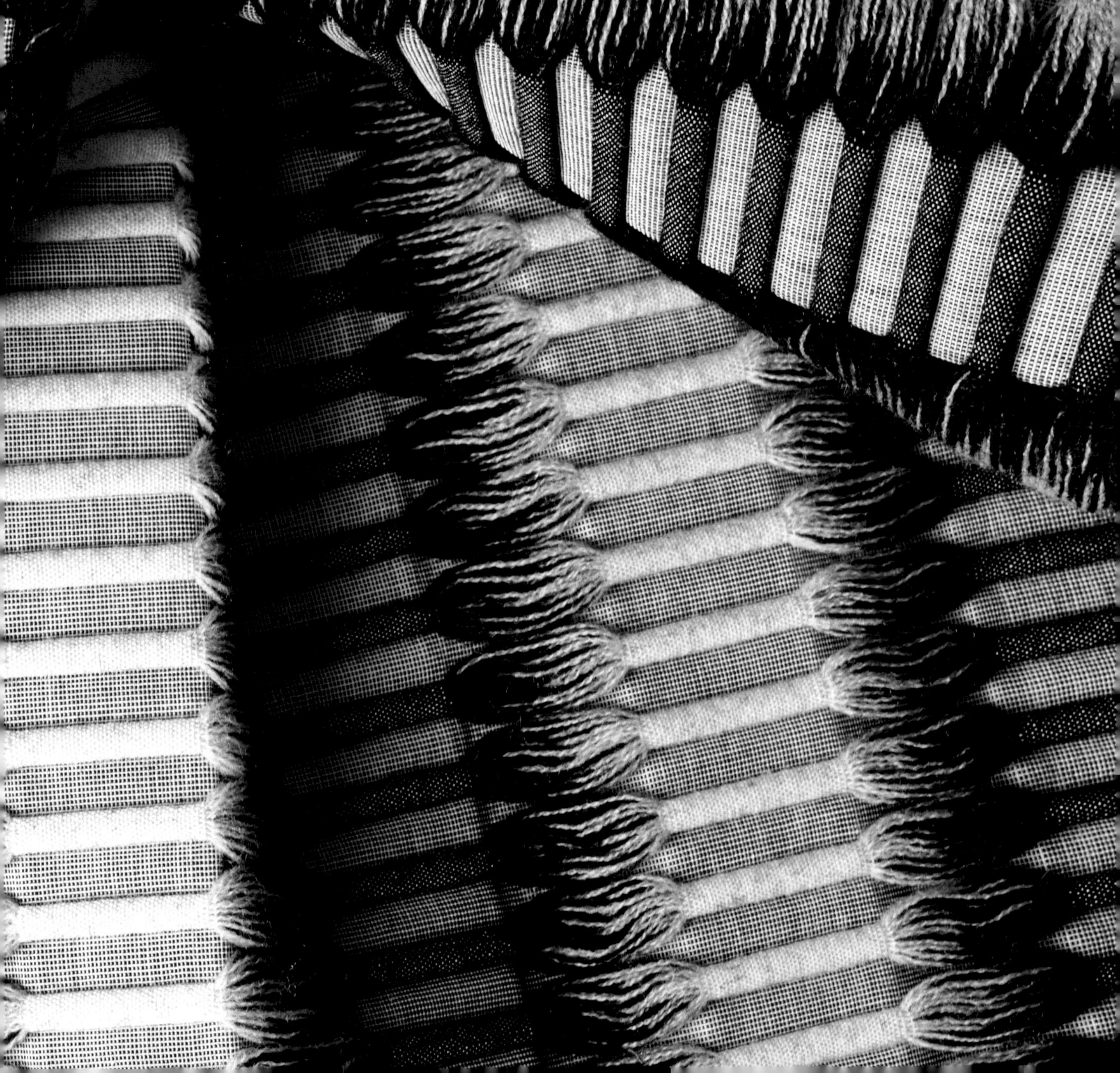

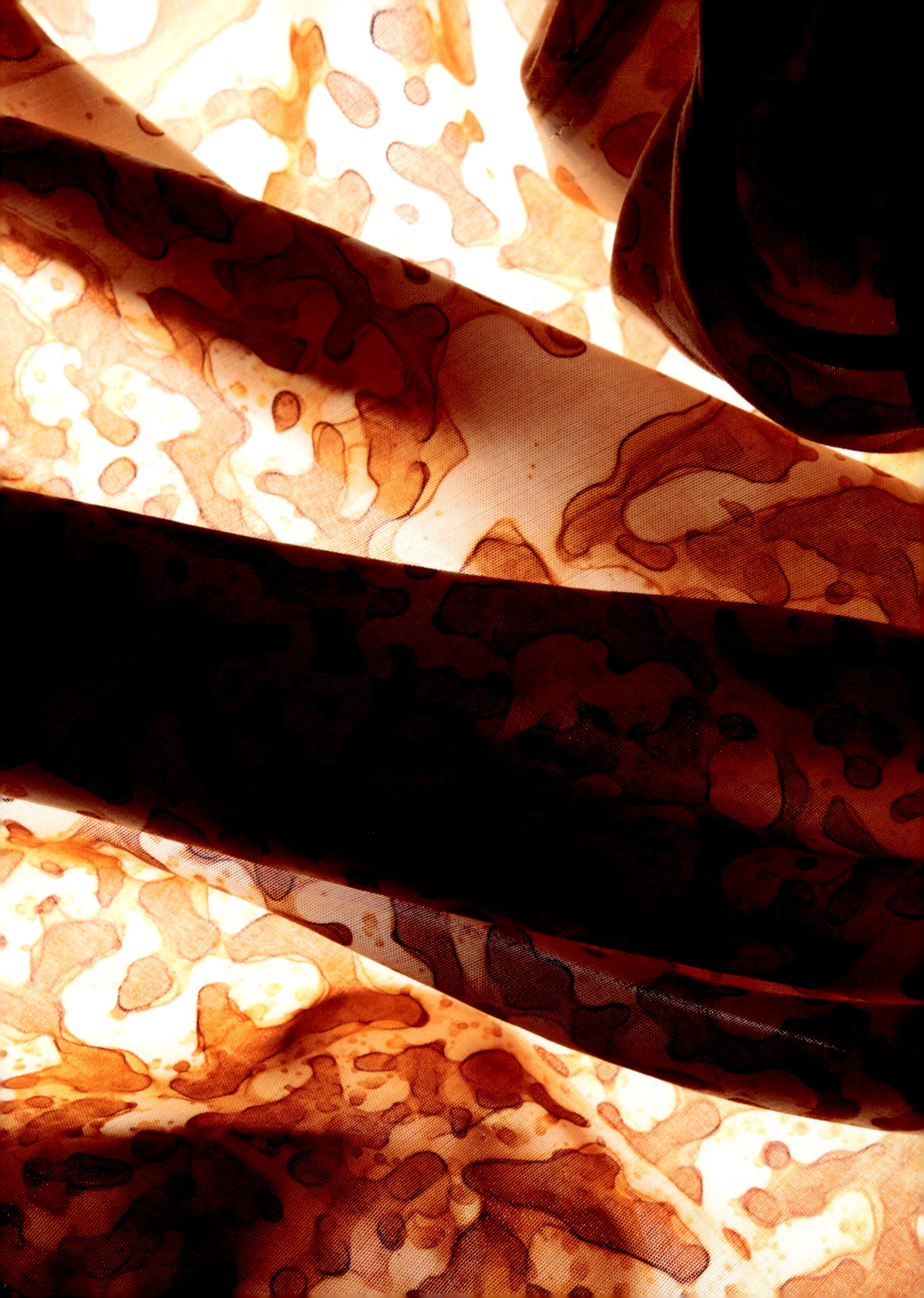

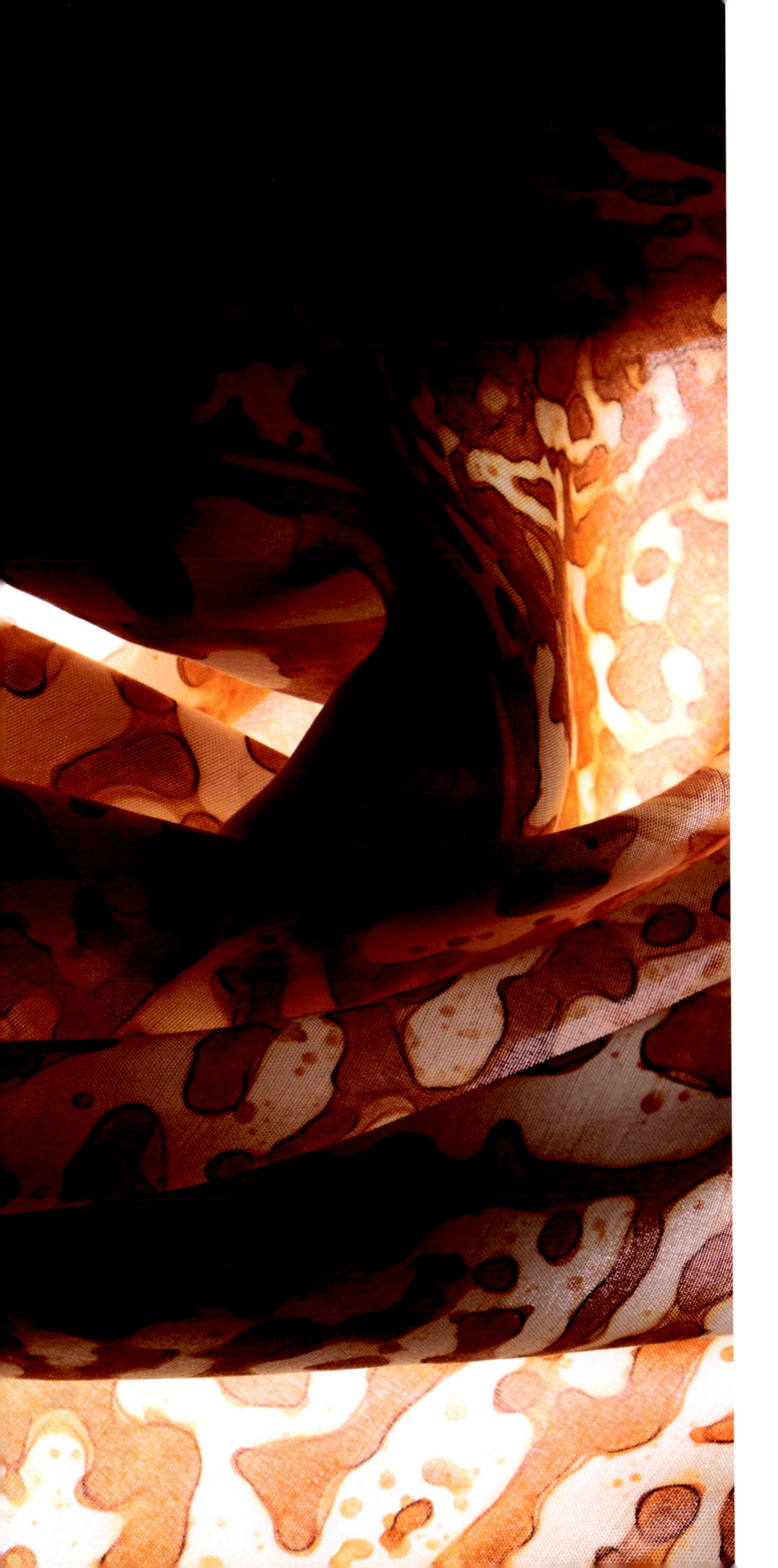

Scrapyard Iron Plates, 1994.
By Reiko Sudo and Hiroko Kobayashi.
Iron oxide – common rust – can create indelible stains, effectively print-dyeing damp fabric. Freeform patterns can be made simply by varying the metal scraps and length of 'weathering' time.

below:
Lath Screen, 2004.
By Reiko Sudo.
A nylon josette balanced with a contrasting soft wool felt in the pattern of the wooden laths in Japanese *shoji* paper screens.

opposite:
Swinging Squares, 2008.
By Reiko Sudo.
The 'chemical lace' technique, used here for collaging embroidered bits, sets loose an array of miniature geometries.

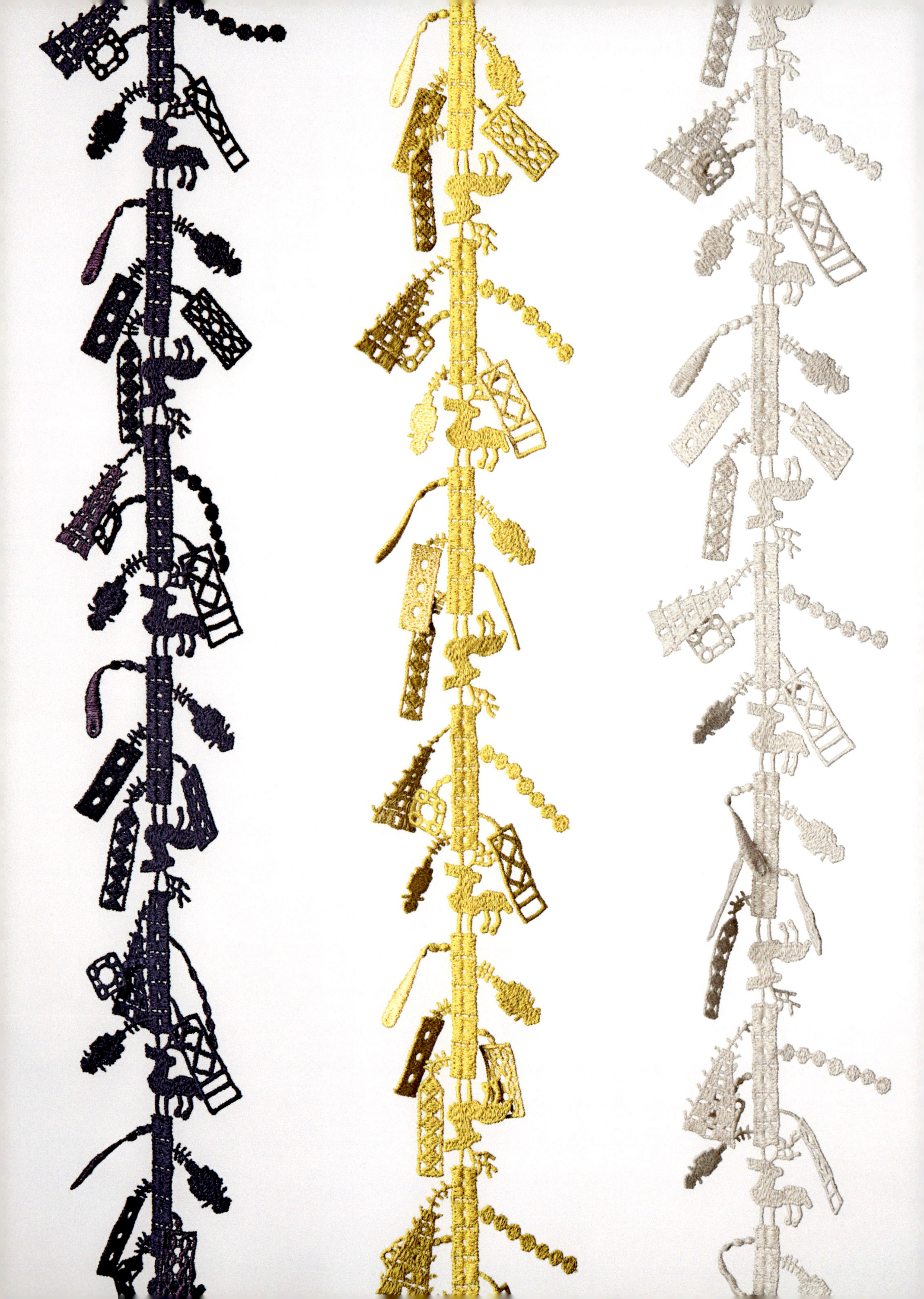

opposite and above:
Stag Horn, 2018.
By Reiko Sudo.
Deer are venerated in Japan as messengers of the gods. Growing new antlers is a symbol of rebirth, so this embroidered deer pattern may bring good luck.

following spread:
Cracked Stripes, 2011.
By Reiko Sudo.
Twill on one side, satin on the other, this thick tri-structured jacquard reveals a third plain-weave middle layer through the cracks.

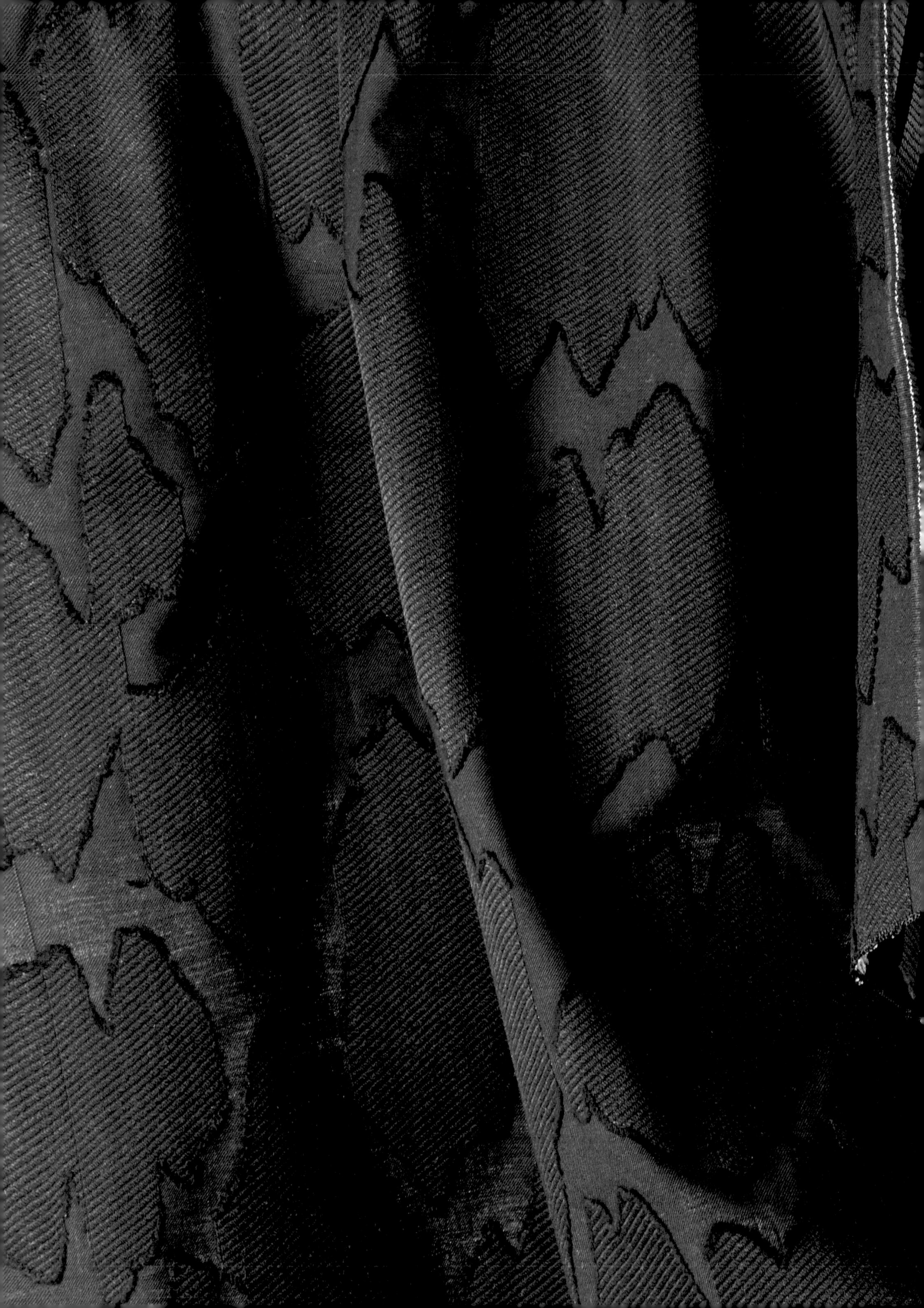

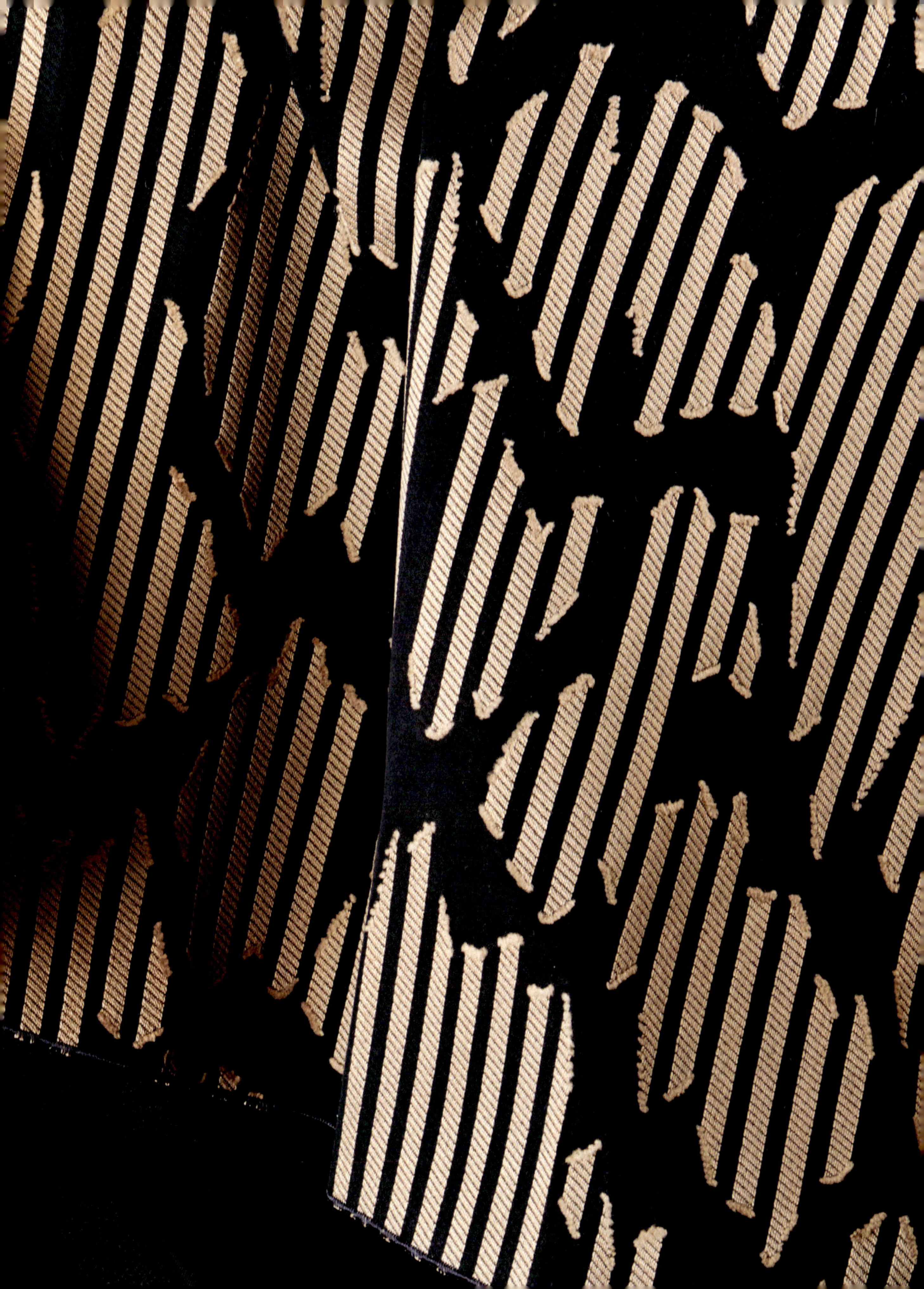

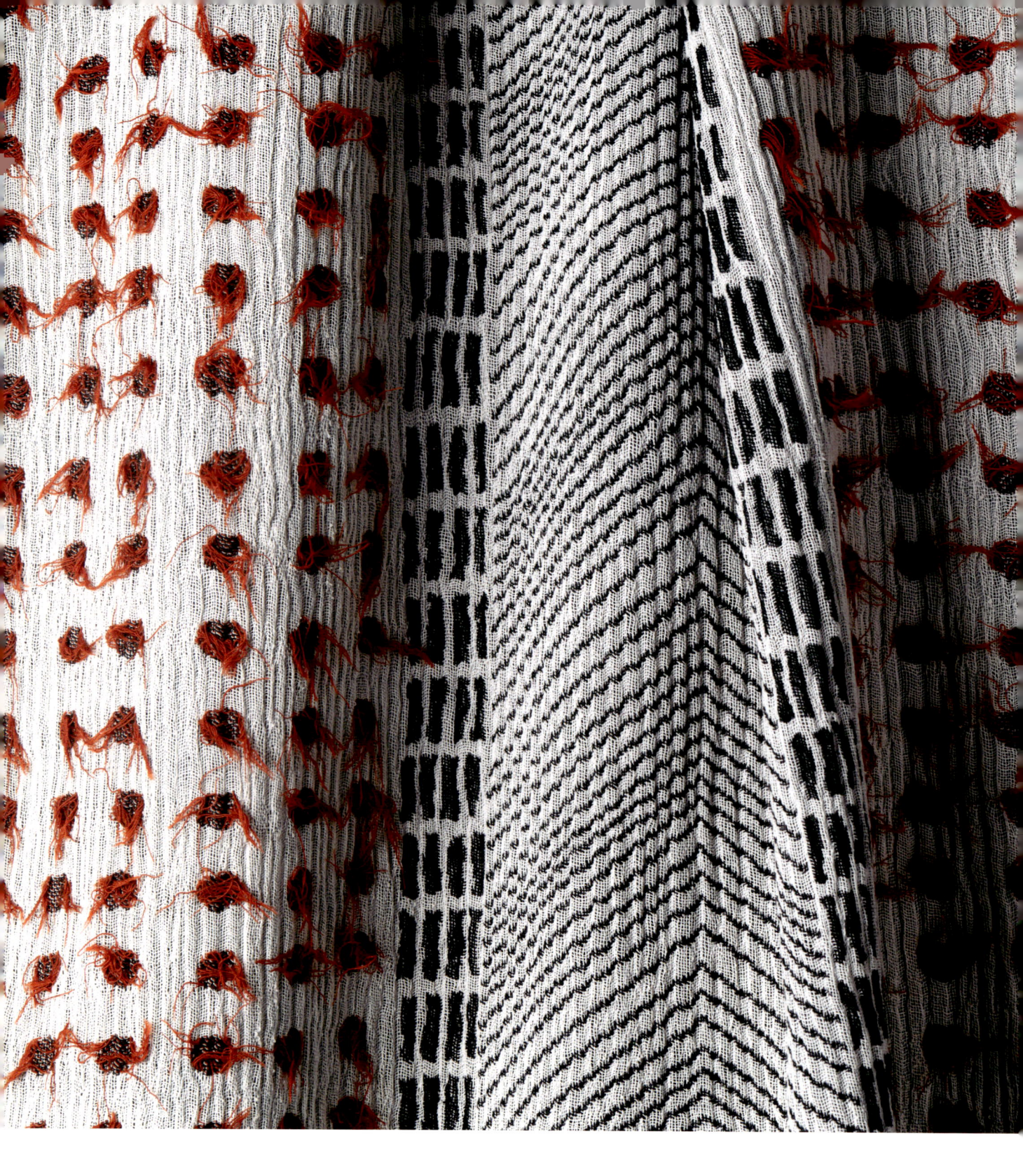

above:
Lentils, 2008.
By Reiko Sudo.
A lentil motif rendered on a narrow-width *obi* sash loom in overspun wool wefts for springy softness.

opposite:
Bean Scatter, 2006.
By Reiko Sudo.
A soft fabric with stretchy warps woven on a narrow-width *kimono* sash loom picks up *azuki* and *kintoki* bean motifs.

following spread:
Fava, 1997.
By Reiko Sudo and Ryoko Sugiura.
A chemical lacework design in wool, inspired by fava beans, or *soramame*, 'sky beans', in Japanese.

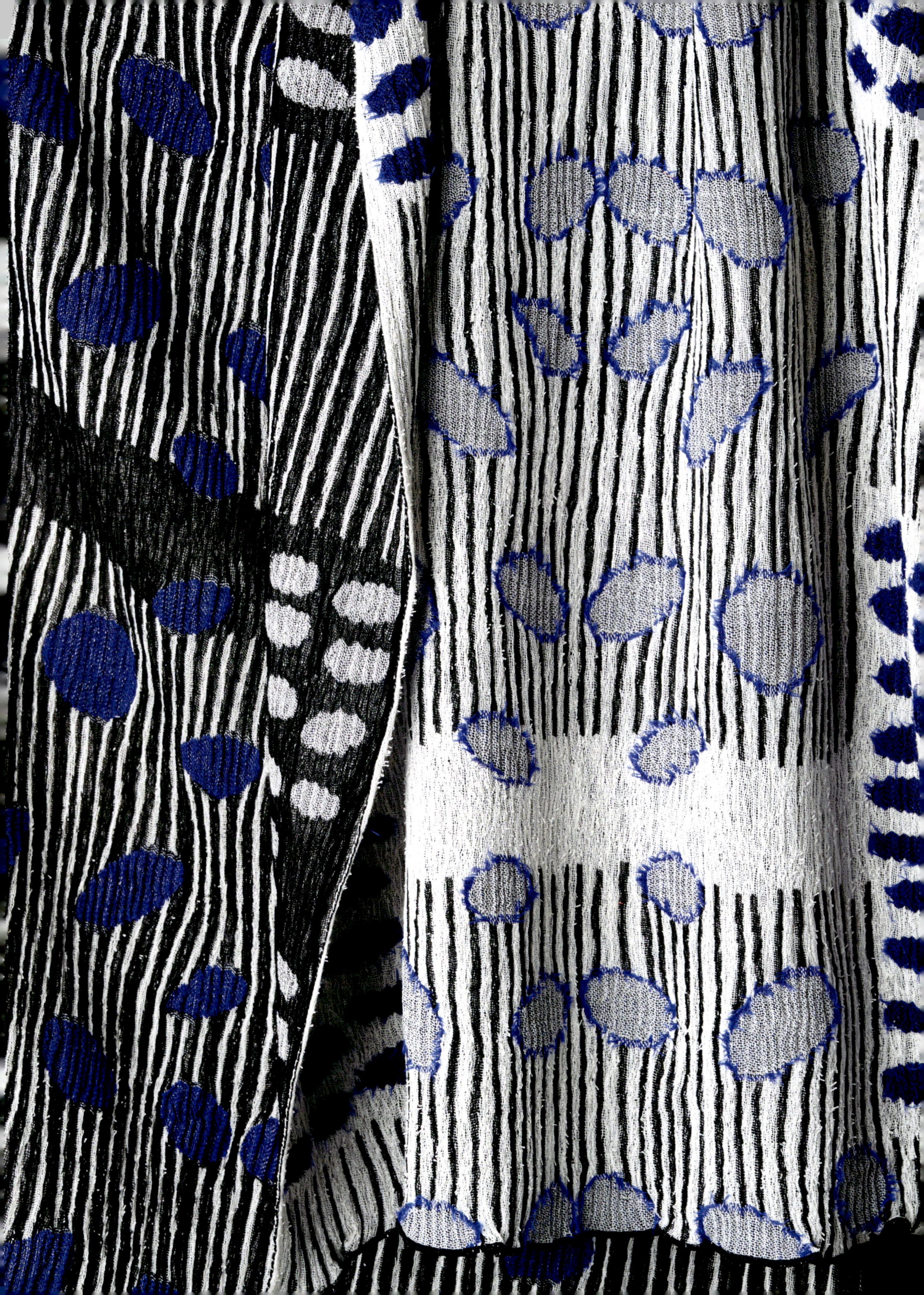

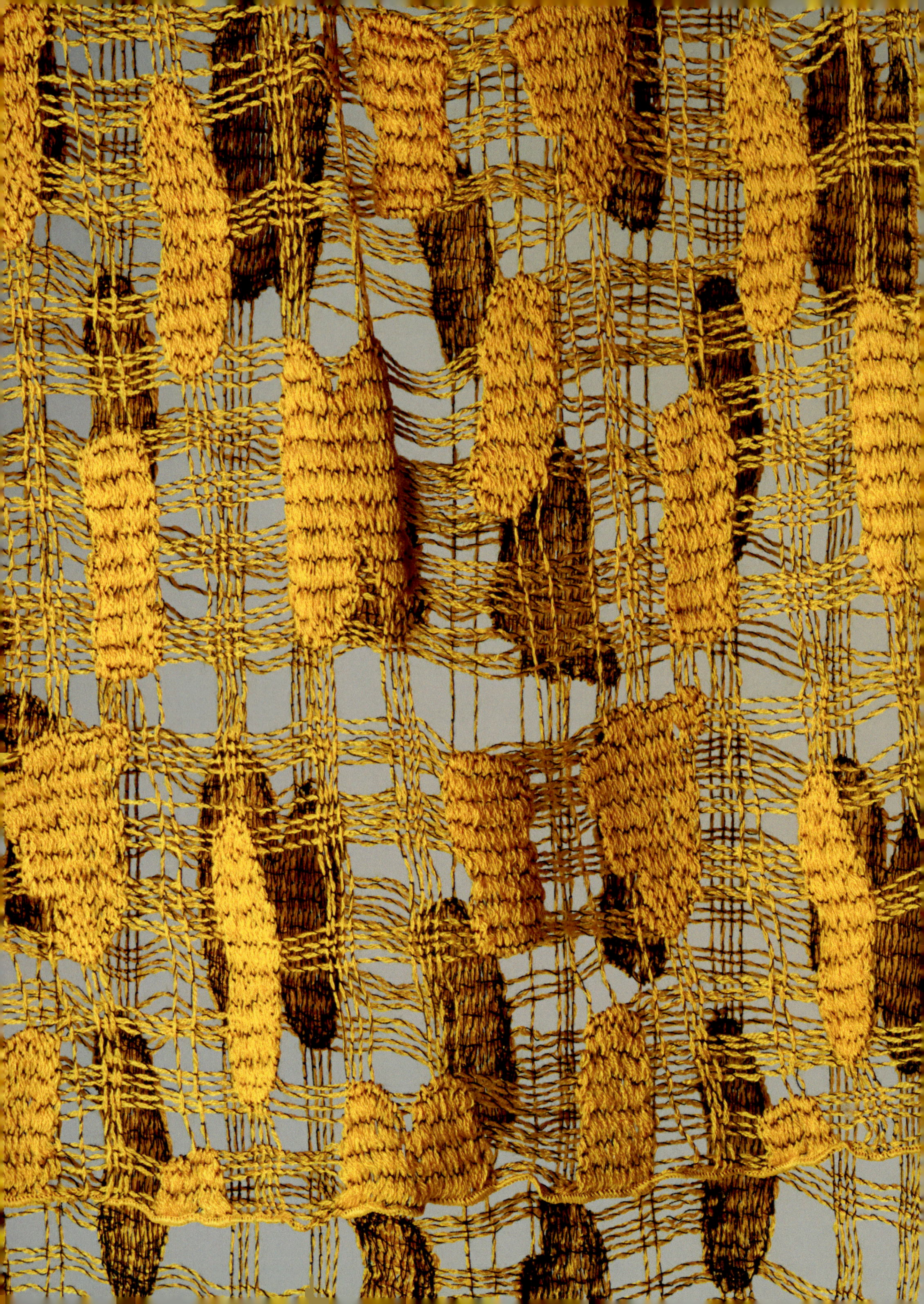

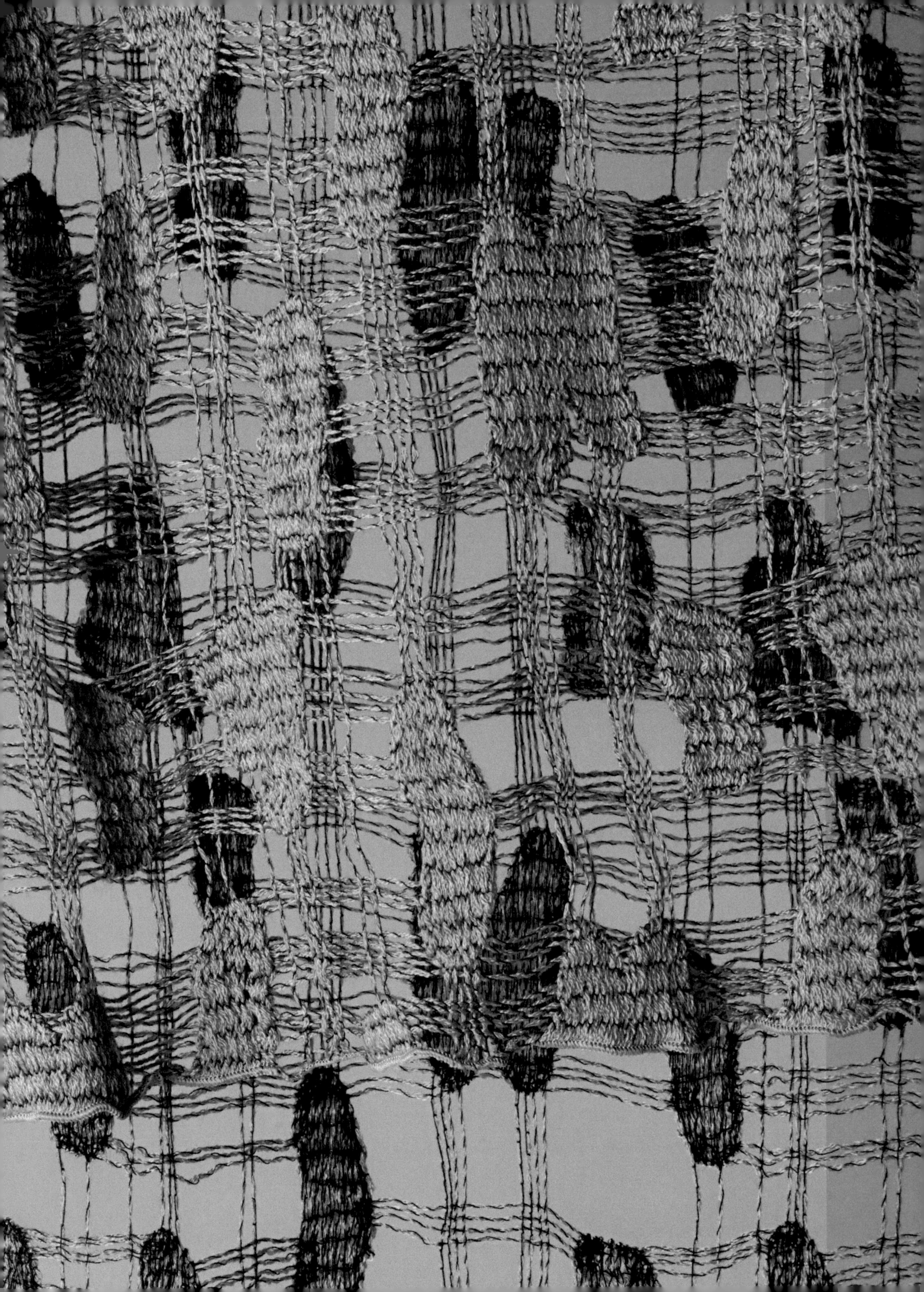

Gouache, 1996.
By Reiko Sudo and Yuka Taniguchi.
A revival of *dobin-zomé* — dyes are poured over wet fabric to create a watercolour effect, then brushed with acid to 'burn out' strokes of pile.

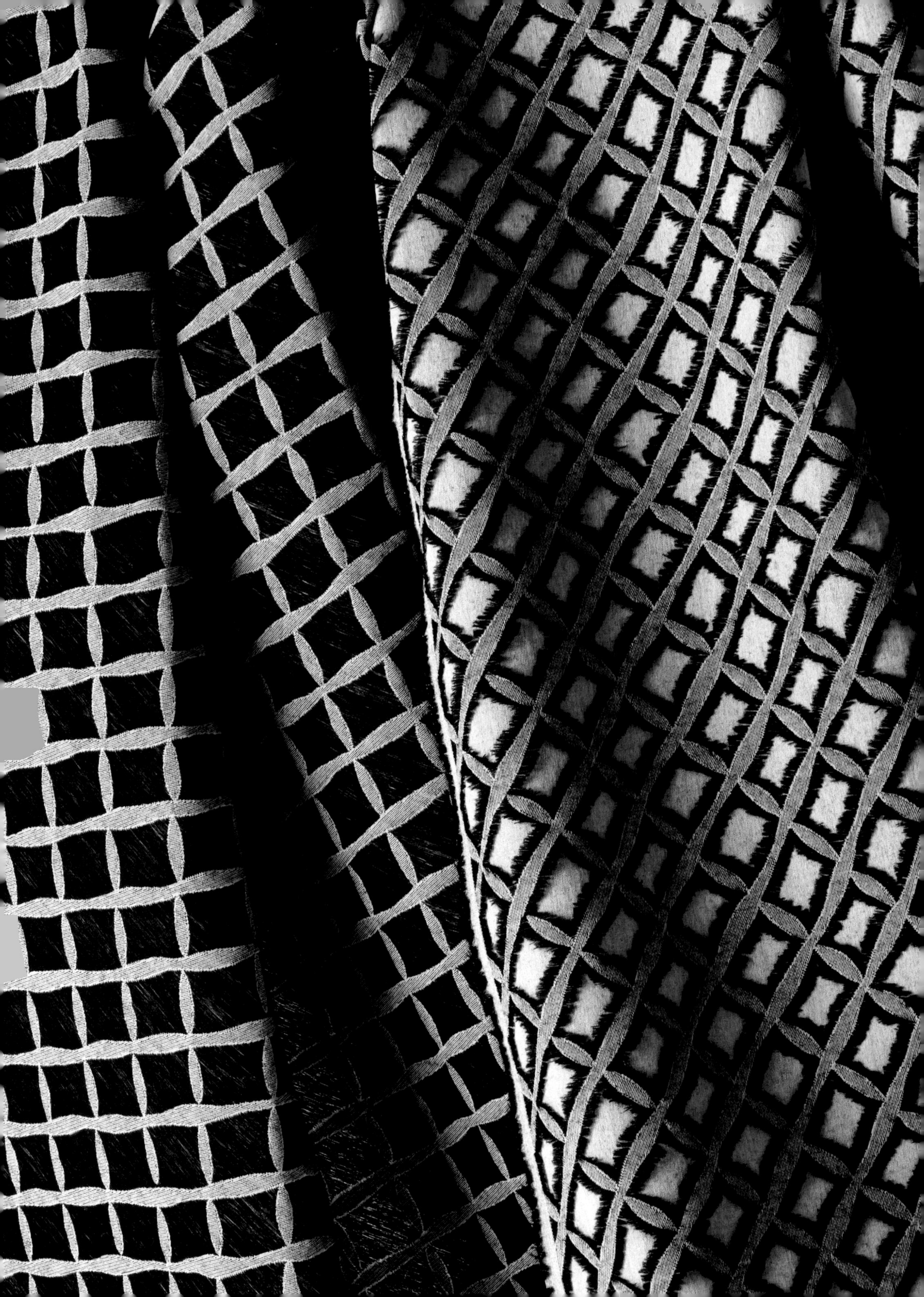

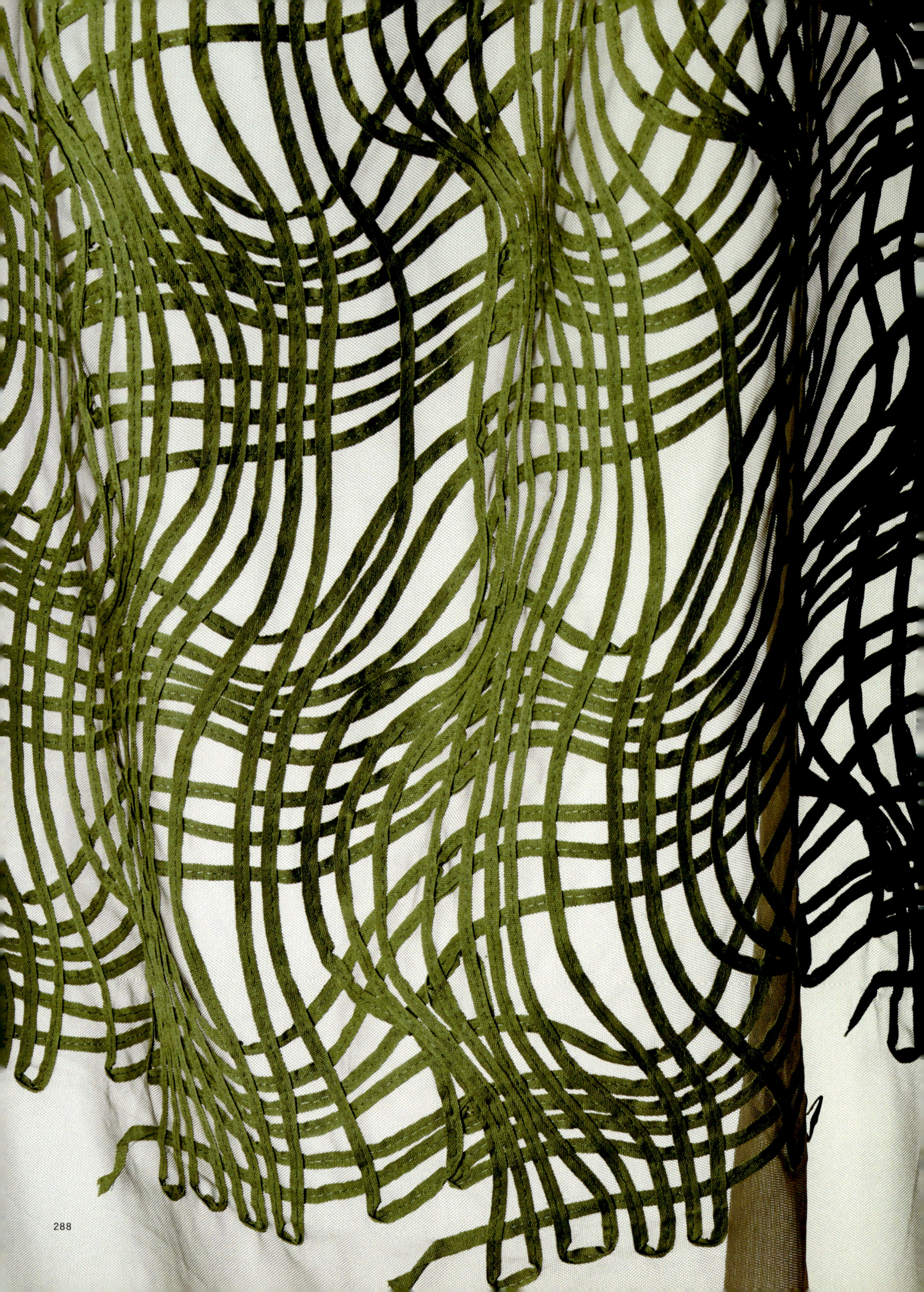

p. 287:
Water Chestnut, 2006.
By Reiko Sudo.
Hand-cut floated wefts
create the diamond shapes
of the water chestnut flower.

on this spread:
Analog Torque, 2003.
By Reiko Sudo.
Computer-drawn curvilinear
stripes are rendered in cord
embroidery using a steering-
wheel embroidery machine
to create a lace-like textile.

Flower Basket, 1997.
By Reiko Sudo and
Yukiko Takahashi.
This 'chemical lace' stitches
down cotton tapes on a
water-soluble base fabric that
is then rinsed away to leave
a flowery openwork pattern.

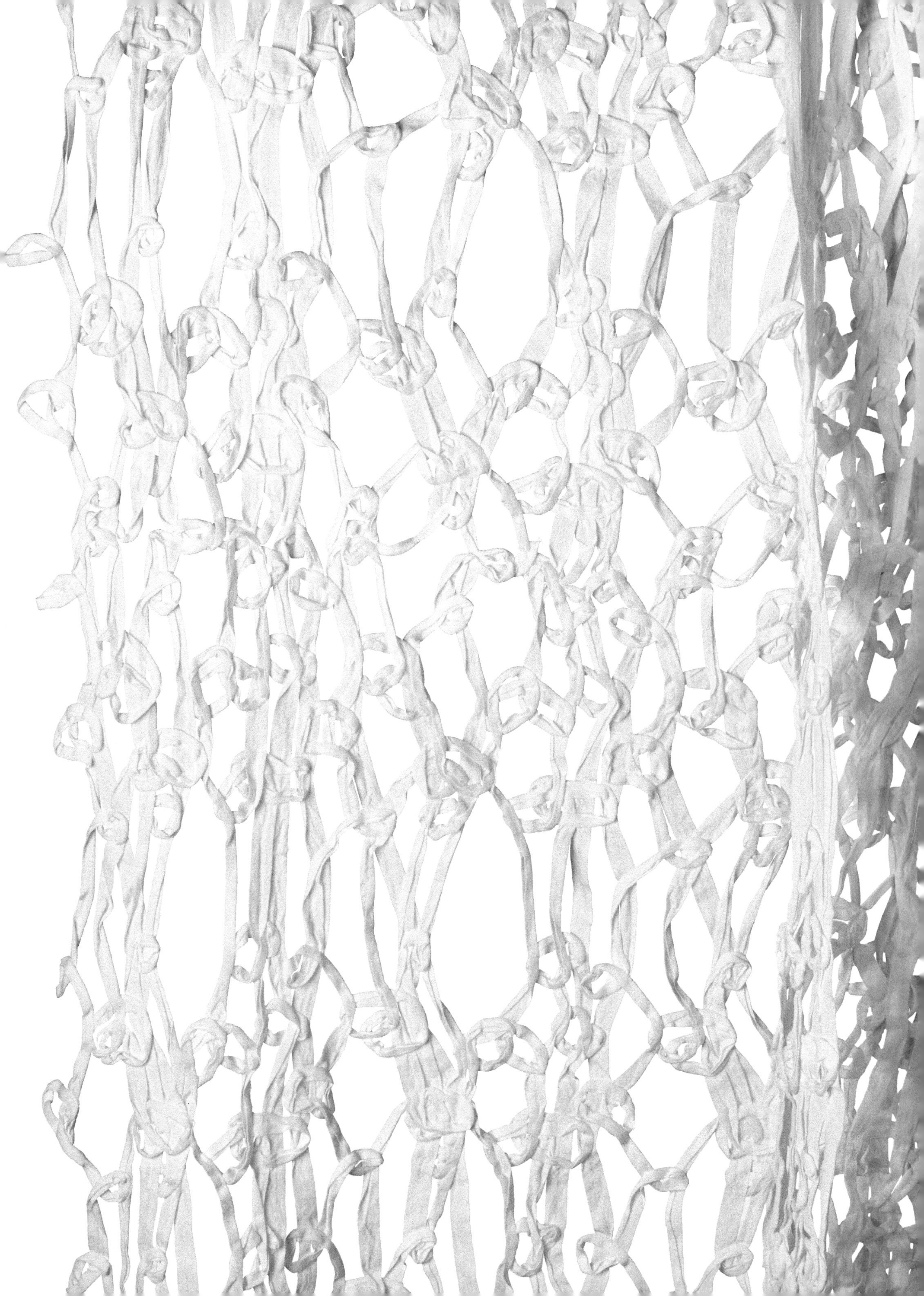

on this spread:
Mongami (Punchcard), 1998.
By Kazuhiro Ueno and
Reiko Sudo.
In homage to the binary
pattern guides used for
jacquard looms, we enlarged
and elongated punch holes
to show more of the colourful
backing on the other side.

following spread:
Heat-moulded Velvet, 1993.
By Reiko Sudo.
Rather than burning the velvet
pile to a uniform length and
calendering to add lustre,
uneven weave patterning to
add random crinkles creates
a crumbly, earthy texture.

293

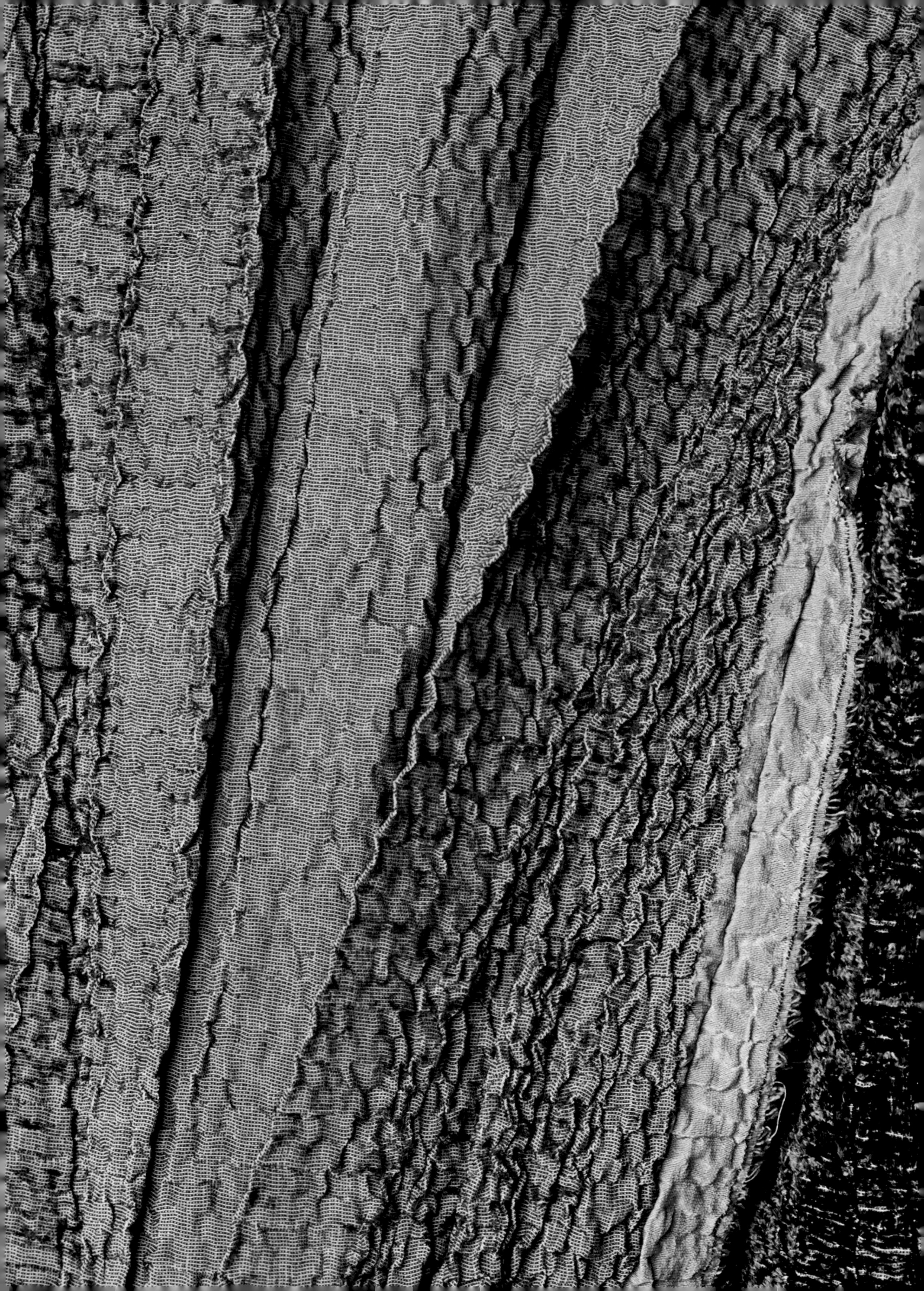

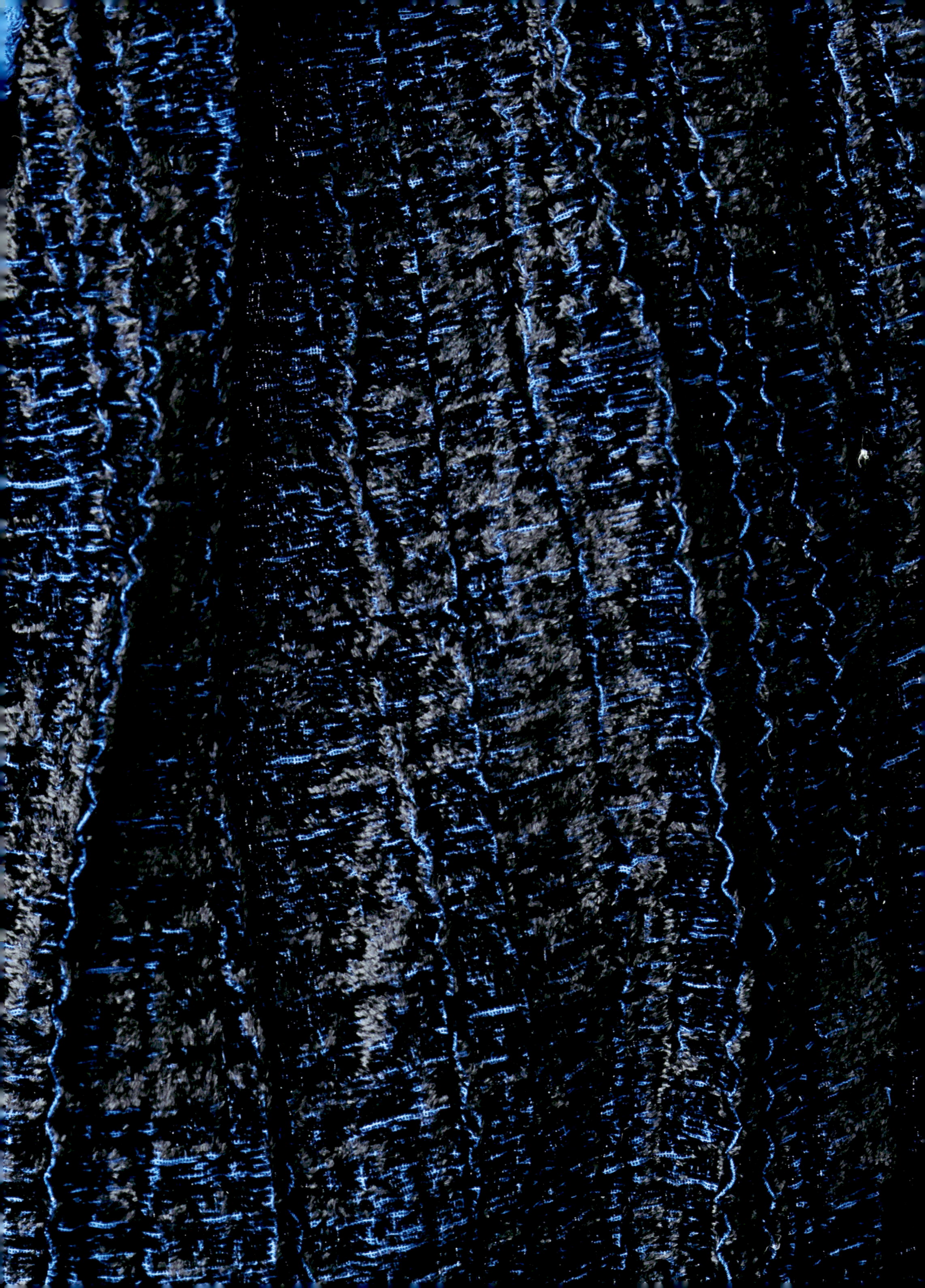

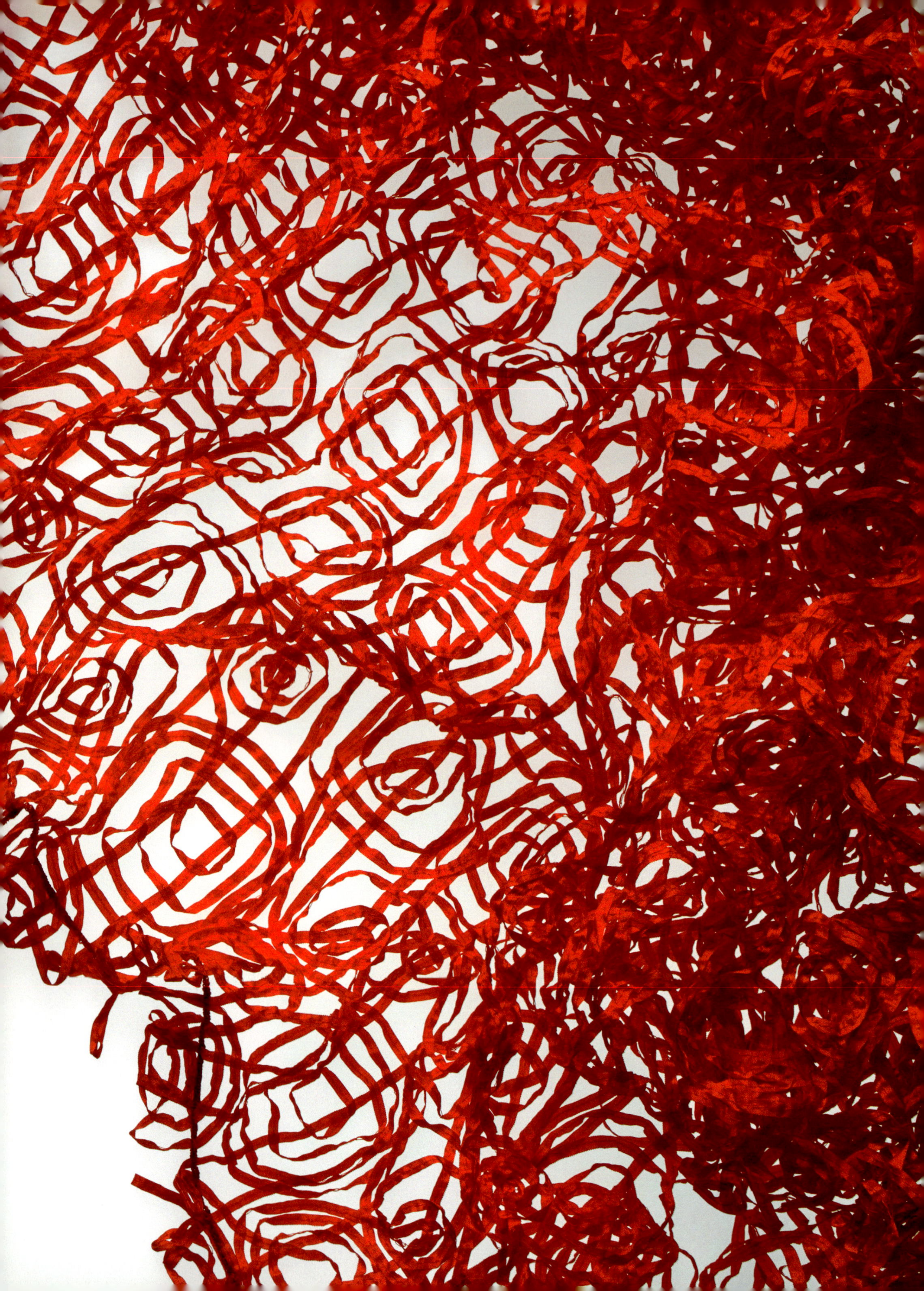

Portrait of a Textile: *Paper Rolls*

How to make a fabric out of springy whorls of paper or rolls of fabric?

Stacked bolts of fabric, the ends tightly rolled, are a wonderful sight. The same goes for deckle-edged rolls of handmade *washi* paper, their uneven spirals alive with coiled energy. But how to make a fabric out of rolled-up paper or cloth? Instead of trying to slice off the roll ends, couldn't we just lay out thin swirls of ribbon? Or stitch down curls of tape? We made several mock-ups, stitching tape onto different backing materials that we then removed, before finally arriving at the so-called 'chemical lace' method. Reputedly invented in Germany in 1883, the original process involved stitching designs onto a silk base that was then dissolved in a lye solution – animal fibres react to alkaline, plant fibres to acid. Today, we use a large steering-wheel embroidery machine to baste ribbon onto a water-soluble base, which is then immersed in water, leaving the lace-like tracery of *Paper Rolls*.

Original design study, 'drawn' in paper strips.

opposite:
Paper Rolls, 2002.
By Reiko Sudo.
Another 'chemical lace', inspired by rolled-up paper viewed in spiral cross-sections.

サワサワ

above
Rolls of *washi* paper served as
an inspiration for *Paper Rolls*.

opposite
Sketch of *washi* paper rolls.

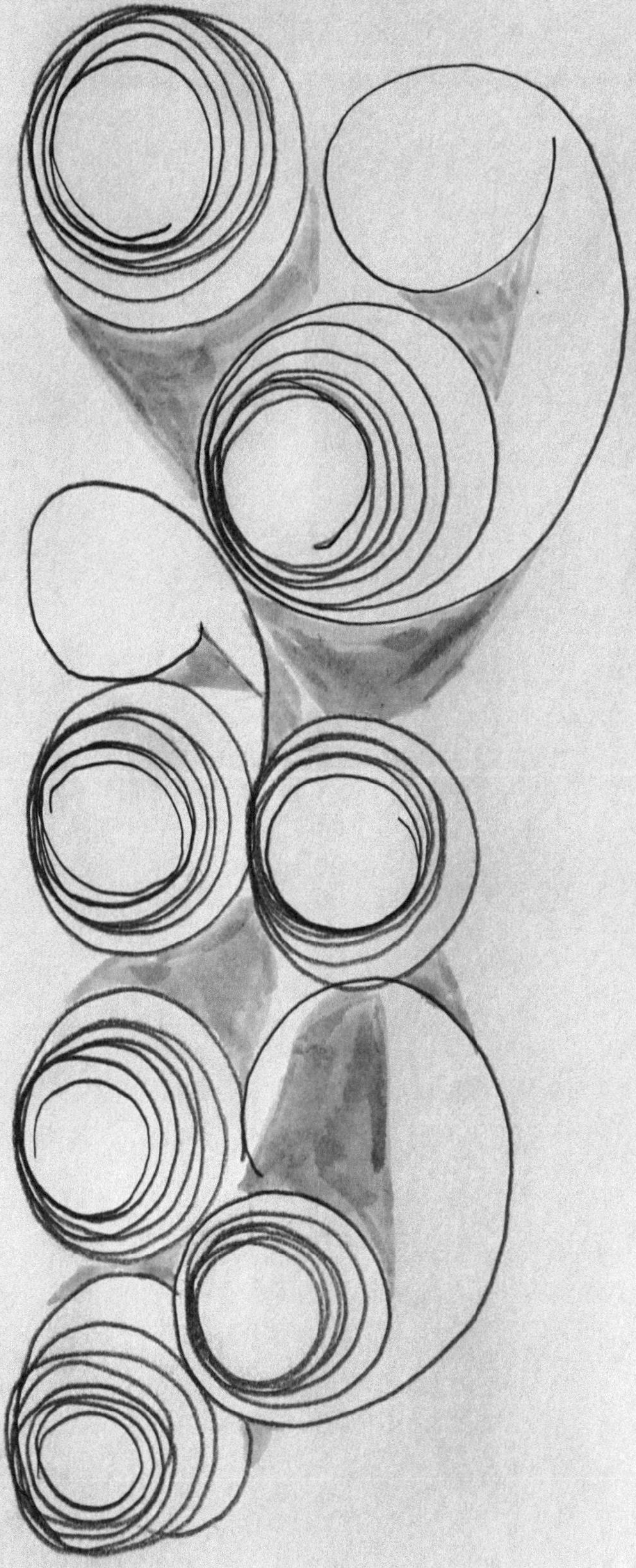

ザワザワ

above
Felt marker sketches of the rolls.

below, left to right
Paper bobbin wound with recycled nylon; plastic embroidery bobbin; under-thread metal bobbin.

Freehand embroidery

A long history of weaving with thinly sliced strips of metal foil affixed to *washi* paper led to today's slit-yarn techniques. Now we can easily slit many different materials besides paper and metal for use in weaving and embroidery. We can even recycle fabrics damaged in weaving for use as slit yarns.

left
A collection of ribbons in different materials and widths.

below left
Limestone is the raw ingredient for water-soluble fabric.

below right
Water-soluble fabric before it is stitched to the whorls of ribbon.

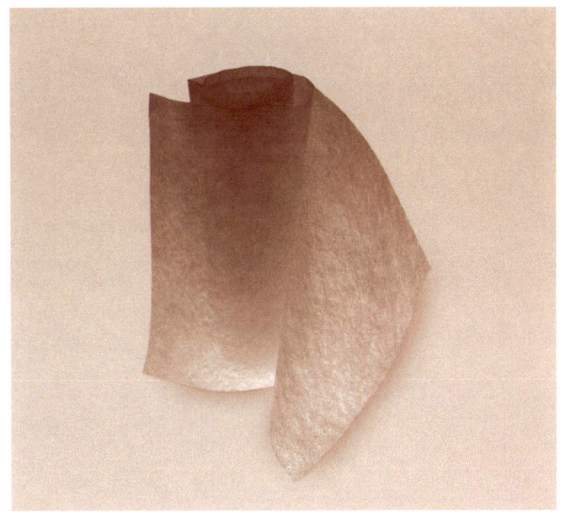

ザワザワ

above
Felt marker sketch on
a design idea sheet.

opposite
A production test of water-
soluble fabric stitched
with ribbon.

ZAWA ZAWA

ザワザワ

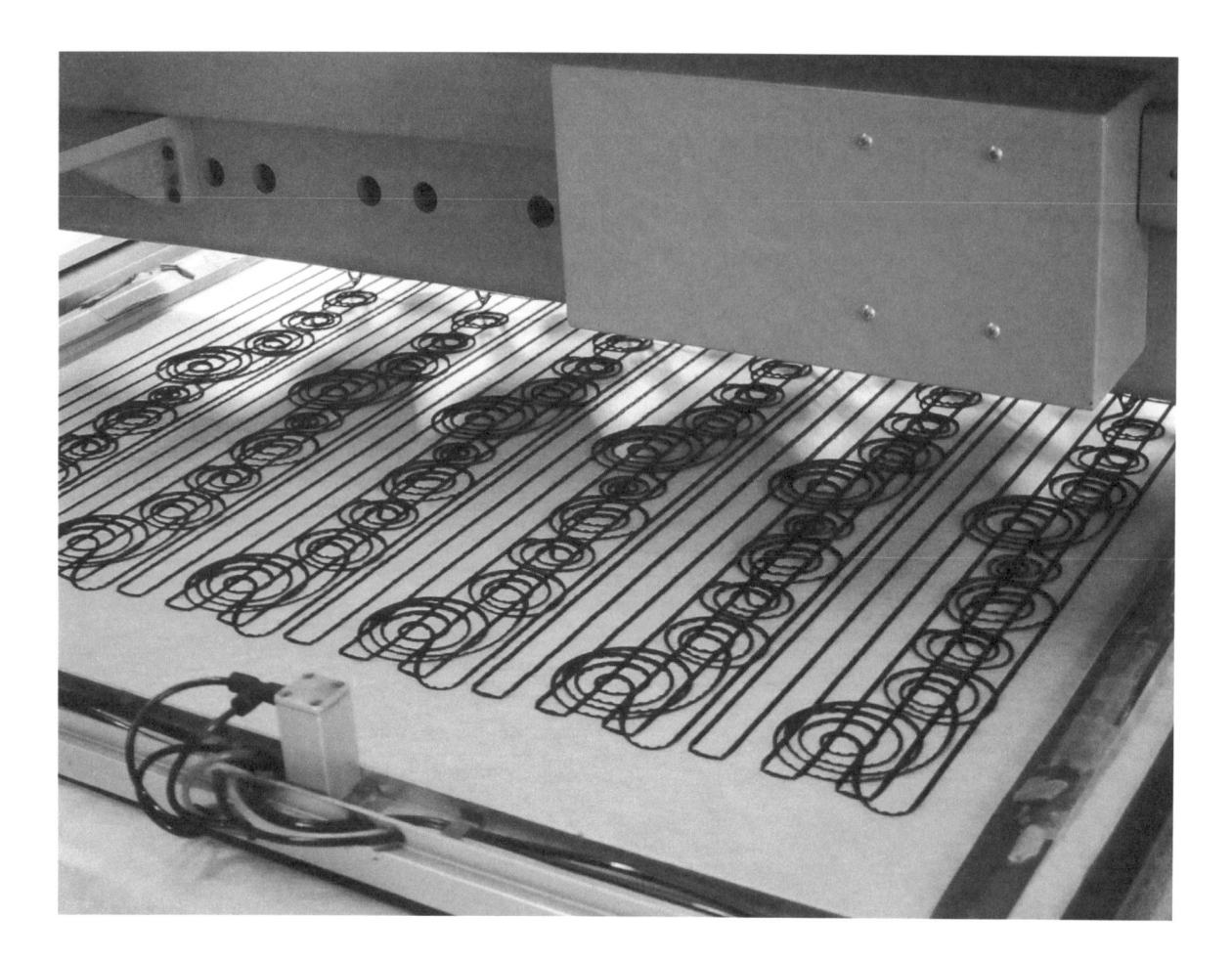

opposite top and above
Stitching recycled nylon tape onto water-soluble fabric using an embroidery machine.

opposite bottom
Paper Rolls before the base fabric is dissolved in water.

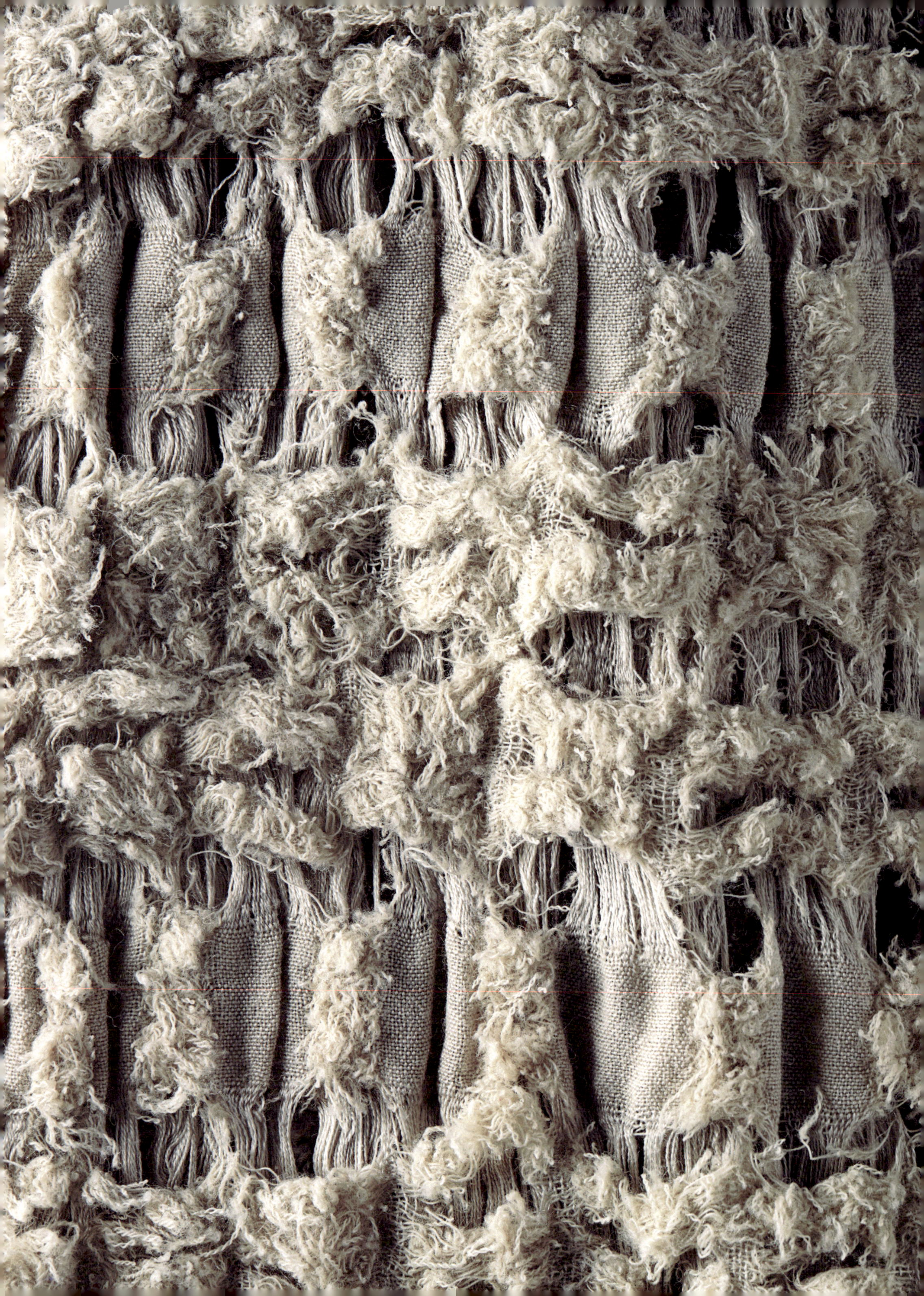

BORO
BORO

boro boro (ボロボロ)

1. Ragged, tattered, worn-out, dilapidated
2. In rags, in tatters, in shreds, in ribbons
3. Crumbly, brittle, fragile
4. Falling (reduced) to pieces, worn to rags (a frazzle), frayed (at the edges)

Cruel and unusual treatment of textiles

The textiles included under *boro boro* have been roasted over burners, dissolved with acid, boiled and stewed, ripped with blades and pulled apart. Whatever did these innocent fabrics do to deserve this rough handling? It's not that they're bad as woven, but rather that stresses and hardships bring out character in even inanimate materials. Mistreatment is not an end in itself (we are not textile sadists), but as anyone who has a favourite old shirt knows, there's an exquisiteness to clothes worn just-so. From riches to rags – and back again.

    Our initial inspiration in creating these *boro boro* fabrics was to emulate the faded glory of things as they age. We only resorted to cruel and unusual means because we couldn't wait for entropy to take effect. We've compressed time from the very beginning by means of purposeful decay, which may involve beating or singeing or tearing or melting. We've burnt-out and felted years of wear and tear into new cloth. We've affixed bits of newsprint and shredded remnants to imprint the past onto the present. Like threadbare heirlooms you just can't throw away, NUNO's *boro boro* textiles tug at our hearts with a mysterious emotional warmth.

p. 306:
Spanish Moss, 1994.
By Reiko Sudo.
Silk warps combine with overspun wool wefts in a complex weave structure. Wefts are then selectively plucked to render a thick 'foliage' of warp fronds.

right:
Website, 1995.
By Reiko Sudo.
Felting adds thickness and fluffiness to wool. The original material here had tightly twisted wool threads woven into a wide mesh, then repeatedly felted down to a quarter of its size.

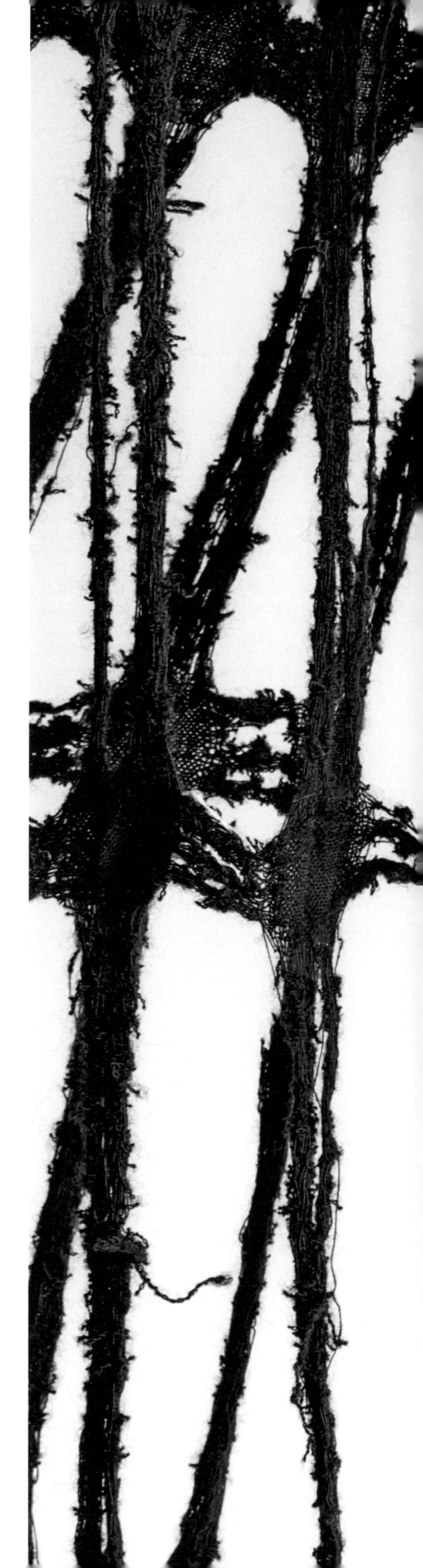

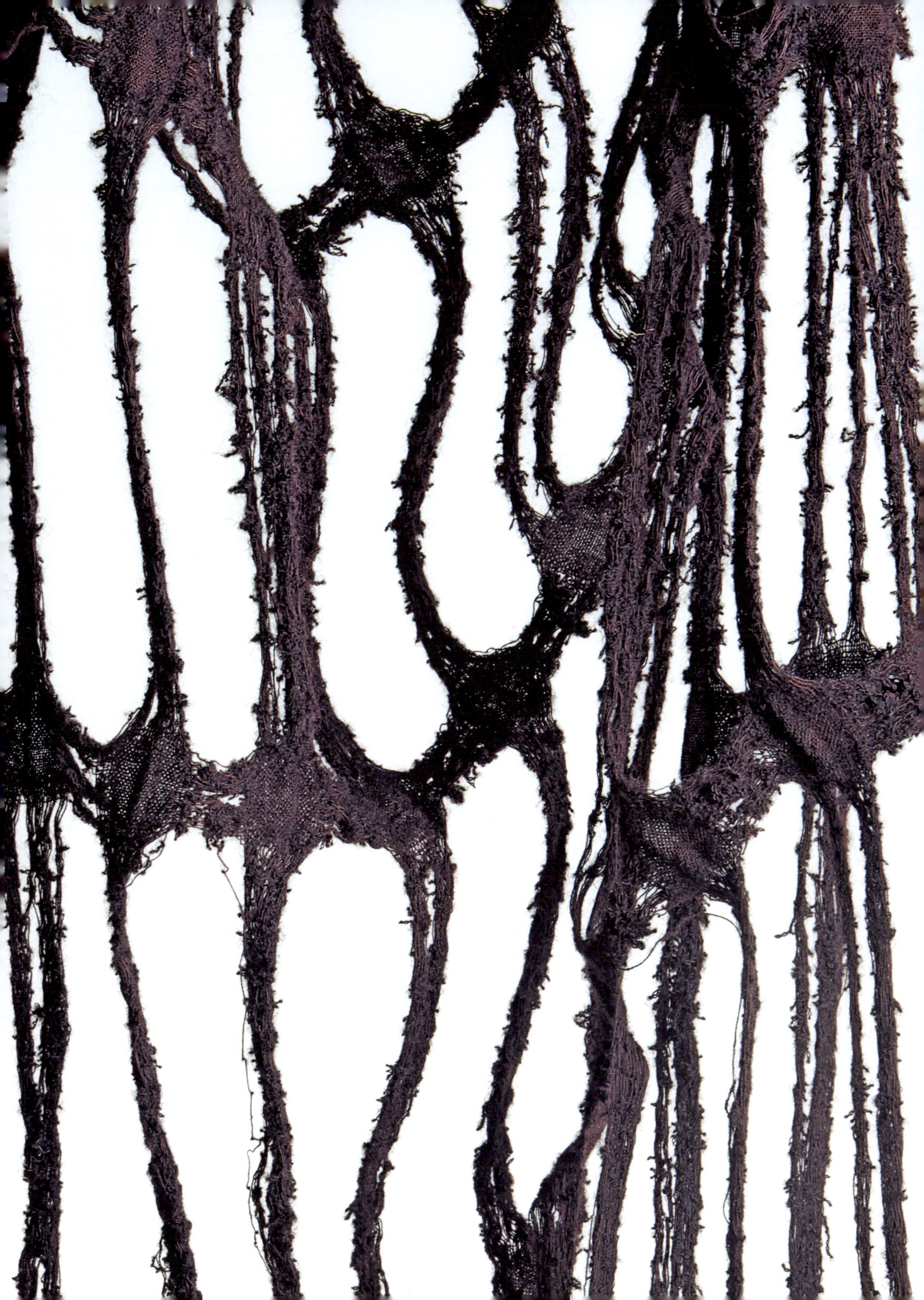

Boro Boro

Anna Jackson

A layered landscape of indigo shades and subtle hues of grey, brown and black, traversed by horizontal, vertical and diagonal stitches. A textured surface that suggests unfathomable depth and a weight that is both visual and literal. A fabric that speaks of simplicity, yet is multifaceted; of austerity, yet is rich.

This distinctive style of Japanese cloth is called *boro*, literally 'rags', often pieced together, patched and reinforced with recycled pieces of fabric. When repeated, *boro boro* means 'tattered', 'ragged', 'crumbling', or 'worn-out'. During the Edo period (1603–1868), the sophisticated silks for which Japan is justly famed were reserved for the wealthy elite, while the majority of Japanese wore plain, striped or simply patterned cottons or bast fibres such as *asa* (hemp) or *fuji* (wisteria). For the poorest in society, particularly those living in rural areas, the fundamental need for warmth and protection meant that every textile, every piece of cloth or clothing, was a highly valued and treasured possession that would be endlessly repaired and re-stitched. This was especially the case in the northeastern region of Tōhoku, where cotton could not be cultivated, although scraps of this warm, soft fabric were salvaged and traded. Clothes and domestic textiles, such as bedding covers, would be repeatedly mended and transformed, creating layered patchworks instilled with a family history that could traverse a number of generations. Reconstituted and revitalized, *boro* textiles convey a compelling story of survival and ingenuity. They reflect the meeting of utilitarian requirement and decorative instinct, and reveal the creative tension between the planned and the spontaneous.

It is important to remember that *boro* textiles were born of necessity rather than philosophy. Yet they have come to exemplify certain key principles of Japanese ethics and aesthetics, such as *mottainai*, the regret over anything wasted; *shibui*, the favouring of subtle, modest beauty; and especially the admiration for imperfection and transience expressed in the aesthetics of *wabi* and *sabi*. *Wabi* initially signified poverty, but evolved to embody an appreciation of rustic simplicity, natural imperfection, understated elegance and humility. *Sabi* originally referred to loneliness or sorrow, but came to signify the beauty or serenity that comes with age, and the impermanence that is shown in patina, wear and repairs.

In the twentieth century, as living standards improved, the Japanese shunned *boro* textiles for new clothes and domestic items. With no pride to be had in an impoverished past, *boro* was viewed negatively and little was done to preserve such pieces. That examples have survived at all is due to serendipity and the efforts of a few folklorists. More recently, *boro* textiles have been rediscovered and become a subject of study, appreciation, acquisition and exhibition. As always with cultural artefacts, meanings change over time. The local nexus of social, economic and artistic needs that led to the creation of these textiles has been replaced by the global connections of curators and collectors. *Boro* is the ultimate rags-to-riches tale. Objects of utility, of poverty, have been appropriated as art and now fetch often incredible prices.

It is not hard to understand the appeal of *boro* textiles. Their visual abstraction gives them a universal quality that chimes with modern sensibilities, while our haptic perceptions are aroused by the obvious variety of their textured surfaces. Most compelling of all, perhaps, is the fact that these textiles are palpably imbued with the very personal history of their creation and use. We are acutely conscious of the time taken and the concentration expended, the movement of the needles and the gestures of the women who worked and re-worked these textiles. Through their worn sleeves and frayed edges, we also perceive the presence of those who used and wore these pieces, whose lives permeate their patchwork surfaces. It is their arresting beauty and particular intimacy that enables us to respond to *boro* in a very imme-

It is important to remember that boro *textiles were born of necessity rather than philosophy. Yet they have come to exemplify certain key principles of Japanese ethics and aesthetics.*

diate way. At a time of growing environmental and social responsibility, these textiles speak to us ever more forcefully. As we increasingly reject a culture of fast, superficial and unrestrained consumption, these works seem to stand as exemplars in the search for models of slow, sincere sustainability.

The legacy of *boro* first appeared in the pioneering work of Japanese designers such as Rei Kawakubo and Yohji Yamamoto, whose assemblage approach to design and interest in imperfection proved such a shocking antithesis to dominant, polished fashion conventions when their collections were launched in Paris in the 1980s. 'Deconstruction' is now a recognized fashion style, marked by the use of exposed seams, raw edges, holes and shreds. However, the production of these items is not always based on efforts of preservation, nor does it often involve recycling.

Both the aesthetic and ethic resonance of *boro* is more directly and consciously reaffirmed in the creative practices and productions of NUNO. In pushing the boundaries of what can be achieved in the making of textiles, NUNO also blurs them; the usual divisions between historic traditions and advanced technology have little meaning. For Reiko Sudo, her colleagues and collaborators, it is the transformative process that is most powerful.

ボロボロ

As in *boro*, the resulting textiles are frequently multilayered, tufted, nubbled, irregular. They are complex but never complicated, intricate but never ornate. The actions of the weavers and dyers are made apparent yet remain enigmatic.

For the environmentally conscious Sudo, *boro* cloth is echoed in more than mere appearance. Sustainability is a key issue, both in terms of supporting the many small textile workshops across Japan with whom NUNO works, and in ensuring that nothing is wasted in the production process. NUNO has long made use of leftover scraps, such as in the delicate, multicoloured *Kasane* ('layering') and the puzzle-like cotton and linen collage of *Tsunagi* ('patching or cobbling together'). Damaged or rejected fabrics are also repurposed in diverse ways, while the creative possibilities offered by other waste materials, such as the feathers left over by poultry farming, are also harnessed. Since 2008, NUNO has been involved in a major project exploring the use of *kibiso*, the tough outer surface of silkworm cocoons, which is normally discarded. The *kibiso* fibre has been refined down to a thickness that allows it to be worked on a machine loom, resulting in a new line of fabrics such as *Hairline* and *Not Knots* with normal silk warps and *kibiso* wefts. All of these endeavours have resulted in extraordinarily varied textile landscapes that are both visually unexpected and inviting of touch.

Japan's textile artistry has always evolved through a combination of respect for the past and passion for the future. Today, this is exemplified by the work of NUNO. Reiko Sudo's appreciation and understanding of historic *boro* has been supplemented and enhanced by the characteristics that make her company such a textile trailblazer: imagination, innovation and ingenuity.

Edgeweiss, 1996.
By Reiko Sudo.
A jacquard overspun cotton weave with float weave wefts that make a striped pattern when cut.

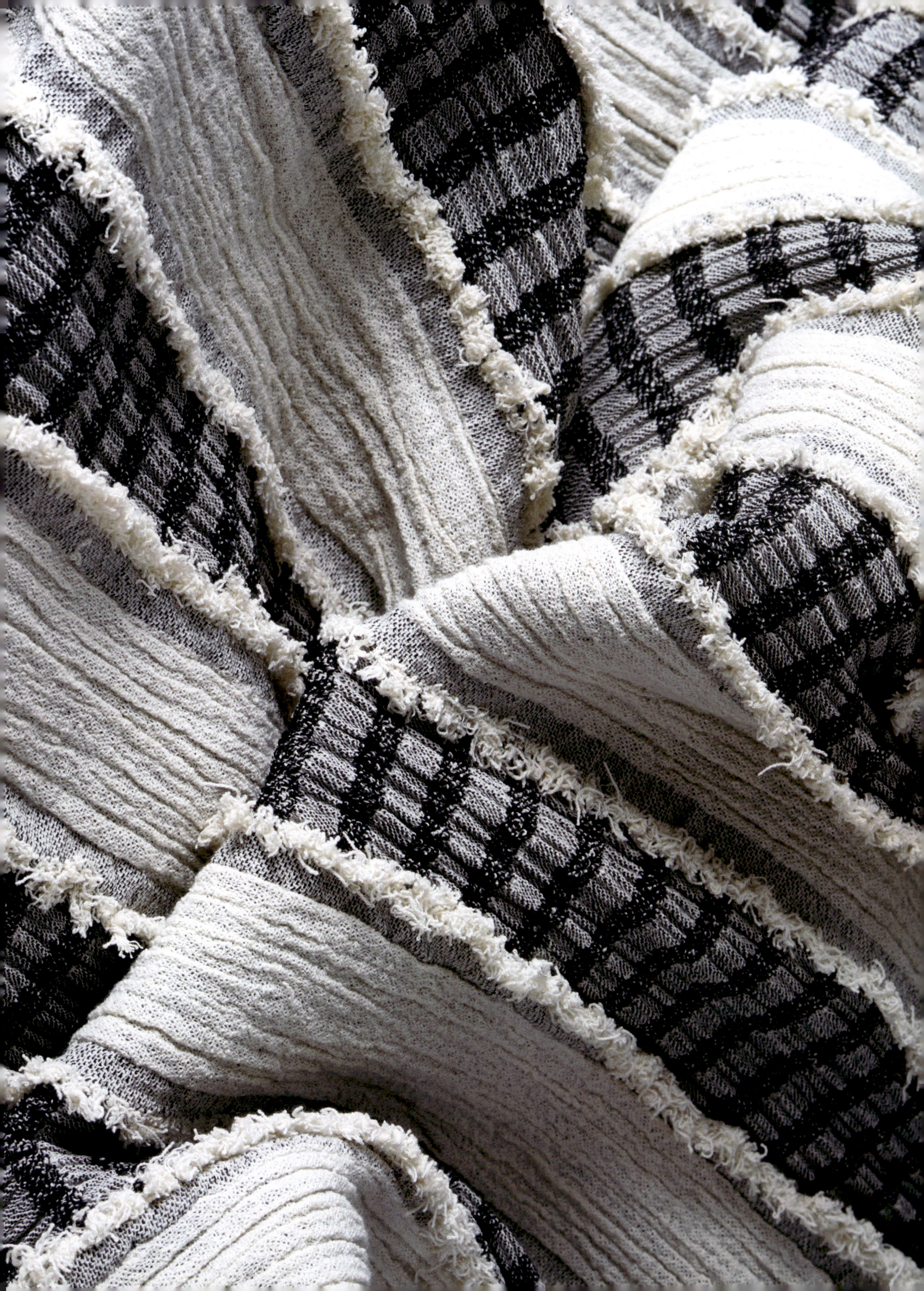

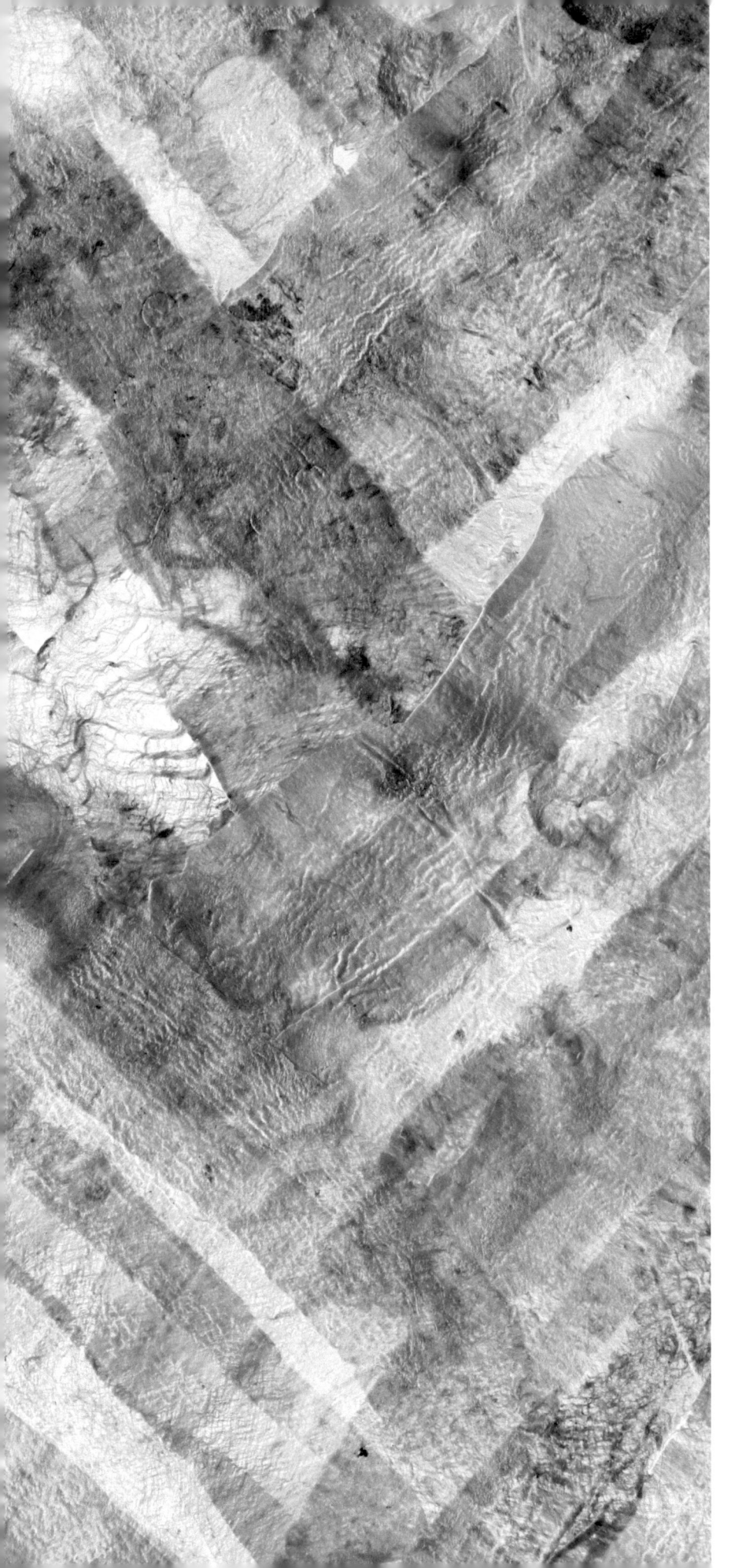

Ogarami-choshi Panel, 2015.
By Reiko Sudo.
One silk cocoon yields 1,300 metres of thread. The last sticky bit, called *ogarami-choshi*, can be peeled off in small flakes that we lay out by hand like a mosaic.

Deep Roots (Stainless Burner Dye), 2000. By Reiko Sudo. Eight-micron stainless-steel fibres for radial tyres are spun into thread with a water-soluble coating, knitted, then finally flamed with a burner.

BORO BORO

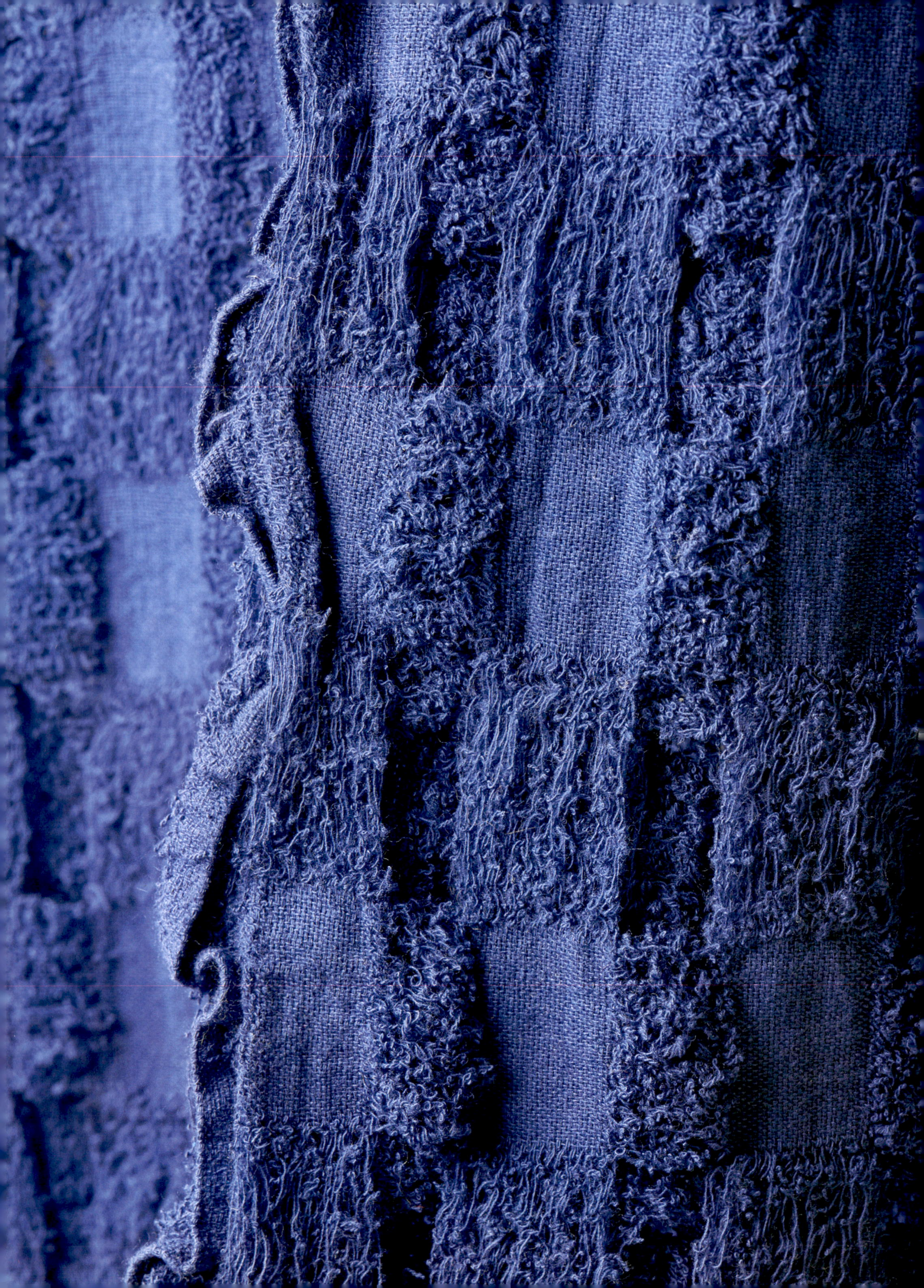

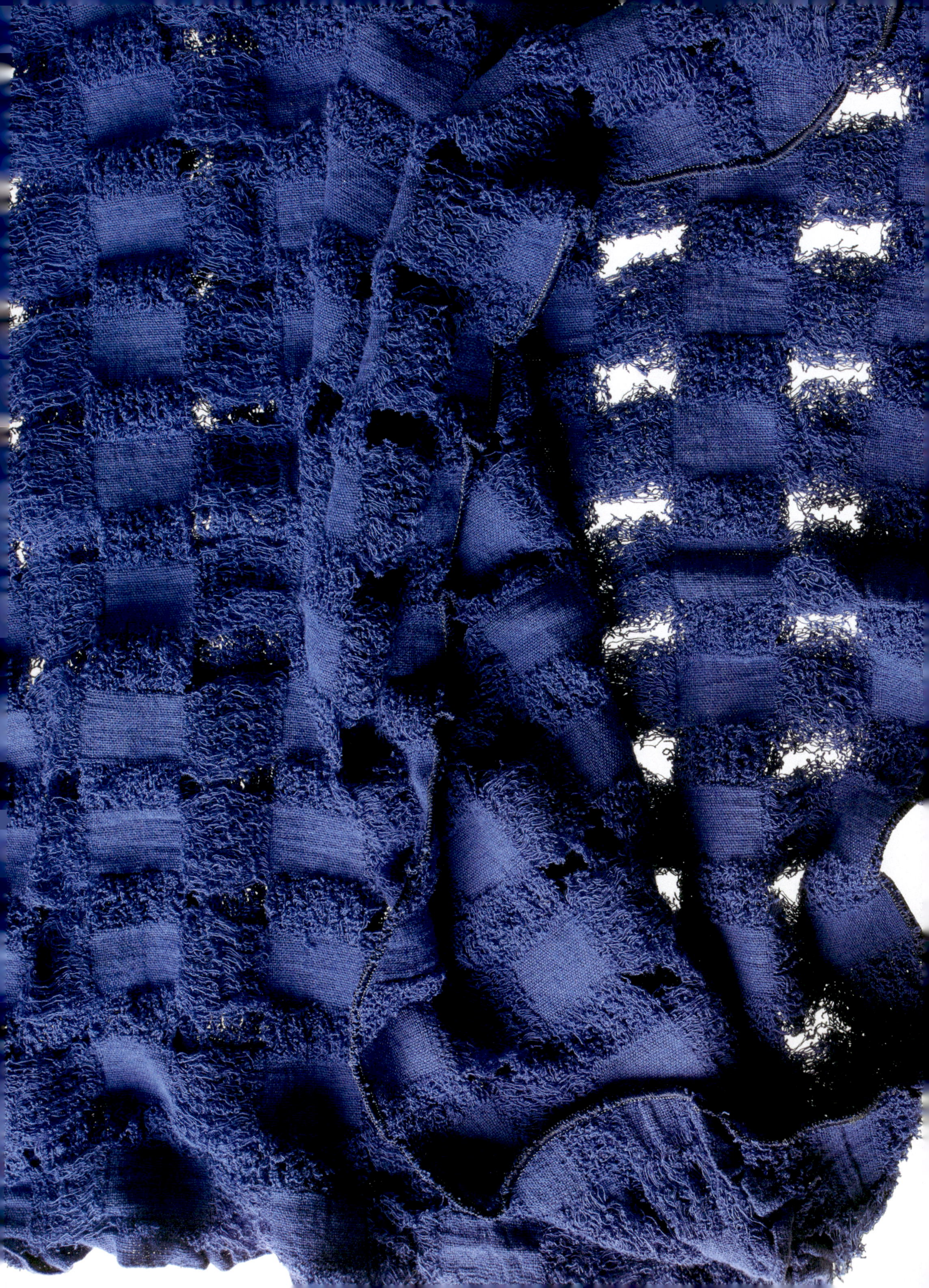

previous spread:
Tubular Weave Mogul, 1987.
By Reiko Sudo.
This four-layer jacquard weave behaves like a single-layer open mesh, with double strands of overspun cotton interlacing to create blocks of raised, rippled texture.

right:
Slink Slub, 2014.
By Reiko Sudo.
Swaying fringes woven in uneven-width slubby silk are left floating in places, and cut by hand.

following spread:
Twig Gather Ohshima, 2017.
By Reiko Sudo.
Part of NUNO's recycled textile series, this *tsugihagi* patchwork combines thin-cut remnant 'twigs' neatly arranged and stitched down on silk organdy.

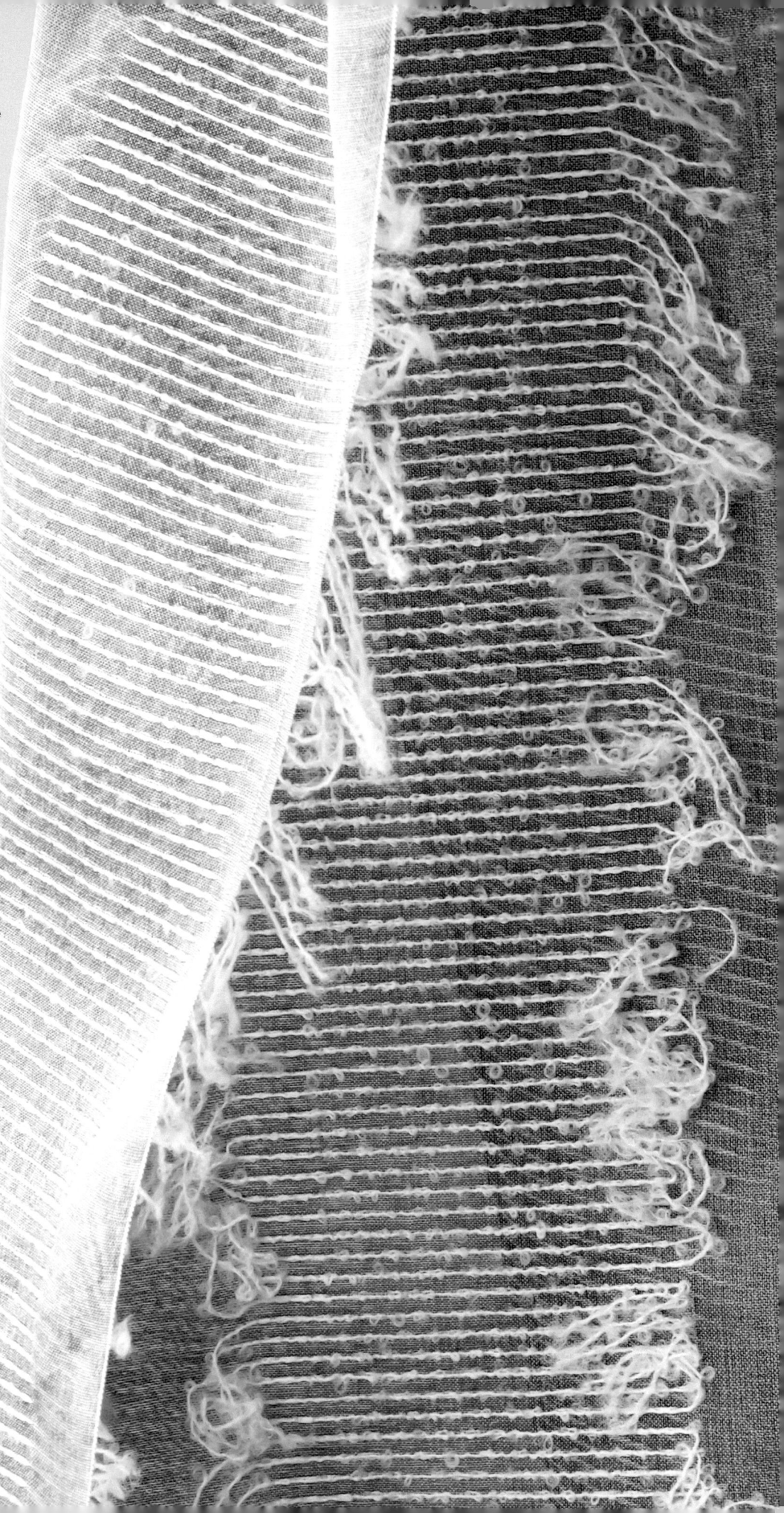

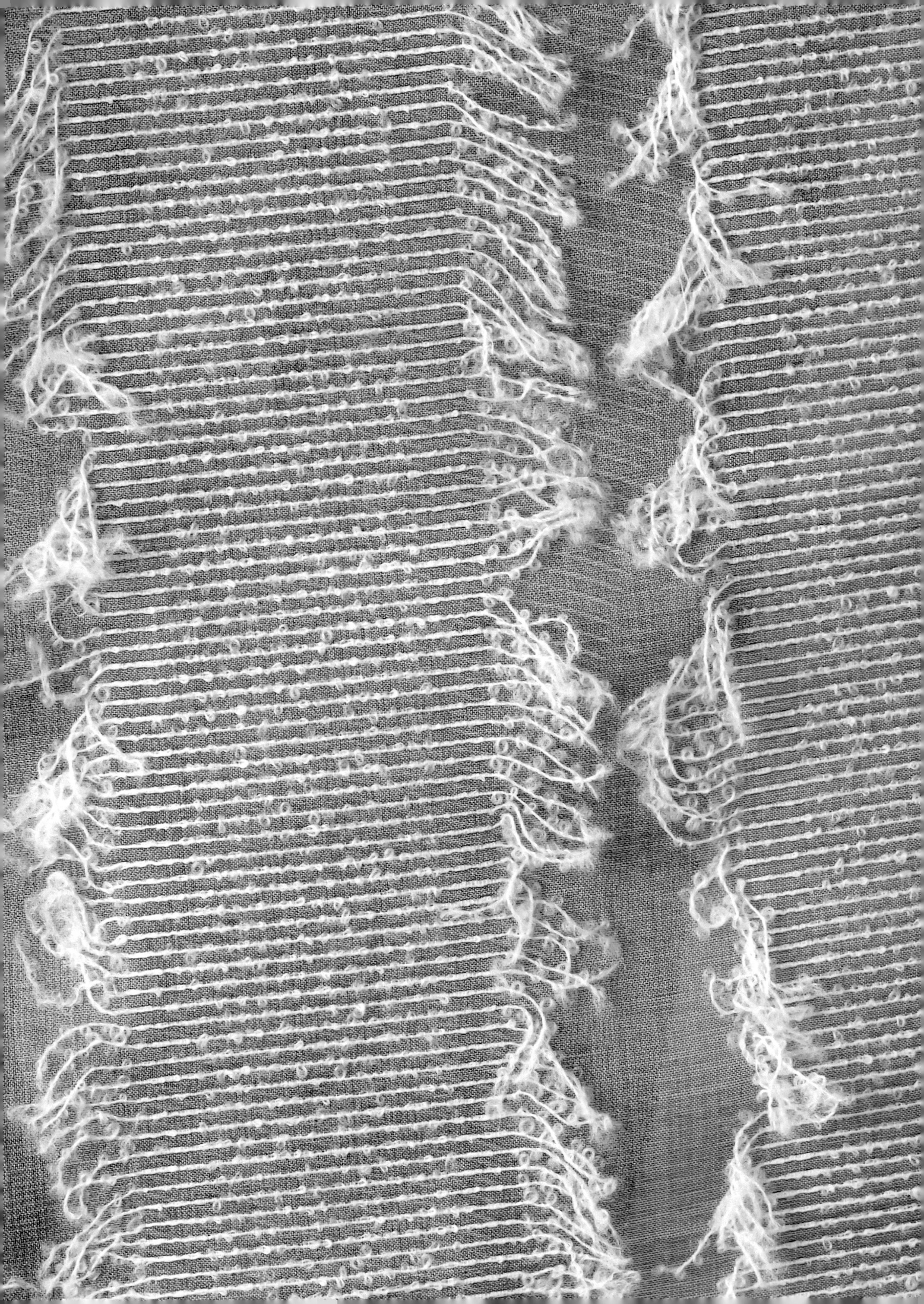

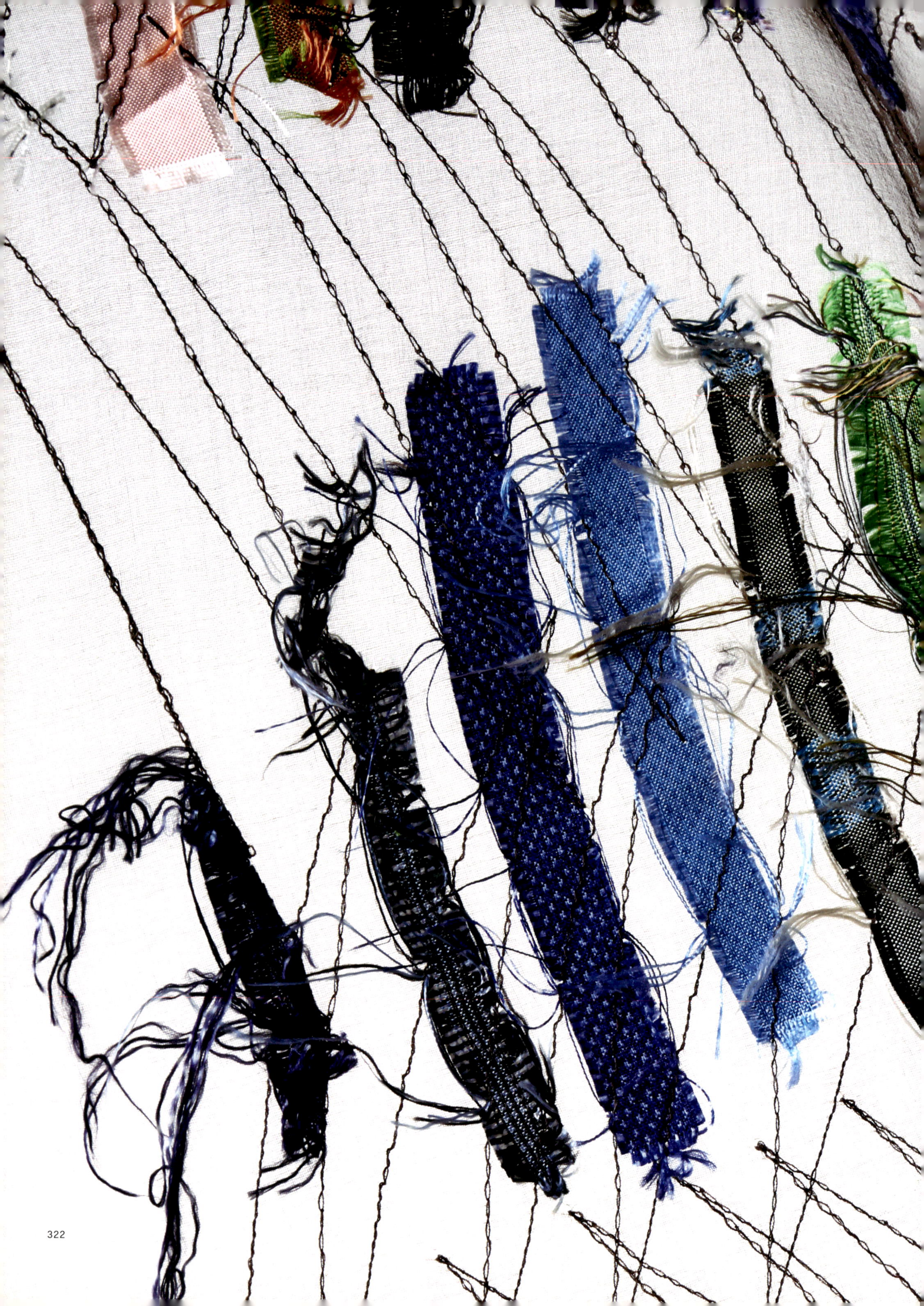

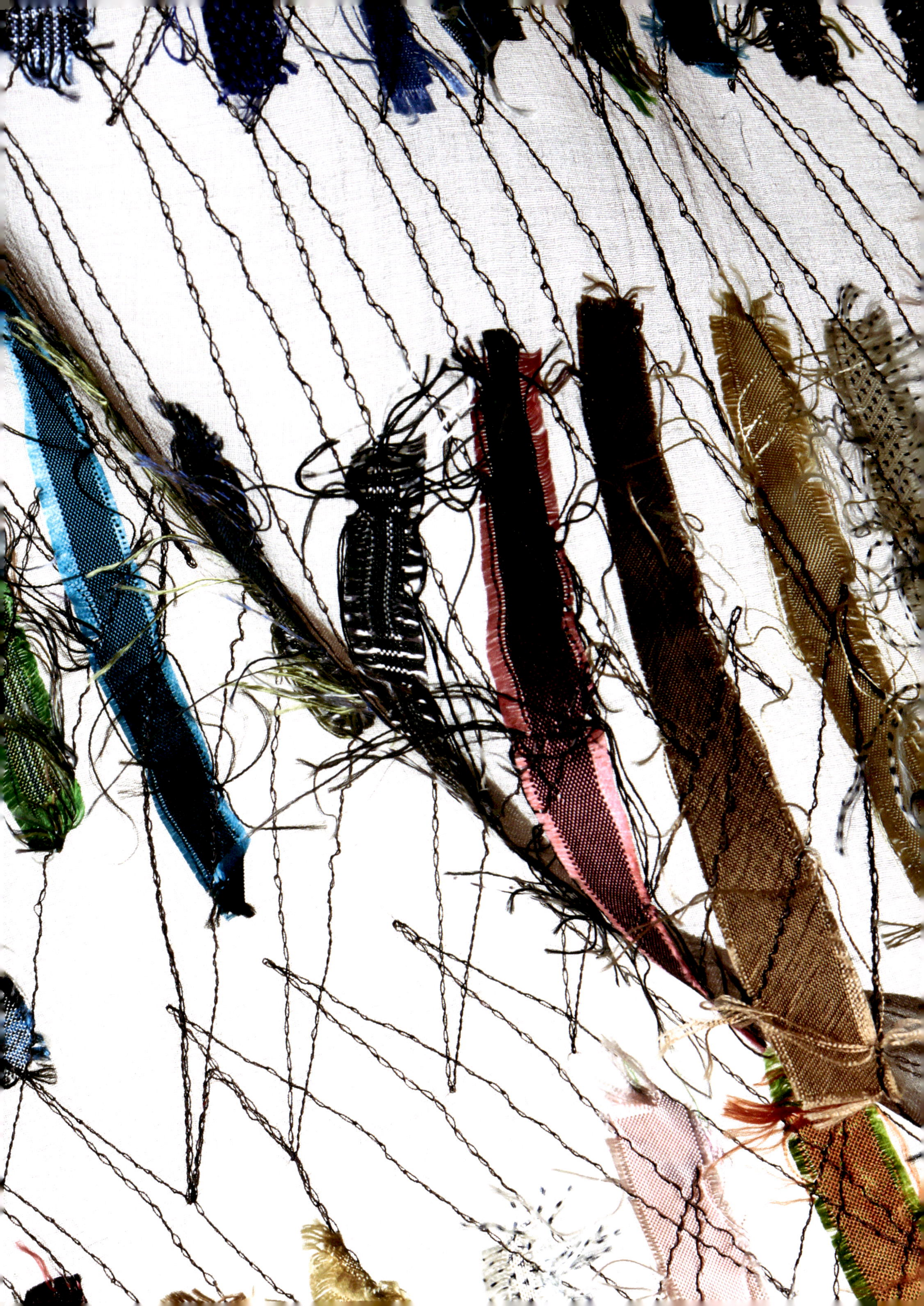

Fuzz, 1987.
By Reiko Sudo
and Junichi Arai.
The surface of this *tsutsu-ori*
tube-woven fabric bristles
with a fine palm fibre-like fuzz.

Ginseng, 1984 (reissued 1992).
By Junichi Arai; reissued
by Reiko Sudo.
Wool shrinks when subjected
to heat or friction, which
allows us to cut loose
protruding strands and
heat-finish each 'finger'
to a different individual
length and thickness.

BORO BORO

Tsugihagi, 1997.
By Reiko Sudo and
Kazuhiro Ueno.
Japanese for 'patchwork'.
Assembled in 'chemical lace'
fashion from whatever fabric
scraps we have on hand, no
two lengths are ever alike.

ボロボロ

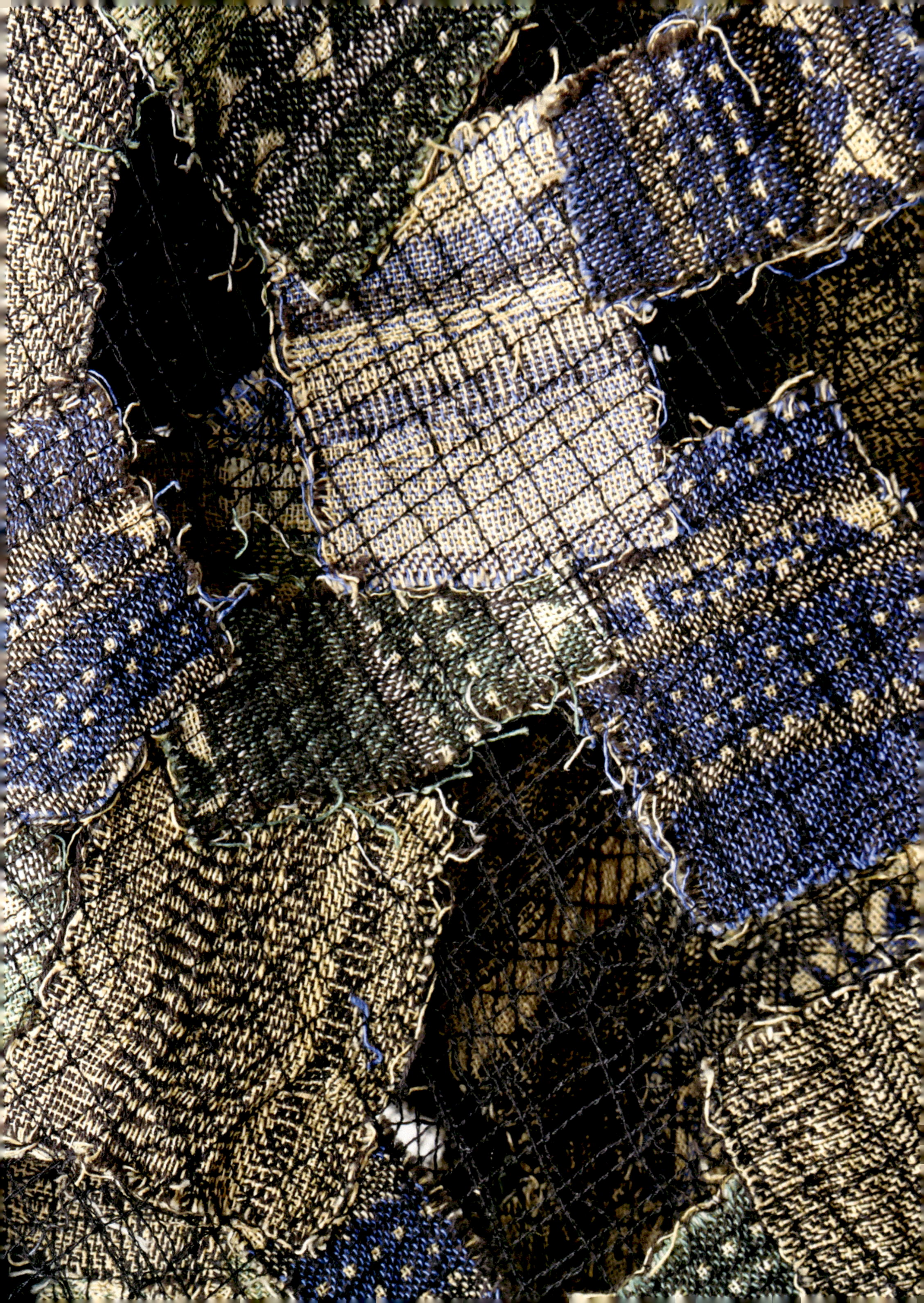

Grater series.
By Reiko Sudo.

left to right:
Grater, 2006.
Diverse rasp patterns inspired this tightly overspun cotton fabric full of body and bounce. Virtually wrinkle-proof, it feels great on the skin.

Stress and Stripe, 2016.
Needle-punching, typically used for padding or lining fabrics, stars as a main actor in this fabric. It is used to create a beautifully crushed texture.

Stress and Check, 2016.
A spiky denim chequerboard is made by needle-punching to raise and mesh fibres just-so: cleverly applied damage.

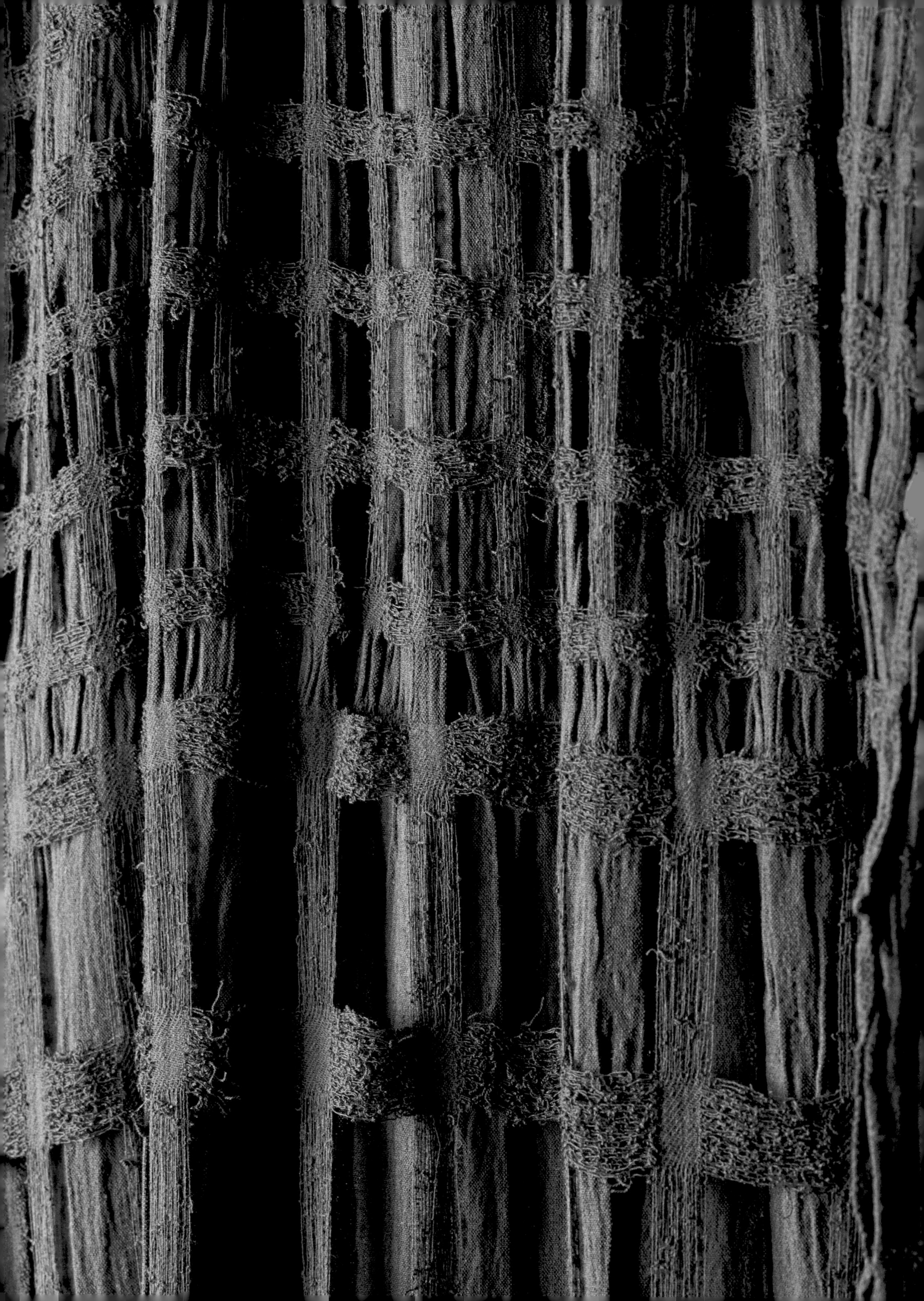

opposite:
Lunatic Fringe, 1982 (reissued 1995).
By Junichi Arai; reissued by Reiko Sudo. A cotton jacquard weave whose top layer is raised in a netted crosshatch that pulls at the backing fabric body to create an all-over wrinkled texture.

left:
Fans, 2011.
By Gaku Masui and Reiko Sudo. A two-sided jacquard weave with rows of auspicious fans front and back. Excess warps and wefts are given a hand-cut finish for added textural interest.

following spread:
Tiggy, 2003.
By Reiko Sudo. This prickly fabric, named after the hedgehog in the children's book *Peter Rabbit*, features flat cotton yarns stiffened with *konyaku* glutinous yam paste, then hand-cut to a bristled effect.

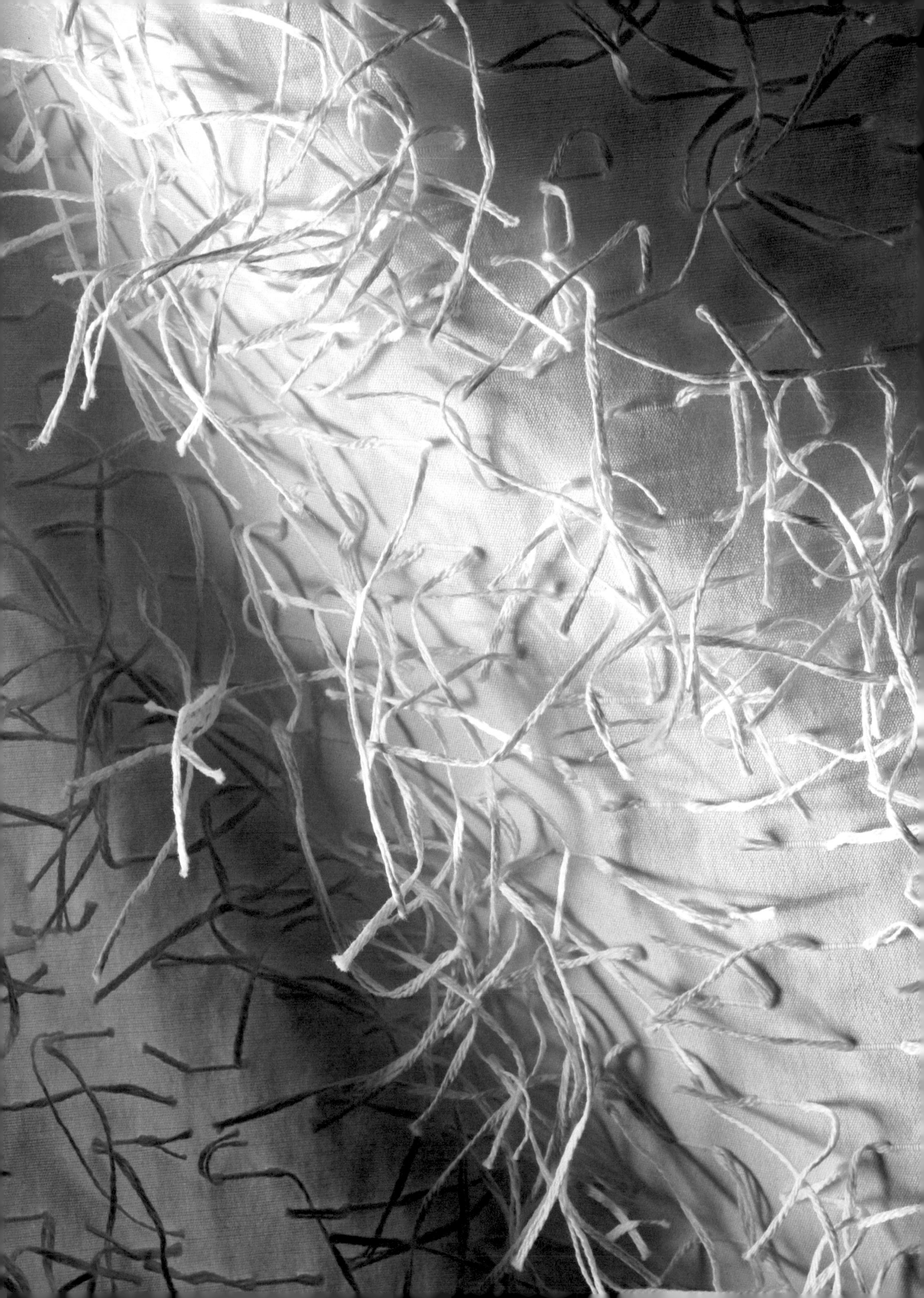

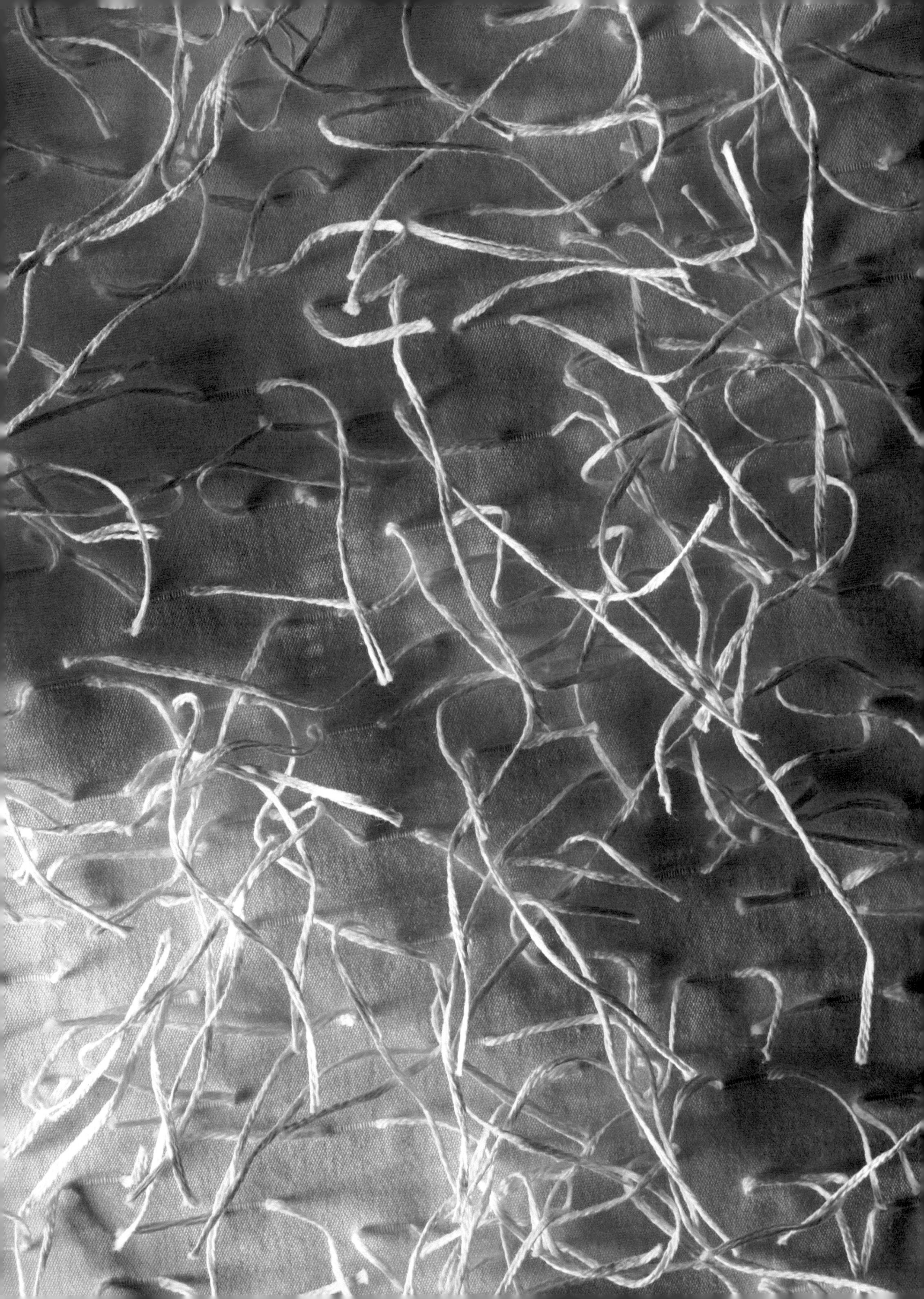

below:
Hoarfrost, 2000.
By Reiko Sudo.
Warps left partially loose on the loom are 'Indian cut' in an image of an ice-bound cascade, with textures reminiscent of frosted tree bark.

opposite:
Eco-green fabric, 2001.
By Reiko Sudo.
Overspun yarns of a biodegradable cornstarch fibre that decomposes to water and carbon dioxide create a delicate textured crepe.

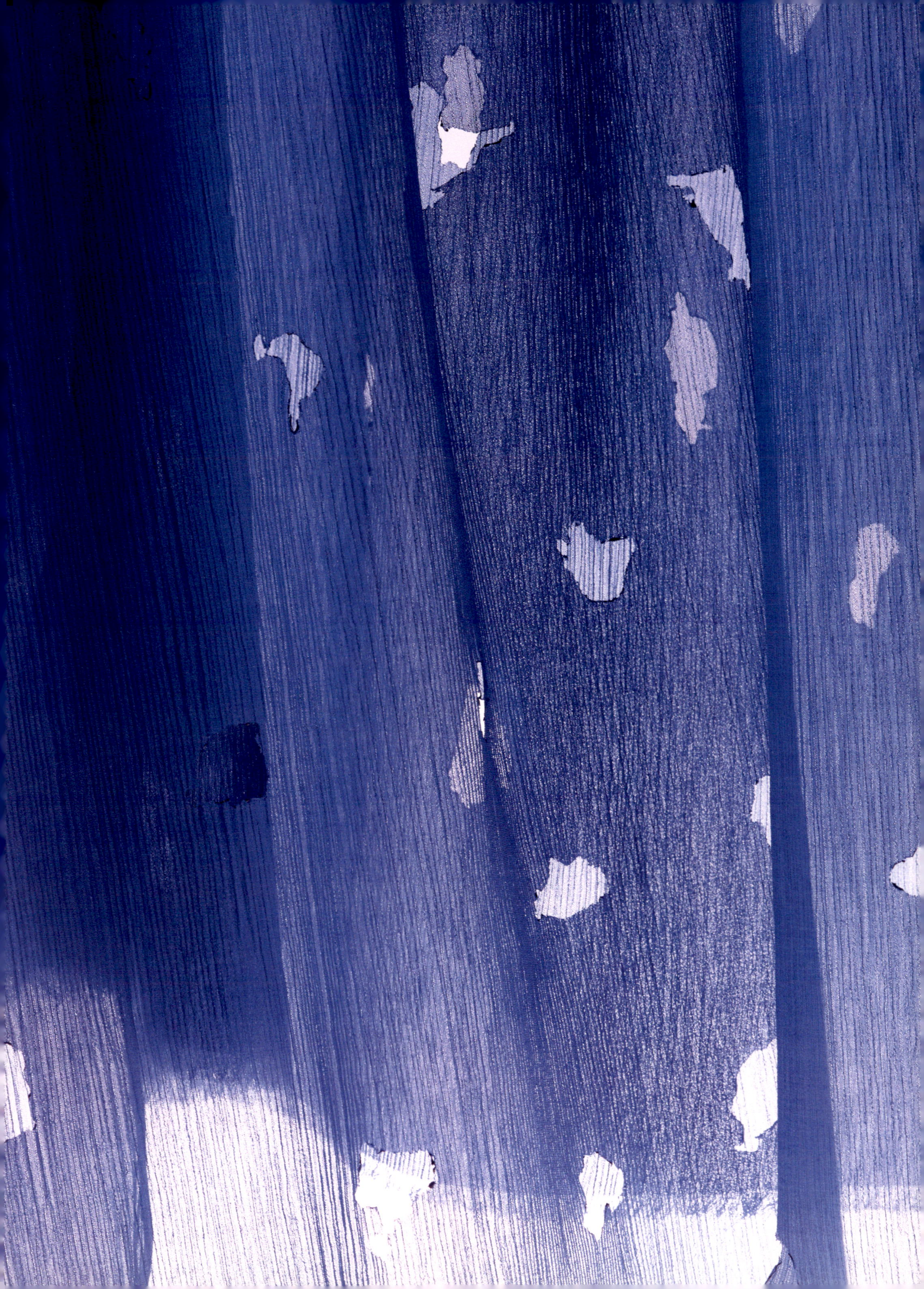

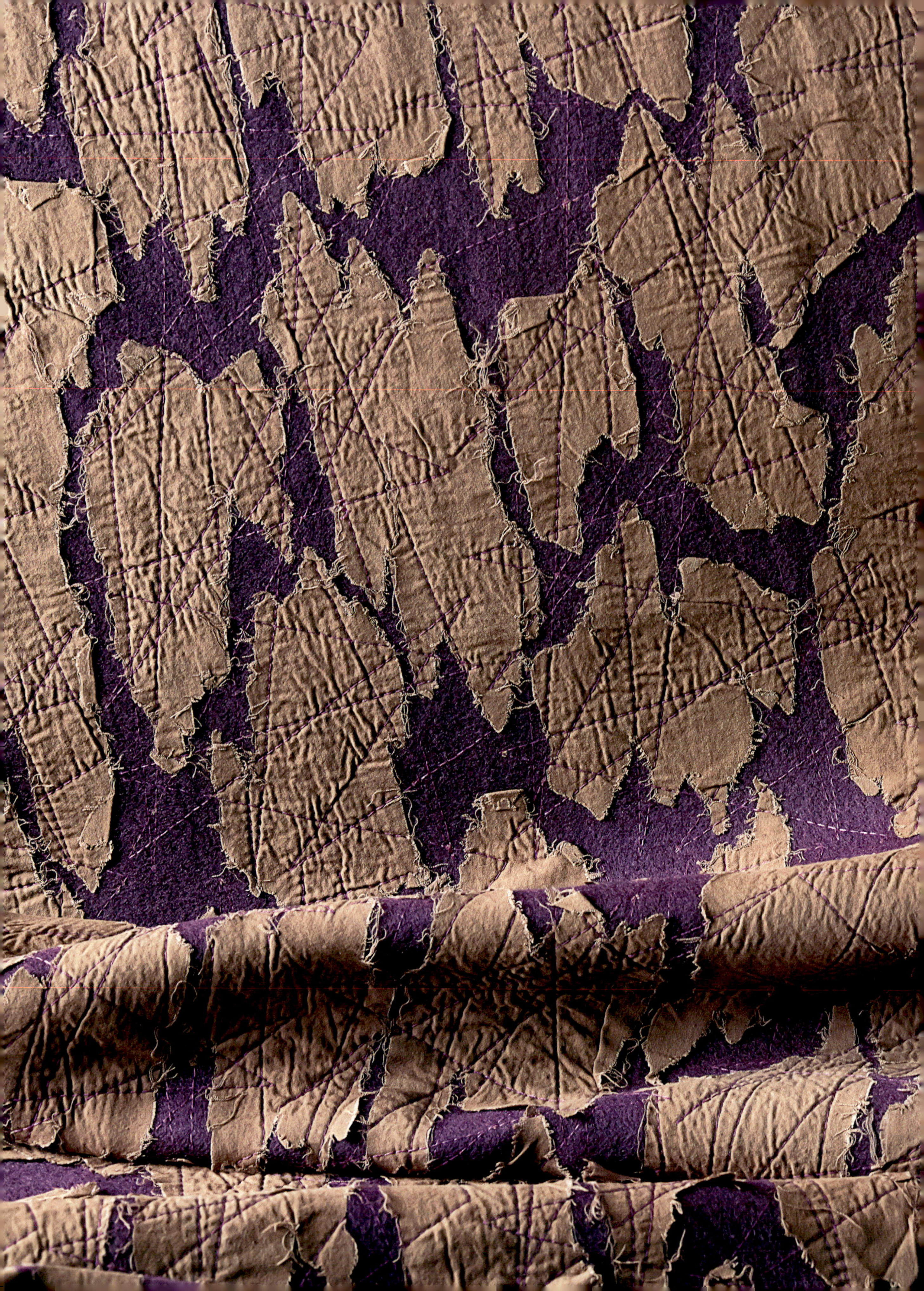

BORO BORO

Cracked Quilt, 1992.
By Reiko Sudo.
A rayon weave quilted to melton wool is printed with an acid that selectively 'burns out' plant fibres to create a crackled surface, then tumble-dried to fray the chemically etched pattern bites.

Spanish Moss, 1994.
By Reiko Sudo.
Silk warps combine in a double-weave structure with overspun wool wefts that are partially thinned out, creating a thick silk 'foliage' reminiscent of air plant garlands.

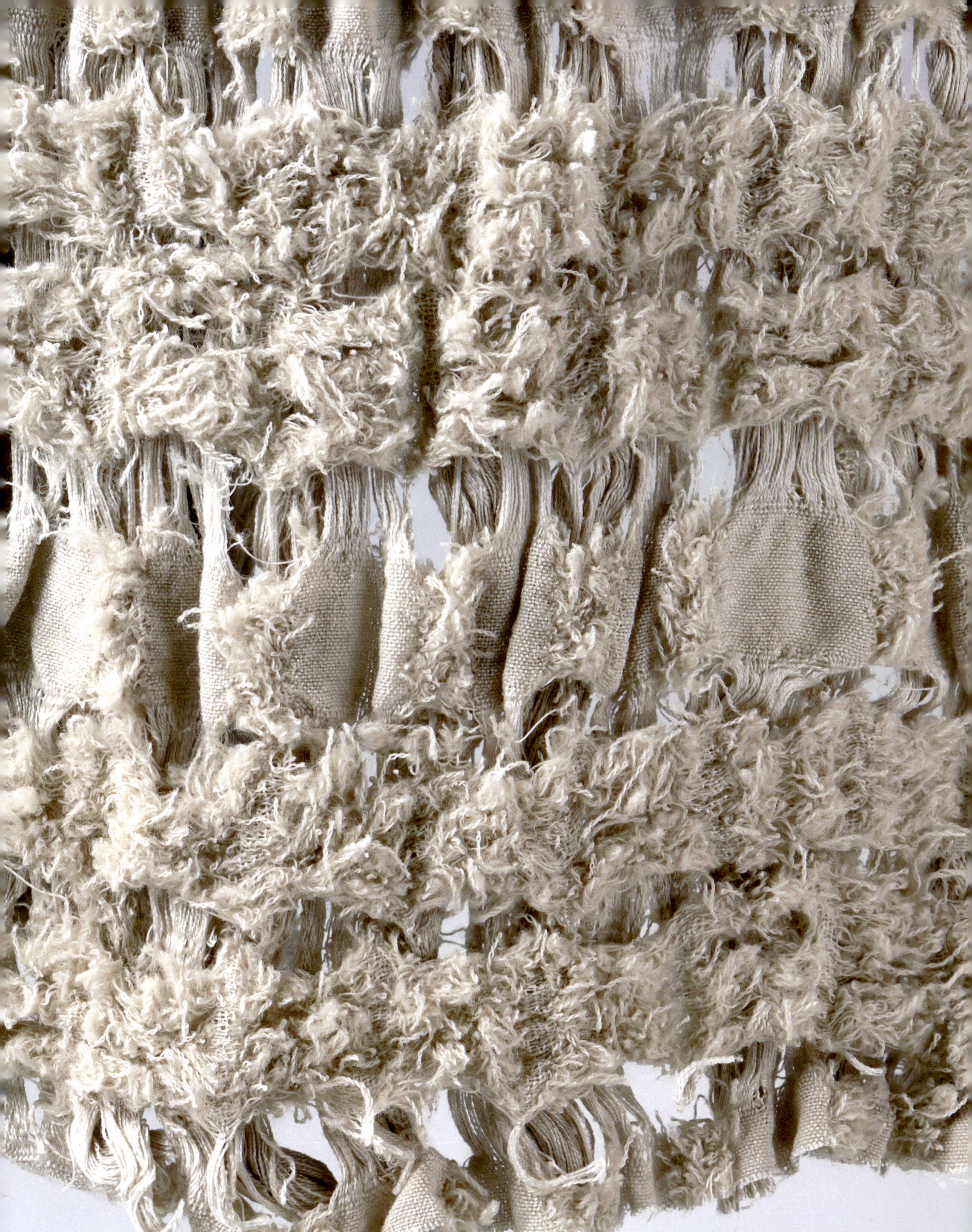

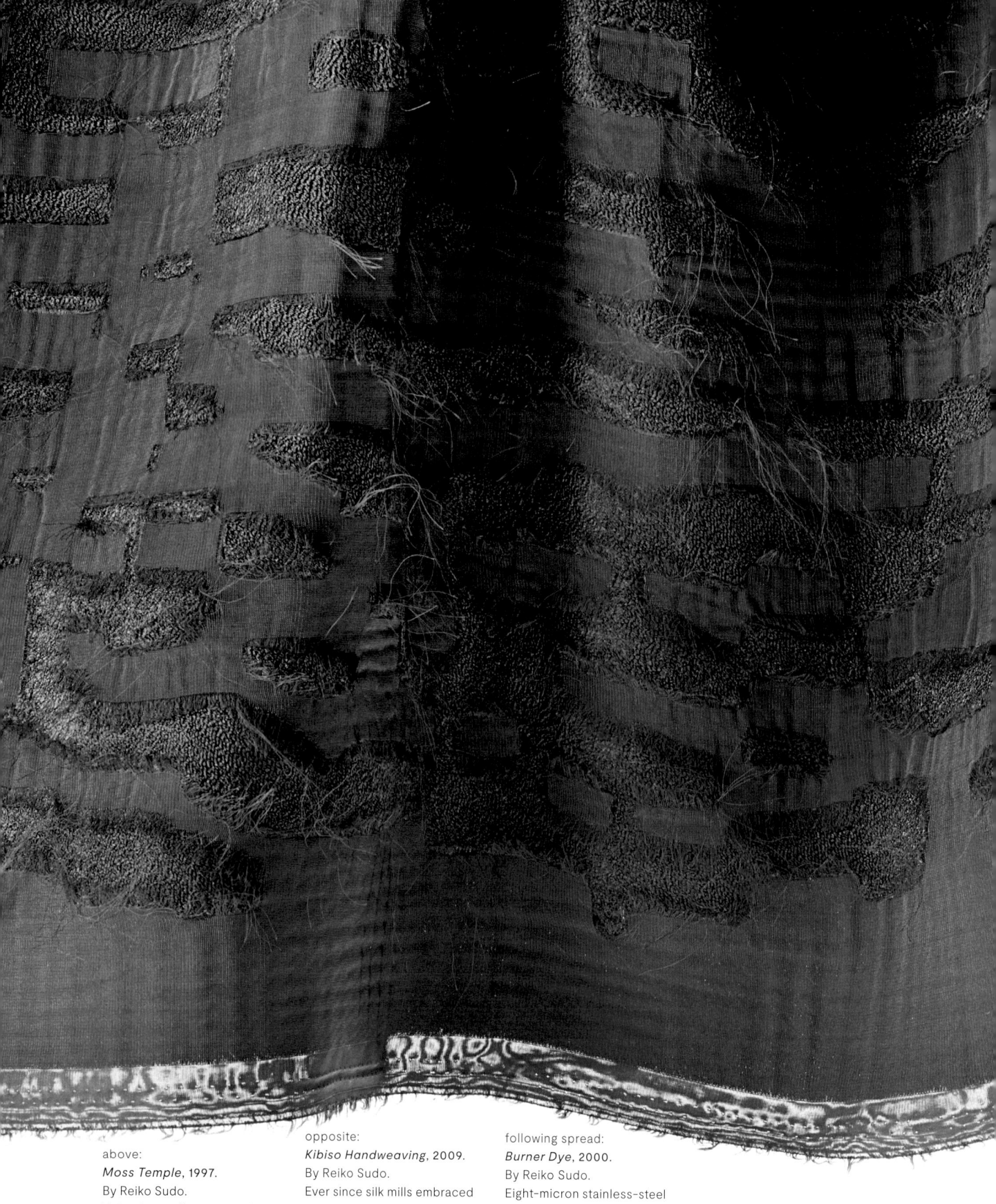

above:
Moss Temple, 1997.
By Reiko Sudo.
Velvet is usually woven with the pile sandwiched between two backing layers that are cut apart to produce two pieces of fabric. Left uncut, the pile peeks through here and there.

opposite:
Kibiso Handweaving, 2009.
By Reiko Sudo.
Ever since silk mills embraced mass production, the hard crusts of cocoons have been discarded as 'waste'; but if processed by hand, amino-rich *kibiso* can make healthful fabrics.

following spread:
Burner Dye, 2000.
By Reiko Sudo.
Eight-micron stainless-steel fibres for tyres are given a water-soluble coating that is dissolved after weaving, then finally flamed with a burner to a beautiful iridescence, like pots on a stove.

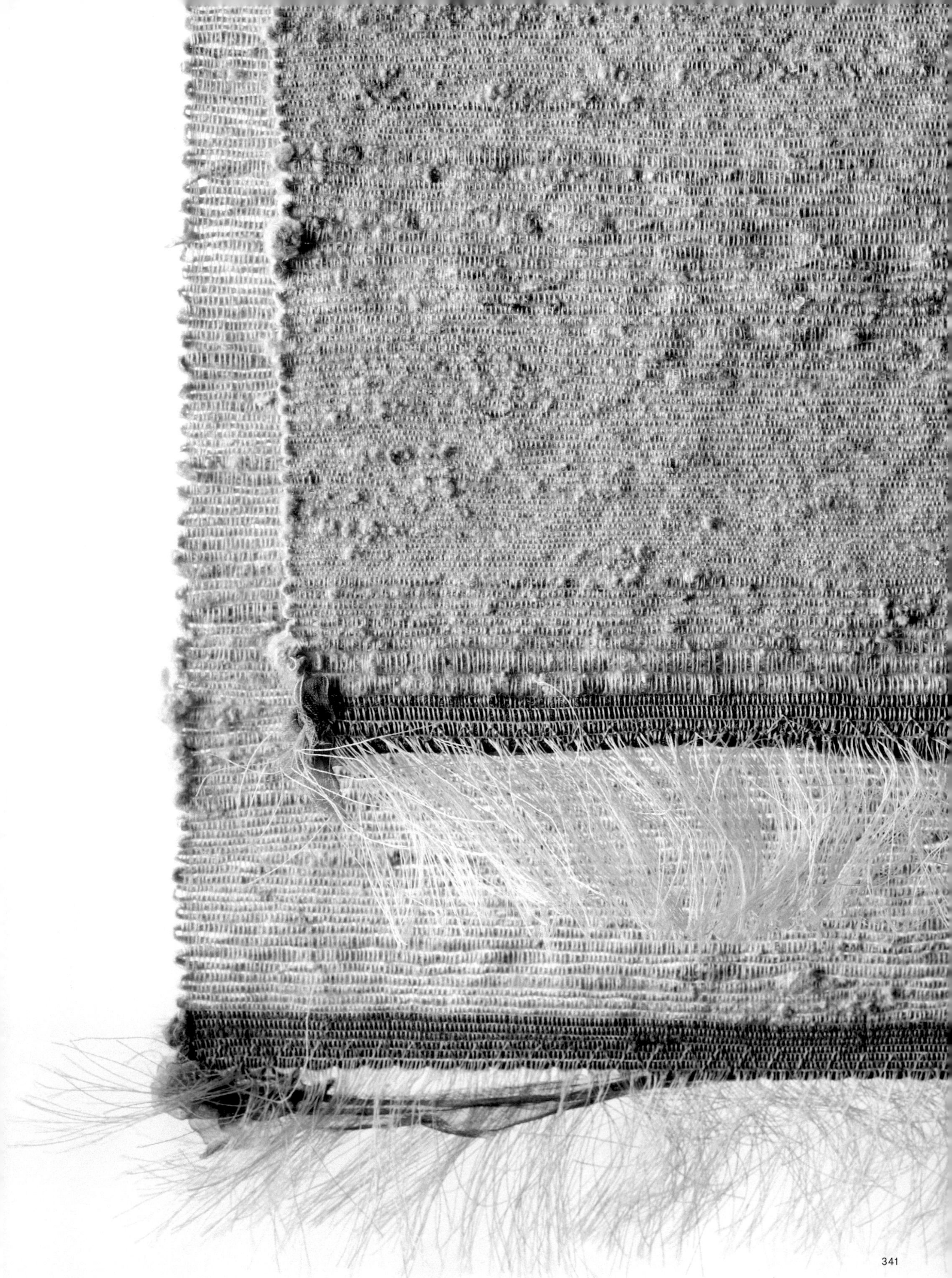

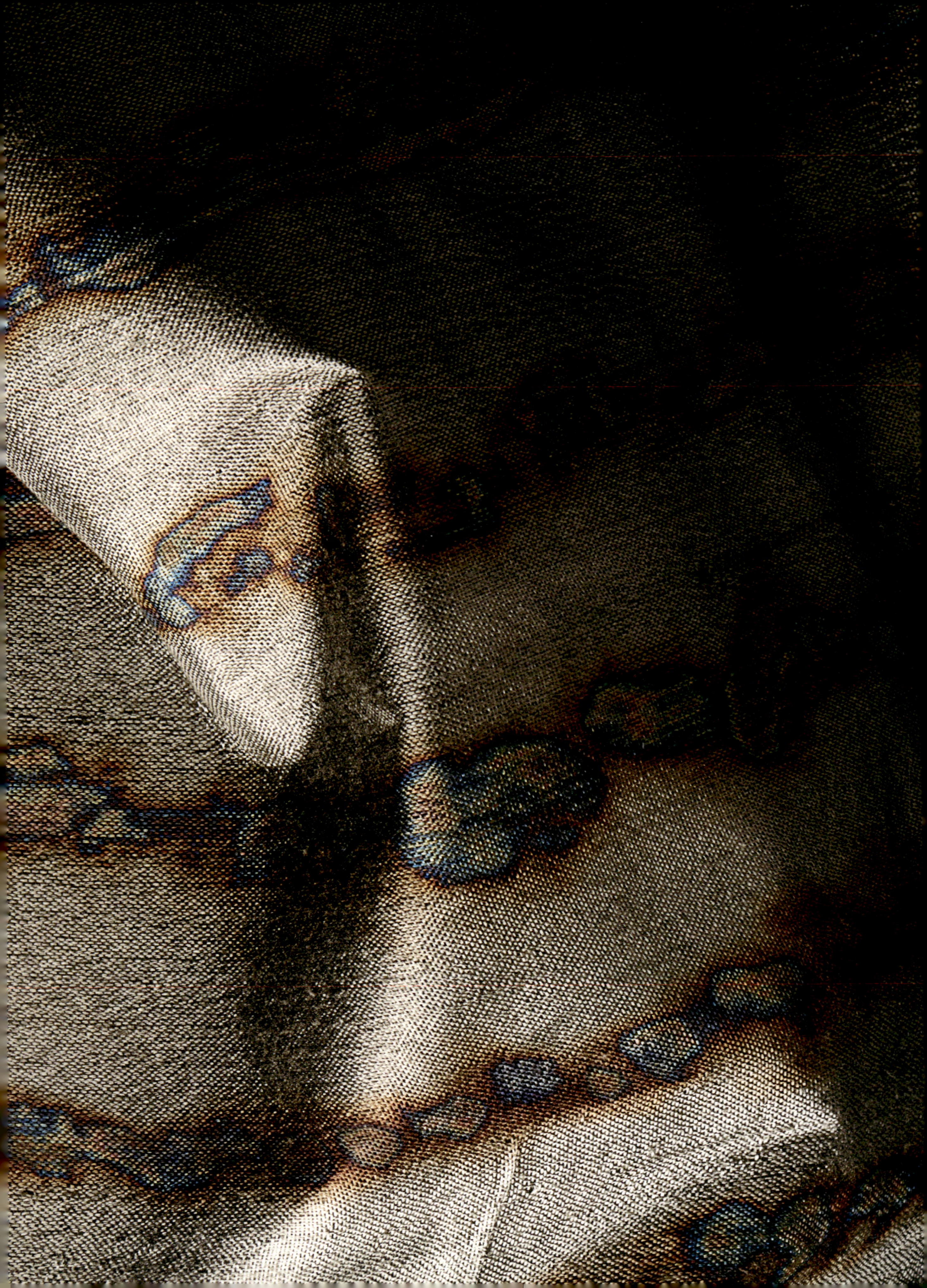

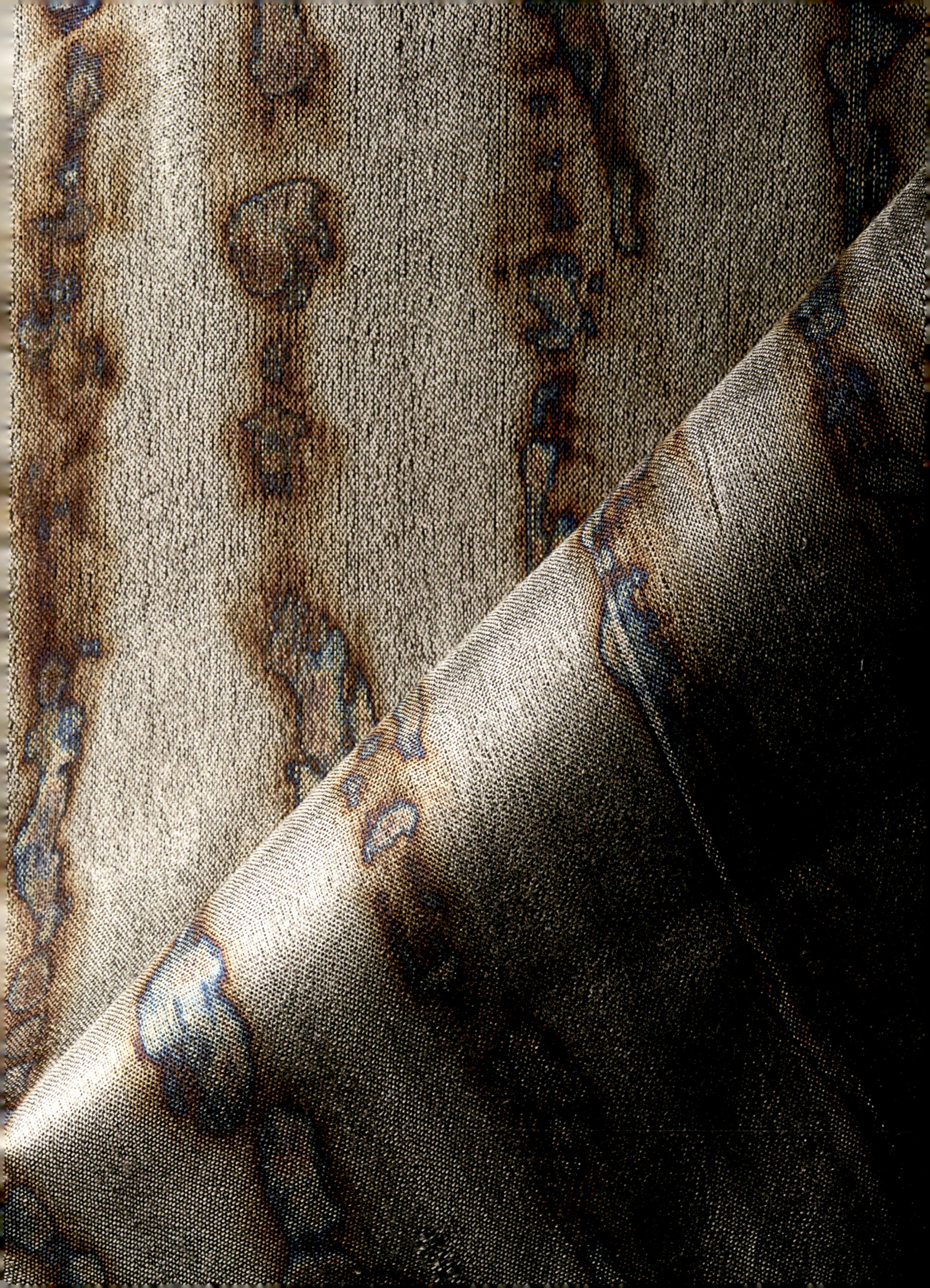

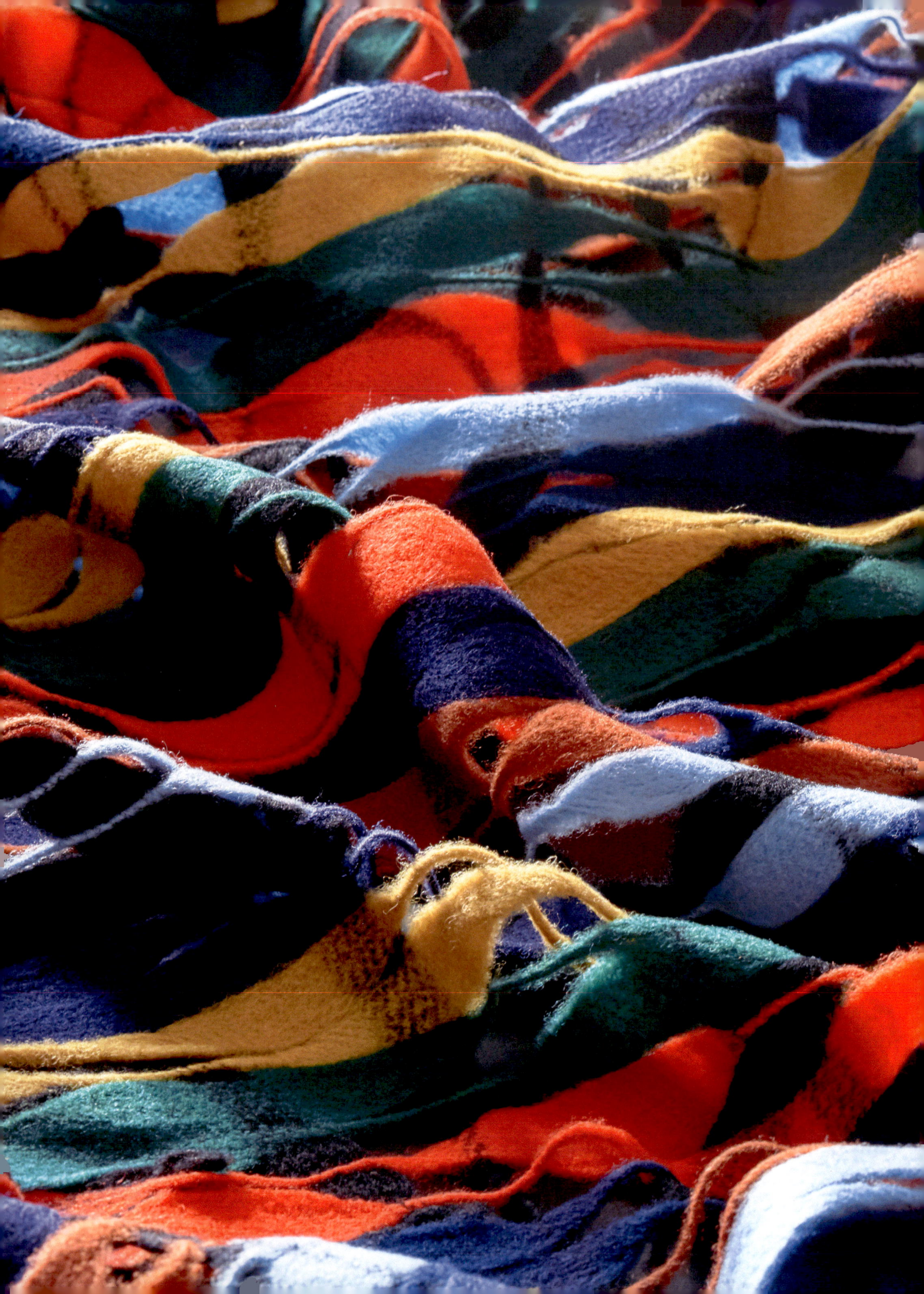

Portrait of a Textile: *Threadstray*

When does textile destruction become textile creation?

Occasionally when I mend things, I enjoy leaving pretty stitch trails across the fabric. But one day, while hemming organdy, my sewing machine needle broke and gouged horrible rips in the material. And yet the torn threads looked quite beautiful in the light. Could we maybe use jagged needles to intentionally scar textiles with different designs? Immediately, I made inquiries of needle-punching firms who process felt, suit linings and other substrates. Our first barbed breakthrough, *Kenzan Stripe* (1987), was selected for the design collection of the Museum of Modern Art, New York. Duly encouraged, we collaborated with the Yamanashi Seiri Kakosho workshop to create *Threadstray*. Spreading our fabric on the needle-punching-machine table, we manually arranged the wool threads ever so slightly to look like hand-loomed warps and wefts, then attacked the wool at blinding speed with a plate of thousands of barbed spikes to create a quasi-felt that seems neither woven nor knitted.

opposite:
Threadstray, 2006.
By Reiko Sudo and Tomoko Iida.
Similar to felting, a barbed needle abrades fibres of thick multicolour merino bouclé warps and wefts to make them mesh together.

Design ideas notebook.

ボロボロ

opposite
0.5-count wool yarns.

above
Original artwork for *Threadstray*.

below
Punching needles.

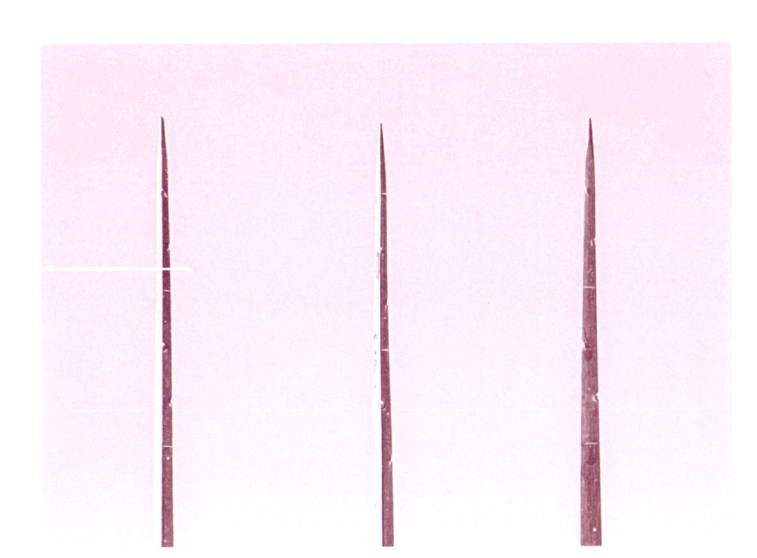

Radical wool

The 1990s Silo-spun 'new generation wool' ushered in an era of lustrous, sheer, draping textiles. Around the same time, NUNO began using New Zealand merino wool with greater spring and overlapping surface 'scale' that made for more lively yarns. Repeated up-and-down abrasion of these yarns with a high-speed, 1,000-needle-punching machine, typically used for making non-woven industrial fabrics, can create a wide range of effects.

opposite
Threadstray, 2006
By Reiko Sudo and
Tomoko Iida.

above
Threadstray after the first
needle-punching run.

following spread
Trial punching on polyester
organdy.

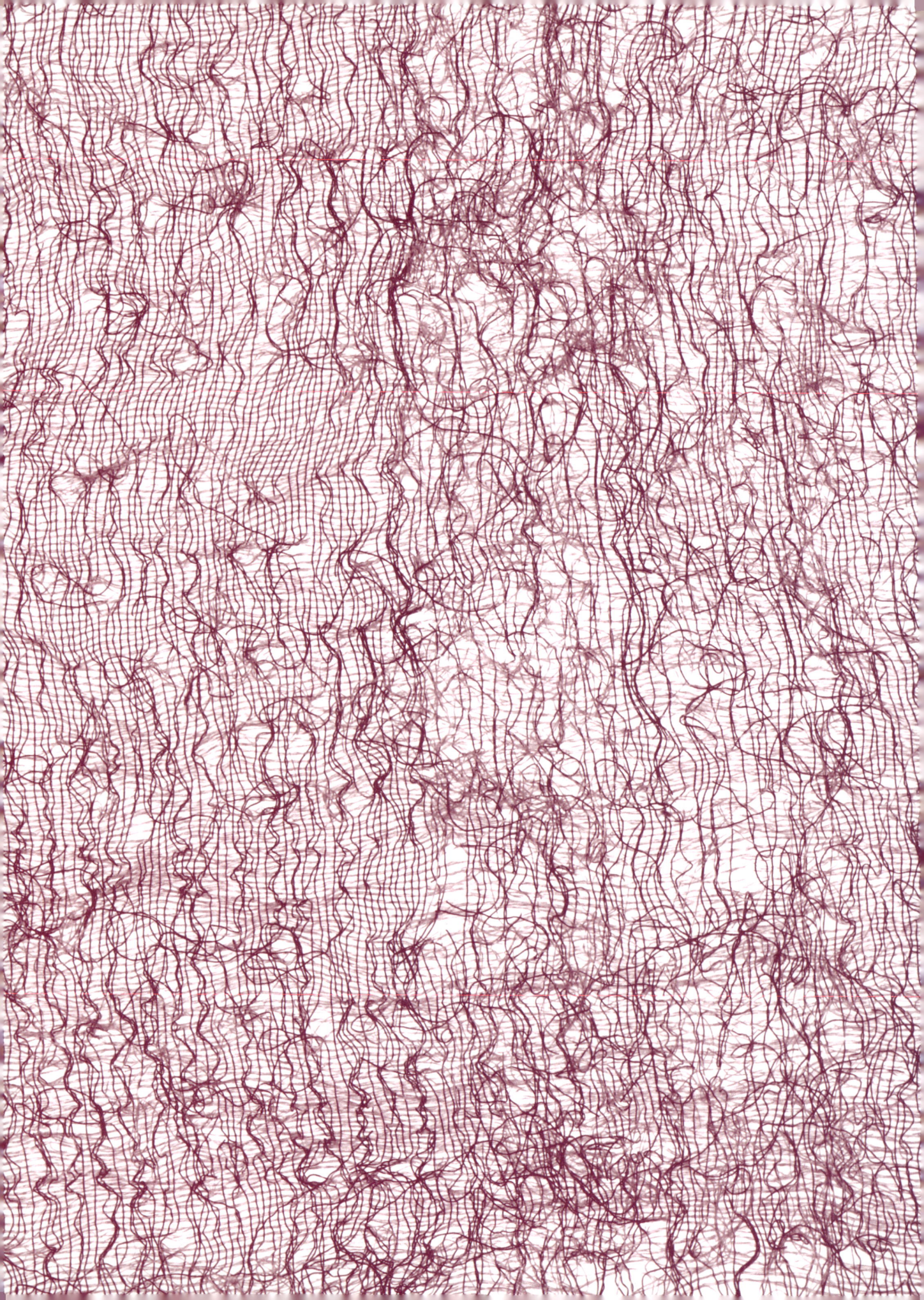

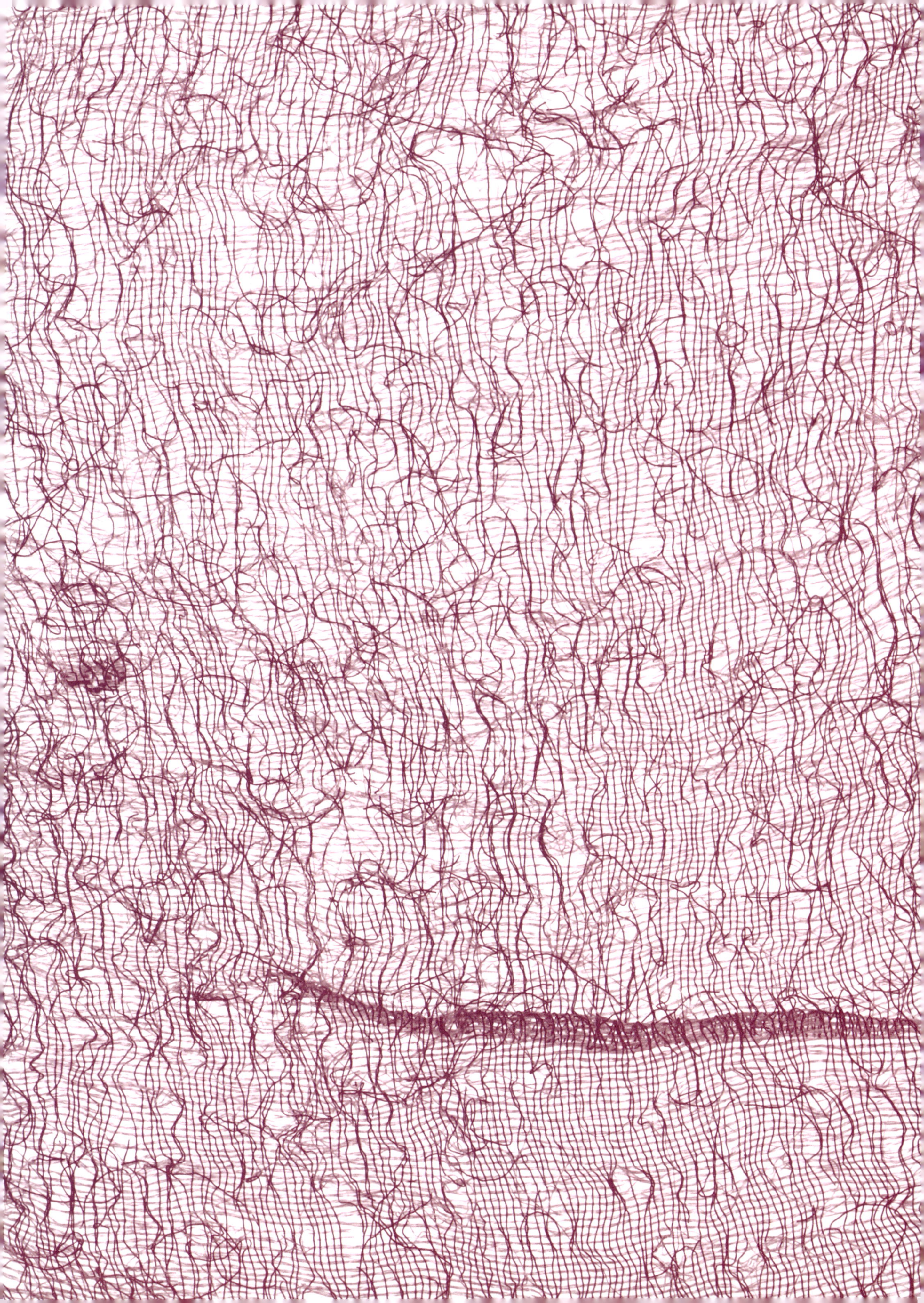

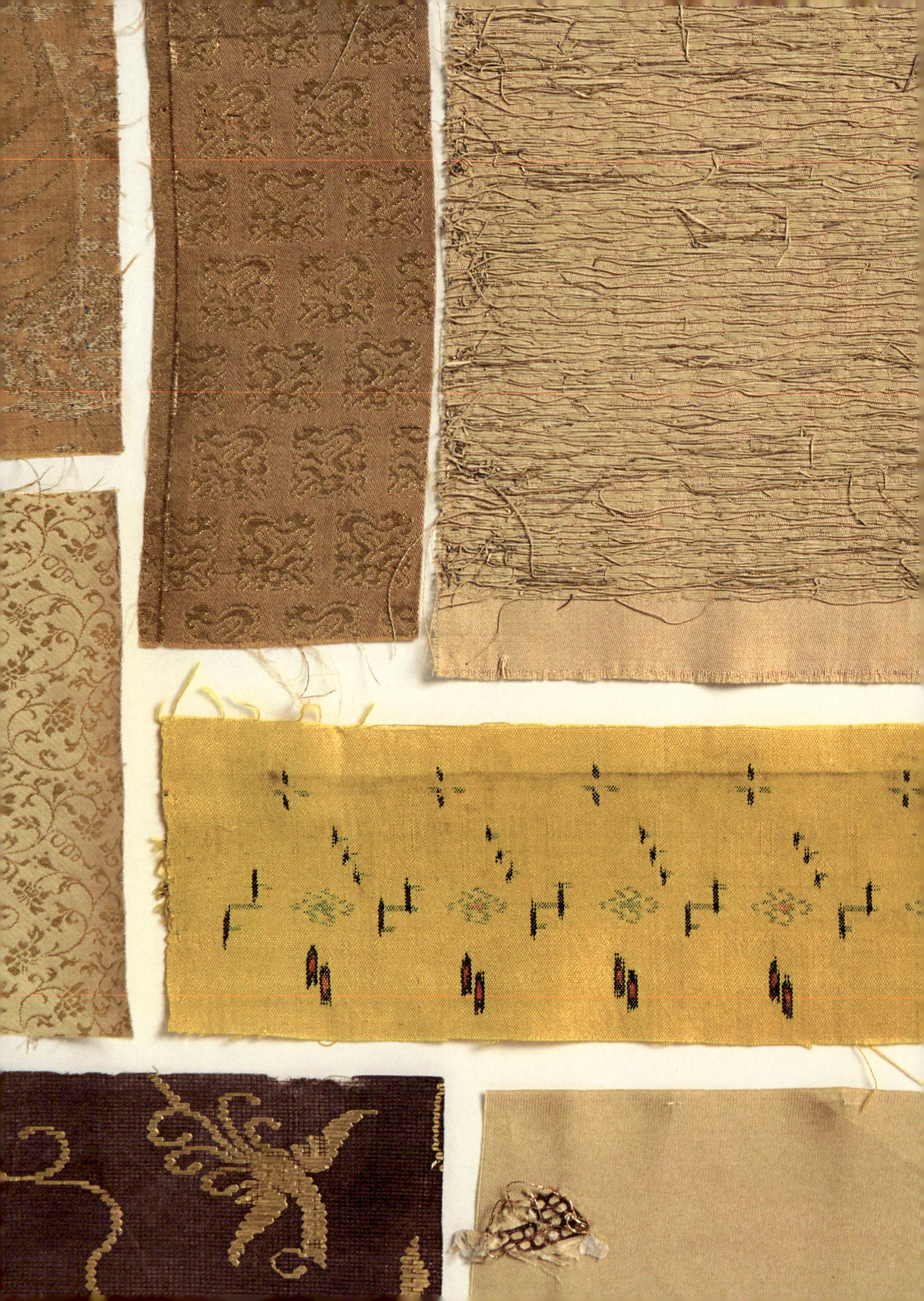

IRO IRO

iro iro (いろいろ)

1. Multicolour(ed), versicolour; kaleidoscopic
2. Layered with different colours; variegated, dappled; pied, piebald
3. Mixed, various, diverse; heterogenous; varied, sundry
4. According to taste or preference; as desired

The Arrow of Time: The Magical Transformation of Surface and Colour

Adam Lowe and Charlotte Skene Catling

Why do we find old and ruined things beautiful? Do they call up a projection from our imagination onto what remains? Or is it a mortal sense of our own transient existence and inevitable destiny? Is it innate in us to perceive beauty in the ragged and decrepit? Or is this learned and peculiar only to some cultures? Ruins have been celebrated in the West since the Enlightenment, while restoration and renewal is often preferred in places not dominated by European thought. Art involves both additive and subtractive processes that can build up material, like a sculptor working in clay, or remove it, like the carving of a block of marble. These processes can be the actions of the artist or of time itself. Creation and ruin are inseparably part of one another.

Art lies in transformation. Material transformations follow the principles of entropic breakdown, with a transfer and release of energy, resulting in objects that inspire and provoke curiosity. The arrow of time is a one-way 'asymmetry' that points towards decomposition. Archaeologists read the past in layers, as they forensically excavate their subject from centuries of decay, revealing glimpses onto which we can map our beliefs. Decay triggers a cascade of associations that prick the imagination. Time's arrow implies loss, but some processes defy entropic flow from perfection to chaos, or coherence to dust. Is a crystal less perfect than the liquid suspension from which it was formed? A soap bubble less coherent than a bar of soap? A butterfly less than the chrysalis?

Cities, buildings and the people, flesh and gestures they contain all swell, sigh and shift with time. Liminal spaces of hard and soft matter are natural environments for artists who celebrate the complexity of the world. Venice is the supreme example, and a place defined by its physical evidence. When Venice subjugated Constantinople, marble from the interior of the Hagia Sophia was looted to clad the south façade of St Mark's Cathedral, the 'trophy wall'. Inside, in Constantinople, remaining slabs retain their polished sheen, in which geological time is frozen, invoking the sublime. Outside, in Venice, salt and humidity have devoured less-resistant veins of marble, carving scars and furrows into a once pristine surface. The markings reveal a complex biography, and the efforts of those who tried to halt its decay. The Victorian art critic John Ruskin was able to read Venice through its stones; stones that erode as this unique city sinks into the marshes, its collective memories absorbed through morphic resonance.

Venice is a liquid city of colour and glass, twin treasures of trade and travel fused through magical alchemy and exposure to the elements. 'Lead white' – an oxide of the metal – is a product of corrosion, as is 'verdigris', an aquamarine breakdown of copper. 'Lapis blue' is a pulverization of stone, purified by chemical sublimation. From this emerges a range of lapis 'ashes', with lowering concentrations of the brilliant lazuli, of increasing poverty but subtle beauty. The dazzling yellow of orpiment and the bruised orange of realgar are sulphides of the poisonous arsenic, while the photosensitive mucus of the predatory 'Murex' sea snail reveals itself as imperial purple only in sunlight.

The mystery of colour appears to lie in the space between material colour and the spectral nature of light. Masters of colour theory struggle with the difference between colour as an idea and as physical fact. Our experience of it is subjective: texture, light and our brains all affect the way we perceive it, while colour is as fugitive as our perceptions. The 'wool scale' was designed to scientifically monitor the fading of colour in yarn, but is now used to calibrate fading in general. It demonstrates the ephemerality of physical colour.

Sanzo Wada founded the Japan Standard Colours Association in 1927, and from 1933 to 1934 produced *Haishoku sokan*, six volumes of mounted colour samples that seem to exist outside time, somewhere conceptually between the work of Victorian French chemist and colour theorist Michel-Eugène Chevreul and Bauhaus artist and educator Josef Albers. Inside the accordion folds of his book, the bodycolour remains as fresh as the day it was applied.

The same was true of the Tomb of Seti I, the largest and most magnificent in the Valley of the Kings in Luxor, until soon after its discovery in 1817 by 'The Great Belzoni'. Belzoni's description of the pristine Hall of Beauties testifies to colours unchanged after three millennia of dry darkness. His admiration for the 'wonderful things' he found didn't stop him (and others) from hacking out sections and carrying them off, adding graffiti and casting surfaces with plaster, papier mâché or wax to take home and exhibit. This triggered the 'Egyptomania' that has distressed the fragile decorations ever since. The tombs were made to last for eternity, but were never to be entered.

As colour ages, it reverts to its raw materials. In 2001, Factum began to document the tomb of Seti I, where the complexity of the colour became crucially important: how to capture the variations of absorbancy, reflectivity, and traces of under- and overpainting that cover relief surfaces? Meaning is fixed in time using pigments of pulverized minerals and oxidized derivatives bound together with gum arabic or animal glue. In the tomb, the texts on the walls began to magically unfold, revealing glimpses into the mystic knowledge needed for the buried Pharaoh to navigate the perilous journey through the dark hours of the sun to rebirth and rejuvenation.

Death is only a necessary decay, a transition that reveals nothing is static. In Pharaonic culture, death is where human life merges with the totality of its environment and the tyranny of intellect is subsumed into the natural order of things. The ultimate transformation is the total loss of sense: sound fades to the buzzing of bees, touch does not respond. We are suddenly sightless – in total darkness – where smell and taste have evaporated. In this state of vulnerability, on the brink of nothingness, a latent energy of life triggers a magical inversion of entropy and a recycling of both sensation and material. In other words: the fabric of life.

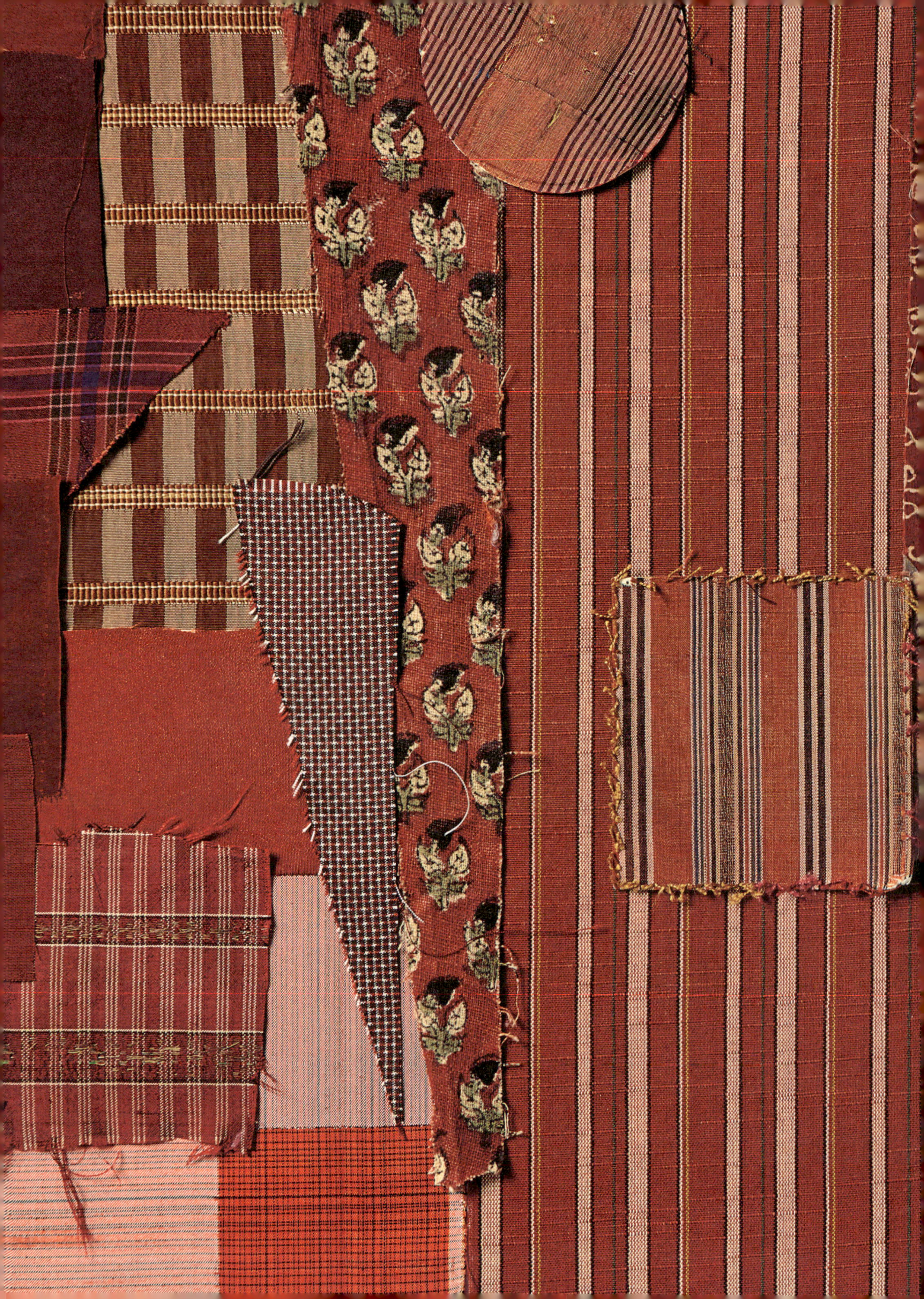

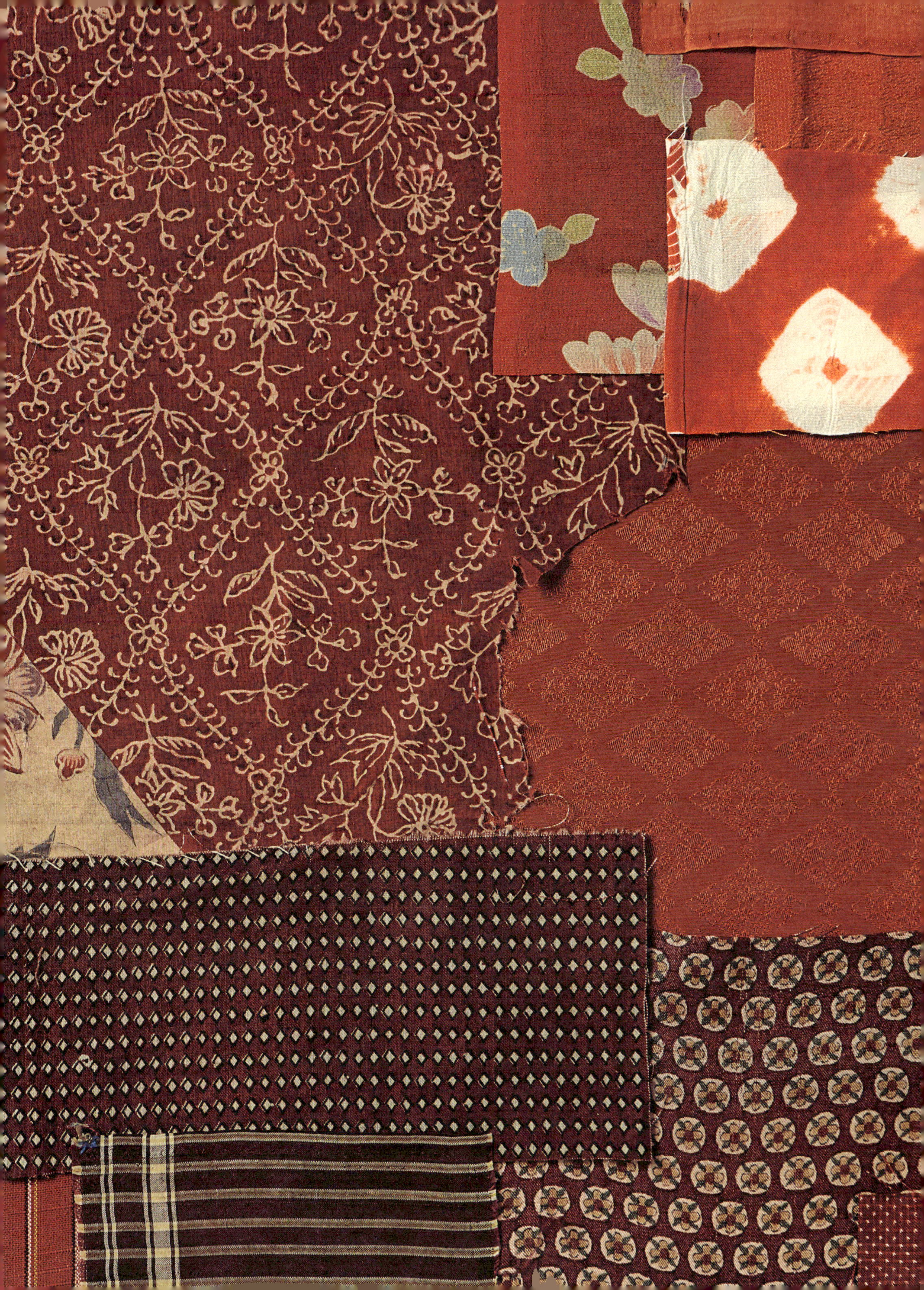

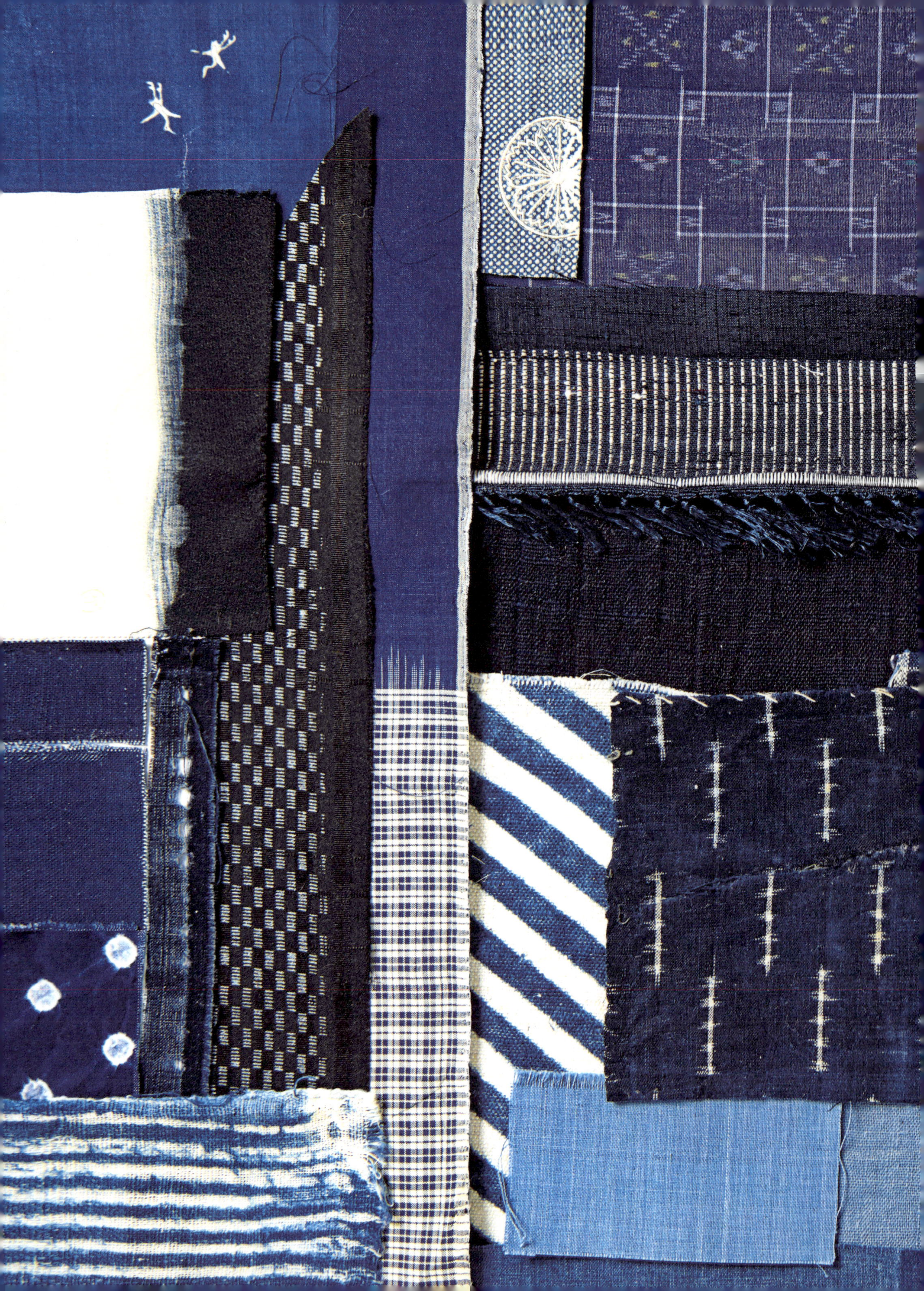

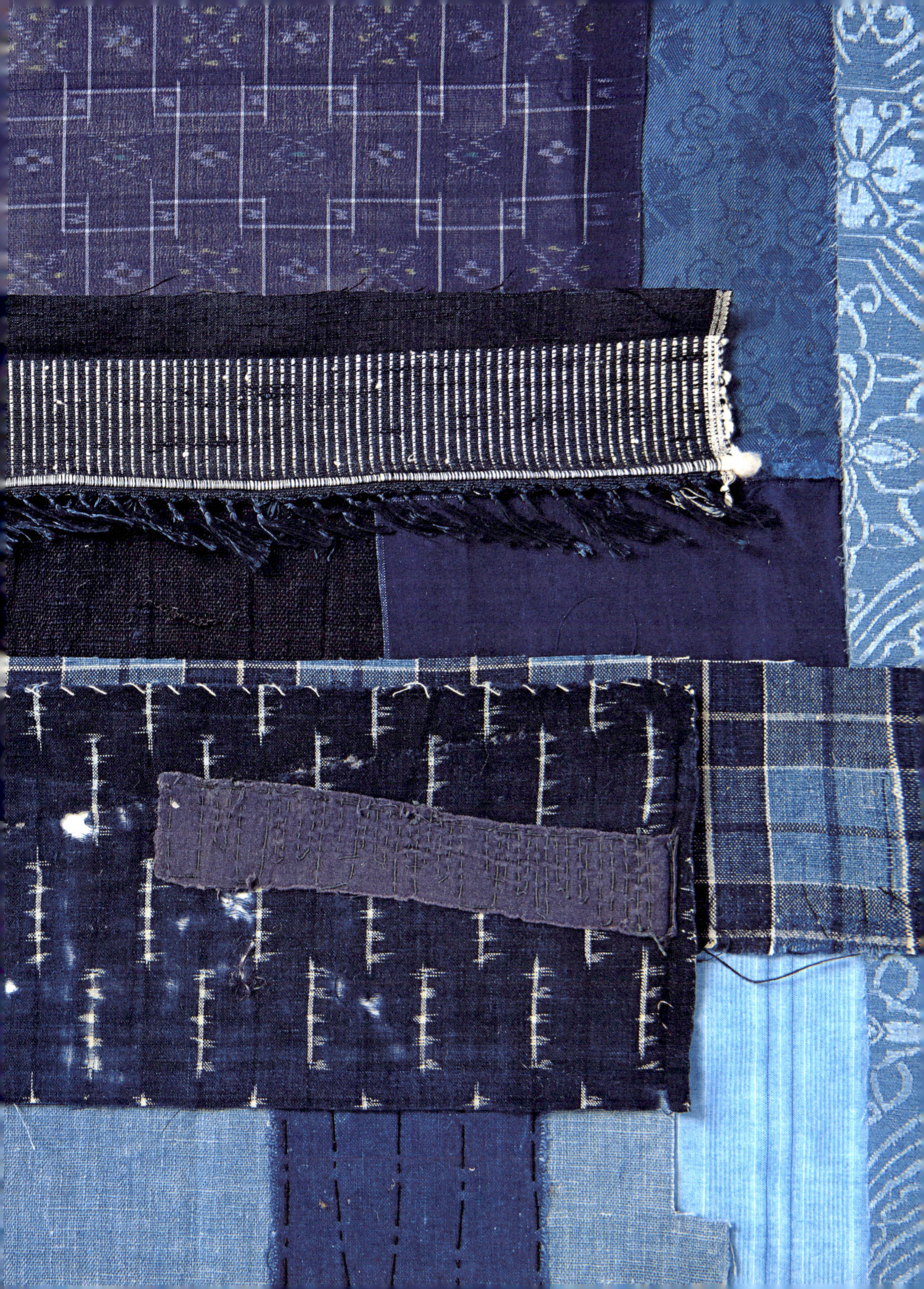

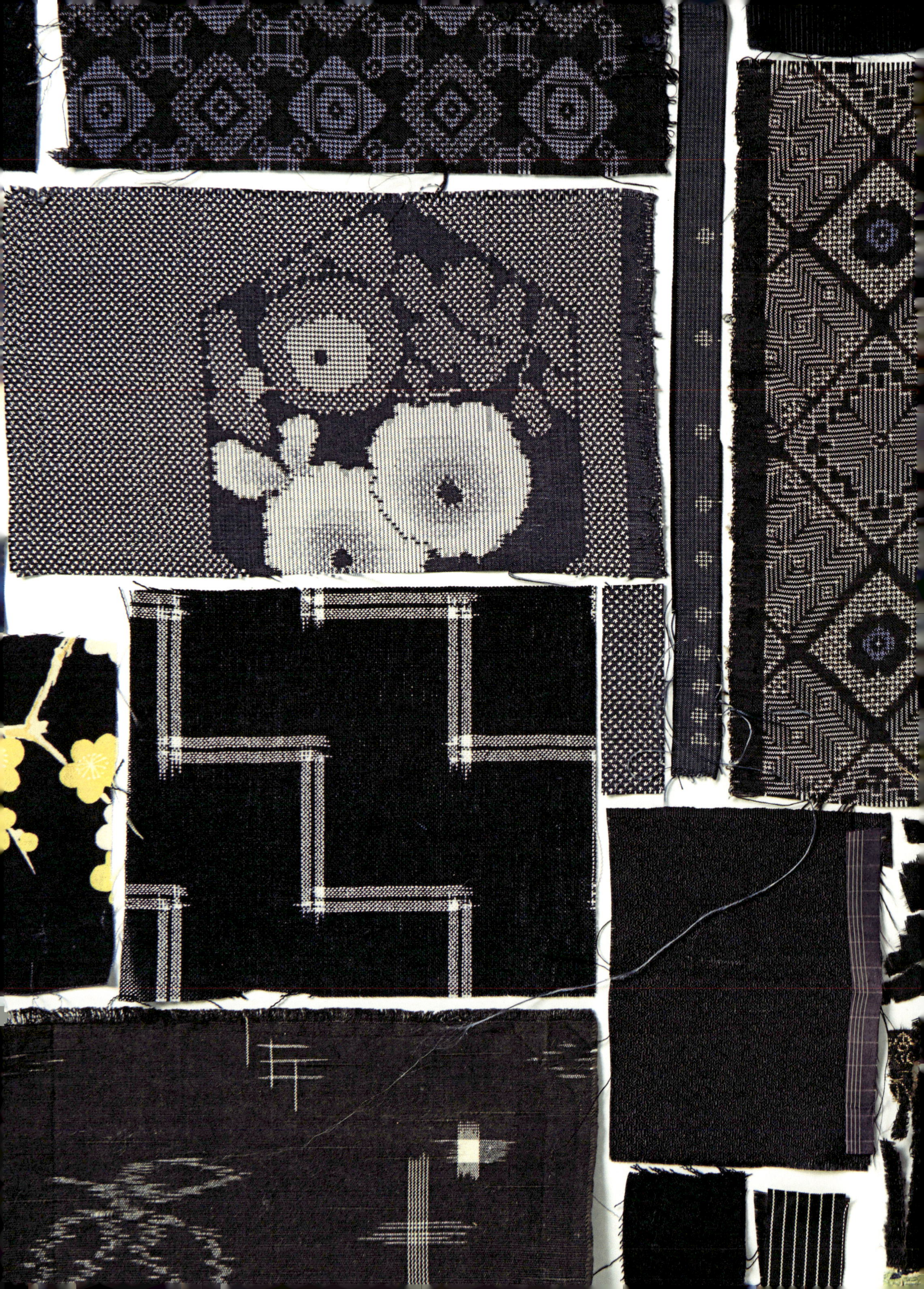

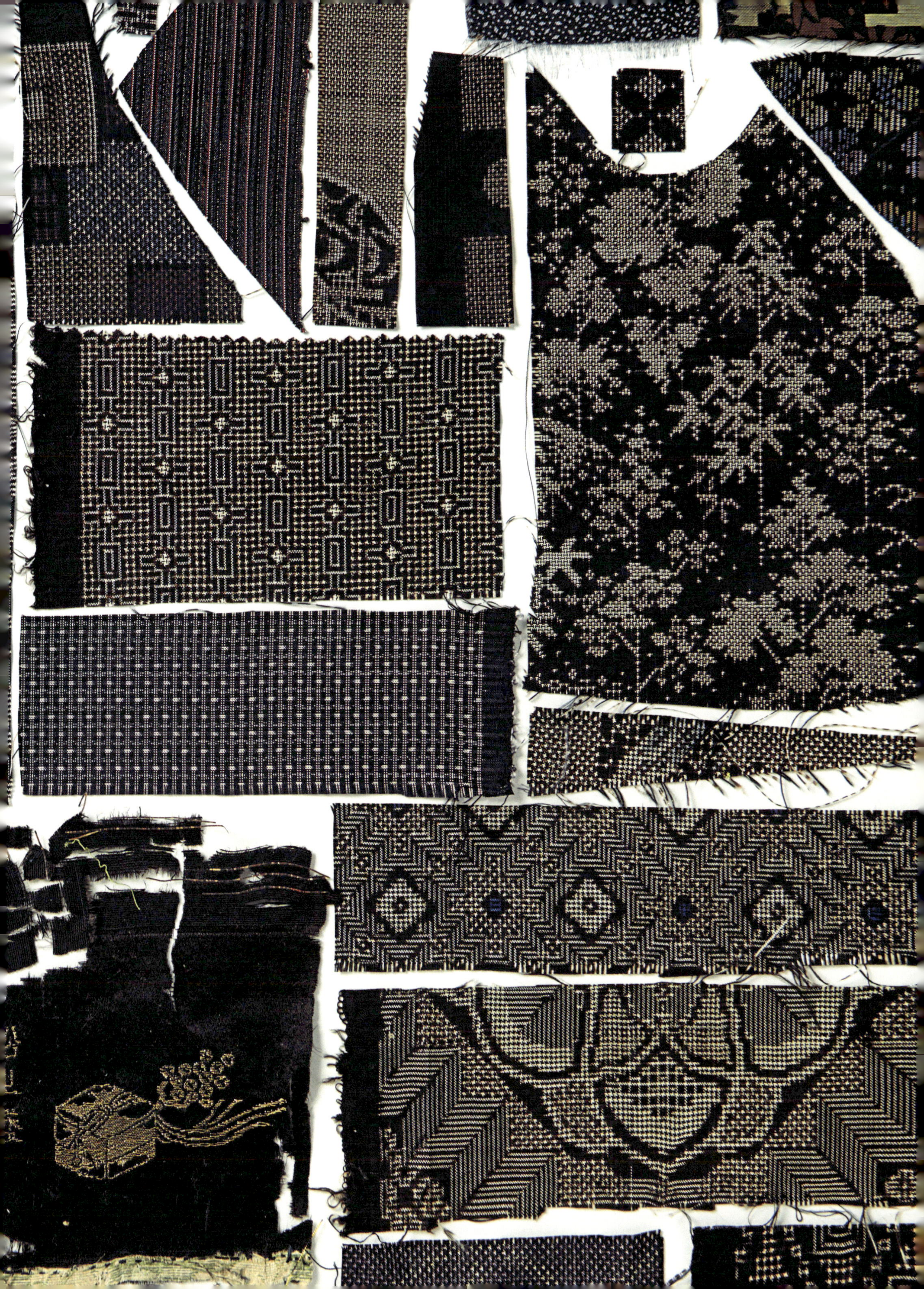

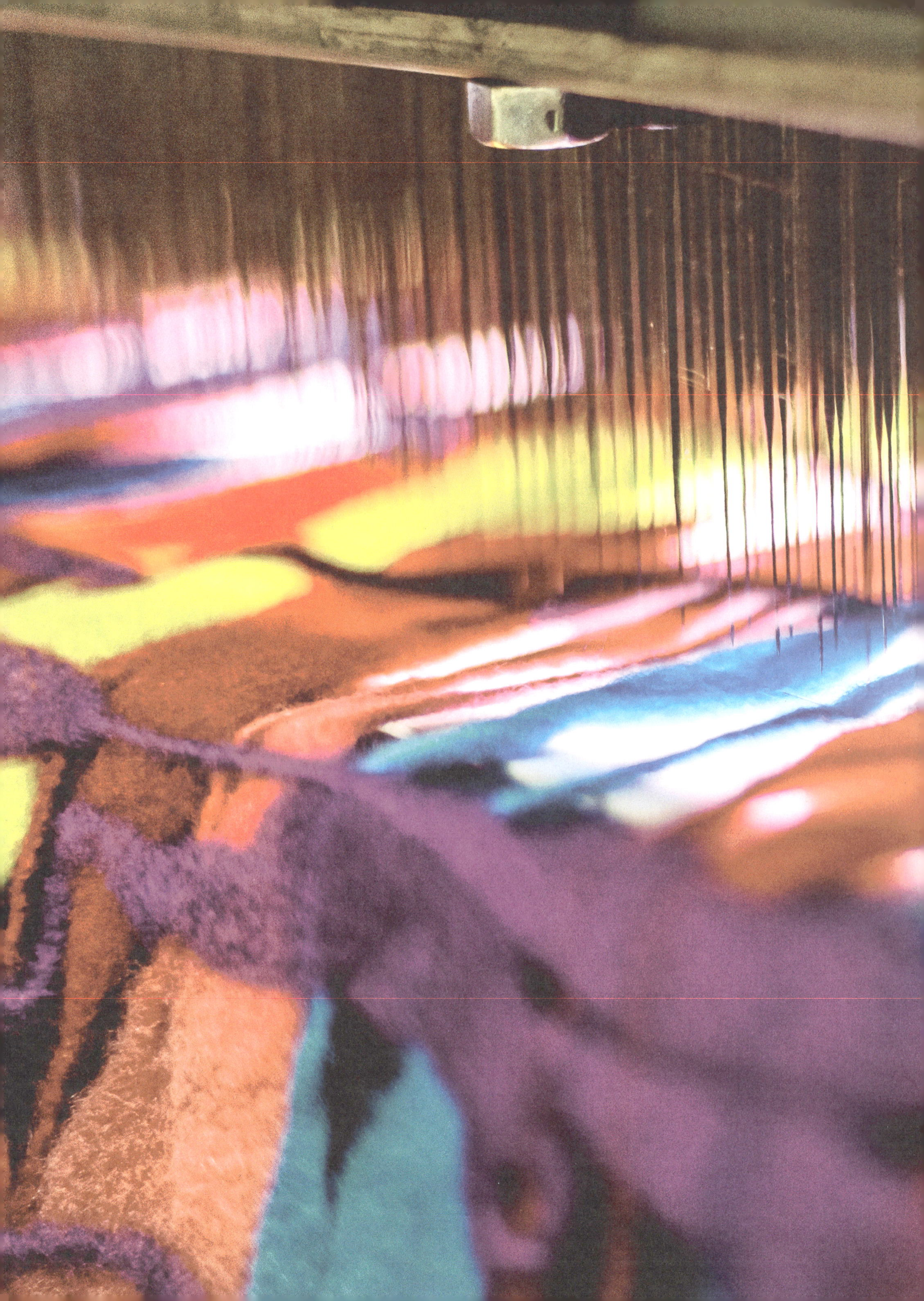

Chronology of Textiles

Puffed Blocks, 1979
(reissued in 1987)
Junichi Arai
Nagai Weaving Inc.
Jacquard weave
60% cotton, 40%
polyester (including
polyurethane).
p. 25

Lunatic Fringe, 1982
(reissued in 1995)
Junichi Arai, reissued
by Reiko Sudo
Onishi Weaving Co.
Jacquard weave
100% cotton
p. 330

Basket Weave Big Pocket, 1984
Junichi Arai
Nagai Weaving Inc.
and Okonogi Knit Co.
Jacquard weave
100% cotton
p. 44

Bashofu 80 Stripes, 1984
Reiko Sudo
Onishi Weaving Co.
Jacquard weave
recycled thread
(*basho* plantain)
100% cotton
pp. 140–41

Chirimen Tazuna Stripes, 1984
(reissued in 2008)
Junichi Arai, reissued
by Reiko Sudo
Nagai Weaving Inc.
(Reissue with SD
Fabric Inc.)
Jacquard weave
100% cotton
p. 139

Film Pattern, 1984
Reiko Sudo
Onishi Weaving Co.
Dobby weave
98% cotton, 2%
polyurethane
p. 128

Embroidery Border, 1984
Reiko Sudo
Fukuma Embroidery Works
Machine embroidery
100% cotton
p. 96

Embroidery Checker, 1984
Reiko Sudo
Fukuma Embroidery Works
Machine embroidery
100% nylon

Woven Structure Pattern, 1984
Junichi Arai
Arai Minoru
Orimono Co.
Jacquard weave
100% cotton
p. 13

Shuro, 1984
(reissued in 1997)
Junichi Arai, reissued
by Reiko Sudo
Onishi Weaving Co.
Jacquard weave
51% wool, 49% cotton
pp. 30–31

Bronze Aluminium Glitz, 1984
Reiko Sudo,
engineering by Junichi Arai
Oike Sangyo Co.
Dobby weave
50% nylon
50% polyester
p. 162

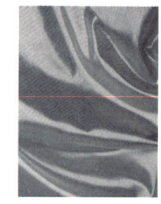

Silver Aluminium Glitz, 1984
Reiko Sudo,
engineering by Junichi Arai
KAYTAY Texinno Inc.
Dobby weave
50% nylon
50% polyester

Ginseng, 1984
(reissued in 1992)
Junichi Arai, reissued
by Reiko Sudo
Onishi Weaving Co.
Jacquard weave,
hand-cutting, felting
100% wool
p. 325

Cotton Candy, 1985
Reiko Sudo
Onishi Weaving Co.
Jacquard weave
51% cotton
49% polyester
p. 18

Demon Crepe, 1985
Reiko Sudo,
engineering by Junichi Arai
Onishi Weaving Co.
Jacquard weave
66% wool
34% cotton
p. 71

Bias Puff, 1985
(reproduced in 2010)
Reiko Sudo,
engineering by Junichi Arai
Onishi Weaving Co.
(reproduction with
Marunaka Weaving Co.)
Jacquard weave,
cross-dyeing
51% cotton, 49% polyester
p. 43

Kakuré Cho (Hidden Butterflies), 1985
Surface design
by Reiko Sudo,
engineering by
Junichi Arai
Onishi Weaving Co.
Jacquard weave
53% cotton, 39%
wool 8% polyurethane
p. 84

Brush Pattern, 1985
Reiko Sudo
Onishi Weaving Co.
Jacquard weave
55% cotton
45% wool

Arrow Ikat, 1985
Junichi Arai
Hyodo Orimono Inc.
Jacquard weave
100% cotton

Big Triangle, 1985
Junichi Arai
Hyodo Orimono Inc.
Jacquard weave
100% cotton

Tubular Weave Cobblestones, 1985
Junichi Arai
Hyodo Orimono Inc.
Jacquard weave
100% cotton

Burned Out Woolly Thistle, 1985
Junichi Arai
Oike Sangyo Co.
Melt-off
100% nylon
(aluminium metallized)

Cedar Bark, 1986
(reissued in 1993)
Junichi Arai, reissued
by Reiko Sudo
Kaneko Weaving Inc.
Dobby weave
43% rayon, 22%
cotton, 21% nylon, 14%
polyester (reissued
with 100% polyester)
pp. 102–3

Monster, 1987
(reproduced in 2010)
Surface design by
Narihiko Joya
Onishi Weaving Co.
(reproduction with
Marunaka Weaving Co.)
Jacquard weave,
cross-dyeing
51% cotton, 49%
polyester

Vortex, 1987
Reiko Sudo
Nagai Weaving Co.
Jacquard weave
51% cotton
49% wool

Mist, 1987
Reiko Sudo
Nagai Weaving Co.
Dobby weave
60% rayon
40% nylon

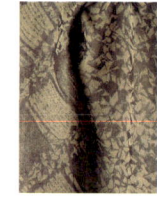

Crumpled Pattern and Comb Shape, 1987
Surface design
by Reiko Sudo,
engineering by
Junichi Arai
Onishi Weaving Co.
Jacquard weave,
multilayer weave
100% cotton

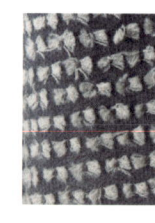

Papillon, 1987
(reissued in 2018)
Reiko Sudo
Nagai Weaving Co.
(reissued with Tayu
Kigyo Inc.)
Jacquard weave,
hand-cutting
89% silk, 11% wool

Fuzz, 1987
Reiko Sudo,
engineering by
Junichi Arai
Onishi Weaving Co.
Jacquard weave
100% cotton
p. 324

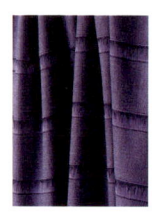

Akiha, 1988
Reiko Sudo
Hyodo Orimono Inc.
Jacquard weave,
spaced weft
51% wool
49% cotton

Contour Line, 1988
Reiko Sudo
Kimura Senko
Dye Works Inc.
Melt-off
100% nylon
(aluminium metallized)
p. 169

Nuno Shelves, 1988
Reiko Sudo
Orimoto
Yamakuchi Inc.
Jacquard weave
100% cotton

House, 1988
Reiko Sudo,
engineering by
Junichi Arai
Onishi Weaving Co.
Jacquard weave,
multilayer weave
100% cotton

Fluffy Hair, 1989
Reiko Sudo
Nagai Weaving Co. and
Hiruma Shearing Inc.
Dobby weave,
hand-cutting
70% polyester,
30% silk
p. 39

Bellows, 1989
(reissued in 1999)
Reiko Sudo
Orimoto Yamakuchi Inc.
(reissued with
Marunaka
Weaving Co.)
Dobby weave
51% rayon, 49% cotton
(reissued with 100%
cotton) pp. 76–77

Giza, 1989
Surface design
by Reiko Sudo,
engineering by
Junichi Arai
Onishi Weaving Co.
Jacquard weave
53% cotton, 39% wool,
8% polyurethane

*Tubular Weave
Border*, 1989
Reiko Sudo
Hyodo Orimono Inc.
Jacquard weave
50% wool, 50% cotton
p. 136

Sputtered Gloss, 1990
(reissued in 1994)
Reiko Sudo,
engineering
by Kanebo Inc.
Suzutora Co.
Sputtering
100% polyester
pp. 174–75

*White Noise
(Boom Bass)*, 1991
Reiko Sudo
Y. M. Textile Inc.
Dobby weave
100% wool
pp. 40–41

*White Noise
(House Remix)*, 1991
Reiko Sudo
Y. M. Textile Inc.
Dobby weave
100% wool

Streambed, 1991
Reiko Sudo
Iizuka Orimono Inc.
Warp-dyeing, dobby
weave, transfer-
printing
76% cotton
24% polyester

First Snow, 1991
Reiko Sudo
Iizuka Orimono Inc.
Warp-dyeing, dobby
weave, transfer-
printing
76% cotton,
24% polyester

Birchbark, 1991
Reiko Sudo
Iizuka Orimono Inc.
Warp-dyeing
Dobby weave
Transfer-printing
76% cotton
24% polyester.

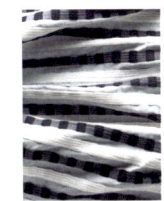

Louvre Block, 1991
Reiko Sudo
Marunaka Weaving Co.
Dobby weave
68% cotton, 32% wool
p. 148

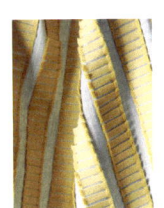

Louvre Stripe, 1991
Reiko Sudo
Marunaka Weaving Co.
Dobby weave,
hand-cutting
61% cotton
39% wool
p. 114

Fuse, 1991
Reiko Sudo
Marunaka Weaving Co.
Dobby weave
66% wool,
34% cotton
pp. 272–73

Sanshuyu Linen, 1991
Surface design by
Sayuri Shimoda,
engineering by
Junichi Arai
Fukuma Embroidery
Works
Machine embroidery
100% linen

Rusted Silver, 1991
Reiko Sudo
Y.M. Textile Inc.
Dobby weave
58% cotton, 39% lamé
(35% rayon, 4% silver),
3% polyester

Embroidery Ajiro, 1992
(reissued in 2010)
Reiko Sudo
Fukuma Embroidery
Works
Machine embroidery
50% cotton, 50%
rayon (reissued
with 100% cotton)
p. 101

Cedar, 1992
Reiko Sudo
Onishi Weaving Co.
Jacquard weave,
cross-dyeing
55% polyester,
45% cotton

Ashanti Stamps, 1992
Reiko Sudo,
engineering by
Junichi Arai
Onishi Weaving Co.
Jacquard weave,
multilayer weave
100% cotton

Cracked Quilt, 1992
Reiko Sudo
Kimura Senko Dye
Works Inc.
Burn-out, multi-
headed embroidery
Ground: 100% wool
Surface: 100% rayon
pp. 336–37

Agitfab, 1992
Reiko Sudo
Kimura Senko Dye
Works Inc.
Bonding
100% polyester,
newspaper from
Myanmar

Leopard Spots, 1992
Reiko Sudo
Y. M. Textile Inc.
Jacquard weave
84% acetate, 16% wool
pp. 192–93

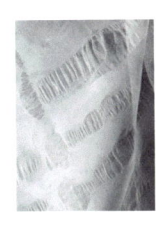

Cirrus, 1992
Reiko Sudo and
Yuka Taniguchi
Nuno Corporation
and Kyo Silk
Maruya Inc.
Hand-painting,
salt-shrinking
100% silk

Nimbus, 1992
Reiko Sudo and
Yuka Taniguchi
Nuno Corporation
and Kyo Silk
Maruya Inc.
Hand-painting,
salt-shrinking
100% silk
p. 242

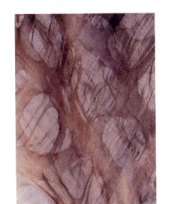

Stratus, 1992
Reiko Sudo and
Yuka Taniguchi
Nuno Corporation and
Kyo Silk Maruya Inc.
Hand-painting,
salt-shrinking
100% silk
p. 243

Tozan Stripe, 1993
Reiko Sudo
Y. M. Textile Inc.
Dobby weave
100% cotton

Kando-Utsushi, 1993
Reiko Sudo
Y. M. Textile Inc.
Dobby weave
100% cotton

Ice House, 1993
Reiko Sudo
Nagai Weaving Inc.
and Okonogi Knit Co.
Jacquard weave,
leno weave, knit cord
50% cotton, 50% wool
p. 45

Willow Crepe, 1993
Reiko Sudo
Y. M. Textile Inc.
Dobby weave
97% silk, 1.5% cotton,
1.5% polyurethane

Fingerplay, 1993
Reiko Sudo
Fukuma Embroidery
Works
Machine embroidery
100% cotton

Copper Mocha, 1993
Reiko Sudo
Tsuguo Inc.
Dobby weave
84% copper,
16% Promix™
pp. 170–71

Jellyfish, 1993
(reissued in 2000)
Reiko Sudo
Kimura Senko Dye
Works Inc. (reissued
with Nakanishi Dye
Works Inc.)
Heat-setting, washing
100% polyester
pp. 56–65

Feather Flurries, 1993
Reiko Sudo
Tsuguo Inc.
Jacquard weave
100% silk with feathers
p. 217

Cherry-Petal Shell, 1993
Reiko Sudo
Tsuguo Inc.
Dobby weave
100% silk

Heat-moulded Velvet, 1993
Reiko Sudo
Yamazaki Velvet Co.
Velvet weave, heat-setting
Ground: 100% polyester
Pile: 100% rayon
pp. 294–95

Sand Dunes, 1993
Reiko Sudo
Y.M. Textile Inc.
Dobby weave
85% wool, 15% cotton
p. 143

Osage-zome 'Braid-Transfer', 1993
Reiko Sudo
Y. M. Textile Inc.
Transfer-printing
100% polyester
p. 92

Stainless Cloth, 1993
Reiko Sudo
Tsuguo Inc.
Dobby weave
60% stainless steel, 40% cotton
pp. 186–87

Wool Slabs, 1993
Kazuhiro Ueno, engineering by Reiko Sudo
Y.M. Textile Inc.
Dobby weave
100% wool

Jonathan Checker, 1993
Reiko Sudo
Y.M. Textile Inc.
Dobby weave
100% cotton

Shigoki-zome 'Squeegee Wipe', 1993
Reiko Sudo
Kimura Senko Dye Works Inc.
Hand screen-printing
100% silk
p. 93

Squared Stripes, 1993
Surface design by Sayuri Shimoda, engineering by Reiko Sudo
Hyodo Orimono Inc.
Jacquard weave
100% cotton
p. 142

Floe, 1994
Reiko Sudo
Nagai Weaving Inc. and Okonogi Knit Co.
Jacquard weave, leno weave, knit cord
51% wool, 49% cotton

Shifu (Paper Cloth), 1994
Reiko Sudo
Tsuguo Inc.
Dobby weave
52% silk, 23% paper, 20% cotton, 5% polyurethane
p. 89

Copper Scarab, 1994
Reiko Sudo
Tsuguo Inc.
Dobby weave
60% copper, 40% cotton
pp. 164–65; p. 185

Brass Cloth, 1994
Reiko Sudo
Tsuguo Inc.
Dobby weave
60% brass, 40% cotton
p. 188

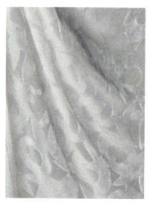

Bamboo Flower, 1994
Reiko Sudo
Kimura Senko Dye Works Inc.
Burn-out, velvet weave, hand screen-printing
Ground: 100% polyester
Pile: 100% rayon
p. 179

Slipstream, 1994
Reiko Sudo
Daifuku Paper Inc. and Tsuguo Inc.
Dobby weave
83% silk, 17% Mino *washi* paper
pp. 234–35

Smokey Quartz, 1994 (reissued in 2007)
Reiko Sudo, engineering by Junichi Arai
KAYTAY Texinno Inc. (reissued with Fuji Chigira Inc.)
Dobby weave, melt-off
100% polyester

Space Suit, 1994 (reissued in 2007)
Reiko Sudo, engineering by Junichi Arai
KAYTAY Texinno Inc. (reissued with Fuji Chigira Inc.)
Dobby weave
100% polyester
p. 181

Copper Comb, 1994
Reiko Sudo
Tsuguo Inc.
Dobby weave
65% wool, 35% copper
p. 194

Honeycomb plaid, 1994
Reiko Sudo
Y. M. Textile Inc.
Dobby weave
100% wool
p. 42

Dobin-Zome 'Kettle-Pouring', 1994
Reiko Sudo
Umetani Dye Works
Hand-painting
100% silk
pp. 238–39

Scrapyard Iron Plates, 1994
Reiko Sudo and Hiroko Kobayashi
Nuno Corporation and Hikari Shoji Inc.
Hand-dyeing
100% rayon
pp. 274–75

Scrapyard Nails, 1994
Reiko Sudo and Hiroko Kobayashi
Nuno Corporation and Hikari Shoji Inc.
Hand-dyeing
100% rayon

Moth-eaten, 1994
Reiko Sudo
Y. M. Textile Inc.
Burn-out
85% cotton, 15% polyester.

Spanish Moss, 1994
Reiko Sudo
Y. M. Textile Inc.
Jacquard weave
60% wool, 40% silk
p. 306; pp. 338–39

Moss, 1994
Reiko Sudo
Y. M. Textile Inc.
Jacquard weave
60% wool, 40% silk
p. 47

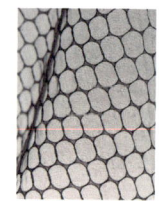

Bubble Pack, 1994
Reiko Sudo
Komori Dye Works and Kyo Silk Maruya Inc.
Hand screen printing, salt-shrinking
100% silk
pp. 218–19

Farm Tools, 1995
Reiko Sudo
Onishi Weaving Co.
Jacquard weave
100% cotton

Rice Hulls, 1995
Reiko Sudo
Hyodo Orimono Inc.
Jacquard weave
100% cotton
p. 270

Furrow, 1995
Reiko Sudo
Onishi Weaving Co.
Jacquard weave
65% cotton, 30% wool, 5% nylon

Bell and Ivy, 1995
Surface design by Sayuri Shimoda, engineering by Reiko Sudo
Onishi Weaving Co.
Jacquard weave
100% cotton
p. 35

Honeycomb Stripes, 1995
Reiko Sudo
Y. M. Textile Inc.
Dobby weave
100% wool

Velvet Melt-off, 1995
Reiko Sudo
Yamazaki Velvet Co.
and Takekura Inc.
Velvet weave, melt-off
100% polyester
(aluminium metallized).

Turkish Wall, 1995
Reiko Sudo
Nakanishi Dye
Works Inc.
Hand screen-printing,
flocking
100% polyester
pigment (titanium
white)
pp. 248–57

Graffiti, 1995
Reiko Sudo
Nakanishi Dye Works
Hand screen-printing,
flocking
100% polyester
pigment (titanium
white)

Ice Floes, 1995
Reiko Sudo
Tsuguo Inc.
Jacquard weave
84% silk, 16% rayon
p. 226

Coal, 1995
Reiko Sudo
Yoshimura
Senmatsu Inc.
Dobby weave
100% polyester

Tubular Weave Mogul,
1995
Reiko Sudo
Onishi Weaving Co.
Jacquard weave
100% cotton
pp. 318–19

Website, 1995
Reiko Sudo
Onishi Weaving Co.
Dobby weave, felting
100% wool
pp. 308–9

Skyscraper, 1995
Reiko Sudo
Hyodo Orimono Inc.
Jacquard weave,
hand-cutting
100% cotton
p. 258

Jungle, 1995
Reiko Sudo
Hyodo Orimono Inc.
Jacquard weave,
hand-cutting
85% cotton, 15% wool

Stainless Leno, 1995
Reiko Sudo
Y. M. Textile Inc.
Leno weave
80% stainless steel,
20% silk

Overhang, 1996
Reiko Sudo
Marunaka Weaving Co.
Dobby weave
100% cotton
pp. 150–51

Wild Corn, 1996
Reiko Sudo
Marunaka Weaving Co.
Jacquard weave
58% wool, 25% cupra,
20% rayon

Crostata, 1996
Reiko Sudo
Onishi Weaving Co.
Jacquard weave
58% nylon, 20%
cotton, 22%
polyurethane
(Spandex™)
pp. 78–79

Biscuit, 1996
Reiko Sudo
Onishi Weaving Co.
Jacquard weave
53% nylon, 24%
cotton, 23%
polyurethane
p. 145

K9 Clip, 1996
Reiko Sudo
Y. M. Textile Inc.
Dobby weave
36% silk, 30% wool,
4% rayon, 21%
paper, 6% nylon, 3%
polyurethane
pp. 50–51

Stretch Kasuri, 1996
Reiko Sudo
Tsuguo Inc.
Dobby weave,
ikat yarn
41% silk, 38% ramie,
15% nylon, 6%
polyurethane

Crazy Stitches, 1996
Surface design
by Kazuhiro Ueno,
engineering by
Reiko Sudo,
Fukuma Embroidery
Works
Machine embroidery
100% cotton

Mica, 1996
(reissued in 2006)
Reiko Sudo
Takekura Inc., KAYTAY
Texinno Inc. and Daito
Pleats Co., Ltd
Melt-off, pleating
100% polyester
p. 227

Delphi, 1996
Reiko Sudo
Daito Pleats Co.Ltd
Dobby weave, pleating
100% polyester
pp. 68–69

Switchboard, 1996
Reiko Sudo
Tsuguo Inc.
Dobby weave
50% copper, 50%
cotton

Teasel, 1996
Reiko Sudo
Fukuma Embroidery
Works
Machine embroidery
100% cotton

Gouache, 1996
Reiko Sudo and
Yuka Taniguchi
Nuno Corporation and
Yamazaki Velvet Co.
Velvet weave, burn-
out, hand-painting
Ground: 100%
polyester
Pile: 100% rayon
p. 286

Edgeweiss, 1996
Reiko Sudo
Onishi Weaving Co.
Jacquard weave,
hand-cutting
100% cotton
p. 313

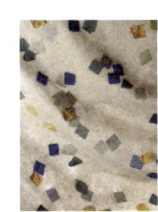

Terrazzo Felt 'Nuno',
1996
Reiko Sudo
Yamanashi
Finishing Co.
Needle-punching
85% wool, 15% alpaca,
remnants of various
Nuno fabrics

Computer Chip, 1996
Reiko Sudo
Hyodo Orimono Inc.
Jacquard weave
100% cotton
p. 271

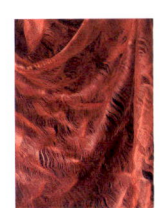

Reed Ripple, 1996
Reiko Sudo,
Saito Sangyo
Dobby weave
50% silk, 50% nylon
pp. 232–33

*Eulalia Crepe /
Cicada*, 1996
Reiko Sudo
Y.M. Textile Inc.
Dobby weave
36% silk, 30% wool
21% paper, 6% nylon
4% rayon, 3%
polyurethane
pp. 86–87

Knossos, 1997
Reiko Sudo
Onishi Weaving Co..
Jacquard weave,
recycled thread
(*basho* plantain)
100% cotton

Shii Tree, 1997
Reiko Sudo
Onishi Weaving Co.
Jacquard weave
51% wool, 49% cotton
pp. 48–49

Wave Head, 1997
Reiko Sudo
Tsuguo Inc.
Jacquard weave
60% silk, 26% rayon,
12% cotton, 2%
polyurethane
p. 80

Fisheye, 1997
Reiko Sudo
Fukuma Embroidery
Works
Machine embroidery
100% cotton
p. 100

Wavelets, 1997
Reiko Sudo
Tsuguo Inc.
Dobby weave
78% polyester,
16% nylon, 5%
polyurethane, 1% Mino
washi paper
p. 149

Stress and Stripes, 1997
Reiko Sudo
Yamanashi Finishing Co.
Needle-punching
100% polyester

Cavern, 1997
Reiko Sudo
Fukuma Embroidery Works
Machine embroidery
70% cotton, 30% rayon

Moss Temple, 1997
Reiko Sudo
Yamazaki Velvet Co. and Urase Co.
Velvet weave, hand screen-printing, heat-setting (near infrared radiation)
76% rayon, 24% polyester
p. 340

Patched Paper, 1997
Reiko Sudo
Daifuku Paper Inc., Tsuguo Inc. and Hiruma Shearing Inc.
Jacquard weave, hand-cutting
57% Mino *washi* paper, 43% polyester

Combed Paper, 1997
Reiko Sudo
Daifuku Paper Inc., Tsuguo Inc. and Hiruma Shearing Inc.
Jacquard weave, hand-cutting
57% Mino *washi* paper, 43% polyester
pp. 230–31

Shutters, 1997
Reiko Sudo
Kato Embroidery Inc.
Multi-headed embroidery, washing, reclaimed thread
100% nylon
p. 6

Heracleum, 1997
Reiko Sudo
Fukuma Embroidery Works
Machine embroidery
100% cotton
Embroidery thread: 100% rayon

Barley Spike, 1997
Surface design by Sayuri Shimoda
Fukuma Embroidery Works
Machine embroidery
100% rayon

Fava, 1997
Reiko Sudo, Hiroko Kobayashi and Ryoko Sugiura
Nuno Corporation and Kato Embroidery Inc.
Multi-headed embroidery, washing
65% acrylic, 25% wool, 10% rayon
pp. 284–85

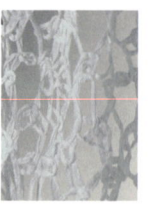

Flower Basket, 1997
Reiko Sudo and Yukiko Takahashi
Kato Embroidery Inc.
Multi-headed embroidery, washing
100% cotton
pp. 290–91

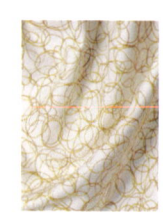

Rubber Band Scatter, 1997
Reiko Sudo
Shiga Asa Kogyou Inc. and Umetani Dye Works
Hand screen-printing
100% linen, pigment (acrylic and silicone)
p. 10

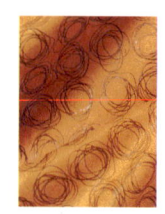

Rubber Band Line-up, 1997
Reiko Sudo
Shiga Asa Kogyou Inc. and Umetani Dye Works
Hand screen-printing
100% linen, pigment (acrylic and silicone)

Waterglass, 1997
Reiko Sudo
Y. M. Textile Inc.
Pleating
100% polyester
carbon fibre

Cloud Chamber, 1997
Surface design by Keiji Otani, engineering by Reiko Sudo
Kimura Senko Dye Works Inc.
Melt-off, hand screen-printing
51% polyester, 49% nylon
p. 195

Tsugihagi, 1997
Reiko Sudo and Kazuhiro Ueno
Kato Embroidery Inc.
Bonding, multi-headed embroidery, recycled thread (*basho* plantain)
100% cotton, remnants of various Nuno *bashofu* fabrics,
pp. 326–27

Origami Pleats, 1997
Reiko Sudo and Mizue Okada
Nuno Corporation
Pleating, transfer-printing
100% polyester
pp. 109–10; p. 208

Whalebone, 1997
Reiko Sudo
Hyodo Orimono Inc.
Jacquard weave
95% wool, 5% acrylic
p. 88

Water Puddles, 1997
Reiko Sudo
Hyodo Orimono Inc.
Jacquard weave
Hand-cutting
100% wool

Mountain (Pinch Puff), 1997
Reiko Sudo, engineering by Hiroko Kobayashi
Nuno Corporation and Takekura Inc.
Heat-setting, transfer-printing
100% polyester
p. 73

Peak (Pinch Puff), 1997
Reiko Sudo, engineering by Hiroko Kobayashi
Nuno Corporation and Takekura Inc.
Heat-setting, transfer-printing
100% polyester
pp. 90–91

Colour Plate, 1997
Reiko Sudo
Hyodo Orimono Inc.
Jacquard weave
100% wool
pp. 152–61

Molt, 1997
Reiko Sudo and Minako Tabane
Kyo Silk Maruya Inc.
Hand screen-printing, salt-shrinking
100% silk

Mercury, 1997
Surface design by Reiko Sudo, engineering by Keiji Otani
Kimura Senko Dye Works Inc.
Bonding, hand screen-printing, foil printing
100% silk
pp. 176–77

Sumi-Zome 'Inking', 1997
Reiko Sudo anf Yuka Taniguchi
Nuno Corporation
Hand-painting
100% pineapple

Brushwood, 1998
Reiko Sudo
Marunaka Weaving Co.
Dobby weave
57% wool, 43% silk

Nesting Instinct, 1998
Surface design by Kazuhiro Ueno, engineering by Reiko Sudo
Onishi Weaving Co.
Jacquard weave
100% cotton
pp. 52–53

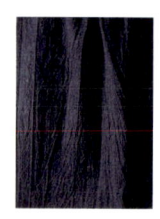

Stainless Sparklers, 1998
Reiko Sudo
Tsuguo Inc.
Dobby weave
53% cotton, 38% stainless, 6% nylon, 3% polyurethane
p. 180

Stained Glass, 1998
Surface design by Sayuri Shimoda, engineering by Reiko Sudo
Tsuguo Inc. and Tsunemi Dye Works
Dobby weave, hand screen-printing, burn-out
70% polyester, 30% cotton

Kase, 1998
Reiko Sudo
Tsuguo Inc. and Tsunemi Dye Works
Dobby weave, hand screen-printing, burn-out
41% wool, 39% cotton, 20% polyester

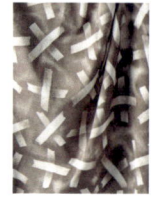

Masking Tape, 1998
Kazuhiro Ueno
Komori Dye Works
Hand screen-printing
100% cotton

Folk Dance, 1998
Kazuhiro Ueno, engineering by Reiko Sudo
Tsuguo Inc.
Jacquard weave, hand-cutting
80% nylon, 20% silk

Karéha, 1998
Reiko Sudo and Yoko Ando
Fukuma Embroidery Works
Machine embroidery, washing
65% acrylic, 25% wool, 10% rayon
pp. 260–61

Chilly Wind, 1998
Reiko Sudo
Tsuguo Inc.
Dobby weave
55% cotton, 45% silk
p. 85

Mongami (Punchcard), 1998
Kazuhiro Ueno, engineering by Reiko Sudo
Tsuguo Inc. and Tsunemi Dye Works
Dobby weave, hand screen-printing, burn-out
70% polyester, 30% cotton pp. 292–93

Hopscotch, 1999
Reiko Sudo
Y. M. Textile Inc.
Dobby weave
100% cotton
p. 137

Garçon Stripe, 1999
Reiko Sudo
Onishi Weaving Co.
Jacquard weave
67% cotton, 33% wool

Imitation Hitta Kanoko, 1999
Reiko Sudo, engineering by Hiroko Kobayashi
Y.M. Textile Inc.
Dobby weave
100% silk
p. 94

Sandwich, 1999
Reiko Sudo
Tsuguo Inc.
Dobby weave, burn-out
55% silk, 45% cotton
p. 144

Suzushi, 1999
Reiko Sudo
Matsuoka Co., Ltd
Dobby weave, leno weave
100% silk
p. 172

Suzushi stripe, 1999
Reiko Sudo
Matsuoka Co., Ltd
Dobby weave, leno weave
100% silk
pp. 122–23

Southern Cross, 1999
Surface design by Ryoko Sugiura, engineering by Reiko Sudo
Y. M. Textile Inc.
Bonding
100% polyester, glass beads
p. 173

Cavex Stripe, 1999
Reiko Sudo
Onishi Weaving Co.
Jacquard weave
60% silk, 30% nylon, 10% polyurethane
p. 128

Millet Craft, 1999
Reiko Sudo, Ryoko Sugiura
Tsuguo Inc.
Jacquard weave
60% cupra, 23% rayon, 17% wool

Sashi-nui, 2000
Reiko Sudo
Tsuguo Inc.
Jacquard weave
100% cotton

Bagheera Velvet Rounds, 2000
Reiko Sudo
Taenaka Pile Weaving Co.
Velvet weave
100% cotton
p. 34

Ichimatsu-Sashi, 2000
Reiko Sudo
Tsuguo Inc. and Hiruma Shearing Inc.
Jacquard weave, hand-cutting, shearing, 55% cotton, 30% silk, 13% polyester, 2% polyurethane
p. 81

Window Box, 2000
Reiko Sudo
SD Fabric Inc.
Jacquard weave
60% wool, 40% nylon

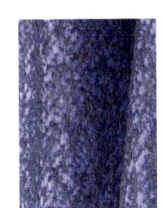

Snowflakes, 2000
Reiko Sudo
Tsuguo Inc. and Hiruma Shearing Inc.
Jacquard weave, hand-cutting, shearing
70% cotton, 30% wool (21% mohair)

Hoarfrost, 2000
Reiko Sudo
Tsuguo Inc. and Hiruma Shearing Inc.
Jacquard weave, hand-cutting, shearing
70% cotton, 30% wool (21% mohair)
p. 334

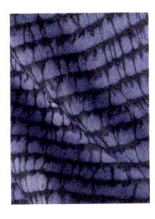

Frozen Cascade, 2000
Reiko Sudo
Tsuguo Inc. and Hiruma Shearing Inc.
Jacquard weave hand-cutting, shearing
70% cotton, 30% wool (21% mohair)

Amate, 2000
Reiko Sudo
Yamazaki Velvet Inc., Taki Paper Inc. and Nakanishi Dye Works
Bonding, hand screen-printing
Ground: 100% polyester; pile: 100% rayon; surface: Echizen *washi* paper
pp. 200–7

Burner Dye, 2000
Reiko Sudo
Tsuguo Inc. and Kyo Silk Maruya Inc.
Dobby weave, burning
Ground: 100% cotton
Surface: 100% stainless steel
pp. 342–43

Arrow Feathers, 2000
Reiko Sudo
Hyodo Orimono Inc.
Jacquard weave
100% wool
pp. 132–33

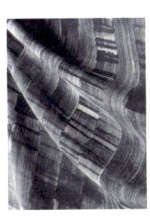

Sumi-Zome 'Inking', 2000
Reiko Sudo and Yuka Taniguchi
Nuno Corporation
Hand-painting
100% rayon.

Deep Roots (Stainless Burner Dye), 2000
Reiko Sudo
Matsui Knitting Crafts Mfg., Ltd.
Raschel lacework, burning
100% stainless steel
pp. 316–17

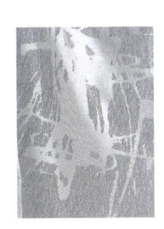

Ink Painting, 2000
Surface design by Yoko Ando, engineering by Reiko Sudo
Mishima Orimono Inc.
Raschel lacework
100% silk

Tanabata, 2000
Reiko Sudo, Hiroko Kobayashi and Tomoko Miura
Nuno Corporation and Takekura Inc.
Pleating, hand-cutting (heat-cut)
100% polyester
p. 108; pp. 220–21

Eco-green fabric, 2001
Reiko Sudo
Y.M. Textile Inc.
Dobby weave, hand-cutting (heat-cut)
100% biodegradable fibre
p. 335

Brush Bamboo, 2001
Reiko Sudo
Tsuguo Inc.
Jacquard weave
45% rayon, 38% silk, 10% nylon, 7% polyurethane

Kogire, 2001
Reiko Sudo
Yamanashi Finishing Co.
Needle-punching
85% wool, 15% nylon

Harmony Stripe, 2002
Reiko Sudo
Omae Inc.
Dobby weave
70% wool, 30% silk
p. 121

Itajime Round, 2002
Reiko Sudo
Yoko Kaneich of NUNO Corporation
Clumped dyeing
100% silk
pp. 246–47

Itajime Rectangle, 2002
Reiko Sudo and Tomoko Iida
Nuno Corporation
Clumped dyeing
100% silk
pp. 222–23

Paper Rolls, 2002
Reiko Sudo
Kato Embroidery Inc.
Multi-headed embroidery, washing
100% polyester
pp. 296–305

Phylum, 2002
Surface design by Sayuri Shimoda, engineering by Reiko Sudo, Fukuma Embroidery Works
Machine embroidery
100% cotton

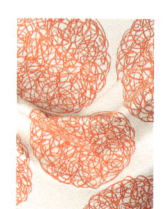

Bow and Arrow, 2002
Reiko Sudo
Tofuku Sangyo Co., Ltd and Uzen Kenren Co. Ltd
Hand screen-printing
100% cotton

Basket Work, 2002
Reiko Sudo
Nakanishi Dye Works Inc.
Hand screen-printing, flocking
100% cotton

Fluff, 2002
Reiko Sudo
Tsuyaei Kogyo Co.Ltd
Dobby weave
95% silk, 5% polyurethane (Spandex™)
pp. 32–33

Cracked Denim Hooptoss, 2002
Reiko Sudo and Yoshihiro Kimura (Kimura Dye Works Inc.)
Nakanishi Dye Works Inc.
Hand screen-printing, burn-out, bonding
80% cotton, 20% polyester

Sashiko Bamboo Basket, 2002 (reissued in 2015)
Reiko Sudo
Onishi Weaving Co. (reissued with Marunaka Weaving Co.)
Jacquard weave, cross-dyeing (reissued with yarn-dyeing)
51% cotton, 49% polyester

Snake Eyes, 2003
Reiko Sudo
Tsuguo Inc.
Jacquard weave
96% cotton, 4% nylon

Kernels, 2003
Reiko Sudo
Tsuguo Inc.
Jacquard weave
85% cotton, 15% polyester (aluminium metallized)
pp. 196–97

Tiggy, 2003
Reiko Sudo
Tsuguo Inc.
Tsunemi Dye Works or Hiruma Shearing Inc.
Jacquard weave, hand-cutting
100% cotton
pp. 332–33

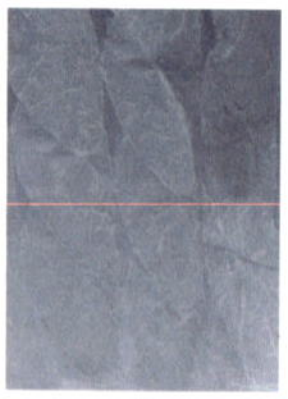

See the Sea, 2003
Reiko Sudo
Tsuguo Inc.
Jacquard weave
53% copper, 47% cotton
p. 184

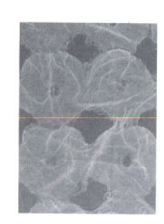

Big Egg, 2003
Reiko Sudo
Taki Paper Inc. and Nakanishi Dye Works
Hand screen-printing, bonding, washing
100% polyester
Echizen *washi* paper

Cookie, 2003
Reiko Sudo
Taki Paper Inc. and Nakanishi Dye Works
Hand screen-printing, bonding, washing
100% polyester
Echizen *washi* paper

Analog Torque, 2003
Reiko Sudo
Kato Embroidery Inc.
Multi-headed embroidery
Base: 100% polyester
Tape: 100% cotton
pp. 288–89

Rhombus, 2003
Reiko Sudo
Hyodo Orimono Inc.
Jacquard weave
100% wool

ReText OHSHIMA Border, 2003
Reiko Sudo
Hyodo Orimono Inc.
Jacquard weave
100% silk (wasted *Ohshima Tsumugi* threads)

Domino Stripe, 2004
Surface design by Sayuri Shimoda, engineering by Reiko Sudo
Tsuguo Inc. and Hiruma Shearing Inc.
Jacquard weave, hand-cutting, shearing
100% cotton
pp. 146–47

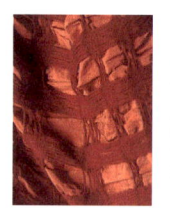

Striped Rounds, 2004
Reiko Sudo
Marunaka Weaving Co. and Hiruma Shearing Inc.
Jacquard weave, hand-cutting, shearing
100% cotton
pp. 126–27

Lath Screen, 2004
Reiko Sudo
SD Fabric Inc.
Jacquard weave
66% rayon, 34% nylon
p. 276

Square Bricks, 2004
Surface design by Sayuri Shimoda, engineering by Reiko Sudo
Marunaka Weaving Co.
Jacquard weave
100% cotton

Paper Honeycomb, 2004
Reiko Sudo
Y. M. Textile Inc.
Dobby weave
100% paper
p. 27

Nuno Tsunagi, 2004
Reiko Sudo and Yuka Taniguchi
Nuno Corporation and Kato Embroidery Inc.
Multi-headed embroidery, bonding
100% silk, remnants of various Nuno fabrics

Round Bricks, 2004
Reiko Sudo
Hyodo Orimono Inc.
Jacquard weave
100% wool

Washigaki, 2004
Reiko Sudo
Yamazaki Velvet Inc. and Taki Paper Inc. and Nakanishi Dye Works Bonding, hand screen-printing
Ground: 100% polyester; pile: 100% rayon; surface: Echizen *washi* paper

Ominaeshi, 2004
Reiko Sudo
Yoshimura Senmatsu Inc. and Fukuma Embroidery Works
Dobby weave, machine embroidery
100% polyester

Chidori Houndstooth, 2005
Reiko Sudo
Marunaka Weaving Co. and Hiruma Shearing Inc.
Jacquard weave, hand-cutting, shearing
100% cotton

Fritter, 2005
Reiko Sudo
Fukuma Embroidery Works
Machine embroidery
100% cotton

Nuno Kasane, 2005
Reiko Sudo and Tomoko Iida
Nuno Corporation and Kato Embroidery Inc.
Multi-headed embroidery, bonding
100% silk, remnants of various NUNO fabrics

Stalagmite, 2005
Kazuhiro Ueno
Kato Embroidery Inc.
Multi-headed embroidery, washing
100% polyester
pp. 266–67

Circle+Square series, 2005–18
Reiko Sudo
Hyodo Orimono Inc.
Jacquard weave
100% cotton

10+5 OHSHIMA, 2005
Reiko Sudo
Hyodo Orimono Inc.
Jacquard weave, hand-cutting
100% silk (wasted *Ohshima Tsumugi* threads)

Tube, 2006
Reiko Sudo
Marunaka Weaving Co. and Hiruma Shearing Inc.
Jacquard weave, hand-cutting, shearing
100% polyester
pp. 210–11

Water Chestnut, 2006
Reiko Sudo
Tsuguo Co. and Hiruma Shearing Inc.
Jacquard weave, hand-cutting
50% cotton, 50% wool
p. 287

Oracle Bone Script, 2006
Reiko Sudo
Marunaka Weaving Co.
Jacquard weave
100% cotton

Coin, 2006
Surface design by Reiko Sudo, engineering by Sayuri Shimoda
Fukuma Embroidery Works
Machine embroidery
100% cotton
Embroidery: Spandex™
p. 97

Flower Almanac, 2006
Reiko Sudo
Kaneko Weaving Inc.
Jacquard weave
100% cotton

Grater series, 2006–16
Reiko Sudo
Yamanashi Finishing Co.
Needle-punching
100% cotton
pp. 328–29

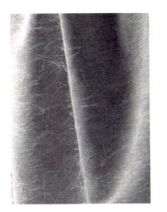

Baby Hairs, 2006
Reiko Sudo
Tsuguo Inc. and Hiruma Shearing
Dobby weave, hand-cutting
75% cotton, 25% saran
pp. 20–21

Threadstray, 2006
Reiko Sudo and Tomoko Iida
Yamanashi Finishing Co.
Needle-punching
100% wool
pp. 344–51

Pastel Drawing, 2006
Reiko Sudo
Nakanishi Dye Works Inc.
Hand screen-printing, flocking
100% polyester

Flyaway, 2006
Reiko Sudo and Yuka Taniguchi
Kato Embroidery Inc.
Multi-headed embroidery
100% polyester
pp. 228–29

Kinugasa Mushroom, 2006
Reiko Sudo
Fukuma Embroidery Works
Machine embroidery, washing
70% cotton, 30% rayon
pp. 244–45

Bean Scatter, 2006
Reiko Sudo
Hyodo Orimono Inc.
Jacquard weave, hand-cutting
64% wool, 36% cotton
p. 283

Kumihira plaid, 2007
Reiko Sudo
Y. M. Textile Inc.
Dobby weave
49% cotton, 37% rayon, 14% wool

Kumihira stripes, 2007
Reiko Sudo
Y. M. Textile Inc.
Dobby weave
42% cotton, 35% rayon, 23% wool
p. 71

Fold Up, 2007
Reiko Sudo
Kaneko Weaving Inc.
Jacquard weave
100% cotton

Kapanese Thistle, 2007
Surface design by Kazuhiro Ueno, engineering by Reiko Sudo
Tsuguo Inc.
Jacquard weave, heat-setting (calendering)
100% polyester
p. 182

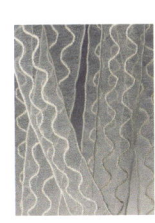

Kata Tatewaku, 2007
Reiko Sudo
Mishima Orimono Inc.
Tricot lacework
70% nylon, 30% cotton

Jigsaw Puzzle, 2007
Reiko Sudo
Fukuma Embroidery Works
Machine embroidery, hand-cutting
100% cotton

Basketweave, 2007
Reiko Sudo
Nakanishi Dye Works Inc.
Hand screen-printing, flocking, heat-setting
100% polyester
pp. 240–41

A – Un, 2007
Reiko Sudo
Hyodo Orimono Inc.
Jacquard weave
100% cotton

Prairie, 2007
Reiko Sudo
Marunaka Weaving Co.
Jacquard weave
70% cotton, 30% linen

Inutadé, 2008
Reiko Sudo
Kaneko Weaving Inc.
Jacquard weave
100% cotton
pp. 82–83

Rice Straw, 2008
Reiko Sudo
Matsuoka Co.
Jacquard weave, hand-cutting
56% cotton, 44% silk

Fort, 2008
Reiko Sudo
Y.M. Textile Inc.
Jacquard weave
100% cotton

Birdies, 2008
Reiko Sudo
Marunaka Weaving Co.
Jacquard weave, cross-dyeing
51% cotton, 49% polyester

Swinging Squares, 2008
Reiko Sudo
Enlarge Inc.
Machine embroidery, washing
100% cotton
p. 277

Wakame, 2008
Reiko Sudo
Nakamura Trading and Fukuma Embroidery Works
Machine embroidery
90% polyester, 10% cotton

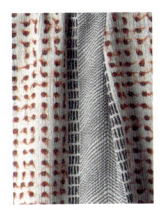

Lentils, 2008
Reiko Sudo
Hyodo Orimono Inc.
Jacquard weave, hand-cutting
64% wool, 36% cotton
p. 282

Kibiso Futsu Crisscross, 2008
Reiko Sudo
Matsuoka Co., Ltd
Dobby weave
62% silk (raw silk and *kibiso*), 38% cotton
p. 125

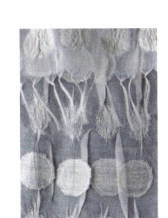

Kibiso Round, 2008
Reiko Sudo
Hyodo Orimono Inc.
Jacquard weave, hand-cutting
100% silk (raw silk and *kibiso*)

Weather Watch, 2009
Surface design by Kazuhiro Ueno, engineering by Reiko Sudo
SD Fabric Inc.
Jacquard weave
100% cotton

Loop de Loop, 2009
Reiko Sudo
Hyodo Orimono Inc.
Jacquard weave
98% wool, 2% nylon
pp. 54–55

Tsugihagi with base fabric, 2009
Reiko Sudo and Kazuhiro Ueno
Kato Embroidery Inc.
Bonding, multi-headed embroidery
100% polyester, remnants of various Nuno fabrics

Satin Stripes, 2009
Reiko Sudo
Yoshimura Senmatsu Inc.
Jacquard weave
45% nylon, 40% wool, 15% polyester
pp. 190–91

Satin Snow, 2009
Reiko Sudo
Yoshimura Senmatsu Inc.
Jacquard weave
45% nylon, 40% wool, 15% polyester
p. 178

Basting Threads, 2009
Reiko Sudo
Matsuoka Co., Ltd
Dobby weave, hand-cutting
88% silk, 7% nylon, 5% linen

Kiwi, 2009
Surface design by Sayuri Shimoda, engineering by Reiko Sudo
Fukuma Embroidery Works
Machine embroidery
64% rayon, 36% cotton

Stripe+Band series, 2009–19
Reiko Sudo
Hyodo Orimono Inc.
Jacquard weave
100% cotton (plus *kibiso* silk thread)
p. 134

Kibiso Itomaki, 2009
Reiko Sudo
Matsuoka Co., Ltd
Dobby weave
100% silk (raw silk and *kibiso*)
p. 131

Kibiso Suzushijima, 2009
Reiko Sudo
Matsuoka Co., Ltd
Dobby weave
100% silk (raw silk and *kibiso*)
pp. 116–17

Kibiso Window, 2009
Reiko Sudo
Hyodo Orimono Inc.
Jacquard weave, hand-cutting
100% silk (raw silk and *kibiso*)

Kibiso Handweaving, 2009
Reiko Sudo
Matsuoka Co., Ltd
Hand weave
100% silk (raw silk and *kibiso*)
p. 341

Kibiso Handweaving Border, 2009
Reiko Sudo
Matsuoka Co., Ltd
Hand weave
100% silk (raw silk and *kibiso*)
p. 124

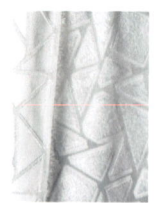

Ice, 2010
Reiko Sudo
Marunaka Weaving Co.
Jacquard weave, hand-cutting, shearing
100% polyester

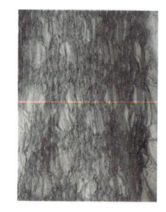

Embroidery Cross, 2010
Reiko Sudo
Fukuma Embroidery Works
Machine embroidery
100% cotton

Polygami, 2010
Reiko Sudo, engineering by Hiroko Kobayashi
Tsuguo Inc.
Jacquard weave, washing
100% polyester
p. 66; pp. 107–8

Pentarystal Crystal, 2010
Reiko Sudo
Enlarge Inc.
Machine embroidery, washing
100% cotton

Cracked Stripes, 2011
Reiko Sudo
Marunaka Weaving Co.
Jacquard weave, hand-cutting, shearing
100% cotton
pp. 280–81

Snowy Branches, 2011
Reiko Sudo
Fukuma Embroidery Works
Machine embroidery
100% polyester
pp. 236–37

Fans, 2011
Surface design by Gaku Masui, engineering by Reiko Sudo
Tsuguo Inc.
Jacquard weave, hand-cutting
70% wool, 30% cotton
p. 331

Waves and Particles, 2012
Reiko Sudo
Tofuku Sangyo Co., Ltd and Uzen Kenren Co. Ltd
Hand screen-printing
100% cotton

NUNO Tataki, 2012
Reiko Sudo
Hiroko Kobayashi of NUNO and Yamanashi Finishing Co.
Needle-punching
Surface: 100% polyester
Ground: 100% wool, remnants of various NUNO fabrics
p. 265

Bobbin Lace Flower, 2012
Surface design by Gaku Masui, engineering by Reiko Sudo
Kato Embroidery Inc.
Multi-headed embroidery, washing
100% polyester

Kamaboko Stripes, 2013
Reiko Sudo
Marunaka Weaving Co.
Jacquard weave, hand-cutting, shearing
100% cotton
p. 137

Azumino Wild Silk, 2013
Reiko Sudo
Hyodo Orimono Inc.
Jacquard weave, hand-cutting
100% silk (Japanese wild silk)
pp. 28–29

Multilayer Weave series, 2013–18
Reiko Sudo and Kazuhiro Ueno
Hyodo Orimono Inc.
Jacquard weave
100% cotton
pp. 268–69

See-thru Swinging Squares, 2014
Reiko Sudo
Enlarge Inc.
Machine embroidery, washing
100% polyester

Fluffy Stars, 2014
Reiko Sudo
Enlarge Inc.
Machine embroidery, washing
100% cotton

Slink Slub, 2014
Reiko Sudo
Hyodo Orimono Inc.
Jacquard weave, hand-cutting
91% silk, 9% wool
pp. 320–21

Trap Circle, 2015
Reiko Sudo
Kaneko Weaving Inc.
Jacquard weave
97% cotton, 2% polyurethane, 1% nylon
p. 46

Space Debris, 2015
Surface design by Gaku Masui
Marunaka Weaving Co.
Jacquard weave, cross-dyeing
51% cotton, 49% polyester

Origami Mosaic, 2015
Gaku Masui, engineering by Reiko Sudo
Hyodo Orimono Inc.
Jacquard weave
94% polyester, 3% polyurethane, 3% nylon
p. 104

Bamboo Flower Opal, 2015
Reiko Sudo
Noguchi Dye Works
Burn-out, machine screen-printing
100% polyester

Kibiso Not Knots, 2015
Reiko Sudo
Matsuoka Co., Ltd
Dobby weave, hand-cutting
100% silk (raw silk and *kibiso*)

Ogarami-Choshi Panel, 2015
Reiko Sudo
Matsuoka Co., Ltd
Bonding
100% silk (*Ogarami-choshi*)
pp. 314–15

Mayumi, 2016
Reiko Sudo
Kaneko Weaving Inc.
Jacquard weave, shearing
100% polyester
p. 183

Pampas Grass, 2016
Surface design
by Gaku Masui,
engineering by
Reiko Sudo
Fukuma Embroidery
Works
Machine embroidery
95% cotton, 5% linen
pp. 98–99

Polka Dots, 2016
Reiko Sudo
Kobatou Orimono Inc.
Jacquard weave,
cross-dyeing
72% acetate,
28% rayon
p. 95

Sweet Pea, 2016
Reiko Sudo
Futaba Lace Co.
Ltd
Raschel lacework
67% cotton, 33% nylon
pp. 36–37

Clematis, 2016
Reiko Sudo
Futaba Lace Co.Ltd
Raschel lacework
62% cotton, 38% nylon

Misty Rain, 2016
Reiko Sudo
Marunaka Weaving Co.
Jacquard weave,
hand-cutting, shearing
100% polyester

Salt-shrink Park, 2016
Reiko Sudo
Tofuku Sangyo Co.,
Ltd and Kyo Silk
Maruya Inc.
Hand screen-printing,
salt-shrinking
100% silk (raw
silk and *kibiso*)
pp. 224–25

Silver Leaf, 2016
Reiko Sudo,
Kyoji Tamiya
Tamiya Raden Inc.
Dobby weave, foil
printing (silver)
75% paper, 25% silk
pp. 198–99

Green Necklace, 2017
Reiko Sudo, Toru
Yamamoto
Creation Studio
Itoasobi
Jacquard weave
59% silk, 36% wool,
5% polyester

*35th Anniversary
Overspun Cotton*,
2017
Reiko Sudo
Hyodo Orimono Inc.
Jacquard weave
100% cotton

Sashiko Woodships,
2017
Reiko Sudo
Marunaka Weaving Co.
Jacquard weave
50% cotton, 50%
polyester

Twig Gather Ohshima,
2017
Reiko Sudo
Kato Embroidery Inc.
Multi-headed
embroidery, bonding
100% silk (wasted
Oshima Tsumugi
remnants)
pp. 322–23

Burn-out Ranma, 2017
Reiko Sudo
Miyashin Inc. and
Tofuku Sangyo Co., Ltd
Dobby weave, hand
screen-printing,
burn-out
63% paper, 37% silk

Ribbon Weave, 2017
Reiko Sudo
Creation Studio
Itoasobi
Dobby weave,
hand-dyeing
100% silk

Snowy Cobblestones,
2018
Reiko Sudo
and Tomoko Iida
Nakanishi Dye
Works Inc.
Burn-out, bonding,
flocking
80% cotton,
20% polyester

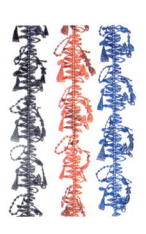

Dunhuang, 2018
Reiko Sudo
Enlarge Inc.
Machine embroidery,
washing
80% cotton, 20%
polyester

Stag Horn, 2018
Reiko Sudo
Enlarge Inc.
Machine embroidery,
washing
80% cotton, 20%
polyester
pp. 278–79

Colour Field, 2018
Reiko Sudo
Hinode Tweeds Inc.
Jacquard weave
100% cotton

Sun Rain, 2018
Reiko Sudo,
Orie Takashige
Kagoshima Prefectual
Institute of Industrial
Technology
Nakanishi Dye
Works Inc.
Hand screen-printing
100% polyester,
volcanic ash

Glass Mosaic, 2018
Reiko Sudo
Hyodo Orimono Inc.
Jacquard weave
100% wool

Papillon, 2018
Reiko Sudo
Tayu Kigyo Inc.
Jacquard weave,
hand-cutting
100% silk
p. 26

Wood Carving, 2019
Reiko Sudo
Hyodo Orimono Inc.
Jacquard weave
67% polyester,
30% cotton,
3% polyurethane

Stripe Stop Stripe,
2019
Reiko Sudo
Kaneko Weaving Inc.
Jacquard weave
41% cotton, 40%
rayon, 17% nylon,
2% polyurethane
p. 135

Circle Z, 2019
Reiko Sudo
Kaneko Weaving Inc.
Jacquard weave
97% cotton, 2%
polyurethane, 1% nylon
pp. 74–75

Hariko Linen, 2019
Reiko Sudo
Fukuma Embroidery
Works
Machine embroidery
100% linen
p. 130

Cause for Gauze,
2019
Reiko Sudo
Fukuma Embroidery
Works
Machine embroidery
100% wool

Travel series, 2019
Reiko Sudo
Hyodo Orimono Inc.
Jacquard weave
100% wool

Burn-out Ball, 2019
Reiko Sudo
Miyashin Inc. and
Tofuku Sangyo Co., Ltd
Dobby weave, hand
screen-printing,
burn-out
63% paper, 37% silk

Marbled series, 2019
Gaku Masui,
Reiko Sudo
Kyoto Marble Inc.
Marble-printing
100% silk

Coin Roll Crepe, 2020
Reiko Sudo
and Bruce Li
Kobatou Orimono Inc.
Dobby weave
42% cotton, 28%
polyester (aluminium
metallized), 14% wool
8% rayon,
8% polyurethane
p. 189

Seal, 2020
Reiko Sudo and
Aono Pile Inc.
Aono Pile Inc.
Pile weave
100% wool

Hairball, 2020
Reiko Sudo and
Aono Pile Inc.
Aono Pile Inc.
Fraise knitting
100% wool
p. 38

Body Scrub, 2020
Reiko Sudo
Miyama Lace Inc.
Raschel lacework
54% silk (raw silk and
kibiso), 33% cashmere,
13% cotton

Glossary

Bashofu: textiles traditionally woven in Okinawa and the Amami Islands from *basho* plantain (*Musa liukiuensis*) fibres.

Bonding: techniques for affixing various materials to a base fabric using acrylic or other adhesives.

Burn-out: process for removing cellulose fibres using acid and heat.

Burning: technique for discolouring metal fibres with a handheld burner.

Calendering: finishing process for smoothing fabric surfaces with hot metal rollers or plates.

Clamp-dyeing: a traditional Japanese technique using tightly pressed boards as a dye-resist. Along with tie-dyeing and wax-coating, one of the three main resist-dyeing techniques.

Chemical lace: technique for simulating lace by embroidering materials onto a base fabric that is later removed, leaving only an openwork fabric of the embroidered elements.

Cross-dyeing: technique for dyeing textiles woven from two or more fibres, each of which reacts to a different dyestuff.

Dobby weave: textiles woven on a Dobby loom using multiple shafts to control a set of warps.Unlike Jacquard weaves, better suited to small repeating patterns.

Felting: non-woven process for abrading animal fibres by means of heat and moisture into solid felt.

Flocking: a technique for affixing short cotton, nylon, rayon or other fibres onto a previously glued textile surface by means of static electricity, to createa velvet-like finish.

Foil-printing: technique for transferring metal foils onto a base fabric using an acrylic adhesive under high heat and pressure.

Fraise knitting: a special stretch-knit fabric with a ribbed design made on a Fraise knitting machine.

Hand-cutting: manual finishing technique where by selected yarns are cut loose or removed by knife or scissors.

Hand-dyeing: any of several manual dyeing techniques, including dipping, pouring or stamping.

Hand-painting: any of several manual surface decorating or patterning techniques using brushes, spatulas, squeegees or similar.

Hand screen-printing: any of several manual surface patterning techniques whereby adhesives or dyes are applied to fabric through a cut-out or photo-generated fine mesh screen.

Hand weave: simple manually woven textiles, typically made on a floor loom.

Heat-setting: a finishing process for shrinking or evening out fabrics by using hot air, vapour, water and other heat sources.

Heat-setting (infrared): technique for creating patterns using resins that melt under near-infrared radiation.

Ikat **yarn:** a technique for resist-dyeing warp and/or weft yarns prior to weaving, to create patterns that exhibit an aesthetically 'slipped' appearance. *Kasuri* is the Japanese name for the Indonesian term *ikat*, originally meaning a bundle or skein of yarns.

Jacquard weave: textiles woven on a loom with a Jacquard device, using punch cards to control warp yarn movements individually, creating flexible patterns.

Kibiso: the outermost protective layer of the silkworm cocoon, typically discarded as too hard or brittle to spin or weave. Rich in sericin protein, with UV-reducing and moisture-retaining properties.

Knit cord: a special ribbon-like cord made on a Raschel knitting machine.

Leno weave: a fabric with dual warps intersecting single wefts, as in traditional Japanese *sha* and *ro* gauzes.

Machine screen-printing: any of several mechanical surface patterning techniques whereby adhesives or dyes are applied to fabric through a cut-out or photo-generated fine mesh screen.

Marble-printing: a special transfer-dyeing technique using cut pieces of kneaded dyestuff arranged like a mosaic on a roller to print meandering patterns onto fabrics.

Melt-off: a finishing process for removing aluminium leaf with an alkaline solution.

Multi-headed embroidery: a mechanized technique for simultaneously stitching repeated copies of a single pattern using a large-scale embroidery machine.

Multilayer weave: textile layered in different weave structures, colours or patterns that are woven simultaneously in a single pass on the loom.

Needle-punching: a mechanized process in which fibres are meshed by means of high-speed vertical jabs with barbed plates. Used to make non-woven industrial fabrics.

Pile weave: textile woven with looped yarns that are then cut to create a fuzzy texture of upright fibres.

Pleating: a process for pressing semi-permanent creases into thermoplastic synthetic fabrics to make a three-dimensional effect.

Raschel lace: a special looped-warp knit fabric made on a Raschel knitting machine. The loops are locked, allowing yarns to be selectively removed to create openwork patterns, as in tulle.

Recycled thread (*basho* plantain): cotton threads coated with a gel of minutely ground and dissolved 'waste' fibres from damaged *basho* plantain stalks.

Reclaimed thread (discarded fabric): damaged or leftover threads from weaving that are reused to make yarns for new weaving.

Salt-shrinking: a finishing technique to selectively shrink silk or other animal fibres using an alkaline solution.

Sashiko: a traditional embroidery technique by which two or more layers of cotton cloth are stitched together in decorative patterns to reinforce and embellish worn fabrics.

Shearing: a technique for trimming stray surface fibres to a smooth, even appearance.

Spaced weft: a weaving technique whereby 'missing' wefts intentionally leave open spaces in the fabric.

Sputtering/Spattering: an industrial method for powder-plating irregular surfaces with metallic coatings. Alloys like stainless steel can be plated by spraying powdered chrome, nickel and iron in rapid succession.

Transfer printing: a technique for transposing designs on inked sheets onto fabric using heat and pressure.

Tricot lacework: a special looped-warp fabric made on a tricot knitting machine. The loops are aligned vertically to create a dense texture.

Velvet weave: a textile woven with long extended warps sandwiched between two outer ground layers, which are then cut apart to create two mirror-image pile fabrics.

Warp-dyeing: a technique for weaving with dyed warp yarns by inserting a transfer paper printed with the desired colour and pattern when winding warps to the loom beam.

Washing: a finishing process using water to shrink/resolve ancillary materials.

Yarn dyeing: any method of dyeing yarns prior to weaving.

Author Biographies

Reiko Sudo, Design Director, Nuno Co., Ltd, was born in Ishioka, Ibaraki Prefecture. She is Professor Emeritus at Tokyo Zokei University and, since 2008, textile design advisor to Ryohin Keikaku, Tsuruoka Textile Industry Cooperative, Yamagata Prefecture and others. Since 2016, she has served on Ryohin Keikaku's Advisory Board. Wielding a vast array of techniques and technologies ranging from traditional Japanese dyeing and weaving to contemporary high-tech textile processes, Sudo has created works included in the permanent collections of MoMA, the Metropolitan Museum of Art, New York, the Museum of Fine Arts, Boston, Los Angeles County Museum of Art, the Victoria and Albert Museum, London and many other institutions worldwide.

Naomi Pollock is an American architect who writes about Japanese design and architecture. Her work has appeared in many publications, such as *Dwell*, *Kinfolk*, *Wallpaper** and *Architectural Record*, for whom she is the Special International Correspondent. She is also the author of numerous books, including *Jutaku: Japanese Houses* and *Japanese Design Since 1945: A Complete Sourcebook*. In 2018, she was invited into the College of Fellows of The American Institute of Architects.

Caroline Kennedy, an attorney and author, served as the Vice-Chair of the NYC Fund for Public Schools from 2002–2012 and the US Ambassador to Japan from 2013–2017. She and her husband, Edwin Schlossberg, have three children.

Haruki Murakami was born in Kyoto in 1949 and now lives near Tokyo. His work has been translated into more than fifty languages, and the most recent of his many international honours is the Hans Christian Andersen Literature Award in 2016.

Kenya Hara is a graphic designer, president of the Nippon Design Center Inc., professor at Musashino Art University and Muji's art director. He has created visual identities for Matsuya Ginza, Mori Building, Tsutaya Shoten, Ginza Six and Mikimoto. In addition, Hara promotes global interest in Japan, serving as Chief Creative Director of the Japan House project for Japan's Ministry of Foreign Affairs and launching the High Resolution Tour website in 2019 as a new approach to tourism.

Brooke Hodge is an independent curator and writer. She has served as Director of Architecture and Design at Palm Springs Art Museum, Deputy Director at the Cooper Hewitt, Smithsonian Design Museum, New York, Director of Exhibitions Management and Publications at the Hammer Museum in Los Angeles, Curator of Architecture and Design at The Museum of Contemporary Art in Los Angeles, and Director of Exhibitions and Publications at Harvard University's Graduate School of Design. In addition, Hodge has written extensively for numerous publications, including *The New York Times T Magazine*, *Wallpaper** and *Metropolis*.

Akane Teshigahara became the fourth *Iemoto* (Headmaster) of the Sogetsu School of Ikebana (Japanese flower arrangement) in 2001. She has pursued the possibilities of new ikebana suitable for an ever-diversified modern space as the leader of Sogetsu, which respects free and liberated creation. She has actively engaged in collaborations with artists in different disciplines, and has also presided over the Akane Junior Class, which aims to develop the sensitivity and independence of children through ikebana.

Toyo Ito was born in 1941. After graduating from the University of Tokyo in 1965, he worked in the office of Kiyonori Kikutake until 1969. In 1971, he founded his own office, Urban Robot (URBOT), which was renamed Toyo Ito & Associates, Architects. Representative projects: Sendai Mediatheque (Japan), Serpentine Gallery Pavilion, 2002 (UK), Tama Art University Library, Hachioji campus (Japan), 'Minna no Mori' Gifu Media Cosmos (Japan), Museo Internacional del Barroco (Mexico).

Arto Lindsay is an artist and musician who lives and works in Rio de Janeiro. He has recorded eleven solo records and has been a band member with DNA, Lounge Lizards, Golden Palominos and Ambitious Lovers. He has produced records for Caetano Veloso, Marisa Monte and David Byrne among others, and collaborated with musicians and visual artists such as Ryuichi Sakamoto, Laurie Anderson and Vito Acconci. Recently, Lindsay has been combining music, technology, choreography and allegorical elements in the form of parades.

Anna Jackson is Keeper of the Asian Department at the Victoria and Albert Museum. A specialist in Japanese textiles and dress, she was the curator of the exhibition 'Kimono: Kyoto to Catwalk' (2020) and editor of the accompanying publication. Her other research interest is the cultural relationship between Asia and Europe, a subject on which she has also published widely.

Charlotte Skene Catling (Skene Catling de la Peña) is a multidisciplinary architect who uses observations about the composition of the earth, historical artefacts and cultural landscapes as the basis for 'geoarchaeological' design. She has written for *The Architectural Review*, *Domus* and other publications, and taught at the Royal College of Art, Karlsruhe Institute of Technology and London School of Architecture.

Adam Lowe is director of Factum Arte and founder of the Factum Foundation for Digital Technology in Conservation, which bridges new technologies and innovative craftsmanship. An adjunct professor in historic preservation at Columbia University, Lowe has worked on major conservation and preservation efforts worldwide, and collaborated with with the Louvre, Prado, British Museum, Hermitage, Victoria and Albert Museum and many other institutions.

Picture Credits

Unless otherwise stated, photographs by Masayuki Hayashi for Nuno Corporation.

p. 8 © Ken Kato, 2021

pp. 11, 107, 156–59, 207 bottom, 304–5 © Nuno Corporation, 2021

p. 14 © Ryohin Keikaku Co., Ltd, 2021

p. 16 © Satoshi Shigeta, 2021

pp. 57–58, 60–62, 153–55, 201–3, 205, 298, 300–1, 303 © Japan House London, 2021. Photographs by Masayuki Hayashi.

pp. 64, 110 bottom, 206, 207 top, 256–57, 349 © Panoramatiks, 2021

pp. 160–61, 362–63 © CHAT (Centre for Heritage, Arts and Textile), Hong Kong, 2021

Acknowledgments

One last little twist of yarn

When I was maybe ten years old, my mother gave me an embroidery frame and several dozen coloured yarns. Young as I was, I thrilled to see how my childish doodle looked so grown up when embroidered. I probably would have felt embarrassed to show anyone what I drew, but suddenly here was something worthy of presenting as a gift. At the time I would never have seen myself as 'creating textiles', I simply enjoyed handing out my handiwork to friends. Nowadays, however, gift-giving is a more complicated affair. While never wanting to force things on others, I am overjoyed to think that a gift of mine might really please them. That has always been my dream for Nuno: to create textiles that would be truly appreciated. I only hope I can keep on making Nuno textiles that elicit grateful smiles of thanks.

Scattered throughout this volume are essays by various names I've had the honour to encounter through Nuno. Former US Ambassador to Japan Caroline Kennedy, who kindly agreed to write a foreword, I first met during a blizzard in February 2014, when she joined me at a family dinner at the Tokyo home of my good friend Naomi Pollock, who has since edited this book. I would like to thank them both. Fortuitous how all these things come together. A few of the essays come from a series of NunoNuno Books based on Japanese onomatopoeia that Nuno self-published from 1994; I'd like to express my appreciation to Haruki Murakami, Toyo Ito and Arto Lindsey for graciously allowing us to reprint their words almost twenty years on. Along with their texts, we now add writings by Kenya Hara, Brooke Hodge, Akane Teshigahara, Anna Jackson, Adam Lowe and Charlotte Skene Catling. To all of them, my heartfelt thanks.

We began preparations toward this book in February 2018. A year later in February 2019 we started photographing, and still another year later in February 2020 I visited Lucas Dietrich at the London offices of Thames & Hudson and received much-needed guidance about the book design, only to see the whole world recoil into a COVID-19 panic the moment I returned to Japan. Like people everywhere, we at Nuno were dealt a big blow psychologically, socially and economically. Luckily, we came through physically unscathed, though of course the entire book production suffered repeated setbacks. It is with great admiration and gratitude, then, that I acknowledge the patience and clarity of T&H staff members Fleur Jones, Kate Edwards, Isabel Roldán, Avni Patel, Christina Twigg and Julie Bosser, and Nuno's own Orie Takashige. Likewise, all Nuno members deserve recognition for their tireless efforts in making sense of our Nuno archives.

Three others also made invaluable contributions: photographer Masayuki Hayashi, who shot the many striking images, our friendly Nuno translator Alfred Birnbaum, who brushed up the English, and my husband, Kazuyoshi Sudo, who helped to shape my original musings. To their visual and verbal skills I owe the strengths of the finished work. They and many other friends, associates and benefactors too numerous to mention have lent me support and guidance for this undertaking.

Lastly, I must offer thanks to all the thousands of artisans and technicians who have been involved in creating our Nuno textiles over the years. Without their precious talents and artistry none of this would have been possible.

Reiko Sudo, June 2021

Cover cloth design: Reiko Sudo and Yuka Taniguchi
Cover cloth production: Kobatou Textile Co., Ltd

First published in the United Kingdom in 2021 by Thames & Hudson Ltd, 181A High Holborn, London WC1V 7QX

First published in the United States of America in 2021 by Thames & Hudson Inc., 500 Fifth Avenue, New York, New York 10110

NUNO: Visionary Japanese Textiles © 2021 Thames & Hudson Ltd, London

Unless otherwise specified, text © 2021 NUNO Corporation

Text by Reiko Sudo

Translation by Alfred Birnbaum

Edited by Naomi Pollock

Special assistance by Kazuyoshi Sudo (Sudo Office), Orie Takashige (Nuno Corporation), Kayo Okamoto (Masayuki Hayashi Studio)

Foreword © 2021 Caroline Kennedy

Introduction © 2021 Naomi Pollock

'Fuwa Fuwa' © 2021 Haruki Murakami, first published in NUNO NUNO BOOKS: FUWA FUWA, NUNO Corporation, 1998

'Shiwa Shiwa' © 2021 Kenya Hara

'Stripes of All Colours' © 2021 Brooke Hodge

'Shining Within' © 2021 Akane Teshigahara

'Three transparencies' © 2021 Toyo Ito, first published in NUNO NUNO BOOKS: SUKE SUKE, NUNO Corporation, 1997

'Four Poems' © 2021 Arto Lindsay, a version of which was first published in NUNO NUNO BOOKS: ZAWA ZAWA, NUNO Corporation, 1999

'Boro Boro' © 2021 Anna Jackson

'Time's Arrow and the Magical Transformation of Colour' © 2021 Adam Lowe and Charlotte Skene Catling

All Rights Reserved. No part of this publication may be reproduced or transmitted in any form or by any means, electronic or mechanical, including photocopy, recording or any other information storage and retrieval system, without prior permission in writing from the publisher.

British Library Cataloguing-in-Publication Data
A catalogue record for this book is available from the British Library

Library of Congress Control Number 2021934193

ISBN 978-0-500-02268-9

Printed in China, by Artron Art (Group) Co., Ltd

Be the first to know about our new releases, exclusive content and author events by visiting
thamesandhudson.com
thamesandhudsonusa.com
thamesandhudson.com.au